Sources of
THE MAKING OF THE WEST

PEOPLES AND CULTURES

Volume I: To 1750

Sources of
THE MAKING OF THE WEST

PEOPLES AND CULTURES

Fourth Edition

Volume I: To 1750

KATHARINE J. LUALDI
University of Southern Maine

BEDFORD/ST. MARTIN'S   Boston ◆ New York

For Bedford/St. Martin's

Publisher for History: Mary Dougherty
Director for Development for History: Jane Knetzger
Developmental Editor: Annette Fantasia
Production Supervisor: Lisa Chow
Senior Executive Marketing Manager: Jenna Bookin Barry
Editorial Assistant: Emily DiPietro
Project Management: DeMasi Design and Publishing Services
Permissions Manager: Kalina K. Ingham
Cover Designer: Billy Boardman
Cover Art: Dwellings on the banks of the Nile, mosaic pavement, c. 80 B.C. Roman, from
   Sanctuary of Fortuna, Praenesta, Italy. Museo Prenestino Palestrina. © The Art Archive,
   New York.
Composition: Jeff Miller Book Design
Printing and Binding: RR Donnelley and Sons

President: Joan E. Feinberg
Editorial Director: Denise B. Wydra
Director of Marketing: Karen R. Soeltz
Director of Production: Susan W. Brown
Associate Director, Editorial Production: Elise S. Kaiser
Manager, Publishing Services: Andrea Cava

Library of Congress Control Number: 2011941808

Manufactured in the United States of America.

7   6   5   4
f   e   d

For information, write: Bedford/St. Martin's, 75 Arlington Street, Boston, MA 02116
(617-399-4000)

ISBN: 978-0-312-57611-0

Preface

D esigned to accompany *The Making of the West: Peoples and Cultures*, Fourth
Edition, and *The Making of the West: A Concise History*, Fourth Edition,
Sources of The Making of the West is intended to help instructors bring the history
of Western civilization to life for their students. This thoroughly revised collection
parallels the major topics and themes covered in each textbook chapter and offers
instructors many opportunities to promote classroom discussion of primary documents and their connection to historical analysis. Thus, the sourcebook helps
reveal that the study of history is not fixed but is an ongoing process of evaluation
and interpretation.

This edition contains over thirty new written and visual sources that comple-
ment the thematic and chronological framework of the textbook and highlight
the intellectual, emotional, and visual landscapes of many different peoples and places.
In response to the many insightful suggestions of reviewers who taught with or examined the previous edition, I selected the documents for this new edition of *Sources of
The Making of the West* both to reflect historians' changing understanding of Western
civilization and to underscore the continued relevance of more conventional written
sources. To this end, several classic sources have been added throughout the collection
to provide fuller evidence of key cultural, social, political, economic, and intellectual
developments, from Homer's *Odyssey* (Chapter 2, Volume I) to Olympe de Gouges's
"Declaration of the Rights of Woman" (Chapter 19, Volume II). These are enhanced
by sources elucidating Europe's connection to the world beyond its borders, such
as the "Decree of General Liberty" calling for the emancipation of slaves in St.
Domingue in 1793, which is paired with insurgent leader Bramantc Lazzary's
response (Chapter 19, Volume II), and African warrior Ndansi Kumalo's personal
account of fighting against British imperialists in the late nineteenth century (Chapter 23, Volume II).

Guided by the textbook's integrated framework, each chapter brings together a
variety of source types illuminating historical experience from many perspectives.
For example, in Chapter 17, "The Atlantic System and Its Consequences, 1700–1750,"
students encounter the social, cultural, political, and intellectual dimensions of the
period, as well as issues of race and gender: Olaudah Equiano's autobiography (Document 1) gives voice to the slaves whose toils fueled the Atlantic system's economy, while
the next source, an advertisement extolling the virtues of coffee (Document 2), reveals
Europeans' growing appetite for one of the many commodities produced by slave
labor. The commercial, technological, and cultural transformations that inspired Russian emperor Peter I's project of Westernization are palpable in his decrees and statutes
that comprise the next document set (Document 3). The final selections by Voltaire
and Mary Astell (Documents 4 and 5) reflect the intellectual products of the era's prosperity, optimism, and contradictions.

Visual primary sources add an exciting dimension to students' ability to see and
interpret the past, and this edition includes several new images, from Myron's statue of
a discus thrower in Chapter 3 (Volume I) to a recent political cartoon on the issue of

EU membership in Chapter 29 (Volume II). These sources visually enrich traditional written documents while challenging students to read the past (and present) in new ways. Along with training their minds to analyze texts for meaning, students learn to view images as an equally valuable window into the past. Furthermore, in this edition, I chose written and nonwritten sources that fit together to elucidate important events and opinions of specific historical eras. For example, Chapter 3 (Volume I) includes an overhead view of a Greek house and asks students to analyze the division of domestic space into male and female domains. It is presented in tandem with the testimony of a man on trial for murdering his wife's lover who, according to the husband, had been sneaking into their house on a regular basis. While defending his actions, the husband brings to life the social values underlying the allocation of space evident in the overhead view. Chapter 21 (Volume II) offers another rich pairing by combining a cartoon lambasting the exploitation of English miners, especially children, with the testimony of miners themselves gathered during parliamentary hearings on working conditions in mines. Through their words, the miners inject the images in the cartoon with the flesh and blood of their own experiences living in the industrial age. These paired visual and written documents thus deepen the interpretive possibilities of the individual sources.

Each document was also selected based on its accessibility, depth in content, and appeal to students. For this reason, when necessary, I have carefully edited documents to speak to specific themes without impairing the documents' overall sense and tone. I have also included documents of varying lengths to increase their utility for both short class exercises and outside writing assignments.

Of course asking the right questions and finding the right answers is at the heart of "doing" history. For this reason, *Sources of The Making of the West*, Fourth Edition, begins with an introduction on how to interpret written and visual primary sources that leads students step-by-step through the process of historical analysis. A brief overview of what this process entails is followed by an extended discussion of the process at work in the analysis of two sources drawn specifically from this collection. I adopted this integrated approach for the Introduction to help students move easily from abstract concepts to concrete examples. As a result, the Introduction does not rely on telling students what to do but rather on showing them how to do it for themselves based on the raw data of history.

To assist students with their journey into the past, each chapter opens with a summary that situates the sources within the broader historical context and addresses their relationship to one another and to the main themes in the corresponding chapter of *The Making of the West* and *The Making of the West: A Concise History*. An explanatory headnote accompanies each source to provide fundamental background information on the author or creator and the source while highlighting its significance. Revised and expanded discussion questions help students examine key points and issues in greater depth. Finally, each chapter concludes with at least four comparative questions intended to encourage students to see both the harmony and discordance among the sources. Although these editorial features intentionally strengthen the coherence of each chapter as a unit, they also allow instructors to choose sources and questions that best suit their specific goals and methods.

Acknowledgments

Many people deserve thanks for helping to bring this fourth edition to fruition. First among them are the authors of *The Making of the West*: Lynn Hunt, Thomas R. Martin, Barbara H. Rosenwein, and Bonnie G. Smith. Many thanks as well to reviewers of the previous edition, who provided valuable insights and suggestions: Veronica Bale, Miracosta College; Daniel F. Callahan, University of Delaware; Jason Coy, College of Charleston; Mary Duarte, Cardinal Stritch University; Meaghan Dwyer-Ryan, Boston College; Brian Elsesser, Harris-Stowe State University; Rebecca Friedman, Florida International University; James E. Higgins, Kutztown University of Pennsylvania; Shereen Ilahi, North Central College; David S. Karr, Columbia College; Matthew Laubacher, Arizona State University; Suzanne LaVere, Indiana University–Purdue University Fort Wayne; Patrice Lewis, Montgomery County Community College; Tanis Lovercheck-Saunders, Casper College; Jeffrey Lee Meriwether, Roger Williams University; Jennifer Morris, College of Mount St. Joseph; Anthony Nardini, Rowan University; Donald S. Prudlo, Jacksonville State University; Debbie Roberts, Yavapai College; Jason L. Strandquist, Pennsylvania State University; Tim Stretton, Saint Mary's University; Miriam Raub Vivian, California State University, Bakersfield; Jason L. Ward, Lee University; Richard Weeks, West Virginia Wesleyan College; Amy Woodson-Boulton, Loyola Marymount University; and Rick L. Woten, Simpson College.

I would also like to thank Anne Thayer, Jeannine Uzzi, Nancy Artz, and Helen Evans for their expertise and editorial assistance with sources new to this edition, as well as the team at Bedford/St. Martin's: Mary Dougherty, Jane Knetzger, Annette Fantasia, Robin Soule, Emily DiPietro, Andrea Cava, and Kalina Ingham.

Contents

Sources of
THE MAKING OF THE WEST

PEOPLES AND CULTURES

Volume I: To 1750

Introduction: Working with Historical Sources

The long history of Western civilization encompasses a broad range of places and cultures. Textbooks provide an essential chronological and thematic framework for understanding the formation of the West as a cultural and geographical entity. Yet the process of historical inquiry extends beyond textbook narratives into the thoughts, words, images, and experiences of people living at the time. Primary sources expose this world so that you can observe, analyze, and interpret the past as it unfolds before you. History is thus not a static collection of facts and dates. Rather, it is an ongoing attempt to make sense of the past and its relationship to the present through the lens of both written and visual primary sources.

Sources of The Making of the West, Fourth Edition, provides this lens for you, with a wide range of engaging sources — from a Mesopotamian epic to a political cartoon of the Old Regime to firsthand accounts of student revolts. When combined, the sources reflect historians' growing appreciation of the need to examine Western civilization from different conceptual angles — political, social, cultural, economic — and geographic viewpoints. The composite picture that emerges reveals a variety of historical experiences shaping each era from both within and outside Europe's borders. Furthermore, the documents here demonstrate that the most historically significant of these experiences are not always those of people in formal positions of power. Men and women from all walks of life have also influenced the course of Western history.

The sources in this reader were selected with an eye toward their ability not only to capture the multifaceted dimensions of the past but also to ignite your intellectual curiosity. Each written and visual document is a unique product of human endeavor and as such is often colored by the personal concerns, biases, and objectives of the author or creator. Among the most exciting challenges facing you is to sift through these nuances to discover what they reveal about the source and its broader historical context.

Interpreting Written Sources

Understanding a written document and its connection to larger historical issues depends on knowing which questions to ask and how to find the right answers. The following six questions will guide you through this process of discovery. Like a detective, you will begin by piecing together basic facts and then move on to more complex levels of analysis, which usually requires reading any given source more than once. You should keep these questions in mind every time you read a document, no matter how long or how short, to help you uncover its meaning and significance.

1. Who wrote this document, when, and where?

The "doing" of history depends on historical records, the existence of which in turn depends on the individuals who composed them in a particular time and place and with specific goals in mind. Therefore before you can begin to understand a document and its significance, you need to determine who wrote it, and when and where it was written. Ultimately, this information will shape your interpretation because the language of documents often reflects the author's social and/ or political status as well as the norms of the society in which the author lived.

2. What type of document is this?

Because all genres have their own defining characteristics, identifying the type of document at hand is vital to elucidating its purpose and meaning. For example, in content and organization, an account of a saint's life looks very different from an imperial edict, which in turn looks very different from a trial record. Each document type follows certain rules of composition that shape what authors say and how they say it.

3. Who is the intended audience of the document?

The type of source often goes hand in hand with the intended audience. For instance, popular songs in the vernacular are designed to reach people across the socioeconomic spectrum, whereas papal bulls written in Latin are directed to a tiny, educated, and predominantly male elite. Moreover, an author often crafts the style and content of a document to appeal to a particular audience and to enhance the effectiveness of his or her message.

4. What are the main points of this document?

All primary sources contain stories whether in numbers, words, and/or images. Before you can begin to analyze their meanings, you need to have a good command of a document's main points. For this reason, while reading, you should mark words, phrases, and passages that strike you as particularly important to create visual and mental markers that will help you navigate the document. Don't worry about mastering all of the details; you can work through them later, once you have sketched out the basic content.

5. Why was this document written?

The simplicity of this question masks the complexity of the possible answers. Historical records are never created in a vacuum; they were produced for a reason, whether public or private, pragmatic or fanciful. Some sources will state outright why they were created, whereas others will not. Yet with or without direct cues, you should look for less obvious signs of the author's intent and rhetorical strategies, as reflected in word choice, for example, or the way in which a point is communicated.

6. What does this document reveal about the particular society and period in question?

This question strikes at the heart of historical analysis and interpretation. In its use of language, its structure, and its biases and assumptions, every source opens a window into its author and time period. Teasing out its deeper significance will allow you to assess the value of a source and to articulate what it adds to our understanding of the historical context in which it is embedded. Thus, as you begin to analyze a source fully, your own interpretive voice will assume center stage.

As you work through each of these questions, you will progress from identifying the basic content of a document to inferring its broader meanings. At its very heart, the study of primary sources centers on the interplay between "facts" and interpretation. To help you engage in this interplay, let us take a concrete example of a historical document. Read it carefully, guided by the questions outlined above. In this way, you will gain insight into this particular text while training yourself in interpreting written primary sources in general.

1.
Legislating Tolerance
Henry IV, *Edict of Nantes* (1598)

The promulgation of the Edict of Nantes in 1598 by King Henry IV (r. 1589–1610) marked the end of the French Wars of Religion by recognizing French Protestants as a legally protected religious minority. Drawing largely on earlier edicts of pacification, the Edict of Nantes was composed of ninety-two general articles, fifty-six secret articles, and two royal warrants. The two series of articles represented the edict proper and were registered by the highest courts of law in the realm (parlements). The following excerpts from the general articles reveal the triumph of political concerns over religious conformity on the one hand, and the limitations of religious tolerance in early modern France on the other.

Henry, by the grace of God, King of France, and Navarre, to all present, and to come, greeting. Among the infinite mercies that it has pleased God to bestow upon us, that most signal and remarkable is, his having given us power and strength not to yield to the dreadful troubles, confusions, and disorders, which were found at

Modernized English text adapted from Edmund Everard, *The Great Pressures and Grievances of the Protestants in France* (London, 1681), 1–5, 10, 14, 16.

our coming to this kingdom, divided into so many parties and factions, that the most legitimate was almost the least, enabling us with constancy in such manner to oppose the storm, as in the end to surmount it, now reaching a part of safety and repose for this state . . . For the general difference among our good subjects, and the particular evils of the soundest parts of the state, we judged might be easily cured, after the principal cause (the continuation of civil war) was taken away. In which having, by the blessing of God, well and happily succeeded, all hostility and wars through the kingdom being now ceased, we hope that we will succeed equally well in other matters remaining to be settled, and that by this means we shall arrive at the establishment of a good peace, with tranquility and rest. . . . Among our said affairs . . . one of the principal has been the complaints we have received from many of our Catholic provinces and cities, that the exercise of the Catholic religion was not universally re-established, as is provided by edicts or statutes heretofore made for the pacification of the troubles arising from religion; as well as the sup- plications and remonstrances which have been made to us by our subjects of the Reformed religion, regarding both the non-fulfillment of what has been granted by the said former laws, and that which they desired to be added for the exercise of their religion, the liberty of their consciences and the security of their persons and fortunes; presuming to have just reasons for desiring some enlargement of articles, as not being without great apprehensions, because their ruin has been the princi- pal pretext and original foundation of the late wars, troubles, and commotions. Now not to burden us with too much business at once, as also that the fury of war was not compatible with the establishment of laws, however good they might be, we have hitherto deferred from time to time giving remedy herein. But now that it has pleased God to give us a beginning of enjoying some rest, we think we cannot employ ourself better than to apply to that which may tend to the glory and service of His holy name, and to provide that He may be adored and prayed unto by all our subjects: and if it has not yet pleased Him to permit it to be in one and the same form of religion, that it may at the least be with one and the same intention, and with such rules that may prevent among them all troubles and tumults. . . . For this cause, we have upon the whole judged it necessary to give to all our said sub- jects one general law, clear, pure, and absolute, by which they shall be regulated in all differences which have heretofore risen among them, or may hereafter rise, wherewith the one and other may be contented, being framed according as the time requires: and having had no other regard in this deliberation than solely the zeal we have to the service of God, praying that He would from this time forward render to all our subjects a durable and established peace. . . . We have by this edict or statute perpetual and irrevocable said, declared, and ordained, saying, declar- ing, and ordaining;

That the memory of all things passed on the one part and the other, since the beginning of the month of March 1585 until our coming to the crown, and also during the other preceding troubles, and the occasion of the same, shall remain extinguished and suppressed, as things that had never been. . . .

We prohibit to all our subjects of whatever state and condition they be, to renew the memory thereof, to attack, resent, injure, or provoke one another by reproaches for what is past, under any pretext or cause whatsoever, by disputing, contesting, quarrelling, reviling, or offending by factious words; but to contain themselves, and live peaceably together as brethren, friends, and fellow-citizens, upon penalty for acting to the contrary, to be punished for breakers of peace, and disturbers of the public quiet.

We ordain, that the Catholic religion shall be restored and re-established in all places, and quarters of this kingdom and country under our obedience, and where the exercise of the same has been interrupted, to be there again, peaceably and freely exercised without any trouble or impediment. . . .

And not to leave any occasion of trouble and difference among our subjects, we have permitted and do permit to those of the Reformed religion, to live and dwell in all the cities and places of this our kingdom and countries under our obedience, without being inquired after, vexed, molested, or compelled to do any thing in religion, contrary to their conscience. . . .

We permit also to those of the said religion to hold, and continue the exercise of the same in all the cities and places under our obedience, where it was by them established and made public at several different times, in the year 1586, and in 1597.

In like manner the said exercise may be established, and re-established in all the cities and places where it has been established or ought to be by the Statute of Pacification, made in the year 1577 . . .

We prohibit most expressly to all those of the said religion, to hold any exercise of it . . . except in places permitted and granted in the present edict. As also not to exercise the said religion in our court, nor in our territories and countries beyond the mountains, nor in our city of Paris, nor within five leagues of the said city. . . .

We prohibit all preachers, readers, and others who speak in public, to use any words, discourse, or propositions tending to excite the people to sedition; and we enjoin them to contain and comport themselves modestly, and to say nothing which shall not be for the instruction and edification of the listeners, and maintaining the peace and tranquility established by us in our said kingdom. . . .

They [French Protestants] shall also be obliged to keep and observe the festivals of the Catholic Church, and shall not on the same days work, sell, or keep open shop, nor likewise the artisans shall not work out of their shops, in their chambers or houses privately on the said festivals, and other days forbidden, of any trade, the noise whereof may be heard outside by those that pass by, or by the neighbors. . . .

We ordain, that there shall not be made any difference or distinction upon the account of the said religion, in receiving scholars to be instructed in the universities, colleges, or schools, nor of the sick or poor into hospitals, sick houses or public almshouses. . . .

We will and ordain, that all those of the Reformed religion, and others who have followed their party, of whatever state, quality or condition they be, shall be obliged and constrained by all due and reasonable ways, and under the penalties contained in the said edict or statute relating thereunto, to pay tithes to the curates, and other ecclesiastics, and to all others to whom they shall appertain. . . .

To the end to re-unite so much the better the minds and good will of our subjects, as is our intention, and to take away all complaints for the future; we declare all those who make or shall make profession of the said Reformed religion, to be capable of holding and exercising all estates, dignities, offices, and public charges whatsoever. . . .

We declare all sentences, judgments, procedures, seizures, sales, and decrees made and given against those of the Reformed religion, as well living as dead, from the death of the deceased King Henry the Second our most honored Lord and father in law, upon the occasion of the said religion, tumults and troubles since happening, as also the execution of the same judgments and decrees, from henceforward canceled, revoked, and annulled. . . .

Those also of the said religion shall depart and desist henceforward from all practices, negotiations, and intelligences, as well within or without our kingdom; and the said assemblies and councils established within the provinces, shall readily separate, and also all the leagues and associations made or to be made under any pretext, to the prejudice of our present edict, shall be cancelled and annulled, . . . prohibiting most expressly to all our subjects to make henceforth any assessments or levies of money, fortifications, enrollments of men, congregations and assemblies of other than such as are permitted by our present edict, and without arms. . . .

We give in command to the people of our said courts of parlement, chambers of our courts, and courts of our aids, bailiffs, chief-justices, provosts and other of our justices and officers to whom it appertains, and to their lieutenants, that they cause to be read, published, and registered this present edict and ordinance in their courts and jurisdictions, and the same keep punctually, and the contents of the same to cause to be enjoined and used fully and peaceably to all those to whom it shall belong, ceasing and making to cease all troubles and obstructions to the contrary, for such is our pleasure: and in witness hereof we have signed these presents with our own hand; and to the end to make it a thing firm and stable for ever, we have caused to put and endorse our seal to the same. Given at *Nantes* in the month of April in the year of Grace 1598, and of our reign the ninth.

Signed

HENRY

1. Who wrote this document, when, and where?

Many documents will not answer these questions directly; therefore, you will have to look elsewhere for clues. In this case, however, the internal evidence is clear. The author is Henry IV, king of France and Navarre, who issued the document in the French town of Nantes in 1598. Aside from the appearance of his name in the edict, there are other, less explicit, markers of his identity. He uses the first person plural ("we") when referring to himself, a grammatical choice that both signals and accentuates his royal stature.

2. What type of document is this?

In this source, you do not have to look far for an answer to this question. Henry IV describes the document as an "edict," "statute," or "law." These words reveal the public and official nature of the document, echoing their use in our own society today. Even if you do not know exactly what an edict, statute, or law meant in late-sixteenth-century terms, the document itself points the way: "we [Henry IV] have upon the whole, judged it necessary to give to all our subjects one general law, clear, pure, and absolute. . . ." Now you know that the document is a body of law issued by King Henry IV in 1598, which helps to explain its formality as well as the predominance of legal language.

3. Who is the intended audience of the document?

The formal and legalistic language of the edict suggests that Henry IV's immediate audience is not the general public but rather some form of political and/or legal body. The final paragraph supports this conclusion. Here Henry IV commands the "people of our said courts of parlement, chambers of our courts, and courts of our aids, bailiffs, chief-justices, provosts, and other of our justices and officers . . ." to read and publish the edict. Reading between the lines, you can detect a mixture of power and dependency in Henry IV's tone. Look carefully at his verb choices throughout the edict: *prohibit, ordain, will, declare, command*. Each of these verbs casts Henry IV as the leader and the audience as his followers. This strategy was essential because the edict would be nothing but empty words without the courts' compliance. Imagine for a moment that Henry IV was not the king of France but rather a soldier writing a letter to his wife or a merchant preparing a contract. In either case, the language chosen would have changed to suit the genre and audience. Thus, identifying the relationship between author and audience can help you to understand both what the document does and does not say.

4. What are the main points of this document?

To answer this question, you should start with the preamble, for it explains why the edict was issued in the first place: to replace the "frightful troubles, confusions, and disorders" in France with "one general law . . . by which they [our subjects] might be regulated in all differences which have heretofore risen among them, or may hereafter rise. . . ." But what differences specifically? Even with no knowledge of the circumstances surrounding the formulation of the edict, you should notice the numerous references to "the Catholic religion" and "the Reformed religion." With this in mind, read the preamble again. Here we learn that Henry IV had received complaints from Catholic provinces and cities and from Protestants ("our subjects of the Reformed religion") regarding the exercise of their respective religions. Furthermore, as the text continues, since "it has pleased God to give us a beginning of enjoying some rest, we think we cannot employ ourself better than to apply to that which may tend to the glory and service of His holy name, and to provide that He may be adored and prayed unto by all our said subjects, and if it has not yet pleased Him to permit it to be in one and the same form of religion, that it may be at the least with one and the same intention, and with such rules that may prevent among them all troubles and tumults. . . ." Now the details of the document fall into place. Each of the articles addresses specific "rules" governing the legal rights and obligations of French Catholics and Protestants, ranging from where they can worship to where they can work.

5. Why was this document written?

As we have already seen, Henry IV relied on the written word to convey information and, at the same time, to express his "power" and "strength." The legalistic and formal nature of the edict aided him in this effort. Yet as Henry IV knew all too well, the gap between law and action could be large indeed. Thus Henry IV compiled the edict not simply to tell people what to do but to persuade them to do it by delineating the terms of religious coexistence point by point and presenting them as the best safeguard against the return of confusion and disorder. He thereby hoped to restore peace to a country that had been divided by civil war for the previous thirty-six years.

6. What does this document reveal about the particular society and period in question?

Historians have mined the Edict of Nantes for insight into various facets of Henry IV's reign and Protestant-Catholic relations at the time. Do not be daunted by such complexity; you should focus instead on what you see as particularly predominant and revealing themes. One of the most striking in the Edict of Nantes is the central place of religion in late-sixteenth-century society. Our contemporary notion of the separation of church and state had no place in the world of Henry IV and his subjects. As he proclaims in the opening lines, he was king "by the Grace of God" who had given him "virtue" and "strength." Furthermore, you might stop to consider why religious differences were the subject of royal legislation in the first place. Note Henry IV's statement that "if it has not yet pleased Him [God] to permit [Christian worship in France] to be in one and the same form of religion, that it may at the least be with one and the same intention. . . ." What does this suggest about sixteenth-century attitudes toward religious difference and tolerance? You cannot answer this question simply by reading the document in black-and-white terms; you need to look beyond the words and between the lines to draw out the document's broader meanings.

Interpreting Visual Sources

Historians do not rely on written records alone to reconstruct the past; they also turn to nonwritten sources, which are equally varied and rich. By drawing on archeological evidence, historians have reconstructed the material dimensions of everyday life in centuries long past; others have used church sculpture to explore popular religious beliefs; and the list continues. This book includes a range of visual representations to enliven your view of history while enhancing your interpretive skills. Interpreting a visual document is very much like interpreting a nonvisual one — you begin with six questions similar to the ones you have already applied to the Edict of Nantes and move from ascertaining the "facts" of the document to a more complex analysis of the visual document's historical meanings and value.

1. Who created this image, when and where?

Just as with written sources, identifying the artist or creator of an image, and when and where it was produced will provide a foundation for your interpretation. Some visual sources, such as a painting or political cartoon signed by the artist, are more forthcoming in this regard. But if the artist is not known (and even if he or she is), there are other paths of inquiry to pursue. Did someone commission the production of the image? What was the historical context in which the image was produced? Piecing together what you know on these two fronts will allow you to draw some basic conclusions about the image.

2. What type of image is this?

The nature of a visual source shapes its form and content because every visual genre has its own conventions. Take a map as an example. At the most basic level, maps are composites of images created to convey topographical and geographical information about a particular place, whether a town, a region, or a continent. Think about how you use maps in your own life. Sometimes they can be fanciful in their designs but typically they have a practical function — to enable the viewer to get from one place to another or at the very least to get a sense of an area's spatial characteristics. A formal portrait, by contrast, would conform to a different set of conventions and, of equal significance, a different set of viewer expectations and uses.

3. Who are the intended viewers of the image?

As with written sources, identifying the relationship between the image's creator and audience is essential to illuminate fully what the artist is trying to convey. Was the image intended for the general public, such as a photograph published in a newspaper? Or was the intended audience more private? Whether public, private, or somewhere in between, the creator's target audience shapes his or her choice of subject matter, format, and style, which in turn should shape your interpretation of its meaning and significance.

4. What is the central message of the image?

Images convey messages just as powerfully as the written word. The challenge is to learn how to "read" pictorial representations accurately. Since artists use images, color, and space to communicate with their audiences, you must train your eyes to look for visual rather than verbal cues. A good place to start is to note the image's main features, followed by a closer examination of its specific details and their interrelationship.

5. Why was this image produced?

Images are produced for a range of reasons—to convey information, to entertain, or to persuade, to name just a few. Understanding the motivations underlying an image's creation is key to unraveling its meaning (or at least what it was supposed to mean) to people at the time. For example, the impressionist painters of the nineteenth century did not paint simply to paint—their style and subject matter intentionally challenged contemporary artistic norms and conventions. Without knowing this, you cannot appreciate the broader context and impact of impressionist art.

6. What does this image reveal about the society and time period in which it was created?

Answering the first five questions will guide your answer here. Identifying the artist, the type of image, and when, where, and for whom it was produced allows you to step beyond a literal reading of the image into the historical setting in which it was produced. Although the meaning of an image can transcend its historical context, its point of origin and intended audience cannot. Therein rests an image's broader value as a window onto the past, for it is a product of human activity in a specific time and place, just like written documents.

Guided by these six questions, you can evaluate visual sources on their own terms and analyze the ways in which they speak to the broader historical context. Once again, let's take an example.

2.
Illustrating a Native Perspective
Lienzo de Tlaxcala (c. 1560)

Like Bernal Díaz del Castillo, the peoples of central Mexico had a stake in recording the momentous events unfolding around them, for they had long believed that remembering the past was essential to their cultural survival. Traditionally, local peoples used pictoriographic representations to record legends, myths, and historical events. After the Spaniards' arrival, indigenous artists borrowed from this tradition to produce their own accounts of the conquest, including the image on page 11. It is one of a series contained in the Lienzo de Tlaxcala, *painted on cloth in the mid-sixteenth century. Apparently, the* Lienzo *was created for the Spanish viceroy to commemorate the alliance of the Tlaxcalans with the Spaniards. The Tlaxcalans were enemies of the Aztecs and after initial resistance to the Spanish invasion decided to join their forces. This particular image depicts two related events. The first is the meeting between the Aztec leader Moctezuma and Hernán Cortés in Tenochtitlán in August 1519. Cortés is accompanied by Doña Marina, his translator and cultural mediator; Moctezuma appears with warriors at his side. Rather than showing Moctezuma in his traditional garb, the artist dressed him in the manner of the Tlaxcalans.*

xff F1219.L58 LAM .06, Courtesy of The Bancroft Library, University of California, Berkeley.

Both sit in European-style chairs, a nod to European artistic influence, and a Tlaxcalan headdress is suspended in the air between them. Game and fowl offered to the Spaniards are portrayed at the bottom. Within a week of this meeting, Cortés imprisoned Moctezuma in his own palaces with the Tlaxcalans' help. Moctezuma the prisoner appears in the upper right of the image as an old, weak ruler whose sun has set.

1. Who created this image, when and where?

In this case, you will have to rely on the headnote to answer these questions. The image was created by an unknown Tlaxcalan artist in the mid-sixteenth century as part of a pictorial series, the *Lienzo de Tlaxcala*, depicting the Spanish conquest of Aztec Mexico. Although the image commemorates events that took place in 1519, it was produced decades later, when Spanish imperial control was firmly entrenched. Thus the image represents a visual point of contact between Spanish and indigenous traditions in the age of European global expansion. Although knowing the identity of the artist would be ideal, the fact that he was Tlaxcalan is of greater value. The Tlaxcalans had allied themselves with the Spanish and considered the *Lienzo* a way of highlighting their role in the Aztecs' defeat.

2. What type of image is this?

On the one hand, this image fits into a long pictorial tradition among the peoples of central Mexico. Before the conquest, they had no alphabetic script. Instead, they drew on a rich repertoire of images and symbols to preserve legends, myths, and historical events. These images and symbols, which included the stylized warriors shown here, were typically painted into books made of deerskin or a plant-based paper. On the other hand, the image also reveals clear European influences, most noticeably in the type of chair in which both Cortés and Moctezuma sit. Looking at the image again with these dual influences in mind, think about how the pictorial markers allowed both indigenous and Spanish viewers to see something recognizable in an event that marked the destruction of one world and the creation of another.

3. Who are the intended viewers of the image?

As the headnote reveals, the image's creator had a specific audience in mind, a Spanish colonial administrator. You should take this fact into account as you think about the image's meaning and significance. Just because a Tlaxcalan artist created the image does not necessarily mean that it represents an unadulterated native point of view. And just because the image documents two historical events does not necessarily mean that the "facts" are objectively presented.

4. What is the central message of the image?

There are many visual components of this image, each of which you should consider individually and then as part of the picture as a whole. As you already know, the artist combined indigenous and European representational traditions. What does this suggest about the image's message? The merging of these two traditions represents the alliance the Tlaxcalans forged with the Spanish. Looking closer, think about how the two leaders, Cortés and Moctezuma, are represented. Cortés is accompanied by his translator, Doña Marina, a Nahua woman. Originally a slave, she had been given to Cortés after his defeat of the Maya at Potonchan. She became a crucial interpreter and cultural mediator for Cortés in the world of the Mexica. Language appears here as a source of his power as well as his alliance with the Tlaxcalans. Although the Spanish contingent was relatively small, thousands of Tlaxcalan and other native warriors entered Tenochtitlán with them, a show of force not lost on local residents. The artist captures this fact by clothing Moctezuma in Tlaxcalan dress — he had once ruled over them but now he was to be ruled. Soon after this meeting, Moctezuma was imprisoned in his own palaces. The artist captures this event in the upper right where Moctezuma is shown as a prisoner.

5. Why was this image produced?

Examining this image reveals the complexity of this question, regardless of the nature of the source. At first glance, the answer is easy: the image was created to commemorate specific events. Yet given what you know about the setting in which the image was produced, the "why" takes on a deeper meaning. The image does not simply record events; it sets a scene in which multiple meanings are embedded — the chairs, Doña Marina, the warriors — that suggest how the Spanish conquest transformed native culture. The image thus served a dual function — to inform the Spanish of the Tlaxcalans' role in the conquest while affirming Spanish dominance over them.

6. What does this image reveal about the society and time period in which it was created?

Answering this question requires you to step beyond a literal meaning of the image into the historical setting in which it was produced. Here you will uncover multiple layers of the image's broader significance. Consider the artist, for example, and his audience. What does the fact that a native artist created the image for a Spanish audience suggest about the nature of Spanish colonization? Clearly, the Spaniards did not make their presence felt as a colonial power simply by seizing land and treasure; they also reshaped indigenous people's understanding of themselves in both the past and present. That the Tlaxcalans expressed this understanding visually in a historical document lent an air of permanence and legitimacy to Spanish colonization and, equally important, to the Tlaxcalans' contributions to it.

Conclusion

Through your analysis of historical sources, you will not only learn details about the world in which the sources were created but also become an active contributor to our understanding of these details' broader significance. Written documents and pictorial representations don't just "tell" historians what happened; they require historians to step into their own imaginations as they strive to reconstitute the past. In this regard, historians' approach to primary sources is exactly that which is described here. They determine the basics of the source — who created it, when, and where — as a springboard for increasingly complex levels of analysis. Each level builds upon the other, just like rungs on a ladder. If you take the time to climb each rung in sequence, you will be able to master the content of a source and to use it to bring history to life. The written and visual primary sources included in *Sources of The Making of the West*, Fourth Edition, will allow you to participate firsthand in the process of historical inquiry by exploring the people, places, and sights of the past and how they shaped their own world and continue to shape ours today.

Early Western Civilization

4000–1000 B.C.E.

The roots of Western culture cut across distant lands and ancient societies. The five documents in this chapter expose the fundamental features of these early civilizations as they developed between the twentieth and tenth centuries B.C.E. The evidence reveals that on the one hand, peoples then living in the Near East, Africa, and the Mediterranean developed their own distinctive beliefs, mythologies, customs, and sense of identity. On the other, they shared many attributes, such as large urban populations, the use of writing, devotion to religion, and economies based on trade and agriculture. This unique mixture of cross-cultural similarities and differences forged the path for the future.

1.
Defining Humanity

Epic of Gilgamesh (c. 2000 B.C.E.)

Invented by the Sumerians in Mesopotamia around 3500 B.C.E., writing was one of the most important products of civilization. People could now record and preserve traditions and beliefs without having to rely exclusively on memory and the spoken word. In this way, writing helped to shape a community's sense of belonging from one generation to the next. Originally written on twelve clay tablets, the poem Epic of Gilgamesh *is one of the oldest recorded stories in the world. The hero is Gilgamesh, the legendary king of the Sumerian city-state of Uruk. His desire to gain immortality drives the plot of the story. The epic's first tablet, excerpted below, sets the tale into motion. It describes Gilgamesh as part god and part man, who heaped abuse on his subjects. Distressed, they beseech the gods to create a match for Gilgamesh's stormy heart. The mother of the gods, Aruru, responds by creating Enkidu, a man of nature, who ultimately befriends Gilgamesh. Over the course of their ensuing adventures together, Enkidu teaches Gilgamesh about his own humanity in life and in death.*

From *The Epic of Gilgamesh*, trans. N. K. Sandars (Baltimore: Penguin Classics, 1972), 61–66.

Gilgamesh King in Uruk

I will proclaim to the world the deeds of Gilgamesh. This was the man to whom all things were known; this was the king who knew the countries of the world. He was wise, he saw mysteries and knew secret things, he brought us a tale of the days before the flood. He went on a long journey, was weary, worn-out with labor, returning he rested, he engraved on a stone the whole story.

When the gods created Gilgamesh they gave him a perfect body. Shamash the glorious sun endowed him with beauty, Adad the god of the storm endowed him with courage, the great gods made his beauty perfect, surpassing all others, terrifying like a great wild bull. Two thirds they made him god and one third man.

In Uruk he built walls, a great rampart, and the temple of blessed Eanna for the god of the firmament Anu, and for Ishtar the goddess of love. Look at it still today: the outer wall where the cornice runs, it shines with the brilliance of copper; and the inner wall, it has no equal. Touch the threshold, it is ancient. Approach Eanna the dwelling of Ishtar, our lady of love and war, the like of which no latter-day king, no man alive can equal. Climb upon the wall of Uruk; walk along it, I say; regard the foundation terrace and examine the masonry: is it not burnt brick and good? The seven sages laid the foundations.

The Coming of Enkidu

Gilgamesh went abroad in the world, but he met with none who could withstand his arms till he came to Uruk. But the men of Uruk muttered in their houses, "Gilgamesh sounds the tocsin[1] for his amusement, his arrogance has no bounds by day or night. No son is left with his father, for Gilgamesh takes them all, even the children; yet the king should be a shepherd to his people. His lust leaves no virgin to her lover, neither the warrior's daughter nor the wife of the noble; yet this is the shepherd of the city, wise, comely, and resolute."

The gods heard their lament, the gods of heaven cried to the Lord of Uruk, to Anu the god of Uruk: "A goddess made him, strong as a savage bull, none can withstand his arms. No son is left with his father, for Gilgamesh takes them all; and is this the king, the shepherd of his people? His lust leaves no virgin to her lover, neither the warrior's daughter nor the wife of the noble." When Anu had heard their lamentation the gods cried to Aruru, the goddess of creation, "You made him, O Aruru, now create his equal; let it be as like him as his own reflection, his second self, stormy heart for stormy heart. Let them contend together and leave Uruk in quiet."

So the goddess conceived an image in her mind, and it was of the stuff of Anu of the firmament. She dipped her hands in water and pinched off clay, she let it fall in the wilderness, and noble Enkidu was created. There was virtue in him of the god of war, of Ninurta himself. His body was rough, he had long hair like a woman's; it waved like the hair of Nisaba, the goddess of corn. His body was covered with matted hair like Samuqan's, the god of cattle. He was innocent of mankind; he knew nothing of the cultivated land.

[1]**tocsin**: bell. [Ed.]

Enkidu ate grass in the hills with the gazelle and lurked with wild beasts at the water-holes; he had joy of the water with the herds of wild game. But there was a trapper who met him one day face to face at the drinking-hole, for the wild game had entered his territory. On three days he met him face to face, and the trapper was frozen with fear. He went back to his house with the game that he had caught, and he was dumb, benumbed with terror. His face was altered like that of one who had made a long journey. With awe in his heart he spoke to his father: "Father, there is a man, unlike any other, who comes down from the hills. He is the strongest in the world, he is like an immortal from heaven. He ranges over the hills with wild beasts and eats grass; he ranges through your land and comes down to the wells. I am afraid and dare not go near him. He fills in the pits which I dig and tears up my traps set for the game; he helps the beasts to escape and now they slip through my fingers."

His father opened his mouth and said to the trapper, "My son, in Uruk lives Gilgamesh; no one has ever prevailed against him, he is strong as a star from heaven. Go to Uruk, find Gilgamesh, extol the strength of this wild man. Ask him to give you a harlot, a wanton from the temple of love; return with her, and let her woman's power overpower this man. When next he comes down to drink at the wells she will be there, stripped naked; and when he sees her beckoning he will embrace her, and then the wild beasts will reject him."

So the trapper set out on his journey to Uruk and addressed himself to Gilgamesh saying, "A man unlike any other is roaming now in the pastures; he is as strong as a star from heaven and I am afraid to approach him. He helps the wild game to escape; he fills in my pits and pulls up my traps." Gilgamesh said, "Trapper, go back, take with you a harlot, a child of pleasure. At the drinking-hole she will strip, and when he sees her beckoning he will embrace her and the game of the wilderness will surely reject him."

Now the trapper returned, taking the harlot with him. After a three days' journey they came to the drinking-hole, and there they sat down; the harlot and the trapper sat facing one another and waited for the game to come. For the first day and for the second day the two sat waiting, but on the third day the herds came; they came down to drink and Enkidu was with them. The small wild creatures of the plains were glad of the water, and Enkidu with them, who ate grass with the gazelle and was born in the hills; and she saw him, the savage man, come from far-off in the hills. The trapper spoke to her: "There he is. Now, woman, make your breasts bare, have no shame, do not delay but welcome his love. Let him see you naked, let him possess your body. When he comes near uncover yourself and lie with him; teach him, the savage man, your woman's art, for when he murmurs love to you the wild beasts that shared his life in the hills will reject him."

She was not ashamed to take him, she made herself naked and welcomed his eagerness; as he lay on her murmuring love she taught him the woman's art. For six days and seven nights they lay together, for Enkidu had forgotten his home in the hills; but when he was satisfied he went back to the wild beasts. Then, when the gazelle saw him, they bolted away; when the wild creatures saw him they fled. Enkidu would have followed, but his body was bound as though with a cord, his knees gave way when he started to run, his swiftness was gone. And now the wild creatures had all fled away; Enkidu was grown weak, for wisdom was in him, and the thoughts of a man were in his heart. So he returned and sat down at the woman's feet, and listened intently to what she said. "You are wise, Enkidu, and now you have become like a god. Why do you want to run wild with the beasts in the hills? Come with me. I will take you to strong-walled Uruk, to the blessed temple of Ishtar and of Anu, of love and of heaven: there Gilgamesh lives, who is very strong, and like a wild bull he lords it over men."

When she had spoken Enkidu was pleased; he longed for a comrade, for one who would understand his heart. "Come, woman, and take me to that holy temple, to the house of Anu and of Ishtar, and to the place where Gilgamesh lords it over the people. I will challenge him boldly, I will cry out aloud in Uruk, 'I am the strongest here, I have come to change the old order, I am he who was born in the hills, I am he who is strongest of all.'"

She said, "Let us go, and let him see your face. I know very well where Gilgamesh is in great Uruk. O Enkidu, there all the people are dressed in their gorgeous robes, every day is holiday, the young men and the girls are wonderful to see. How sweet they smell! All the great ones are roused from their beds. O Enkidu, you who love life, I will show you Gilgamesh, a man of many moods; you shall look at him well in his radiant manhood. His body is perfect in strength and maturity; he never rests by night or day. He is stronger than you, so leave your boasting. Shamash the glorious sun has given favors to Gilgamesh, and Anu of the heavens, and Enlil, and Ea the wise has given him deep understanding. I tell you, even before you have left the wilderness, Gilgamesh will know in his dreams that you are coming."

Discussion Questions

1. How does the poem describe Gilgamesh and Enkidu before their first meeting? What do they look like physically? What is the source of their strength?

2. Why does Enkidu need to be tamed? What does he gain in the process?

3. What does the creation of Enkidu suggest about how Mesopotamians understood the relationship between the gods and humans, between nature and civilization?

2.
Establishing Law and Justice

King Hammurabi, *The Code of Hammurabi*
(Early Eighteenth Century b.c.e.)

The law code promulgated by King Hammurabi (r. c. 1792–1750 b.c.e.) of Babylon elucidates the inner workings of Mesopotamian society, the cradle of the world's first civilization. The copy of the code excerpted here is inscribed on a stone pillar, crowned by a sculptural relief depicting the god of justice commissioning Hammurabi to write

From James B. Pritchard, ed., *Ancient Near Eastern Texts Relating to the Old Testament*, 3rd ed. with supplement (Princeton, NJ: Princeton University Press, 1969), 164–78.

the laws. This image embodies the Mesopotamian belief that kings were divinely appointed and thereby responsible for imparting justice and promoting their subjects' well-being. As a messenger of the divine will, King Hammurabi influenced both the public and private lives of his people. As the following selection reveals, he was especially concerned with protecting property rights and a social hierarchy that positioned slaves at the bottom and free persons at the top. By codifying laws in writing, Hammurabi helped set an enduring precedent in the Western tradition.

When lofty Anum,[1] king of the Anunnaki,[2]
(and) Enlil, lord of heaven and earth,
the determiner of the destinies of the land,
determined for Marduk,[3] the first-born of Enki,[4]
the Enlil functions over all mankind,
made him great among the Igigi,[5]
called Babylon by its exalted name,
made it supreme in the world,
established for him in its midst an enduring kingship,
whose foundations are as firm as heaven and earth —
at that time Anum and Enlil named me
to promote the welfare of the people,[6]
me, Hammurabi, the devout, god-fearing prince,
to cause justice to prevail in the land,
to destroy the wicked and the evil,
that the strong might not oppress the weak,
to rise like the sun over the black-headed (people),[7]
and to light up the land. . . .

(v)

When Marduk commissioned me to guide the people aright,
     to direct the land,
I established law and justice in the language of the land,
thereby promoting the welfare of the people.
At that time (I decreed):

---

[1]The sky-god, the leader of the pantheon, worshiped especially in the temple of Eanna in Uruk, along with the goddess Inanna.

[2]In this inscription the Anunnaki are the lesser gods attendant upon Anum, and the Igigi are the lesser gods attendant on Enlil.

[3]The storm-god, the chief executive of the pantheon, worshiped especially in the temple of Ekur in Nippur in central Babylonia, modern Nuffar.

[4]The son of Enki and consort of Sarpanit; the god of Babylon and in Hammurabi's time the god of the Babylonian Empire with the functions of Enlil delegated to him; worshiped especially in the temple of Esagila in Babylon.

[5]Lord of the earth and the mass of life-giving waters within it, issuing in streams and fountains; the father of Marduk; worshiped especially in the temple of Eabzu in Eridu, in southern Babylonia, modern Abu Shahrein.

[6]Lit., "to make good the flesh of the people."

[7]The late-Sumerian expression for men in general.

The Laws

If a seignior[8] accused a(nother) seignior and brought a charge of murder against him, but has not proved it, his accuser shall be put to death.[9]

If a seignior brought a charge of sorcery against a(nother) seignior, but has not proved it, the one against whom the charge of sorcery was brought, upon going to the river,[10] shall throw himself into the river, and if the river has then overpowered him, his accuser shall take over his estate; if the river has shown that seignior to be innocent and he has accordingly come forth safe, the one who brought the charge of sorcery against him shall be put to death, while the one who threw himself into the river shall take over the estate of his accuser.

If a seignior came forward with false testimony in a case, and has not proved the word which he spoke, if that case was a case involving life, that seignior shall be put to death. . . .

If a seignior has purchased or he received for safe-keeping either silver or gold or a male slave or a female slave or an ox or a sheep or an ass or any sort of thing from the hand of a seignior's son or a seignior's slave without witnesses and contracts, since that seignior is a thief, he shall be put to death.

If a seignior stole either an ox or a sheep or an ass or a pig or a boat, if it belonged to the church (or) if it belonged to the state, he shall make thirtyfold restitution; if it belonged to a private citizen, he shall make good tenfold. If the thief does not have sufficient to make restitution, he shall be put to death. . . .

If a seignior has stolen the young son of a(nother) seignior, he shall be put to death.[11]

If a seignior has helped either a male slave of the state or a female slave of the state or a male slave of a private citizen or a female slave of a private citizen to escape through the city-gate, he shall be put to death.

If a seignior has harbored in his house either a fugitive male or female slave belonging to the state or to a private citizen and has not brought him forth at the summons of the police, that householder shall be put to death. . . .

If a seignior made a breach in a house, they shall put him to death in front of that breach and wall him in.[12]

---

[8]The word *awēlum*, used here, is literally "man," but in the legal literature it seems to be used in at least three senses: (1) sometimes to indicate a man of the higher class; (2) sometimes to suggest a free man of any class; and (3) occasionally, to indicate a man of any class. For the last, I use the inclusive word *man*, but for the first two, since it is seldom clear which of the two is intended in a given context, I follow the ambiguity of the original and use the rather general term *seignior* in Italian and Spanish, to indicate any free man of standing, and not in the strict feudal sense, although the ancient Near East did have something approximating the feudal system, and that is another reason for using *seignior*.

[9]With this law and the three following, cf. Deut. 5:20, 19:16 ff. and Exod. 23:1–3.

[10]The word for "river" throughout this section has the determinative of deity, indicating that the Euphrates river, as judge in the case, was regarded as god.

[11]Cf. Exod. 21:16 and Deut. 24:7.

[12]Cf. Exod. 22:2, 3a.

If a seignior committed robbery and has been caught, that seignior shall be put to death.

If the robber has not been caught, the robbed seignior shall set forth the particulars regarding his lost property in the presence of god, and the city and governor, in whose territory and district the robbery was committed, shall make good to him his lost property.

If it was a life (that was lost), the city and governor shall pay one mina[13] of silver to his people. . . .[14]

If a seignior rented a field for cultivation, but has not produced grain in the field, they shall prove that he did no work on the field and he shall give grain to the owner of the field on the basis of those adjoining it.

If he did not cultivate the field, but has neglected (it), he shall give grain to the owner of the field on the basis of those adjoining it; furthermore, the field which he neglected he shall break up with mattocks, harrow and return to the owner of the field. . . .

If a shepherd has not come to an agreement with the owner of a field to pasture sheep on the grass, but has pastured sheep on the field without the consent of the owner of the field, when the owner of the field harvests his field, the shepherd who pastured the sheep on the field without the consent of the owner of the field shall give in addition twenty *kur* of grain per eighteen *iku* to the owner of the field. . . .

If a merchant lent grain, wool, oil, or any goods at all to a trader to retail, the trader shall write down the value and pay (it) back to the merchant, with the trader obtaining a sealed receipt for the money which he pays to the merchant.

If the trader has been careless and so has not obtained a sealed receipt for the money which he paid to the merchant, the money with no sealed receipt may not be credited to the account.

If a trader borrowed money from a merchant and has then disputed (the fact) with his merchant, that merchant in the presence of god and witnesses shall prove that the trader borrowed the money and the trader shall pay to the merchant threefold the full amount of money that he borrowed.

When a merchant entrusted (something) to a trader and the trader has returned to his merchant whatever the merchant gave him, if the merchant has then disputed with him whatever the trader gave him, that trader shall prove it against the merchant in the presence of god and witnesses and the merchant shall pay to the trader sixfold whatever he received because he had a dispute with his trader.

If a woman wine seller, instead of receiving grain for the price of a drink, has received money by the large weight and so has made the value of the drink less than the value of the grain, they shall prove it against that wine seller[15] and throw her into the water.

---

[13]A weight of about 500 grams, divided into 60 shekels.
[14]For this and the preceding law, cf. Deut. 21:1 ff.
[15]This has also been translated as "they shall bind that wine seller."

If outlaws have congregated in the establishment of a woman wine seller and she has not arrested those outlaws and did not take them to the palace, that wine seller shall be put to death. . . .

If a seignior pointed the finger at a nun or the wife of a(nother) seignior, but has proved nothing, they shall drag that seignior into the presence of the judges and also cut off half his (hair).

If a seignior acquired a wife, but did not draw up the contracts for her, that woman is no wife.

If the wife of a seignior has been caught while lying with another man, they shall bind them and throw them into the water. If the husband[16] of the woman wishes to spare his wife, then the king in turn may spare his subject.[17]

If a seignior bound the (betrothed) wife of a(nother) seignior, who had had no intercourse with[18] a male and was still living in her father's house, and he has lain in her bosom and they have caught him, that seignior shall be put to death, while that woman shall go free.[19]

If a seignior's wife was accused by her husband,[20] but she was not caught while lying with another man, she shall make affirmation by god and return to her house.

If the finger was pointed at the wife of a seignior because of another man, but she has not been caught while lying with the other man, she shall throw herself into the river[21] for the sake of her husband.[22]

If a seignior was taken captive, but there was sufficient to live on in his house, his wife [shall not leave her house, but she shall take care of her person by not] entering [the house of another].[23]

If that woman did not take care of her person, but has entered the house of another, they shall prove it against that woman and throw her into the water.[24]

If the seignior was taken captive and there was not sufficient to live on in his house, his wife may enter the house of another, with that woman incurring no blame at all.

If, when a seignior was taken captive and there was not sufficient to live on in his house, his wife has then entered the house of another before his (return) and has borne children, (and) later her husband has returned and has reached his city, that woman shall return to her first husband, while the children shall go with their father.

If, when a seignior deserted his city and then ran away, his wife has entered the house of another after his (departure), if that seignior has returned and wishes to take back his wife, the wife of the fugitive shall not return to her husband because he scorned his city and ran away. . . .

---

[16]Lit., "owner, master."
[17]Lit., "his slave." With this law cf. Deut. 22:22.
[18]Lit., "had not known."
[19]Cf. Deut. 22:23–27.
[20]Lit., "If with respect to a seignior's wife (casus pendens) her husband accused her."
[21]I.e., submit to the water ordeal, with the river as divine judge; cf. note 10.
[22]Cf. Num. 5:11–31.
[23]I.e., in order to live there as another man's wife.
[24]I.e., to be drowned.

If a seignior wishes to divorce his wife who did not bear him children, he shall give her money to the full amount of her marriage-price and he shall also make good to her the dowry which she brought from her father's house and then he may divorce her.

If there was no marriage-price, he shall give her one mina of silver as the divorce-settlement.

If he is a peasant, he shall give her one-third mina of silver.

If a seignior's wife, who was living in the house of the seignior, has made up her mind to leave in order that she may engage in business, thus neglecting her house (and) humiliating her husband, they shall prove it against her; and if her husband has then decided on her divorce, he may divorce her, with nothing to be given her as her divorce-settlement upon her departure.[25] If her husband has not decided on her divorce, her husband may marry another woman, with the former woman[26] living in the house of her husband like a maidservant.

If a woman so hated her husband that she has declared, "You may not have me," her record shall be investigated at her city council, and if she was careful and was not at fault, even though her husband has been going out and disparaging her greatly, that woman, without incurring any blame at all, may take her dowry and go off to her father's house.

If she was not careful, but was a gadabout, thus neglecting her house (and) humiliating her husband, they shall throw that woman into the water. . . .

When a seignior married a woman and a fever[27] has then seized her, if he has made up his mind to marry another, he may marry (her), without divorcing his wife whom the fever seized; she shall live in the house which he built and he shall continue to support her as long as she lives.

If that woman has refused to live in her husband's house, he shall make good her dowry to her which she brought from her father's house and then she may leave.

If a seignior, upon presenting a field, orchard, house, or goods to his wife, left a sealed document with her, her children may not enter a claim against her after (the death of) her husband, since the mother may give her inheritance to that son of hers whom she likes, (but) she may not give (it) to an outsider. . . .

If a seignior's wife has brought about the death of her husband because of another man, they shall impale that woman on stakes. . . .

If, when a seignior acquired a wife, she bore him children and that woman has then gone to (her) fate, her father may not lay claim to her dowry, since her dowry belongs to her children.

If a seignior acquired a wife and that woman has gone to (her) fate without providing him with children, if his father-in-law has then returned to him the marriage-price which that seignior brought to the house of his father-in-law, her husband may not lay claim to the dowry of that woman, since her dowry belongs to her father's house. . . .

---

[25]Lit., "her journey," a noun in the adverbial accusative of manner.
[26]Lit., "that woman."
[27]The exact meaning of the word used here, *la'bum*, is not known.

If a member of the artisan class[28] took a son as a foster child and has taught him his handicraft, he may never be reclaimed. . . .

If a son has struck his father, they shall cut off his hand.[29]

If a seignior has destroyed the eye of a member of the aristocracy,[30] they shall destroy his eye.[31]

If he has broken a(nother) seignior's bone, they shall break his bone.[32]

If he has destroyed the eye of a commoner or broken the bone of a commoner, he shall pay one mina of silver.

If he has destroyed the eye of a seignior's slave or broken the bone of a seignior's slave, he shall pay one-half his value.

If a seignior has knocked out a tooth of a seignior of his own rank, they shall knock out his tooth.[33]

If he has knocked out a commoner's tooth, he shall pay one-third mina of silver.

If a seignior has struck the cheek of a seignior who is superior to him, he shall be beaten sixty (times) with an oxtail whip in the assembly.

If a member of the aristocracy has struck the cheek of a(nother) member of the aristocracy who is of the same rank as[34] himself, he shall pay one mina of silver.

If a commoner has struck the cheek of a(nother) commoner, he shall pay ten shekels of silver.

If a seignior's slave has struck the cheek of a member of the aristocracy, they shall cut off his ear.

If a seignior has struck a(nother) seignior in a brawl and has inflicted an injury on him, that seignior shall swear, "I did not strike him deliberately";[35] and he shall also pay for the physician.

If he has died because of his blow, he shall swear (as before), and if it was a member of the aristocracy, he shall pay one-half mina of silver.

If it was a member of the commonalty, he shall pay one-third mina of silver.

If a seignior struck a(nother) seignior's daughter and has caused her to have a miscarriage,[36] he shall pay ten shekels of silver for her fetus.

---

[28]Lit., "the son of an artisan," where "son" is used in the technical sense of "belonging to the class or species of," which is so common in the Semitic languages.

[29]Cf. Exod. 21:15. For the whole collection of laws dealing with personal injuries (laws 195–214), cf. the similar collection in Exod. 21:12–27.

[30]Lit., "the son of a man," where "son" is used in the technical sense explained before and "man" is used in the sense of "noble or aristocrat." It is also possible that "son" here is intended to be taken in its regular sense to indicate a person younger than the assailant.

[31]Cf. Exod. 21:23–25.

[32]Cf. Lev. 24:19f.

[33]Cf. Deut. 19:21.

[34]Lit., "who is like."

[35]Lit., "while I was aware of (it)."

[36]Lit., "caused her to drop that of her womb (her fetus)." With this and the following five laws, cf. Exod. 21:22–25.

If that woman has died, they shall put his daughter to death.

If by a blow he has caused a commoner's daughter to have a miscarriage, he shall pay five shekels of silver.

If that woman has died, he shall pay one-half mina of silver.

If he struck a seignior's female slave and has caused her to have a miscarriage, he shall pay two shekels of silver.

If that female slave has died, he shall pay one-third mina of silver. . . .

If an ox, when it was walking along the street, gored a seignior to death,[37] that case is not subject to claim.

If a seignior's ox was a gorer and his city council made it known to him that it was a gorer, but he did not pad its horns (or) tie up his ox, and that ox gored to death a member of the aristocracy, he shall give one-half mina of silver.[38]

If it was a seignior's slave, he shall give one-third mina of silver. . . .

The Epilogue

The laws of justice, which Hammurabi, the efficient king, set up,
and by which he caused the land to take the right way and have good government.
I, Hammurabi, the perfect king,
was not careless (or) neglectful of the black-headed (people),
whom Enlil had presented to me,
(and) whose shepherding Marduk had committed to me;
I sought out peaceful regions for them;
I overcame grievous difficulties;
I caused light to rise on them.
With the mighty weapon which Zababa and Inanna entrusted to me,
with the insight that Enki allotted to me,
with the ability that Marduk gave me,
I rooted out the enemy above and below;
I made an end of war;
I promoted the welfare of the land;
I made the peoples rest in friendly habitations;
I did not let them have anyone to terrorize them.
The great gods called me,
so I became the beneficent shepherd whose scepter is righteous;
my benign shadow is spread over my city.
In my bosom I carried the peoples of the land of Sumer and Akkad;
they prospered under my protection;
I always governed them in peace;
I sheltered them in my wisdom.
In order that the strong might not oppress the weak,
that justice might be dealt the orphan (and) the widow,
in Babylon, the city whose head Anum and Enlil raised aloft,

---

[37]Lit., "and has caused his death."
[38]Cf. Exod. 21:28–36.

in Esagila, the temple whose foundations stand firm like heaven and earth,
I wrote my precious words on my stela,
and in the presence of the statue of me, the king of justice,
I set (it) up in order to administer the law of the land,
to prescribe the ordinances of the land,
to give justice to the oppressed.

DISCUSSION QUESTIONS

1. What do the Prologue and Epilogue indicate about the status of Mesopotamian rulers?

2. What values or ideals governing the code are expressed in these excerpts?

3. What does the code reveal in particular about women's position in Mesopotamian society?

3.
Praising the One God

Hymn to the Aten (Fourteenth Century B.C.E.)

In the fourth and third millennia B.C.E., Egypt emerged as a great civilization to rival that of Mesopotamia. Guided by a succession of powerful kings, Egypt became a prosperous, unified country despite intermittent periods of turmoil and disarray. Among the reasons for Egypt's rise as a large-scale state was a deeply held belief in the gods as a model for central authority and stability. Egyptians considered their kings, ultimately known as pharaohs, to be divinity in human form; as such, they had a particular responsibility to pay tribute to the traditional gods. The New Kingdom pharaoh Akhenaten (r. 1372–1355 B.C.E.) sought to reform this tradition. Instead of honoring the older state and local gods, he ordered that all worship center on the god Aten, who represented the sun. The "Hymn to the Aten" points to Akhenaten's special relationship with Aten as his "son"; it was most likely composed by his scribes to reflect basic royal doctrine. Although Egyptians had long revered Aten as a manifestation of the sun god Re, their religion remained fundamentally polytheistic. By contrast, through hymns such as this one Akhenaten elevated Aten to new heights of importance as the sole god. His religion never received popular support and consequently did not survive Akhenaten's death; even so, it reveals both the profound religiosity of the Egyptian people and also their inherent conservatism.

Adoration of *Re-Harakhti-who-rejoices-in-lightland In-his-name-Shu-who-is-Aten*, who gives life forever, by the King who lives by Maat,[1] the Lord of the Two Lands:

From Miriam Lichtheim, *Ancient Egyptian Literature: Volume II: The New Kingdom* (Berkeley: University of California Press, 1976), 91–92.

[1]**Maat:** The divine principle of order and justice. Egyptians believed that their rulers were responsible for providing Maat for the gods. [Ed.]

Neferkheprure, Sole-one-of-Re; the Son of Re who lives by Maat, the Lord of crowns: *Akhenaten*, great in his lifetime, given life forever.[2]

Splendid you rise, O living Aten, eternal lord!
You are radiant, beauteous, mighty,
Your love is great, immense.
Your rays light up all faces,
Your bright hue gives life to hearts,
When you fill the Two Lands with your love.
August God who fashioned himself,
Who made very land, created what is in it,
All peoples, herds, and flocks,
All trees that grow from soil;
They live when you dawn for them,
You are mother and father of all that you made.

When you dawn their eyes observe you,
As your rays light the whole earth;
Every heart acclaims your sight,
When you are risen as their lord.
When you set in sky's western lightland,
They lie down as if to die,
Their heads covered, their noses stopped,
Until you dawn in sky's eastern lightland.
Their arms adore your *ka*,[3]
As you nourish the hearts by your beauty;
One lives when you cast your rays,
Every land is in festivity.

Singers, musicians, shout with joy,
In the court of the *benben*-shrine,[4]
And in all temples in Akhet-Aten,
The place of truth in which you rejoice.
Foods are offered in their midst,
Your holy son performs your praises,
O Aten living in his risings,
And all your creatures leap before you.
Your august son exults in joy,
O Aten living daily content in the sky,

---

[2]As originally composed, the hymn was recited by the king, hence this introduction. In the final portion of the hymn, the king speaks in the first person. . . .

[3]*ka*: In ancient Egyptian religion, *ka* was a primary aspect of the soul of a human being or of a god. [Ed.]

[4]A sanctuary of Aten at El Amarna which seems to have been named after the sanctuary of Re at Heliopolis that bore this name.

Your offspring, your august son, Sole one of Re;[5]
Your Son of Re does not cease to extol his beauty,[6]
Neferkheprure, Sole-one-of-Re.

I am your son who serves you, who exalts your name,
Your power, your strength, are firm in my heart;
You are the living Aten whose image endures,
You have made the far sky to shine in it,
To observe all that you made.
You are One yet a million lives are in you,
To make them live <you give> the breath of life to their noses;
By the sight of your rays all flowers exist,
What lives and sprouts from the soil grows when you shine.
Drinking deep of your sight all flocks frisk,
The birds in the nest fly up in joy;
Their folded wings unfold in praise
Of the living Aten, their maker.

DISCUSSION QUESTIONS

1. Describe Aten as he is presented in this hymn. What are his attributes?

2. How do these attributes reflect Egyptian beliefs about the role of the gods in the everyday world?

3. What does this hymn suggest about the relationship between Aten and Akhenaten? Why do you think the pharaoh wanted to celebrate this relationship?

4. Some scholars argue that the cult of Aten represents an early form of monotheism. Is there any evidence in this hymn to support this argument?

4.
Writing Experiences

Egyptian Scribal Exercise Book (Twelfth Century B.C.E.)

After a period of political troubles, the successors of the Middle Kingdom rulers transformed Egypt into an imperial power. Key to the success of the New Kingdom was a legion of professional scribes who oversaw governmental affairs both at home and abroad. To ensure they were fit for civil service, a new literary genre known as "school texts" was developed for the use of scribes in training and their teachers. The book excerpted here was compiled with just such a purpose in mind. In it, a high-ranking

---

From Miriam Lichtheim, *Ancient Egyptian Literature: Volume II: The New Kingdom* (Berkeley: University of California Press, 1976), 168–72.

[5]The epithet which forms part of Akhenaten's throne name.
[6]One expects "your beauty."

scribe, frustrated by his apprentice's poor performance, contrasts the prestige and comfort of the scribal profession to other forms of employment. Although the text is clearly biased in favor of scribes, it provides insight into their special status in Egyptian society as masters of the technology of writing.

Title

(1,1) [Beginning of the instruction in letter writing made by the royal scribe and chief overseer of the cattle of Amen-Re, King of Gods, Nebmare-nakht] for his apprentice, the scribe Wenemdiamun.

The Idle Scribe Is Worthless

The royal scribe and chief overseer of the cattle of Amen-Re, King of Gods, Nebmare-nakht, speaks to the scribe Wenemdiamun, as follows. You are busy coming and going, and don't think of writing. You resist listening to me; (3,5) you neglect my teachings.

You are worse than the goose of the shore, that is busy with mischief. It spends the summer destroying the dates, the winter destroying the seed-grain. It spends the balance of the year in pursuit of the cultivators. It does not let seed be cast to the ground without snatching it in its fall. One cannot catch it by snaring. One does not offer it in the temple. The evil, sharp-eyed bird that does no work!

You are worse than the desert antelope that lives by running. It spends no day in plowing. Never at all does it tread on the threshing-floor. It lives on the oxen's labor, without entering among them. But though I spend the day telling you "Write," it seems like a plague to you. Writing is very (4,1) pleasant! ———.

All Occupations Are Bad Except That of the Scribe

See for yourself with your own eye. The occupations lie before you.

The washerman's day is going up, going down. All his limbs are weak, [from] whitening his neighbors' clothes every day, from washing their linen.

The maker of pots is smeared with soil, like one whose relations have died. His hands, (4,5) his feet are full of clay; he is like one who lives in the bog.

The cobbler mingles with vats. His odor is penetrating. His hands are red with madder, like one who is smeared with blood. He looks behind him for the kite, like one whose flesh is exposed.

The watchman[1] prepares garlands and polishes vase-stands. He spends a night of toil just as one on whom the sun shines.

The merchants travel downstream and upstream. They are as busy as can be, carrying goods from one town to another. They supply him who has wants. But the tax collectors carry off the gold, that most precious of metals.

---

[1]This word is obscure but the context suggests a man who guards and cleans the temple at night and makes it ready for the morning service. [Ed.]

The ships' crews from every house (of commerce), they receive their loads. (5,1) They depart from Egypt for Syria, and each man's god is with him. (But) not one of them says: "We shall see Egypt again!"

The carpenter who is in the shipyard carries the timber and stacks it. If he gives today the output of yesterday, woe to his limbs! The shipwright stands behind him to tell him evil things.

His outworker who is in the fields, his is the toughest of all the jobs. He spends the day loaded (5,5) with his tools, tied to his tool-box. When he returns home at night, he is loaded with the tool-box and the timbers, his drinking mug, and his whetstones.

The scribe, he alone, records the output of all of them. Take note of it!

The Misfortunes of the Peasant

Let me also expound to you the situation of the peasant, that other tough occupation. [Comes] the inundation and soaks him, he attends to his equipment. By day he cuts his farming tools; (6,1) by night he twists rope. Even his midday hour he spends on farm labor. He equips himself to go to the field as if he were a warrior. The dried field lies before him; he goes out to get his team. When he has been after the herdsman for many days, he gets his team and comes back with it. He makes for it a place in the field. (6,5) Comes dawn, he goes to make a start and does not find it in its place. He spends three days searching for it; he finds it in the bog. He finds no hides on them; the jackals have chewed them. He comes out, his garment in his hand, to beg for himself a team.

When he reaches his field he finds [it] broken up. He spends time cultivating, and the snake is after him. It finishes off the seed as it is cast to the ground. He does not see a green blade. He does three plowings with borrowed grain. His wife (7,1) has gone down to the merchants and found nothing for barter. Now the scribe lands on the shore. He surveys the harvest. Attendants are behind him with staffs, Nubians with clubs. One says (to him): "Give grain." "There is none." He is beaten savagely. He is bound, thrown in the well, submerged head down. His wife is bound in his presence. His children are in fetters. His neighbors (7,5) abandon them and flee. When it's over, there's no grain.

If you have any sense, be a scribe. If you have learned about the peasant, you will not be able to be one. Take note of it!

Be a Scribe

The scribe of the army and commander[2] of the cattle of the house of Amun, Nebmare-nakht, speaks to the scribe Wenemdiamun, as follows. Be a scribe! Your body will be sleek; your hand will be soft. You will not flicker like a flame, like one whose body is feeble. For there is not the bone of a man in you. You are tall and thin. If you lifted a load to carry it, you would stagger, your legs would tremble. You are lacking in strength; (8,1) you are weak in all your limbs; you are poor in body.

---

[2]A joking alteration of the teacher's title.

Set your sight on being a scribe; a fine profession that suits you. You call for one; a thousand answer you. You stride freely on the road. You will not be like a hired ox. You are in front of others.

I spend the day instructing you. You do not listen! Your heart is like an [empty] room. My teachings are not in it. Take their [meaning] to yourself!

The marsh thicket is before you each day, as a nestling is after its mother. You follow the path of (8,5) pleasure; you make friends with revellers. You have made your home in the brewery, as one who thirsts for beer. You sit in the parlor with an idler.[3] You hold the writings in contempt. You visit the whore. Do not do these things! What are they for? They are of no use. Take note of it!

The Scribe Does Not Suffer Like the Soldier

Furthermore. Look, I instruct you to make you sound; to make you hold the palette freely. To make you become one whom the king trusts; to make you gain entrance to treasury and granary. To make you receive the ship-load at the gate of the granary. To make you issue the offerings on feast days. You are dressed in fine clothes; you own horses. Your boat is on (9,1) the river; you are supplied with attendants. You stride about inspecting. A mansion is built in your town. You have a powerful office, given you by the king. Male and female slaves are about you. Those who are in the fields grasp your hand, on plots that you have made. Look, I make you into a staff of life! Put the writings in your heart, and you will be protected from all kinds of toil. You will become a worthy official.

Do you not recall the (fate of) the unskilled man? His name is not known. He is ever burdened [like an ass carrying] in front of the scribe who knows what he is about.

Come, [let me tell] you the woes of (9,5) the soldier, and how many are his superiors: the general, the troop-commander, the officer who leads, the standard-bearer, the lieutenant, the scribe, the commander of fifty, and the garrison-captain. They go in and out in the halls of the palace, saying: "Get laborers!" He is awakened at any hour. One is after him as (after) a donkey. He toils until the Aten sets in his darkness of night. He is hungry, his belly hurts; he is dead while yet alive. When he receives the grain-ration, having been released from duty, it is not good for grinding.

He is called up for Syria. He may not rest. There are no clothes, no sandals. The weapons of war are assembled at the fortress of Sile. (10,1) His march is uphill through mountains. He drinks water every third day; it is smelly and tastes of salt. His body is ravaged by illness. The enemy comes, surrounds him with missiles, and life recedes from him. He is told: "Quick, forward, valiant soldier! Win for yourself a good name!" He does not know what he is about. His body is weak, his legs fail him. When victory is won, the captives are handed over to his majesty, to be taken to Egypt. The foreign woman faints on the march; she hangs herself [on] (10,5) the soldier's neck. His knapsack drops, another grabs it while he is burdened with the woman. His wife and children are in their village; he dies and does not

---

[3]Lit., "He whose back is turned to his job."

reach it. If he comes out alive, he is worn out from marching. Be he at large, be he detained, the soldier suffers. If he leaps and joins the deserters, all his people are imprisoned. He dies on the edge of the desert, and there is none to perpetuate his name. He suffers in death as in life. A big sack is brought for him; he does not know his resting place.

Be a scribe, and be spared from soldiering! You call and one says: "Here I am." You are safe from torments. Every man seeks to raise himself up. Take note of it!

DISCUSSION QUESTIONS

1. What specific examples does the teacher give of a scribe's place in Egypt's political, religious, and economic life?
2. What sets the scribe apart from the other trades and professions identified in the document?
3. What does this document reveal about the structure of both the Egyptian economy and society in the New Kingdom?

5.
Allying for Peace

The "Eternal Treaty" between the Egyptians and Hittites
(C. 1259 B.C.E.)

Even after the emergence of great civilizations in Mesopotamia and Egypt, new societies took root in the Mediterranean. The Hittites were the most ambitious of these newcomers. By around 1750 B.C.E., they had forged a powerful and wealthy kingdom in Anatolia. Their success depended largely on an aggressive campaign of territorial expansion, a strategy that brought them into direct military conflict with New Kingdom Egypt. Since neither was able to gain the upper hand, and with new threats brewing, the Egyptian pharaoh Ramses II (r. 1304–1237 B.C.E.), and Hittite king Hattusilis III (r. 1267–1237 B.C.E.), agreed to make peace. Both Egyptian and Hittite versions of their agreement survive. Although their content is largely the same, the Hittite version (excerpted below) may be a closer rendition of the formally agreed on text. In it, Ramses and Hattusilis forged an "eternal" alliance aimed at protecting their rule both at home and abroad. As a result, the two countries remained close allies until the Hittite Empire collapsed in the late twelfth and early eleventh centuries B.C.E. A copy of the treaty appears above the entrance to the Security Council Chamber of the United Nations, a nod to the treaty's emphasis on the power of diplomacy as an instrument of peace.

From James B. Pritchard, ed., *Ancient Near Eastern Texts Relating to the Old Testament*, 3rd ed. with supplement (Princeton, NJ: Princeton University Press, 1969), 202–3.

Title

Treaty of Rea-mashesha mai Amana, the great king, the king of the land of Egypt, the valiant, with Hattusilis, the king of the Hatti land, his brother, for establishing [good] peace [and] good brotherhood [worthy of] great [king]ship between them forever.

Preamble

These are the words of Rea-mashesha mai Amana, the great king of the land of Egypt, the valiant of all lands, . . . (spoken) to Hattusilis, the great king, the king of the Hatti land, the valiant. . . .

Relations up to the Conclusion of the Treaty

Now I have established good brotherhood (and) good peace between us forever. In order to establish good peace (and) good brotherhood in [the relationship] of the land of Egypt with the Hatti land forever (I speak) thus: Behold, as for the relationship between the land of Egypt and the Hatti land, since eternity the god does not permit the making of hostility between them because of a treaty (valid) forever. Behold, Rea-mashesha mai Amana, the great king, the king of the land of Egypt, in order to bring about the relationship that the Sun-god[1] and the Storm-god[2] have effected for the land of Egypt with the Hatti land finds himself in a relationship valid since eternity which [does not permi]t the making of hostility between [them] until all and everlasting time.

The Present Treaty

Rea-mashesha mai Amana, the great king, the king of the land of Egypt, has entered into a treaty (written) upon a silver tablet with Hattusilis, the great king, the king of the Hatti land, [his] brother, [from] this [da]y on to establish good peace (and) good brotherhood be[tween us] forever. He is a brother [to me] and I am a brother to him and at peace with him forever. And as for us, our brotherhood and our peace is being brought about and it will be better than the brotherhood and the peace which existed formerly for the land of Egypt with the Hatti land.

Future Relations of the Two Countries

Behold, Rea-mashesha mai Amana, the king of the land of Egypt, is a good peace (and) in good brotherhood with [Hattusilis], the great king, the king of the Hatti land.

Behold the sons of Rea-mashesha mai Amana, the king of the land of Egypt, are in peace with (and) brothers of the sons of Hattusilis, the great king, the king

---

[1]Rea (Re), the chief god of the Egyptians.
[2]The chief god of the Hittites.

of the Hatti land, forever. They are in the same relationship of brotherhood and peace as we.

And as for (the relationship of) the land of Egypt with the Hatti land, they are at peace and brothers like us forever.

Mutual Renunciation of Aggression

Rea-mashesha mai Amana, the great king, the king of the land of Egypt, shall not trespass into the Hatti land to take anything therefrom in the future. And Hattusilis, the great king, the king of the Hatti land, shall not trespass into the land of Egypt to take anything therefrom in the future.

Behold, the holy ordinance (valid) forever which the Sun-god and the Storm-god had brought about for the land of Egypt with the Hatti land (calls for) peace and brotherhood so as not to make hostility between them. Behold, Rea-mashesha mai Amana, the great king, the king of the land of Egypt, has seized hold of it in order to bring about well-being from this day on. Behold, the land of Egypt (in its relation) with the Hatti land — they are at peace and brothers forever.

Defensive Alliance

If an enemy from abroad comes against the Hatti land, and Hattusilis, the great king, the king of the Hatti land, sends to me saying: "Come to me to help me against him," Rea-mashesha mai Amana, the great king, the king of the land of Egypt, shall send his foot soldiers (and) his charioteers and they shall slay [his enemy and] take revenge upon him for the sake of the Hatti land.

And if Hattusilis, the great king, the king of the Hatti land, is angry with servants belonging to him (and if) they have failed against him and sends to Rea-mashesha mai Amana, the great king, the king of the land of Egypt, on their account — lo! Rea-mashesha mai Amana shall send his foot soldiers (and) his charioteers and they shall destroy all those with whom he is angry.

If an enemy from abroad comes against the land of Egypt and Rea-mashesha mai Amana, the king of the land of Egypt, your brother, sends to Hattusilis, the king of the Hatti land, his brother, saying: "Come here to help me against him" — lo! Hattusilis, the king of the Hatti land, shall send his foot soldiers (and) his charioteers and shall slay my enemies.

And if Rea-mashesha ma[i Amana, the king of] the land of Egypt, is angry with servants belonging to him (and if) they have committed sin again[st him and I send] to Hattusilis, the king of the Hatti land, my brother, on his account — lo! Hattusilis, [the king of the Hatti land,] my brother, shall send his foot soldiers (and) his charioteers and they shall destroy all those with whom he is angry.

Succession to the Throne

Behold, the son of Hattusilis, the king of the Hatti land, shall be made king of the Hatti land in place of Hattusilis, his father, after the many years of Hattusilis, the king of the Hatti land. If the noblemen of the Hatti land commit sin against him —

lo! [Rea-mashesha mai Amana, the king of Egypt, shall send foot soldiers] (and) charioteers to take revenge upon them [for the sake of the Hatti land. And after they have reestablished order] in the country of the king of the Hatti land, [they shall return] to the country [of Egypt].

[Corresponding provision concerning Egypt lost in a gap.]

Extradition of Fugitives

[If a nobleman flees from the Hatti land and i]f one (such) man comes [to Rea-mashesha mai Amana, the great king, the king of the land of Egypt,] in order to enter his services . . . [Rea-mashesha mai Amana, the great king, the king of the land of Egypt, shall seize them and] shall have them brought back to the king of the Hatti land.

[several badly broken lines]

[If a nobleman] flees [from Rea-mashesha mai Amana, the king of the land of Egypt, and if one (such) man] comes to the [Hatti] land, [Ha]ttusilis, [the great king, the king of the Hatti land, shall seize him and] shall have him brought back to R[ea-mashesha mai] Amana, the great king, the king of Egypt, his brother.

If one man flees from the [Hatti land or] two men, [or three men and come to] Rea-mashesha mai [Amana, the great king, the king of the land of Egyp]t, [Rea-mashesha] mai Amana, the great king, [the king of the land of Egypt, shall seize them and have them brought back t]o Hattusilis, his brother. [Rea-mashesha mai Amana and Hattusilis are verily] brothers; hence [let them not *exact punishment for*] their sins, [let them not] tear out [their eyes; let them not *take revenge upon*] their people [. . . together with] their [wives and wi]th their children.

If [one man flees from Egypt] or two men or three men [and come to Hattusilis, the great king, the king of the Hatti land, Hattusilis, the great king], the king of the Hatti land, his brother, shall seize them and have them brought [back to Rea-mashesha mai Amana, the great king, the king of] the land of Egypt. [Hattusilis, the king of the Hatti land], and Rea-mashesha, the great king, the k[ing of the land of Egypt, are verily brothers; hence let them not *exact punishment for* their sins,] [. . .] let them not tear out their eyes; [let them not *take revenge upon* their people . . . together with] their wives (and) with their children.[3]

DISCUSSION QUESTIONS

1. What are the central terms of the alliance? What does each ruler want to guard against, and why?

2. What do these terms suggest about the nature of Egyptian and Hittite rule? What was the basis of Ramses II and Hattusilis III's power?

3. How does religion come into play in the treaty? What gods does it invoke, and why?

---

[3]After some fragmentary lines the text breaks off altogether. With the end of the treaty the list of the gods who were invoked as witnesses is missing.

COMPARATIVE QUESTIONS

1. Using evidence from all five sources, compare and contrast social, political, and religious life in ancient Mesopotamia, Egypt, and the Mediterranean.

2. How do deities function in the different societies? Why are some rulers portrayed as gods or godlike? How would this affect their governance? In what ways did Akhenaten both build upon and depart from these precedents in his worship of Aten?

3. What qualities and characteristics are associated with women in the *Epic of Gilgamesh* and Hammurabi's code? What do these sources say about gender attitudes in the two societies?

4. Historians traditionally view cities, formal political systems, knowledge of writing, and diverse crafts as defining features of civilization. In what ways do these documents reflect such definitions?

Empires in the Near East and the Reemergence of Civilization in Greece

1000–500 B.C.E.

Although dire economic conditions and foreign invasions caused havoc across the Near East and the Mediterranean from 1200 to 1000 B.C.E., by the eighth century B.C.E., local economies and societies were well on their way to recovery. The documents in this chapter allow us to chart the course of renewal in both regions, beginning with the Persian Empire. Between the sixth and fifth centuries, Persian rulers enhanced the traditional Near Eastern model of monarchical government, with its emphasis on a king's divine right to rule, by conquering new territories and enriching their treasury. The second document reveals that a new religion — Judaism — took shape against this backdrop. With its exclusive worship of a single God, Judaism forever changed the religious landscape of Western civilization. The third and fourth documents illuminate important facets of Greek society at the time, which soon became a target of Persia's imperial ambitions. As these documents demonstrate, Greeks shaped a sense of their own distinctive identity through innovative social, political, and cultural forms, ranging from city-states based on the concept of citizenship to epic poetry celebrating the individual's quest for excellence. At the same time, however, the last document reveals that Greeks shared a fundamental similarity with their Near Eastern neighbors: the acceptance of slavery as an essential element in public and private life.

1.
Empires and Divine Right

Inscription Honoring Cyrus, King of Persia (r. c. 557–530 B.C.E.)

The Persian king Cyrus founded the third in a series of powerful kingdoms that emerged from the shadows of the Dark Age in the Near East. Following the example of his Babylonian and Assyrian counterparts, Cyrus embraced imperial monarchy as a model of government while striving to expand his wealth and territorial holdings. The inscription that follows, etched originally on a clay barrel, describes a pivotal event in Cyrus's reign — his conquest of Babylon in 539 B.C.E. Like the Epic of Gilgamesh, it begins with a tale of woe. The ruler of Babylon was tormenting its inhabitants and dishonoring the gods. Upon hearing the people's complaints, Marduk, the king of the gods, decided to take action. In its account of the ensuing events, the inscription glorifies Cyrus's success while exposing its foundations — military might, cultural tolerance, and the belief in his divine right to rule. Following his lead, his successors built an even more formidable empire that threatened everything in its path, including the Greek city-states.

. . . He [Marduk] scanned and looked (through) all the countries, searching for a righteous ruler willing to lead him. . . . (Then) he pronounced the name of Cyrus, king of Anshan, [Persia] declared him . . . the ruler of all the world. He made the Guti country and all the Manda-hordes bow in submission to his (i.e., Cyrus') feet. And he (Cyrus) did always endeavor to treat according to justice the black-headed whom he (Marduk) has made him conquer. Marduk, the great lord, a protector of his people/worshipers, beheld with pleasure his (i.e., Cyrus') good deeds and his upright mind (lit.: heart) (and therefore) ordered him to march against his city Babylon. He made him set out on the road to Babylon going at his side like a real friend. His widespread troops — their number, like that of the water of a river, could not be established — strolled along, their weapons packed away. Without any battle, he made him enter his town Babylon, sparing Babylon any calamity. He delivered into his (i.e., Cyrus') hands Nabonidus, the king who did not worship him (i.e., Marduk). All the inhabitants of Babylon as well as of the entire country of Sumer and Akkad, princes and governors (included), bowed to him (Cyrus) and kissed his feet, jubilant that he (had received) the kingship, and with shining faces. Happily they greeted him as a master through whose help they had come (again) to life from death (and) had all been spared damage and disaster, and they worshiped his (very) name.

I am Cyrus, king of the world, great king, legitimate king, king of Babylon, king of Sumer and Akkad, king of the four rims (of the earth), son of Cambyses, great king, king of Anshan, grandson of Cyrus, great king, king of Anshan, descendant of Teipes, great king, king of Anshan, of a family (which) always (exercised) kingship; whose rule Bel and Nebo love, whom they want as king to please their hearts.

When I entered Babylon as a friend and (when) I established the seat of the government in the palace of the ruler under jubilation and rejoicing, Marduk, the great lord, [induced] the magnanimous inhabitants of Babylon [to love me], and I was daily endeavoring to worship him. My numerous troops walked around in Babylon in peace, I did not allow anybody to terrorize (any place) of the [country of Sumer] and Akkad. I strove for peace in Babylon and in all his (other) sacred cities. As to the inhabitants of Babylon, [who] against the will of the gods [had/ were . . . , I abolished] the corvé (lit.: yoke) which was against their (social) stand-

From James B. Pritchard, ed., *Ancient Near Eastern Texts Relating to the Old Testament*, 3rd ed. with supplement (Princeton, NJ: Princeton University Press, 1969), 315–16.

ing. I brought relief to their dilapidated housing, putting (thus) an end to their (main) complaints. Marduk, the great lord, was well pleased with my deeds and sent friendly blessings to myself, Cyrus, the king who worships him, to Cambyses, my son, the offspring of [my] loins, as well as to all my troops, and we all [praised] his great [godhead] joyously, standing before him in peace.

All the kings of the entire world from the Upper to the Lower Sea, those who are seated in throne rooms, (those who) live in other [types of buildings as well as] all the kings of the West land living in tents, brought their heavy tributes and kissed my feet in Babylon. (As to the region) from . . . as far as Ashur and Susa, Agade, Eshnunna, the towns Zamban, Me-Turnu, Der as well as the region of the Gutians, I returned to (these) sacred cities on the other side of the Tigris, the sanctuaries of which have been ruins for a long time, the images which (used) to live therein and established for them permanent sanctuaries. I (also) gathered all their (former) inhabitants and returned (to them) their habitations. Furthermore, I resettled upon the command of Marduk, the great lord, all the gods of Sumer and Akkad whom Nabonidus has brought into Babylon to the anger of the lord of the gods, unharmed, in their (former) chapels, the places which make them happy.

May all the gods whom I have resettled in their sacred cities ask daily Bel and Nebo for a long life for me and may they recommend me (to him); to Marduk, my lord, they may say this: "Cyrus, the king who worships you, and Cambyses, his son, . . ." . . . all of them I settled in a peaceful place . . . ducks and doves, . . . I endeavored to fortify/repair their dwelling places.

DISCUSSION QUESTIONS

1. According to the inscription, why did Cyrus conquer Babylon? What does this reveal about the relationship between political and religious beliefs at the time?

2. How did the residents of the city and the neighboring regions respond to the Persian conquest, and why?

3. What specific examples does the inscription provide of Cyrus's religious tolerance?

4. What might have been the purpose of this inscription, and who was its intended audience?

2.
Monotheism and Mosaic Law

The Book of Exodus, Chapters 19–20
(c. Tenth–Sixth Centuries B.C.E.)

The Hebrews were among the many peoples caught up in the web of King Cyrus's empire. Upon conquering Babylon, he allowed them to return to Canaan and freely practice their religion after years in exile. The region had long been central to the Hebrews' identity. They believed that centuries earlier, their god, Yahweh, had chosen

From *The Jerusalem Bible: Reader's Edition* (New York and London: Doubleday, 1966), 80–86.

them to be his special agents in the world. The relationship between Yahweh and the Hebrews was definitively forged when Yahweh led them out of slavery in Egypt into this "promised land" and gave them laws by which to live. The Book of Exodus includes the best known of these laws, the Ten Commandments, which God revealed to the Hebrew leader Moses on Mount Sinai. The biblical story casts him in much the same role as that of Hammurabi in his code — both are agents of divine justice and protection. Although the Hebrews did not deny the existence of other gods, their covenant with Yahweh was a crucial stage in the development of monotheism. In gradually accepting Yahweh as the only God, the Hebrews created a new religion that transformed the course of religious history in Western civilization.

III. The Covenant at Sinai

A. The Covenant and the Decalogue

The Israelites Come to Sinai   19 Three months after they came out of the land of Egypt . . . on that day the sons of Israel came to the wilderness of Sinai.[1] From Rephidim they set out again; and when they reached the wilderness of Sinai, there in the wilderness they pitched their camp; there facing the mountain Israel pitched camp.

Yahweh Promises a Covenant   Moses then went up to God, and Yahweh called to him from the mountain, saying, "Say this to the House of Jacob, declare this to the sons of Israel, 'You yourselves have seen what I did with the Egyptians, how I carried you on eagle's wings and brought you to myself. From this you know that now, if you obey my voice and hold fast to my covenant, you of all the nations shall be my very own for all the earth is mine. I will count you a kingdom of priests, a consecrated nation.' Those are the words you are to speak to the sons of Israel." So Moses went and summoned the elders of the people, putting before them all that Yahweh had bidden him. Then all the people answered as one, "All that Yahweh has said, we will do." And Moses took the people's reply back to Yahweh.

Preparing for the Covenant   Yahweh said to Moses, "I am coming to you in a dense cloud so that the people may hear when I speak to you and may trust you always." And Moses took the people's reply back to Yahweh.

Yahweh said to Moses, "Go to the people and tell them to prepare themselves today and tomorrow. Let them wash their clothing and hold themselves in readiness for the third day, because on the third day Yahweh will descend on the mountain of Sinai in the sight of all the people. You will mark out the limits of the mountain and say, 'Take care not to go up the mountain or to touch the foot of it. Whoever touches the mountain will be put to death. No one must lay a hand on him: he must be stoned or shot down by arrow, whether man or beast; he must not remain alive.' When the ram's horn sounds a long blast, they are to go up the mountain."

---

[1]According to tradition, Mount Sinai was at Jebel Musa in the southern region of the Sinai peninsula.

So Moses came down from the mountain to the people and bade them prepare themselves; and they washed their clothing. Then he said to the people, "Be ready for the third day; do not go near any woman."

The Theophany on Sinai   Now at daybreak on the third day there were peals of thunder on the mountain and lightning flashes, a dense cloud, and a loud trumpet blast, and inside the camp all the people trembled. Then Moses led the people out of the camp to meet God; and they stood at the bottom of the mountain. The mountain of Sinai was entirely wrapped in smoke, because Yahweh had descended on it in the form of fire. Like smoke from a furnace the smoke went up, and the whole mountain shook violently. Louder and louder grew the sound of the trumpet. Moses spoke, and God answered him with peals of thunder. Yahweh came down on the mountain of Sinai, on the mountain top, and Yahweh called Moses to the top of the mountain; and Moses went up. Yahweh said to Moses, "Go down and warn the people not to pass beyond their bounds to come and look on Yahweh, or many of them will lose their lives. The priests, the men who do approach Yahweh, even these must purify themselves, or Yahweh will break out against them." Moses answered Yahweh, "The people cannot come up the mountain of Sinai because you warned us yourself when you said, 'Mark out the limits of the mountain and declare it sacred.'" "Go down," said Yahweh to him, "and come up again bringing Aaron with you. But do not allow the priests or the people to pass beyond their bounds to come up to Yahweh, or he will break out against them." So Moses went down to the people and spoke to them. . . .

The Decalogue   20 Then God spoke all these words. He said, "I am Yahweh your God who brought you out of the land of Egypt, out of the house of slavery.

"You shall have no gods except me.

"You shall not make yourself a carved image or any likeness of anything in heaven or on earth beneath or in the waters under the earth; you shall not bow down to them or serve them. For I, Yahweh your God, am a jealous God and I punish the father's fault in the sons, the grandsons, and the great-grandsons of those who hate me; but I show kindness to thousands of those who love me and keep my commandments.

"You shall not utter the name of Yahweh your God to misuse it,[2] for Yahweh will not leave unpunished the man who utters his name to misuse it.

"Remember the Sabbath day and keep it holy. For six days you shall labor and do all your work, but the seventh day is a Sabbath for Yahweh your God. You shall do no work that day, neither you nor your son nor your daughter nor your servants, men or women, nor your animals nor the stranger who lives with you. For in six days Yahweh made the heavens and the earth and the sea and all that these hold, but on the seventh day he rested; that is why Yahweh has blessed the Sabbath day and made it sacred.

"Honor your father and your mother so that you may have a long life in the land that Yahweh your God has given to you.

"You shall not kill.

---

[2]Either in a false oath or irreverently.

"You shall not commit adultery.

"You shall not steal.

"You shall not bear false witness against your neighbor.

"You shall not covet your neighbor's house. You shall not covet your neighbor's wife, or his servant, man or woman, or his ox, or his donkey, or anything that is his."

All the people shook with fear at the peals of thunder and the lightning flashes, the sound of the trumpet, and the smoking mountain; and they kept their distance. "Speak to us yourself" they said to Moses "and we will listen; but do not let God speak to us, or we shall die." Moses answered the people, "Do not be afraid; God has come to test you, so that your fear of him, being always in your mind, may keep you from sinning." So the people kept their distance while Moses approached the dark cloud where God was.

DISCUSSION QUESTIONS

1. What does God mean by his "covenant," and what is its significance for the Hebrew people?

2. What do the Ten Commandments delineated here reveal about the Hebrews' way of life?

3. How does the Book of Exodus cast light on the development of Hebrew monotheism?

3.
The Quest for Individual Excellence (*Arête*)

Homer, *The Odyssey* (Eighth Century b.c.e.)

Economic and political turmoil engulfed Greece during what scholars have dubbed the "Dark Age," but this period also set the stage for the remaking of Greek civilization. Greece's geography encouraged continued contact with other peoples, thereby allowing for economic, cultural, and political recovery and innovation. In the process, Greeks fashioned a new sense of identity centered on the value of individual excellence (arête in Greek). Drawing on long-standing oral tradition, the Greek poet Homer celebrated this value in his epic poem The Odyssey. *Composed in the eighth century* b.c.e., *the poem recounts the adventures of Odysseus, who sets sail for his home off the west coast of Greece after having fought in the Trojan War. (Homer told the tale of this war in* The Iliad, *his other epic poem.) Odysseus's homecoming proves to be no easy feat; he faces one peril after another during his ten-year journey back to Ithaca. The excerpt below from Book 9 describes his visit to the "land of the Cyclops." What begins as a reconnaissance mission turns into a battle for his and his men's lives. Odysseus rises to the challenge, all the while displaying characteristics highly prized by Homer's audience as they reshaped Greek society.*

From "Book 9: In the One-Eyed Giant's Cave" by Homer, from *The Odyssey* by Homer, trans. Robert Fagles (New York: Penguin Group, 1996), 214–27.

   From there we sailed on, our spirits now at a low ebb,
and reached the land of the high and mighty Cyclops,
lawless brutes, who trust so to the everlasting gods
they never plant with their own hands or plow the soil.
Unsown, unplowed, the earth teems with all they need,
wheat, barley and vines, swelled by the rains of Zeus[1]
to yield a big full-bodied wine from clustered grapes.
They have no meeting place for council, no laws either,
no, up on the mountain peaks they live in arching caverns —
each a law to himself, ruling his wives and children,
not a care in the world for any neighbor.
                                        Now,
a level island stretches flat across the harbor,
not close inshore to the Cyclops' coast, not too far out,
thick with woods where the wild goats breed by hundreds.
No trampling of men to start them from their lairs,
no hunters roughing it out on the woody ridges,
stalking quarry, ever raid their haven.
No flocks browse, no plowlands roll with wheat;
unplowed, unsown forever — empty of humankind —
the island just feeds droves of bleating goats.
For the Cyclops have no ships with crimson prows,
no shipwrights there to build them good trim craft
that could sail them out to foreign ports of call
as most men risk the seas to trade with other men.
Such artisans would have made this island too
a decent place to live in . . . No mean spot,
it could bear you any crop you like in season.
The water-meadows along the low foaming shore
run soft and moist, and your vines would never flag.
The land's clear for plowing. Harvest on harvest,
a man could reap a healthy stand of grain —
the subsoil's dark and rich.
There's a snug deep-water harbor there, what's more,
no need for mooring-gear, no anchor-stones to heave,
no cables to make fast. Just beach your keels, ride out
the days till your shipmates' spirit stirs for open sea
and a fair wind blows. And last, at the harbor's head
there's a spring that rushes fresh from beneath a cave
and black poplars flourish round its mouth.

.   .   .   .

When young Dawn with her rose-red fingers shone once more
I called a muster briskly, commanding all the hands,

---

[1]**Zeus:** The supreme god of Olympus; known as the father of gods and men. [Ed.]

"The rest of you stay here, my friends-in-arms.
I'll go across with my own ship and crew
and probe the natives living over there.
What *are* they — violent, savage, lawless?
or friendly strangers, god-fearing men?"

    With that I boarded ship and told the crew
to embark at once and cast off cables quickly.
They swung aboard, they sat to the oars in ranks
and in rhythm churned the water white with stroke on stroke.
But as soon as we reached the coast I mentioned — no long trip —
we spied a cavern just at the shore, gaping above the surf,
towering, overgrown with laurel. And here big flocks,
sheep and goats, were stalled to spend the nights,
and around its mouth a yard was walled up
with quarried boulders sunk deep in the earth
and enormous pines and oak-trees looming darkly . . .
Here was a giant's lair, in fact, who always pastured
his sheepflocks far afield and never mixed with others.
A grim loner, dead set in his own lawless ways.
Here was a piece of work, by god, a monster
built like no mortal who ever supped on bread,
no, like a shaggy peak, I'd say — a man-mountain
rearing head and shoulders over the world.

. . . .

    Our party quickly made its way to his cave
but we failed to find our host himself inside;
he was off in his pasture, ranging his sleek flocks.
So we explored his den, gazing wide-eyed at it all,
the large flat racks loaded with drying cheeses,
the folds crowded with young lambs and kids,
split into three groups — here the spring-born,
here mid-yearlings, here the fresh sucklings
off to the side — each sort was penned apart.
And all his vessels, pails and hammered buckets
he used for milking, were brimming full with whey.
From the start my comrades pressed me, pleading hard,
"Let's make away with the cheeses, then come back —
hurry, drive the lambs and kids from the pens
to our swift ship, put out to sea at once!"
But I would not give way —
and how much better it would have been —
not till I saw him, saw what gifts he'd give.
But he proved no lovely sight to my companions.

There we built a fire, set our hands on the cheeses,
offered some to the gods and ate the bulk ourselves
and settled down inside, awaiting his return . . .
And back he came from pasture, late in the day,
herding his flocks home, and lugging a huge load
of good dry logs to fuel his fire at supper.
He flung them down in the cave — a jolting crash —
we scuttled in panic into the deepest dark recess.

.   .   .   .

As soon as he'd briskly finished all his chores
he lit his fire and spied us in the blaze and
"Strangers!" he thundered out, "now who are you?
Where did you sail from, over the running sea-lanes?
Out on a trading spree or roving the waves like pirates,
sea-wolves raiding at will, who risk their lives
to plunder other men?"
                                    The hearts inside us shook,
terrified by his rumbling voice and monstrous hulk.
Nevertheless I found the nerve to answer, firmly,
"Men of Achaea we are and bound now from Troy!
Driven far off course by the warring winds,
over the vast gulf of the sea — battling home
on a strange tack, a route that's off the map,
and so we've come to you . . .
so it must please King Zeus's plotting heart.
We're glad to say we're men of Atrides Agamemnon,[2]
whose fame is the proudest thing on earth these days,
so great a city he sacked, such multitudes he killed!
But since we've chanced on you, we're at your knees
in hopes of a warm welcome, even a guest-gift,
the sort that hosts give strangers. That's the custom.
Respect the gods, my friend. We're suppliants — at your mercy!
Zeus of the Strangers guards all guests and suppliants:
strangers are sacred — Zeus will avenge their rights!"

    "Stranger," he grumbled back from his brutal heart,
"you must be a fool, stranger, or come from nowhere,
telling *me* to fear the gods or avoid their wrath!
We Cyclops never blink at Zeus and Zeus's shield
of storm and thunder, or any other blessed god —
we've got more force by far.

---

[2]**Agamemnon**: According to Greek mythology, the king of Mycenae and head commander of the attack on Troy. [Ed.]

I'd never spare you in fear of Zeus's hatred,
you or your comrades here, unless I had the urge.
But tell me, where did you moor your sturdy ship
when you arrived? Up the coast or close in?
I'd just like to know."
               So he laid his trap
but he never caught me, no, wise to the world
I shot back in my crafty way, "My ship?
Poseidon[3] god of the earthquake smashed my ship,
he drove it against the rocks at your island's far cape,
dashed it against a cliff as the winds rode us in.
I and the men you see escaped a sudden death."

    Not a word in reply to that, the ruthless brute.
Lurching up, he lunged out with his hands toward my men
and snatching two at once, rapping them on the ground
he knocked them dead like pups —
their brains gushed out all over, soaked the floor —
and ripping them limb from limb to fix his meal
he bolted them down like a mountain-lion, left no scrap,
devoured entrails, flesh and bones, marrow and all!
We flung our arms to Zeus, we wept and cried aloud,
looking on at his grisly work — paralyzed, appalled.
But once the Cyclops had stuffed his enormous gut
with human flesh, washing it down with raw milk,
he slept in his cave, stretched out along his flocks.
And I with my fighting heart, I thought at first
to steal up to him, draw the sharp sword at my hip
and stab his chest where the midriff packs the liver —
I groped for the fatal spot but a fresh thought held me back.
There at a stroke we'd finish off ourselves as well —
how could *we* with our bare hands heave back
that slab he set to block his cavern's gaping maw?

. . . .

he left me there, the heart inside me brooding on revenge:
how could I pay him back? would Athena give me glory?
Here was the plan that struck my mind as best . . .
the Cyclops' great club: there it lay by the pens,
olivewood, full of sap. He'd lopped it off to brandish
once it dried. Looking it over, we judged it big enough
to be the mast of a pitch-black ship with her twenty oars,
a freighter broad in the beam that plows through miles of sea —
so long, so thick it bulked before our eyes. Well,

---

[3]**Poseidon:** The god of the sea. [Ed.]

flanking it now, I chopped off a fathom's length,
pushed it to comrades, told them to plane it down,
and they made the club smooth as I bent and shaved
the tip to a stabbing point. I turned it over
the blazing fire to char it good and hard,
then hid it well, buried deep under the dung
that littered the cavern's floor in thick wet clumps.
And now I ordered my shipmates all to cast lots —
who'd brave it out with me
to hoist our stake and grind it into his eye
when sleep had overcome him? Luck of the draw:
I got the very ones I would have picked myself,
four good men, and I in the lead made five . . .

     Nightfall brought him back herding his woolly sheep
and he quickly drove the sleek flock into the vaulted cavern,
rams and all — none left outside in the walled yard —
his own idea, perhaps, or a god led him on.
Then he hoisted the huge slab to block the door
and squatted to milk his sheep and bleating goats,
each in order, putting a suckling underneath each dam,
and as soon as he'd briskly finished all his chores
he snatched up two more men and fixed his meal.
But this time I lifted a carved wooden bowl,
brimful of my ruddy wine,
and went right up to the Cyclops, enticing,
"Here, Cyclops, try this wine — to top off
the banquet of human flesh you've bolted down!
Judge for yourself what stock our ship had stored.
I brought it here to make you a fine libation,
hoping you would pity me, Cyclops, send me home,
but your rages are insufferable. You barbarian —
how can any man on earth come visit you after *this*?
What you've done outrages all that's right!"

     At that he seized the bowl and tossed it off
and the heady wine pleased him immensely. "More" —
he demanded a second bowl — "a hearty helping!

. . . .

     I poured him another fiery bowl —
three bowls I brimmed and three he drank to the last drop,
the fool, and then, when the wine was swirling round his brain,
I approached my host with a cordial, winning word:
"So, you ask me the name I'm known by, Cyclops?
I will tell you. But you must give me a guest-gift

as you've promised. Nobody — that's my name. Nobody —
so my mother and father call me, all my friends."

But he boomed back at me from his ruthless heart,
"*Nobody?* I'll eat Nobody last of all his friends —
I'll eat the others first! That's my gift to *you!*"
                                                    With that
he toppled over, sprawled full-length, flat on his back
and lay there, his massive neck slumping to one side,
and sleep that conquers all overwhelmed him now
as wine came spurting, flooding up from his gullet
with chunks of human flesh — he vomited, blind drunk.
Now, at last, I thrust our stake in a bed of embers
to get it red-hot and rallied all my comrades:
"Courage — no panic, no one hang back now!"
And green as it was, just as the olive stake
was about to catch fire — the glow terrific, yes —
I dragged it from the flames, my men clustering round
as some god breathed enormous courage through us all.
Hoisting high that olive stake with its stabbing point,
straight into the monster's eye they rammed it hard —
I drove my weight on it from above and bored it home
as a shipwright bores his beam with a shipwright's drill
that men below, whipping the strap back and forth, whirl
and the drill keeps twisting faster, never stopping —
So we seized our stake with its fiery tip
and bored it round and round in the giant's eye
till blood came boiling up around that smoking shaft
and the hot blast singed his brow and eyelids round the core
and the broiling eyeball burst —
                                   its crackling roots blazed
and hissed —
              as a blacksmith plunges a glowing ax or adze
in an ice-cold bath and the metal screeches steam
and its temper hardens — that's the iron's strength —
so the eye of the Cyclops sizzled round that stake!
He loosed a hideous roar, the rock walls echoed round
and we scuttled back in terror. The monster wrenched the spike
from his eye and out it came with a red geyser of blood —
he flung it aside with frantic hands, and mad with pain
he bellowed out for help from his neighbor Cyclops
living round about in caves on windswept crags.
Hearing his cries, they lumbered up from every side
and hulking round his cavern, asked what ailed him:
"What, Polyphemus, what in the world's the trouble?
Roaring out in the godsent night to rob us of our sleep.

Surely no one's rustling your flocks against your will —
surely no one's trying to kill you now by fraud or force!"

     "*Nobody*, friends" — Polyphemus bellowed back from his cave —
"Nobody's killing me now by fraud and not by force!"

     "*If* you're alone," his friends boomed back at once,
"and nobody's trying to overpower you now — look,
it must be a plague sent here by mighty Zeus
and there's no escape from *that*.
You'd better pray to your father, Lord Poseidon."

     They lumbered off, but laughter filled my heart
to think how nobody's name — my great cunning stroke —
had duped them one and all. But the Cyclops there,
still groaning, racked with agony, groped around
for the huge slab, and heaving it from the doorway,
down he sat in the cave's mouth, his arms spread wide,
hoping to catch a comrade stealing out with sheep —
such a blithering fool he took me for!
But I was already plotting . . .
what was the best way out? how could I find
escape from death for my crew, myself as well?
My wits kept weaving, weaving cunning schemes —
Life at stake, monstrous death staring us in the face —
till this plan struck my mind as best. That flock,
those well-fed rams with their splendid thick fleece,
sturdy, handsome beasts sporting their dark weight of wool:
I lashed them abreast, quietly, twisting the willow-twigs
the Cyclops slept on — giant, lawless brute — I took them
three by three; each ram in the middle bore a man
while the two rams either side would shield him well.
So three beasts to bear each man, but as for myself?
There was one bellwether ram, the prize of all the flock,
And clutching him by his back, tucked up under
his shaggy belly, there I hung, face upward,
both hands locked in his marvelous deep fleece,
clinging for dear life, my spirit steeled, enduring . . .
So we held on, desperate, waiting Dawn's first light.
                                                  As soon
as young Dawn with her rose-red fingers shone once more
the rams went rumbling out of the cave toward pasture,
the ewes kept bleating round the pens, unmilked,
their udders about to burst. Their master now,
heaving in torment, felt the back of each animal
halting before him here, but the idiot never sensed

my men were trussed up under their thick fleecy ribs.
And last of them all came my great ram now, striding out,
weighed down with his dense wool and my deep plots.
Stroking him gently, powerful Polyphemus murmured,
"Dear old ram, why last of the flock to quit the cave?
In the good old days you'd never lag behind the rest —
you with your long marching strides, first by far
of the flock to graze the fresh young grasses,
first by far to reach the rippling streams,
first to turn back home, keen for your fold
when night comes on — but now you're last of all.
And why? Sick at heart for your master's eye
that coward gouged out with his wicked crew? —
only, after he'd stunned my wits with wine —
that, that Nobody . . .
who's not escaped his death, I swear, not yet.

.   .   .   .

    And with that threat he let my ram go free outside,
But soon as we'd got one foot past cave and courtyard,
first I loosed myself from the ram, then loosed my men,
then quickly, glancing back again and again we drove
our flock, good plump beasts with their long shanks,
straight to the ship, and a welcome sight we were
to loyal comrades — we who'd escaped our deaths —

.   .   .   .

But once offshore as far as a man's shout can carry,
I called back to the Cyclops, stinging taunts:
"So, Cyclops, no weak coward it was whose crew
you bent to devour there in your vaulted cave —
you with your brute force! Your filthy crimes
came down on your own head, you shameless cannibal,
daring to eat your guests in your own house —
so Zeus and the other gods have paid you back!"

    That made the rage of the monster boil over.
Ripping off the peak of a towering crag, he heaved it
so hard the boulder landed just in from of our dark prow
and a huge swell reared up as the rock went plunging under —
a tidal wave from the open sea. The sudden backwash
drove us landward again, forcing us close inshore
but grabbing a long pole, I thrust us off and away,
tossing my head for dear life, signaling crews
to put their backs in the oars, escape grim death.
They threw themselves in the labor, rowed on fast

but once we'd plowed the breakers twice as far,
again I began to taunt the Cyclops — men around me
trying to check me, calm me, left and right:
"So headstrong — why? Why rile the beast again?"

    "That rock he flung in the sea just now, hurling our ship
to shore once more — we thought we'd die on the spot!"

    "If he'd caught a sound from *one* of us, just a whisper,
he would have crushed our heads and ship timbers
with one heave of another flashing, jagged rock!"

    "Good god, the brute can throw!"
                               So they begged
but they could not bring my fighting spirit round.
I called back with another burst of anger, "Cyclops —
if any man on the face of the earth should ask you
who blinded you, shamed you so — say Odysseus,
raider of cities, *he* gouged out your eye,
Laertes' son who makes his home in Ithaca!"

DISCUSSION QUESTIONS

1. How does Odysseus describe the land of the Cyclops and its inhabitants?
2. What does this description suggest about Odysseus's understanding of the nature of Greek society and how it compares to other societies?
3. Describe Odysseus's initial encounter with the Cyclops. How does he expect to be treated and why? How does the Cyclops respond?
4. How does Odysseus outwit the Cyclops? What values do you see reflected in Odysseus's treatment of him?

4.
Two Visions of the City-State

Tyrtaeus of Sparta and Solon of Athens, *Poems*
(Seventh–Sixth Centuries B.C.E.)

Among the most remarkable products of Greece's recovery from its Dark Age was the creation of a new social and political entity, the city-state. These poems elucidate the values shaping two of these communities, Sparta and Athens. The author of the first, Tyrtaeus of Sparta (originally from Athens, according to some ancient sources), was active when Sparta launched the Second Messenian War in the mid-sixth century

From *Early Greek Lyric Poetry*, trans. David Mulroy (Ann Arbor: University of Michigan Press, 1992), 48–49, 68–69.

b.c.e. *His poem reveals the preeminent importance of military glory to the Spartans'* *communal identity. The author of the second work, the Athenian statesman Solon,* *emphasizes shared justice as the ideal basis of society. Democratic reforms instituted* *in the late sixth century* b.c.e. *transformed his vision into reality. Both poems are* *written in the elegiac meter, a style often used at the time to instruct the public.*

Tyrtaeus

It is a beautiful thing when a good man falls
    and dies fighting for his country.
The worst pain is leaving one's city and fertile
    fields for the life of a beggar,
wandering with mother, old father, little
    children, and wedded wife.
The man beaten by need and odious poverty
    is detested everywhere he goes,
a disgrace to his family and noble appearance, trailed
    by every dishonor and evil.
If no one takes care of the wanderer or gives him
    honor, respect, or pity,
we must fight to the death for our land and children, giving
    no thought to lengthening life.
Fight in a stubborn, close array, my boys!
    Never waver or retreat!
Feel your anger swell. There is no place
    in combat for love of life.
Older soldiers, whose knees are not so light,
    need you to stand and protect them.
An aging warrior cut down in the vanguard of battle
    disgraces the young. His head
is white, his beard is grey, and now he is spilling
    his powerful spirit in dust,
naked, clutching his bloody groin: a sight
    for shame and anger. But youthful
warriors always look good, until the blossom
    withers. Men gape
at them in life and women sigh, and dying
    in combat they are handsome still.
Now is the time for a man to stand, planting
    his feet and biting his lip.

Solon

Our city will never perish by decree of Zeus
    or whim of the immortals; such
is the great-hearted protector, child of thunder, who holds
    her hands over us: Athena.

But by thoughtless devotion to money, the citizens are willing
    to destroy our great city.
Our leaders' minds are unjust; soon they will suffer
    The pangs of great arrogance.
They cannot control their greed and enjoy the cheerful
    feast at hand in peace . . .[1]
    Their wealth depends on crime. . . .
    They seize and steal at random
without regard for the holy, the public good,
    or the sacred foundations of Justice,
who is silent but knows present and past, and comes
    for full retribution in time.
The deadly infection spreads throughout the city,
    rushing it into slavery,
which wakens internal strife and war that kills
    so many beautiful youths.
Malicious conspiracies easily ruin a city,
    though the people love it dearly.
These are the evils stalking the people: many
    impoverished leave for foreign
soil, bound and sold in chains of disgrace. . . .
The public evil visits every home;
    undeterred by courtyard gates,
it leaps the high hedge and finds its man,
    though he runs to his bedroom to hide.
My heart bids me to teach the Athenians that lawless
    behavior is the bane of a city,
but respect for law spreads order and beauty;
    it shackles the legs of the unjust,
smooths and moderates, diminishes arrogance and withers
    delusion's burgeoning blossoms;
it straightens crooked judgments, humbles pride,
    halts partisanship and the anger
born of faction. Everything righteous and wise
    depends on respect for the law.

DISCUSSION QUESTIONS

1. What does Tyrtaeus reveal about the values and conduct that Spartan warriors were expected to embody?

2. How does Tyrtaeus describe warriors who do not live up to these expectations? What do his criticisms reveal about Spartan culture?

3. Why does Solon think Athenian citizens pose a threat to the polis?

4. What message does Solon seek to convey to Athenian citizens in this poem?

---

[1] The ellipses here and below indicate at least one missing line in the original Greek text. [Ed.]

5.
Economics and the Expansion of Slavery

Xenophon, *Revenues* (Fourth Century B.C.E.)

The creation of slavery went hand in hand with the creation of civilization, from its beginnings in Mesopotamia to its refashioning in Greece during the Archaic Age (c. 750–500 B.C.E.). The Greek author Xenophon (c. 430–355 B.C.E.) had no doubt as to the importance of slavery to a society's well-being. He addressed it explicitly in Revenues, *his proposal to reform the state finances of Athens. The issue at hand was how the government could maximize the economic benefit of its silver mines. In the excerpt below, Xenophon argues that the city-state could increase its income by buying a large number of slaves, who would then be leased out at a set amount per slave to private subcontractors working the mines. Although Xenophon's advice dates from the fourth century B.C.E. and does not appear to have been followed, he explicitly refers to the past to give credence to his argument. Slavery had been expanding in Greece since the days of Homer; both private individuals and city-states owned slaves to such an extent that by the time Xenophon was writing, they made up close to a third of the total population in some places. Xenophon gives voice to the attitudes that drove this expansion.*

As for the silver mines, I believe that if a proper system of working were introduced, a vast amount of money would be obtained from them apart from our other sources of revenue. I want to point out the possibilities of these mines to those who do not know. For, once you realize their possibilities, you will be in a better position to consider how the mines should be managed.

Now, we all agree that the mines have been worked for many generations. At any rate, no one even attempts to date the beginning of mining operations. And yet, although digging and the removal of the silver ore have been carried on for so long a time, note how small is the size of the dumps compared with the virgin and silver-laden hills. And it is continually being found that, so far from shrinking, the silver-yielding area extends further and further.

Well, so long as the maximum number of workmen was employed in them, no one ever wanted a job; in fact, there were always more jobs than the labourers could deal with. And even at the present day no owner of slaves employed in the mines reduces the number of his men; on the contrary, every master obtains as many more as he can. The fact is, I imagine, that when there are few diggers and searchers, the amount of metal recovered is small, and when there are many, the total of ore discovered is multiplied. Hence of all the industries with which I am acquainted this is the only one in which expansion of business excites no jealousy.

Further than this, every farmer can tell just how many yoke of oxen are enough for the farm and how many labourers. To put more on the land than the requisite number is counted loss. In mining undertakings, on the contrary, every-

From Xenophon, *Scripta Minora*, trans. E. C. Marchant (London: William Heinemann, New York: G. P. Putnam's Sons, 1925), 205, 207, 209, 211, 213.

one tells you that he is short of labour. Mining, in fact, is quite different from other industries. An increase in the number of coppersmiths, for example, produces a fall in the price of copper work, and the coppersmiths retire from business. The same thing happens in the iron trade. Again, when corn and wine are abundant, the crops are cheap, and the profit derived from growing them disappears, so that many give up farming and set up as merchants or shopkeepers or moneylenders. But an increase in the amount of the silver ore discovered and of the metal won is accompanied by an increase in the number of persons who take up this industry. Neither is silver like furniture, of which a man never buys more when once he has got enough for his house. No one ever yet possessed so much silver as to want no more; if a man finds himself with a huge amount of it, he takes as much pleasure in burying the surplus as in using it.

Mark too that, whenever states are prosperous, silver is in strong demand. The men will spend money on fine arms and good horses and magnificent houses and establishments, and the women go in for expensive clothes and gold jewelry. If, on the other hand, the body politic is diseased owing to failure of the harvest or to war, the land goes out of cultivation and there is a much more insistent demand for cash to pay for food and mercenaries.

If anyone says that gold is quite as useful as silver, I am not going to contradict him; but I know this, that when gold is plentiful, silver rises and gold falls in value.

With these facts before us, we need not hesitate to bring as much labour as we can get into the mines and carry on work in them, feeling confident that the ore will never give out and that silver will never lose its value. . . .

To make myself clearer on the subject . . . I will now explain how the mines may be worked with the greatest advantage to the state. Not that I expect to surprise you by what I am going to say, as if I had found the solution of a difficult problem. For, some things that I shall mention are still to be seen by anyone at the present day, and as for conditions in the past, our fathers have told us that they were similar. But what may well excite surprise is that the state, being aware that many private individuals are making money out of her, does not imitate them. Those of us who have given thought to the matter have heard long ago, I imagine, that Nicias son of Niceratus, once owned a thousand men in the mines, and let them out to Sosias the Thracian, on condition that Sosias paid him an *obol* a day per man net and filled all vacancies as they occurred. Hipponicus, again, had six hundred slaves let out on the same terms and received a rent of a *mina* a day net. Philemonides had three hundred, and received half a *mina*. There were others too, owning numbers in proportion, I presume, to their capital. But why dwell on the past? At this day there are many men in the mines let out in this way. Were my proposals adopted, the only innovation would be, that just as private individuals have built up a permanent income by becoming slave owners, so the state would become possessed of public slaves, until there were three for every citizen. Whether my plan is workable, let anyone who chooses judge for himself by examining it in detail.

So let us take first the cost of the men. Clearly the treasury is in a better position to provide the money than private individuals. Moreover the Council can easily issue a notice inviting all and sundry to bring slaves, and can buy those that are brought to it. When once they are purchased, why should there be more hesitation about hiring from the treasury than from a private person, the terms offered being the same? At any rate men hire consecrated lands and houses, and farm taxes under the state.

The treasury can insure the slaves purchased by requiring some of the lessees to become guarantors, as it does in the case of the tax-farmers.[1] In fact a tax-farmer can swindle the state more easily than a lessee of slaves. For how are you to detect the export of public money? Money looks the same whether it is private property or belongs to the state. But how is a man to steal slaves when they are branded with the public mark and it is a penal offence to sell or export them?

So far, then, it appears to be possible for the state to acquire and to keep men. But, one may ask, when labour is abundant, how will a sufficient number of persons be found to hire it? Well, if anyone feels doubtful about that, let him comfort himself with the thought that many men in the business will hire the state slaves as additional hands, since they have abundance of capital, and that among those now working in the mines many are growing old. Moreover there are many others, both Athenians and foreigners, who have neither will nor strength to work with their own hands, but would be glad to make a living by becoming managers.

Discussion Questions

1. Why does Xenophon think the Athenian government should adopt his proposal? What does he think the government has to gain?

2. What role do slaves play in his plan? How does he describe them and their value to the state and to private citizens?

3. The Greeks are credited with creating a unique political model in the ancient world based on the concept of citizenship and shared governance. Does Xenophon's proposal offer any insights as to why Greek slavery expanded at the same time?

Comparative Questions

1. Based on these documents, what similarities and differences do you see between Near Eastern and Greek social and political organization?

2. What do Homer, Tyrtaeus, Solon, and Xenophon reveal about how Greeks forged their own distinct sense of cultural identity? What would you describe as some of its key attributes?

3. According to Solon, what should be the basis of society and why? In appealing to the Athenian government to adopt his proposal for the state-owned mines, in what ways does Xenophon build on Solon's ideal while revealing its paradoxes?

4. What role does the divine play in the accounts of the conquest of Babylon and the Hebrews' flight from Egypt? What does this suggest about the place of religion in the Near East at the time?

---

[1]**tax-farmers:** Tax-farmers were independent bidders in an annual, state-run auction for the contract to collect taxes. In exchange for the contract, tax-farmers had to pay a guaranteed set amount to the state while keeping something additional above that amount as their profit. [Ed.]

The Greek Golden Age
C. 500–C. 400 B.C.E.

In the fifth century, Greece enjoyed a period of extraordinary prosperity and achievement, with Athens leading the way. Its economy was booming and its culture flourishing. At the same time, its male citizens developed the first democracy in history, and under their guidance, Athens became the leader of the Greek world. The first four documents attest to the dynamic nature of Greek politics, art, philosophy, and science. They also reveal that, even as innovation fueled Greece's rise to glory, the pull of traditional beliefs remained strong. Such beliefs were especially influential in establishing expected behavior for both women and men. As the last two selections demonstrate, a woman's status was inextricably linked to her roles as wife and mother. To put either in jeopardy threatened the very foundations of Greek society.

1.

The Golden Age of Athens

Thucydides, *The Funeral Oration of Pericles* (429 B.C.E.)

The most renowned Athenian politician in his day, Pericles (c. 495–429 B.C.E.) contributed greatly to the brilliance of Athens's Golden Age. Not only did he help to build the city-state's empire abroad, but he also devoted much of his career to strengthening democracy at home. In his History of the Peloponnesian War, *Thucydides brings Pericles to life in a description of a speech he delivered to honor those who had died during the first year of fighting. The Peloponnesian War pitted Athens against its authoritarian rival, Sparta, from 431 to 404 B.C.E., ending ultimately with Athens's defeat. As Pericles' words in this excerpt reveal, however, at the time of his speech, Athens was still brimming with confidence in the greatness of its people and government.*

From Thucydides, *The Peloponnesian Wars*, trans. Benjamin Jowett (New York: Twayne Publishers, 1963), 65–72.

During the same winter, in accordance with traditional custom, the funeral of those who first fell in this war was celebrated by the Athenians at the public charge. . . .

Over the first who were buried, Pericles was chosen to speak. At the fitting moment he advanced from the sepulcher to a lofty stage, which had been erected in order that he might be heard as far away as possible by the crowd, and spoke somewhat as follows: . . .

"I will speak of our ancestors first, for it is right and seemly that on such an occasion as this we should also render this honor to their memory. Men of the same stock, ever dwelling in this land, in successive generations to this very day, by their valor handed it down as a free land. They are worthy of praise, and still more are our fathers, who added to their inheritance, and after many a struggle bequeathed to us, their sons, the great empire we possess. . . . But before I praise the dead, I shall first proceed to show by what kind of practices we attained to our position, and under what kind of institutions and manner of life our empire became great. For I conceive that it would not be unsuited to the occasion that this should be told, and that this whole assembly of citizens and foreigners may profitably listen to it.

"Our institutions do not emulate the laws of others. We do not copy our neighbors: rather, we are an example to them. Our system is called a democracy, for it respects the majority and not the few; but while the law secures equality to all alike in their private disputes, the claim of excellence is also recognized; and when a citizen is in any way distinguished, he is generally preferred to the public service, not in rotation, but for merit. Nor again is there any bar in poverty and obscurity of rank to a man who can do the state some service. It is as free men that we conduct our public life, and in our daily occupations we avoid mutual suspicions; we are not angry with our neighbor if he does what he likes; we do not put on sour looks at him which, though harmless, are not pleasant. While we give no offense in our private intercourse, in our public acts we are prevented from doing wrong by fear; we respect the authorities and the laws, especially those which are ordained for the protection of the injured as well as those unwritten laws which bring upon the transgressor admitted dishonor.

"Furthermore, none have provided more relaxations for the spirit from toil; we have regular games and sacrifices throughout the year; our homes are furnished with elegance; and the delight which we daily feel in all these things banishes melancholy. Because of the greatness of our city, the fruits of the whole earth flow in upon us so that we enjoy the goods of other countries as freely as our own.

"Then, again, in military training we are superior to our adversaries, as I shall show. Our city is thrown open to the world, and we never expel a foreigner or prevent him from seeing or learning anything which, if not concealed, it might profit an enemy to see. We rely not so much upon preparations or stratagems, as upon our own courage in action. And in the matter of education, whereas from early youth they are always undergoing laborious exercises which are to make them brave, we live at ease and yet are equally ready to face perils to which our strength is equal. And here is the evidence. The Lacedaemonians march against our land not by themselves, but with all their allies: we invade a neighbor's country alone;

and although our opponents are fighting for their homes and we are on a foreign soil, we seldom have any difficulty in overcoming them. . . .

"Nor is this the only cause for marveling at our city. We are lovers of beauty without extravagance and of learning without loss of vigor. Wealth we employ less for talk and ostentation than when there is a real use for it. To avow poverty with us is no disgrace: the true disgrace is in doing nothing to avoid it. The same persons attend at once to the concerns of their households and of the city, and men of diverse employments have a very fair idea of politics. If a man takes no interest in public affairs, we alone do not commend him as quiet but condemn him as useless; and if few of us are originators, we are all sound judges of a policy. In our opinion action does not suffer from discussion but, rather, from the want of that instruction which is gained by discussion preparatory to the action required. For we have an exceptional gift of acting with audacity after calculating the prospects of our enterprises, whereas other men are bold from ignorance but hesitate upon reflection. But it would be right to esteem those men bravest in spirit who have the clearest understanding of the pains and pleasures of life and do not on that account shrink from danger. . . .

"This is why I have dwelt upon the greatness of Athens, showing you that we are contending for a higher prize than those who enjoy no like advantages, and establishing by manifest proof the merit of these men whom I am now commemorating. Their loftiest praise has been already spoken; for in descanting on the city, I have honored the qualities which earned renown for them and for men such as they. And of how few Hellenes can it be said as of them, that their deeds matched their fame! In my belief an end such as theirs proves a man's worth; it is at once its first revelation and final seal. For even those who come short in other ways may justly plead the valor with which they have fought for their country; they have blotted out evil with good, and their public services have outweighed the harm they have done in their private actions. . . . And when the moment for fighting came, they held it nobler to suffer death than to yield and save their lives; it was the report of dishonor from which they fled, but on the battlefield their feet stood fast; and while for a moment they were in the hands of fortune, at the height, less of terror than of glory, they departed.

"Such was the conduct of these men; they were worthy of Athens. The rest of us must pray for a safer issue to our courage and yet disdain to show any less daring towards our enemies. We must not consider only what words can be uttered on the utility of such a spirit. Anyone might discourse to you at length on all the advantages of resisting the enemy bravely, but you know them just as well yourselves. It is better that you should actually gaze day by day on the power of the city until you are filled with the love of her; and when you are convinced of her greatness, reflect that it was acquired by men of daring who knew their duty and feared dishonor in the hour of action, men who if they ever failed in an enterprise, even then disdained to deprive the city of their prowess but offered themselves up as the finest contribution to the common cause. . . .

"To you who are the sons and brothers of the departed, I see that the struggle to emulate them will be arduous. For all men praise the dead; and, however preeminent your virtue may be, you would hardly be thought their equals, but somewhat inferior. The living have their rivals and detractors; but when a man is out of the way, the honor and good will which he receives is uncontested. And, if I am also to speak of womanly virtues to those of you who will now be widows, let me sum them up in one short admonition: 'Your glory will be great if you show no more than the infirmities of your nature, a glory that consists in being least the subjects of report among men, for good or evil.'

"I have spoken in obedience to the law, making use of such fitting words as I had. The tribute of deeds has been paid in part, for the dead have been honorably interred; it remains only that their children shall be maintained at the public charge until they are grown up: this is the solid prize with which, as with a garland, Athens crowns these men and those left behind after such contests. For where the rewards of virtue are greatest, there men do the greatest services to their cities. And now, when you have duly lamented, everyone his own dead, you may depart."

Discussion Questions

1. According to Pericles, what sets Athens apart from its neighbors and adversaries?

2. As described here, what are the guiding principles of Athenian democracy?

3. How does Pericles characterize his fellow Athenians and their contributions to the city's glory?

4. What obligations does Pericles believe Athenian citizens have to the state?

2.
Movement in Stone
Myron of Eleutherai, *Discus Thrower* (c. 450 b.c.e.)

According to Thucydides, Athenians were innovators, not emulators. Although this statement applies to many facets of the Greek Golden Age, it is perhaps nowhere more visible than in its art. Greek sculptors abandoned the stiffness characteristic of earlier statues and replaced it with a new style of human movement. The Discus Thrower by Myron (c. 480–440 b.c.e.) is among the most renowned examples of this type of statuary. The figure is presented in arrested motion as he swings his arm back, about to fling the discus. A favorite sport in ancient Greece, discus throwing was part of the Olympic pentathlon competition. Originally sculpted in bronze, the Discus Thrower is known today only through later Roman copies; even then it inspired admiration among viewers. As the Roman rhetorician Quintilian proclaimed in the first century c.e., "Where can we find a more violent and elaborate attitude than that of the Discus Thrower of Myron? Yet the critic who disapproved of the figure because it was not upright, would merely show his utter failure to understand the sculptor's art, in which the very novelty and difficulty of execution is what most deserves our praise."

The Art Archive/Museo Nazionale Terme Rome/Gianni Dagli Orti

DISCUSSION QUESTIONS

1. Why do you think Myron chose this pose rather than an upright one? How did his choice contribute to the statue's sense of motion?

2. Compare the ways in which the athlete's body and face are portrayed in the sculpture. What differences do you see? Do these differences add anything to the statue's overall visual effect?

3. In what ways does this statue reflect the Greeks' newfound confidence in human potential for beauty and perfection?

3.
The Emergence of Philosophy

Plato, *The Apology of Socrates* (399 B.C.E.)

Political innovation was not the only distinctive feature of fifth-century Athens. Socrates (469–399 B.C.E.) was a famous philosopher of the day, and his views on ethics and morality challenged conventional values while steering Greek philosophy in new directions. Unlike the Sophists, Socrates offered no classes and did not write his ideas down. He relied instead on conversation and critical questioning to draw people into his way of thinking. In this document, we hear Socrates speaking for himself before a jury as described by his pupil Plato. At the time, Socrates was on trial for impiety, and he spoke these words to convince his fellow citizens of his innocence. In the process, he revealed key elements of his philosophy that would have an enduring influence on Western thought. Sadly, his efforts were in vain; he was convicted and sentenced to death.

How you, O Athenians, have been affected by my accusers, I cannot tell; but I know that they almost made me forget who I was — so persuasively did they speak; and yet they have hardly uttered a word of truth. But of the many falsehoods told by them, there was one which quite amazed me; — I mean when they said that you should be upon your guard and not allow yourselves to be deceived by the force of my eloquence. To say this, when they were certain to be detected as soon as I opened my lips and proved myself to be anything but a great speaker, did indeed appear to me most shameless — unless by the force of eloquence they mean the force of truth; for if such is their meaning, I admit that I am eloquent. But in how different a way from theirs! Well, as I was saying, they have scarcely spoken the truth at all; but from me you shall hear the whole truth: not, however, delivered after their manner in a set oration duly ornamented with words and phrases. No, by heaven! but I shall use the words and arguments which occur to me at the moment; for I am confident in the justice of my cause. . . .

From Plato, *The Dialogues of Plato*, vol. 2, 3rd ed., trans. Benjamin Jowett (New York: Macmillan and Co., 1892), 109, 111–16, 121–23.

I will begin at the beginning, and ask what is the accusation which has given rise to the slander of me, and in fact has encouraged Meletus to prefer this charge against me. Well, what do the slanderers say? They shall be my prosecutors, and I will sum up their words in an affidavit: "Socrates is an evil-doer, and a curious person, who searches into things under the earth and in heaven, and he makes the worse appear the better cause; and he teaches the aforesaid doctrines to others." Such is the nature of the accusation: it is just what you have yourselves seen in the comedy of Aristophanes, who has introduced a man whom he calls Socrates, going about and saying that he walks in air, and talking a deal of nonsense concerning matters of which I do not pretend to know either much or little — not that I mean to speak disparagingly of any one who is a student of natural philosophy. I should be very sorry if Meletus could bring so grave a charge against me. But the simple truth is, O Athenians, that I have nothing to do with physical speculations. Very many of those here present are witnesses to the truth of this, and to them I appeal. . . .

Men of Athens, this reputation of mine has come of a certain sort of wisdom which I possess. If you ask me what kind of wisdom, I reply, wisdom such as may perhaps be attained by man, for to that extent I am inclined to believe that I am wise; whereas the persons of whom I was speaking have a superhuman wisdom, which I may fail to describe, because I have it not myself; and he who says that I have, speaks falsely, and is taking away my character. And here, O men of Athens, I must beg you not to interrupt me, even if I seem to say something extravagant. For the word which I will speak is not mine. I will refer you to a witness who is worthy of credit; that witness shall be the God of Delphi — he will tell you about my wisdom, if I have any, and of what sort it is. You must have known Chaerephon; he was early a friend of mine, and also a friend of yours, for he shared in the recent exile of the people, and returned with you. Well, Chaerephon, as you know, was very impetuous in all his doings, and he went to Delphi and boldly asked the oracle to tell him whether — as I was saying, I must beg you not to interrupt — he asked the oracle to tell him whether any one was wiser than I was, and the Pythian prophetess answered, that there was no man wiser. Chaerephon is dead himself; but his brother, who is in court, will confirm the truth of what I am saying.

Why do I mention this? Because I am going to explain to you why I have such an evil name. When I heard the answer, I said to myself, What can the god mean? and what is the interpretation of his riddle? for I know that I have no wisdom, small or great. What then can he mean when he says that I am the wisest of men? And yet he is a god, and cannot lie; that would be against his nature. After long consideration, I thought of a method of trying the question. I reflected that if I could only find a man wiser than myself, then I might go to the god with a refutation in my hand. I should say to him, "Here is a man who is wiser than I am; but you said that I was the wisest." Accordingly I went to one who had the reputation of wisdom, and observed him — his name I need not mention; he was a politician whom I selected for examination — and the result was as follows: When I began to talk with him, I could not help thinking that he was not really wise, although he was thought wise by many, and still wiser by himself; and thereupon I tried to explain to him that he thought himself wise, but was not really wise; and the consequence was that he hated me, and his enmity was shared by several who were present and heard me. So I left him, saying to myself, as I went away: Well, although I do not suppose that either of us knows anything really beautiful and good, I am better off than he is, — for he knows nothing, and thinks that he knows; I neither know nor think that I know. In this latter particular, then, I seem to have slightly the advantage of him. Then I went to another who had still higher pretensions to wisdom, and my conclusion was exactly the same. Whereupon I made another enemy of him, and of many others besides him.

Then I went to one man after another, being not unconscious of the enmity which I provoked, and I lamented and feared this: but necessity was laid upon me, — the word of God, I thought, ought to be considered first. And I said to myself, Go I must to all who appear to know, and find out the meaning of the oracle. And I swear to you, Athenians, by the dog I swear! — for I must tell you the truth — the result of my mission was just this: I found that the men most in repute were all but the most foolish; and that others less esteemed were really wiser and better. I will tell you the tale of my wanderings and of the "Herculean" labors, as I may call them, which I endured only to find at last the oracle irrefutable. After the politicians, I went to the poets; tragic, dithyrambic, and all sorts. And there, I said to myself, you will be instantly detected; now you will find out that you are more ignorant than they are. Accordingly, I took them some of the most elaborate passages in their own writings, and asked what was the meaning of them — thinking that they would teach me something. Will you believe me? I am almost ashamed to confess the truth, but I must say that there is hardly a person present who would not have talked better about their poetry than they did themselves. Then I knew that not by wisdom do poets write poetry, but by a sort of genius and inspiration; they are like diviners or soothsayers who also say many fine things, but do not understand the meaning of them. The poets appeared to me to be much in the same case; and I further observed that upon the strength of their poetry they believed themselves to be the wisest of men in other things in which they were not wise. So I departed, conceiving myself to be superior to them for the same reason that I was superior to the politicians.

At last I went to the artisans, for I was conscious that I knew nothing at all, as I may say, and I was sure that they knew many fine things; and here I was not mistaken, for they did know many things of which I was ignorant, and in this they certainly were wiser than I was. But I observed that even the good artisans fell into the same error as the poets; — because they were good workmen they thought that they also knew all sorts of high matters, and this defect in them overshadowed their wisdom; and therefore I asked myself on behalf of the oracle, whether I would like to be as I was, neither having their knowledge nor their ignorance, or like them in both; and I made answer to myself and to the oracle that I was better off as I was.

This inquisition has led to my having many enemies of the worst and most dangerous kind, and has given occasion also to many calumnies. And I am called wise, for my hearers always imagine that I myself possess the wisdom which I find wanting in others: but the truth is, O men of Athens, that God only is wise; and by his answer he intends to show that the wisdom of men is worth little or nothing; he is not speaking of Socrates, he is only using my name by way of illustration, as if he said, He, O men, is the wisest, who, like Socrates, knows that his wisdom is in truth worth nothing. And so I go about the world, obedient to the god, and search and make enquiry into the wisdom of any one, whether citizen or stranger, who appears to be wise; and if he is not wise, then in vindication of the oracle I show him that he is not wise; and my occupation quite absorbs me, and I have no time to give either to any public matter of interest or to any concern of my own, but I am in utter poverty by reason of my devotion to the god.

There is another thing: — young men of the richer classes, who have not much to do, come about me of their own accord; they like to hear the pretenders examined, and they often imitate me, and proceed to examine others; there are plenty of persons, as they quickly discover, who think that they know something, but really know little or nothing; and then those who are examined by them instead of being angry with themselves are angry with me: This confounded Socrates, they say; this villainous misleader of youth! — and then if somebody asks them, Why, what evil does he practice or teach? they do not know, and cannot tell; but in order that they may not appear to be at a loss, they repeat the ready-made charges which are used against all philosophers about teaching things up in the clouds and under the earth, and having no gods, and making the worse appear the better cause; for they do not like to confess that their pretense of knowledge has been detected — which is the truth; and as they are numerous and ambitious and energetic, and are drawn up in battle array and have persuasive tongues, they have filled your ears with their loud and inveterate calumnies. And this is the reason why my three accusers, Meletus and Anytus and Lycon, have set upon me; Meletus, who has a quarrel with me on behalf of the poets; Anytus, on behalf of the craftsmen and politicians; Lycon, on behalf of the rhetoricians: and, as I said at the beginning, I cannot expect to get rid of such a mass of calumny all in a moment. And this, O men of Athens, is the truth and the whole truth; I have concealed nothing, I have dissembled nothing. And yet, I know that my plainness of speech makes them hate me, and what is their hatred but a proof that I am speaking the truth? — Hence has arisen the prejudice against me; and this is the reason of it. . . .

Some one will say: And are you not ashamed, Socrates, of a course of life which is likely to bring you to an untimely end? To him I may fairly answer: There you are mistaken: a man who is good for anything ought not to calculate the chance of living or dying; he ought only to consider whether in doing anything he is doing right or wrong — acting the part of a good man or of a bad. . . .

For the fear of death is indeed the pretense of wisdom, and not real wisdom, being a pretense of knowing the unknown; and no one knows whether death, which men in their fear apprehend to be the greatest evil, may not be the greatest good. Is not this ignorance of a disgraceful sort, the ignorance which is the conceit that a man knows what he does not know? And in this respect only I believe myself to differ from men in general, and may perhaps claim to be wiser than they are: — that whereas I know but little of the world below, I do not suppose that I know: but I do know that injustice and disobedience to a better, whether God or man, is evil and dishonorable, and I will never fear or avoid a possible good rather than a certain evil. And therefore if you let me go now, and are not convinced by Anytus, who said that since I had been prosecuted I must be put to death; (or if not that I ought never to have been prosecuted at all); and that if I escape now, your sons will all be utterly ruined by listening to my words — if you say to me, Socrates, this time we will not mind Anytus, and you shall be let off, but upon one condition, that you are not to enquire and speculate in this way any more, and that if you are caught doing so again you shall die; — if this was the condition on which you let me go, I should reply: Men of Athens, I honor and love you; but I shall obey God rather than you, and while I have life and strength I shall never cease from the practice and teaching of philosophy, exhorting any one whom I meet and saying to him after my manner: You, my friend, — a citizen of the great and mighty and wise city of Athens, — are you not ashamed of heaping up the greatest amount of money and honor and reputation, and caring so little about wisdom and truth and the greatest improvement of the soul, which you never regard or heed at all? And if the person with whom I am arguing, says: Yes, but I do care; then I do not leave him or let him go at once; but I proceed to interrogate and examine and cross-examine him, and if I think that he has no virtue in him, but only says that he has, I reproach him with undervaluing the greater, and overvaluing the less. And I shall repeat the same words to every one whom I meet, young and old, citizen and alien, but especially to the citizens, inasmuch as they are my brethren. For know that this is the command of God; and I believe that no greater good has ever happened in the State than my service to the God. For I do nothing but go about persuading you all, old and young alike, not to take thought for your persons or your properties, but first and chiefly to care about the greatest improvement of the soul. I tell you that virtue is not given by money, but that from virtue comes money and every other good of man, public as well as private. This is my teaching, and if this is the doctrine which corrupts the youth, I am a mischievous person. But if any one says that this is not my teaching, he is speaking an untruth. Wherefore, O men of Athens, I say to you, do as Anytus bids or not as Anytus bids, and either acquit me or not; but whichever you do, understand that I shall never alter my ways, not even if I have to die many times.

Discussion Questions

1. According to Socrates, what accusations have been levied against him, and why?

2. In refuting these accusations, what does Socrates reveal about his fundamental intellectual beliefs and methods?

3. Why do you think many of Socrates' contemporaries found his views so threatening?

4. What impressions do Socrates' words give you of him as a man?

4.
The Advance of Science

Hippocrates of Cos, *On the Sacred Disease* (400 b.c.e.)

Science was yet another forum for innovation and change during Greece's Golden Age. Hippocrates of Cos (c. 460–377 b.c.e.) gained fame across the Hellenic world as an exceptional medical teacher and practitioner who helped to transform contempo-

rary theories regarding the cause and treatment of disease. Traditional Greek medicine looked to religion and magic to understand and heal illness. By contrast, Hippocrates emphasized the need to view disease as a physical ailment rooted in the natural world. The text excerpted below, On the Sacred Disease, *is one of the earliest of the many treatises attributed to Hippocrates. The "sacred disease" in question is epilepsy. Although scholars cannot prove definitively that Hippocrates wrote the work, they agree that its advocation of rational, observation-based medicine represents a key feature of his scientific legacy.*

The Sacred Disease

I am about to discuss the disease called "sacred." It is not, in my opinion, any more divine or more sacred than other diseases, but has a natural cause, and its supposed divine origin is due to men's inexperience, and to their wonder at its peculiar character. Now while men continue to believe in its divine origin because they are at a loss to understand it, they really disprove its divinity by the facile method of healing which they adopt, consisting as it does of purifications and incantations. But if it is to be considered divine just because it is wonderful, there will be not one sacred disease but many, for I will show that other diseases are no less wonderful and portentous, and yet nobody considers them sacred. For instance, quotidian fevers, tertians, and quartans seem to me to be no less sacred and god-sent than this disease,[1] but nobody wonders at them. Then again one can see men who are mad and delirious from no obvious cause, and committing many strange acts; while in their sleep, to my knowledge, many groan and shriek, others choke, others dart up and rush out of doors, being delirious until they wake, when they become as healthy and rational as they were before, though pale and weak; and this happens not once but many times. Many other instances, of various kinds, could be given, but time does not permit us to speak of each separately.

My own view is that those who first attributed a sacred character to this malady were like the magicians, purifiers, charlatans, and quacks of our own day, men who claim great piety and superior knowledge. Being at a loss, and having no treatment which would help, they concealed and sheltered themselves behind superstition, and called this illness sacred, in order that their utter ignorance might not be manifest. They added a plausible story, and established a method of treatment that secured their own position. They used purifications and incantations; they forbade the use of baths, and of many foods that are unsuitable for sick folk . . . [they forbade] the wearing of black (black is the sign of death); not to lie on or wear goat-skin, not to put foot on foot or hand on hand. . . . These observances they impose because of the divine origin of the disease, claiming superior knowledge and alleging other causes, so that, should the patient recover, the

---

From *Hippocrates*, vol. 2, trans. W. H. S. Jones (Cambridge, MA: Harvard University Press, 1959), 139, 141, 143, 145, 153, 175, 179, 181, 183.

[1]Because of the regularity of the attacks of fever, which occur every day (quotidians), every other day (tertians), or with intermissions of two whole days (quartans).

reputation for cleverness may be theirs; but should he die, they may have a sure fund of excuses, with the defense that they are not at all to blame, but the gods. Having given nothing to eat or drink, and not having steeped their patients in baths, no blame can be laid, they say, upon them. So I suppose that no Libyan dwelling in the interior can enjoy good health, since they lie on goat-skins and eat goats' flesh, possessing neither coverlet nor cloak nor footgear that is not from the goat; in fact they possess no cattle save goats. But if to eat or apply these things engenders and increases the disease, while to refrain works a cure, then neither is godhead[2] to blame nor are the purifications beneficial; it is the foods that cure or hurt, and the power of godhead disappears.

Accordingly I hold that those who attempt in this manner to cure these diseases cannot consider them either sacred or divine; for when they are removed by such purifications and by such treatment as this, there is nothing to prevent the production of attacks in men by devices that are similar. If so, something human is to blame, and not godhead. He who by purifications and magic can take away such an affection can also by similar means bring it on, so that by this argument the action of godhead is disproved. By these sayings and devices they claim superior knowledge, and deceive men by prescribing for them purifications and cleansings, most of their talk turning on the intervention of gods and spirits. . . .

The fact is that the cause of this affection, as of the more serious diseases generally, is the brain. . . .

Men ought to know that from the brain, and from the brain only, arise our pleasures, joys, laughter, and jests, as well as our sorrows, pains, griefs, and tears. Through it, in particular, we think, see, hear, and distinguish the ugly from the beautiful, the bad from the good, the pleasant from the unpleasant, in some cases using custom as a test, in others perceiving them from their utility. It is the same thing which makes us mad or delirious, inspires us with dread and fear, whether by night or by day, brings sleeplessness, inopportune mistakes, aimless anxieties, absent-mindedness, and acts that are contrary to habit. These things that we suffer all come from the brain, when it is not healthy, but becomes abnormally hot, cold, moist, or dry, or suffers any other unnatural affection to which it was not accustomed. . . .

In these ways I hold that the brain is the most powerful organ of the human body, for when it is healthy it is an interpreter to us of the phenomena caused by the air, as it is the air that gives it intelligence. Eyes, ears, tongue, hands, and feet act in accordance with the discernment of the brain; in fact the whole body participates in intelligence in proportion to its participation in air. To consciousness the brain is the messenger. For when a man draws breath into himself, the air first reaches the brain, and so is dispersed through the rest of the body. . . .

. . . As therefore it is the first of the bodily organs to perceive the intelligence coming from the air, so too if any violent change has occurred in the air owing to the seasons, the brain also becomes different from what it was. Therefore I assert

---

[2][The Greek word for godhead] does not imply any sort of monotheism. The article is generic, and the phrase therefore means "*a* god" rather than "*the* god."

that the diseases too that attack it are the most acute, most serious, most fatal, and the hardest for the inexperienced to judge of.

This disease styled sacred comes from the same causes as others, from the things that come to and go from the body, from cold, sun, and from the changing restlessness of winds. . . . Each has a nature and power of its own; none is hopeless or incapable of treatment. Most are cured by the same things as caused them. One thing is food for one thing, and another for another, though occasionally each actually does harm. So the physician must know how, by distinguishing the seasons for individual things, he may assign to one thing nutriment and growth, and to another diminution and harm. For in this disease as in all others it is necessary, not to increase the illness, but to wear it down by applying to each what is most hostile to it, not that to which it is conformable. For what is conformity gives vigor and increase; what is hostile causes weakness and decay. Whoever knows how to cause in men by regimen moist or dry, hot or cold, he can cure this disease also, if he distinguish the seasons for useful treatment, without having recourse to purifications and magic.

DISCUSSION QUESTIONS

1. According to traditional medicine, what was the cause of epilepsy? Why does Hippocrates reject this belief?

2. What course of treatment does Hippocrates think physicians should follow when treating this disease, and why?

3. Many scholars regard Hippocrates as the father of scientific medicine. Do you view his explanation of the causes and treatment of epilepsy as scientific? Why or why not?

5.
Domestic Boundaries

Euphiletus, *A Husband Speaks in His Own Defense*
(c. 400 B.C.E.)
and
Overhead Views of a House on the North Slope of the Areopagus (Fifth Century B.C.E.)

Despite momentous changes during Greece's Golden Age, ancient traditions retained their grip on much of society, especially women. Defined by their roles as daughters, wives, and widows, women were closely supervised and had limited legal and political

---

From Kathleen Freeman, ed., *The Murder of Herodes and Other Trials from the Athenian Law Courts* (Indianapolis: Hackett Publishing, 1994), 43–52; and Susan Walker, "Women and Housing in Classical Greece: The Archaeological Evidence," in *Images of Women in Antiquity*, ed. Averil Cameron and Amélie Kuhrt (Detroit: Wayne State University Press, 1993), 87.

*rights. The testimony below is that of a man named Euphiletus who was put on trial
for murdering his wife's lover. He presented the following arguments in his own
defense, as prepared for him by the speechwriter Lysias (c. 440–380 B.C.E.). Although
not directly related to Euphiletus's case, the overhead views of a Greek house illuminate the physical geography of the domestic values underlying his defense. Most
women spent a significant portion of their lives segregated in their own quarters
(gynakeion), usually on the second floor of the house to limit access to the street.
Typically, men's quarters (andron) were on the first floor, intended in part to prevent
unsupervised meetings between women and men from outside the family. The draw-
ings show the first floor of an excavated house on the north slope of Areopagus, a
rocky hill west of the Acropolis in Athens.*

I would give a great deal, members of the jury, to find you, as judges of this case,
taking the same attitude towards me as you would adopt towards your own behavior in similar circumstances. I am sure that if you felt about others in the same way
as you did about yourselves, not one of you would fail to be angered by these deeds,
and all of you would consider the punishment a small one for those guilty of such
conduct.

Moreover, the same opinion would be found prevailing not only among you,
but everywhere throughout Greece. This is the one crime for which, under any
government, democratic or exclusive, equal satisfaction is granted to the meanest
against the mightiest, so that the least of them receives the same justice as the most
exalted. Such is the detestation, members of the jury, in which this outrage is held
by all mankind.

Concerning the severity of the penalty, therefore, you are, I imagine, all of the
same opinion: not one of you is so easy-going as to believe that those guilty of such
great offenses should obtain pardon, or are deserving of a light penalty. What I have
to prove, I take it, is just this: that Eratosthenes seduced my wife, and that in corrupting her he brought shame upon my children and outrage upon me, by entering my home; that there was no other enmity between him and me except this; and
that I did not commit this act for the sake of money, in order to rise from poverty
to wealth, nor for any other advantage except the satisfaction allowed by law.

I shall expound my case to you in full from the beginning, omitting nothing
and telling the truth. In this alone lies my salvation, I imagine — if I can explain to
you everything that happened.

Members of the jury: when I decided to marry and had brought a wife home,
at first my attitude towards her was this: I did not wish to annoy her, but neither
was she to have too much of her own way. I watched her as well as I could, and kept
an eye on her as was proper. But later, after my child had been born, I came to trust
her, and I handed all my possessions over to her, believing that this was the greatest possible proof of affection.

Well, members of the jury, in the beginning she was the best of women. She
was a clever housewife, economical and exact in her management of everything.
But then, my mother died; and her death has proved to be the source of all my
troubles, because it was when my wife went to the funeral that this man Eratosthenes saw her; and as time went on, he was able to seduce her. He kept a look out

for our maid who goes to market; and approaching her with his suggestions, he succeeded in corrupting her mistress.

Now first of all, gentlemen, I must explain that I have a small house which is divided into two — the men's quarters and the women's — each having the same space, the women upstairs and the men downstairs.

After the birth of my child, his mother nursed him; but I did not want her to run the risk of going downstairs every time she had to give him a bath, so I myself took over the upper story, and let the women have the ground floor. And so it came about that by this time it was quite customary for my wife often to go downstairs and sleep with the child, so that she could give him the breast and stop him from crying.

This went on for a long while, and I had not the slightest suspicion. On the contrary, I was in such a fool's paradise that I believed my wife to be the chastest woman in all the city.

Time passed, gentlemen. One day, when I had come home unexpectedly from the country, after dinner, the child began crying and complaining. Actually it was the maid who was pinching him on purpose to make him behave so, because — as I found out later — this man was in the house.

Well, I told my wife to go and feed the child, to stop his crying. But at first she refused, pretending that she was so glad to see me back after my long absence. At last I began to get annoyed, and I insisted on her going.

"Oh, yes!" she said. "To leave *you* alone with the maid up here! You mauled her about before, when you were drunk!"

I laughed. She got up, went out, closed the door — pretending that it was a joke — and locked it. As for me, I thought no harm of all this, and I had not the slightest suspicion. I went to sleep, glad to do so after my journey from the country.

Towards morning, she returned and unlocked the door.

I asked her why the doors had been creaking during the night. She explained that the lamp beside the baby had gone out, and that she had then gone to get a light from the neighbors.

I said no more. I thought it really was so. But it did seem to me, members of the jury, that she had done up her face with cosmetics, in spite of the fact that her brother had died only a month before. Still, even so, I said nothing about it. I just went off, without a word.

After this, members of the jury, an interval elapsed, during which my injuries had progressed, leaving me far behind. Then, one day, I was approached by an old hag. She had been sent by a woman — Eratosthenes' previous mistress, as I found out later. This woman, furious because he no longer came to see her as before, had been on the look-out until she had discovered the reason. The old crone, therefore, had come and was lying in wait for me near my house.

"Euphiletus," she said, "please don't think that my approaching you is in any way due to a wish to interfere. The fact is, the man who is wronging you and your wife is an enemy of ours. Now if you catch the woman who does your shopping and works for you, and put her through an examination, you will discover all. The culprit," she added, "is Eratosthenes from Oea. Your wife is not the only one he has seduced — there are plenty of others. It's his profession."

With these words, members of the jury, she went off.

At once I was overwhelmed. Everything rushed into my mind, and I was filled with suspicion. I reflected how I had been locked into the bedroom. I remembered how on that night the middle and outer doors had creaked, a thing that had never happened before; and how I had had the idea that my wife's face was rouged. All these things rushed into my mind, and I was filled with suspicion.

I went back home, and told the servant to come with me to market. I took her instead to the house of one of my friends; and there I informed her that I had discovered all that was going on in my house.

"As for you," I said, "two courses are open to you: either to be flogged and sent to the tread-mill, and never be released from a life of utter misery; or to confess the whole truth and suffer no punishment, but win pardon from me for your wrong-doing. Tell me no lies. Speak the whole truth."

At first she tried denial, and told me that I could do as I pleased — she knew nothing. But when I named Eratosthenes to her face, and said that he was the man who had been visiting my wife, she was dumbfounded, thinking that I had found out everything exactly. And then at last, falling at my feet and exacting a promise from me that no harm should be done to her, she denounced the villain. She described how he had first approached her after the funeral, and then how in the end she had passed the message on, and in course of time my wife had been over-persuaded. She explained the way in which he had contrived to get into the house, and how when I was in the country my wife had gone to a religious service with this man's mother, and everything else that had happened. She recounted it all exactly.

When she had told all, I said:

"See to it that nobody gets to know of this; otherwise the promise I made you will not hold good. And furthermore, I expect you to show me this actually happening. I have no use for words. I want the *fact* to be exhibited, if it really is so."

She agreed to do this.

Four or five days then elapsed, as I shall prove to you by important evidence. But before I do so, I wish to narrate the events of the last day.

I had a friend and relative named Sôstratus. He was coming home from the country after sunset when I met him. I knew that as he had got back so late, he would not find any of his own people at home; so I asked him to dine with me. We went home to my place, and going upstairs to the upper story, we had dinner there. When he felt restored, he went off; and I went to bed.

Then, members of the jury, Eratosthenes made his entry; and the maid wakened me and told me that he was in the house.

I told her to watch the door; and going downstairs, I slipped out noiselessly.

I went to the houses of one man after another. Some I found at home; others, I was told, were out of town. So collecting as many as I could of those who were there, I went back. We procured torches from the shop near by, and entered my house. The door had been left open by arrangement with the maid.

We forced the bedroom door. The first of us to enter saw him still lying beside my wife. Those who followed saw him standing naked on the bed.

I knocked him down, members of the jury, with one blow. I then twisted his hands behind his back and tied them. And then I asked him why he was committing this crime against me, of breaking into my house.

He answered that he admitted his guilt; but he begged and besought me not to kill him — to accept a money-payment instead.

But I replied:

"It is not I who shall be killing you, but the law of the State, which you, in transgressing, have valued less highly than your own pleasures. You have preferred to commit this great crime against my wife and my children, rather than to obey the law and be of decent behavior."

Thus, members of the jury, this man met the fate which the laws prescribe for wrong-doers of his kind.

Eratosthenes was not seized in the street and carried off, nor had he taken refuge at the altar, as the prosecution alleges. The facts do not admit of it: he was struck in the bedroom, he fell at once, and I bound his hands behind his back. There were so many present that he could not possibly escape through their midst, since he had neither steel nor wood nor any other weapon with which he could have defended himself against all those who had entered the room.

No, members of the jury: you know as well as I do how wrong-doers will not admit that their adversaries are speaking the truth, and attempt by lies and trickery of other kinds to excite the anger of the hearers against those whose acts are in accordance with Justice.

[To the Clerk of the Court]:

Read the Law.

[The Law of Solon is read, that an adulterer may be put to death by the man who catches him.]

He made no denial, members of the jury. He admitted his guilt, and begged and implored that he should not be put to death, offering to pay compensation. But I would not accept his estimate. I preferred to accord a higher authority to the law of the State, and I took that satisfaction which you, because you thought it the most just, have decreed for those who commit such offenses. . . .

You have heard the witnesses, members of the jury. Now consider the case further in your own minds, inquiring whether there had ever existed between Eratosthenes and myself any other enmity but this. You will find none. He never brought any malicious charge against me, nor tried to secure my banishment, nor prosecuted me in any private suit. Neither had he knowledge of any crime of which I feared the revelation, so that I desired to kill him; nor by carrying out this act did I hope to gain money. So far from ever having had any dispute with him, or drunken brawl, or any other quarrel, I had never even set eyes on the man before that night. What possible object could I have had, therefore, in running so great a risk, except that I had suffered the greatest of all injuries at his hands? Again, would I myself have called in witnesses to my crime, when it was possible for me, if I desired to murder him without justification, to have had no confidants?

It is my belief, members of the jury, that this punishment was inflicted not in my own interests, but in those of the whole community. Such villains, seeing the rewards which await their crimes, will be less ready to commit offenses against others if they see that you too hold the same opinion of them. Otherwise it would be far better to wipe out the existing laws and make different ones, which will penalize those who keep guard over their own wives, and grant full immunity to those who criminally pursue them. This would be a far more just procedure than to set a trap for citizens by means of the laws, which urge the man who catches an adulterer to do with him whatever he will, and yet allow the injured party to undergo a trial far more perilous than that which faces the law-breaker who seduces other men's wives. Of this, I am an example — I, who now stand in danger of losing life, property, everything, because I have obeyed the laws of the State.

House on the North Slope of the Areopagus: probable functions of rooms

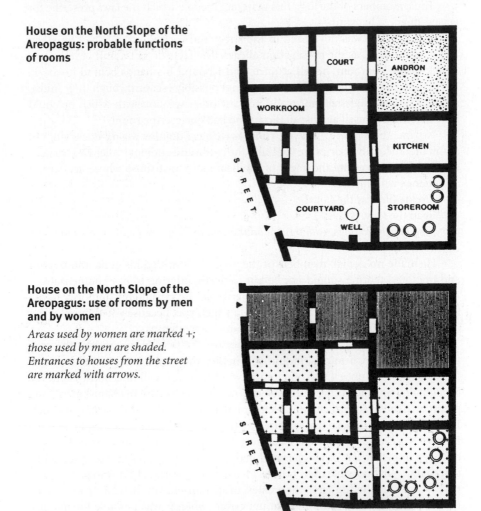

House on the North Slope of the Areopagus: use of rooms by men and by women

Areas used by women are marked +; those used by men are shaded. Entrances to houses from the street are marked with arrows.

From *Images of Women in Antiquity*, ed. Averil Cameron and Amelie Kuhrt (London: Routledge, 1993), 87.

DISCUSSION QUESTIONS

1. What does Euphiletus's testimony suggest about the roles both men and women were expected to play in Athenian society in general and within the home in particular?

2. How did these expectations shape the physical geography of domestic space as revealed in the overhead views of a Greek house?

3. According to Euphiletus, why did his wife cross the boundaries of this geography? How did this set the stage for his woes?

6.
Protesting War, Performing Satire
Aristophanes, *Lysistrata* (411 B.C.E.)

The plays of Aristophanes (450–386 B.C.E.) are the only comedies to survive from Greece's Golden Age. Although he was a wellborn Athenian, Aristophanes held the leaders of his city-state responsible for starting the Peloponnesian War (431–404) and refusing to make peace. He produced Acharnians, *the first antiwar play, in 425.* Lysistrata, *Aristophanes' most famous comedy, describes a meeting of women who come together to decide how to end the war. The play opens with the group's Athenian leader, Lysistrata, waiting impatiently for the women to arrive. When they do, she suggests a bold strategy to convince their husbands to desist from war and make peace — a sex strike. To force the hand of Athenians in general, Lysistrata has another plan in place. As she tells the gathering, women are about to seize the Acropolis, the geographic, political, and religious center of Athens. Although the work was satiric, Aristophanes' antiwar stance signaled increasing dissatisfaction with conditions in Athens as a result of the war. As the excerpt here reveals, his message in* Lysistrata *is so powerful and timeless that the play is still performed throughout the world.*

> [*Lysistrata comes out of one of the flanking doors of the stage-house. She looks off to right and left, but sees no one approaching.*]

> LYSISTRATA [*annoyed*]: Now if someone had invited them to a Bacchic revel, or to Pan's shrine, or to Genetyllis' shrine at Colias[1] — you'd

From *The Comedies of Aristophanes, vol. 7: Lysistrata*, ed. and trans. Alan H. Sommerstein (Warminster, England: Arris & Phillips, 1990), 15, 17, 19, 21, 23, 25, 27, 29, 31, 33, 35, 39, 41, 43.

[1]In Greek a Bacchic revel can mean either a society organized for the worship of Dionysus or such a society's place of meeting. Pan had strong associations with music and dancing, and was worshipped by young women with all-night celebrations. A well-known sanctuary of the goddesses of procreation known as the Genetyllides was at the headland of Colias. This sanctuary appears to have been a favorite resort of well-to-do Athenian women.

never have been able to get through the crowd, what with the drums! But as it is, there's not a woman turned up here.

[*Seeing the far door open*] Except that here's my neighbour coming out.

[*Calonice comes out.*] Good morning, Calonice.

CALONICE: Same to you, Lysistrata. [*Coming closer*] What's disturbed you so terribly? Don't look cross, child. Knitted brows don't look good on you.

LYSISTRATA: My heart's burning, Calonice, and I'm feeling *very* sore about us women: because in men's opinion we're thought to be such utter rascals —

CALONICE: And so we are, by Zeus!

LYSISTRATA: But when they've been told to meet here to have a discussion about a far from trivial matter, they lie asleep and don't come.

CALONICE: They'll come, darling. For women to get out of the house is quite some trouble, you know. One of us may be hanging round her husband, another rousing a servant, another putting her baby to bed or bathing it or feeding it with titbits.

LYSISTRATA: But the point is, there were other things that should matter more to them than all those!

CALONICE: What actually *is* it, Lysistrata dear, that you're calling us women together for? What is this thing? What's the size of it?

LYSISTRATA: It's big —

CALONICE: you don't mean big *and meaty*?

LYSISTRATA: — and meaty too, I tell you.

CALONICE: Then how come we're not all here?

LYSISTRATA: Not in *that* sense! We'd have assembled fast enough if it was. No, it's something that I've been examining and tossing about through many a sleepless night.

CALONICE: Tossing about? Must be a dainty little thing.

LYSISTRATA: So very *dainty* that the salvation of all Greece is actually in the hands of her women.

CALONICE: In the hands of her women? Then it's resting on very little!

LYSISTRATA: I tell you that the fortunes of the country depend on us. Either there will be no more Peloponnesians —[2]

CALONICE: Well, that would be splendid, by Zeus, for them to be no more!

LYSISTRATA: — and the Boeotians will all be utterly destroyed —

CALONICE: Oh, please not *all* of them — do make an exception for the eels![3]

---

[2]**Peloponnesians**: People of Peloponnese, a region forming the southern Greek peninsula. [Ed].

[3]**exception for the eels**: Eels from Lake Copaïs in Boeotia, a region in south-central Greece, were a culinary delicacy. [Ed.]

LYSISTRATA: I won't utter any words of that kind about Athens, but you can infer my meaning. But if the wives come together here — those from Boeotia, those of the Peloponnesians, and ourselves — united we'll save Greece.

CALONICE: But what can women achieve that is clever or glorious — we who sit at home all dolled up, wearing saffron gowns and cosmetics and Cimberic[4] straight-liners and riverboat slippers?

LYSISTRATA: Why, that's exactly what I'm counting on to save Greece — our pretty saffron gowns and our perfumes and our riverboat slippers and our rouge and our see-through shifts.

CALONICE: How on earth do you mean?

LYSISTRATA: To make it that none of the men living today will take up the spear against each other —

CALONICE: In that case, by the Two Goddesses,[5] I'm going to dye a gown with saffron!

LYSISTRATA: — or take up a shield —

CALONICE: I'm going to put on a Cimberic!

LYSISTRATA: — or even a little toy sword.

CALONICE: I'm going to buy riverboat slippers!

LYSISTRATA: So shouldn't the women be here now?

CALONICE: Not *now*, in heaven's name — they should have taken wing and been here long ago!

LYSISTRATA: Ah, I tell you, my good friend, you'll see they're thoroughly Athenian — everything they do is too late. Why, there isn't even a single woman here from the Paralia, nor from Salamis.[6]

CALONICE: Oh, as for them, they'll have been working over on their pinnaces well before daylight.

LYSISTRATA: And the Acharnian[7] women too, whom I was expecting and counting on their being first here, they haven't come.

CALONICE: Well, at any rate Theogenes'[8] wife was putting on all sail to come here. [*Pointing offstage*] But look, here you are, some of them are arriving now.

LYSISTRATA: [*looking in the other direction*]: And here come some others.

CALONICE [*recoiling as if from a foul smell*]: Ugh! where are they from?

---

[4]**Cimberic**: negligée [Ed.]
[5]Reference to Demeter and her daughter Persephone; oaths in their name were used only by women.
[6]**Paralia . . . Salamis**: The Paralia and Salamis were key strategic areas under Athens' jurisdiction. [Ed.]
[7]The district of Acharnae was in the central part of the Athenian polis.
[8]Theogenes of Acharnae was a merchant and shipowner who had the reputation of a vain boaster pretending to be much richer than he was.

LYSISTRATA: Lousia.

CALONICE: Dead right; seems to me we've opened a real *can* of lice!

[*During this dialogue women have been coming on from both sides, and a fair-sized group has now gathered. One of them is Myrrhine.*]

MYRRHINE: We haven't come late, Lysistrata, have we? [*Lysistrata ignores the question.*] What do you say? Why don't you speak?

LYSISTRATA [*severely*]: Myrrhine, I don't thank anyone for only arriving now, on a matter of this importance.

MYRRHINE: The thing was, I had trouble finding my waistband in the dark. But if it really is vital, speak to those of us who are here.

LYSISTRATA: No, no; let's wait — it's only a matter of a few minutes — for the women from Boeotia and the Peloponnese to come.

MYRRHINE: Yours is a much better idea. [*Looking off*] And look, here comes Lampito now.

[*Enter Lampito, accompanied by a Theban woman (Ismenia) and a Corinthian woman, and followed by several other Spartan women. Their garments, unlike those of the Athenian women, are open at the side in the Doric fashion.*]

LYSISTRATA: Welcome, Lampito, my very dear Laconian[9] friend! Darling, what beauty you display! What a fine colour, and what a robust frame you've got! You could throttle a bull.

LAMPITO [*in Laconian dialect*]: Yes, indeed, I reckon, by the Two Gods;[10] at any rate I do gymnastics and jump heel-to-buttocks.

CALONICE [*feeling Lampito's breasts*]: What a splendid pair of tits you've got!

LAMPITO [*annoyed*]: Really, you're feeling me over like a victim for sacrifice!

LYSISTRATA: And where does this other young lady come from [*indicating Ismenia*]?

LAMPITO: She's come to you, don't you know, by the Two Gods, as a representative of Boeotia.

MYRRHINE [*looking inside Ismenia's revealing costume*]: Yes, she represents Boeotia all right, with that fine lowland region she's got!

CALONICE: And, by Zeus, with the mint shoots very neatly plucked out!

LYSISTRATA: And who's the other girl?

LAMPITO: A lady of noble line, by the Two Gods, a Corinthian.

CALONICE: Yes, it's certainly obvious she *does* have noble lines — here and here [*pointing to the Corinthian's belly and buttocks*]!

LAMPITO: Now who has convened this gathering of women?

---

[9]**Laconian:** A term sometimes used to refer to the people of Sparta. [Ed.]
[10]To a Spartan, the "Two Gods" are Castor and Pollux, brothers of Helen and special patrons of Sparta.

LYSISTRATA: Here I am; I did.

LAMPITO: Tell us, pray, what you wish of us.

CALONICE: Yes, indeed, dear lady, do tell us what this important business of yours is.

LYSISTRATA: I will tell you now. But before doing so, I will ask you this one small question.

CALONICE: Whatever you like.

LYSISTRATA: Don't you miss the fathers of your children badly, when they're away on campaign? I know that every one of you has a man away from home.

CALONICE: *My* husband, my dear, anyway, has been off on the Thracian Coast for five months, keeping a watch on Eucrates.[11]

MYRRHINE: And *mine's* been seven solid months at Pylos.[12]

LAMPITO: And *mine*, even when he does ever come home from his active service, right away he's fastened on his shield-band and gone flying off again.

LYSISTRATA: Why, there isn't even a *lover* left us now — not the least glimmer of one. Since the Milesians[13] deserted us, I haven't even seen a six-inch dildo that might have given us some slender comfort. If I were to find a plan, then, would you be willing to join me in bringing the war to an end?

CALONICE: By the Two Goddesses, I would, for one, even if I had to pawn this mantle and drink my purse dry all in one day!

MYRRHINE: And *I* think I'd even be ready to slice myself in two like a flounder and donate half of my body!

LAMPITO: And I would climb right to the top of Mount Taÿgetum,[14] if I was going to be able to see peace from there.

LYSISTRATA: I will say it: there's no need for the idea to stay hidden. What we must do, women, if we mean to compel the men to live in peace, is to abstain —

CALONICE: From what? Tell us.

LYSISTRATA: You'll do it, then?

CALONICE: We'll do it, even if we have to give our lives. [*The others indicate enthusiastic agreement.*]

---

[11]**Eucrates:** An Athenian general of questionable loyalty. [Ed.]

[12]A strategic promontory on the west coast of the Peloponnese, seized by the Athenians in 425 and held ever since by an Athenian garrison.

[13]**Milesians:** Miletus was an important Greek city in Asia Minor. Once an ally of Athens, it revolted in 412. Apparently it was known for the production of artificial leather penises. [Ed.]

[14]This range forms the western boundary of Laconia. From the plain of Sparta, its highest peak would have seemed to an ancient Spartan literally impossible to climb.

LYSISTRATA: Well then: we must abstain from — cock and balls. [*Strong murmurs of dissent; some of the women seem on the point of quitting the meeting.*] Why are you turning your backs on me? Where are you going? I ask you, why are you pursing your lips and tossing your heads? "Why pales your colour, why this flow of tears?" Will you do it or will you not? or why do you hesitate?

CALONICE: I won't do it. Let the war carry on.

MYRRHINE: By Zeus, nor will I. Let the war carry on.

LYSISTRATA: *You* say that, Madam Flounder? Why, a moment ago you were saying you'd be ready to slice off half of your body!

CALONICE: Anything else you want — anything! And if need be, I'm willing to walk through fire — rather that than cock and balls! There is nothing, Lysistrata dear, nothing like it!

LYSISTRATA [*turning to another of the women*]: And what about you?

WOMAN: I'd rather go through fire too!

LYSISTRATA: What an absolute race of nymphomaniacs we are, the lot of us! No wonder the tragedies get written round us: we're nothing but Poseidon and a tub. [*To Lampito*] Look, my dear Laconian friend, if you, just you, join with me, we can still save the situation. Do cast your vote on my side.

LAMPITO: Well, by the Two Gods, it's a hard thing for women to sleep alone without Big Red. But all the same, yes; we do need peace back again.

LYSISTRATA: Oh my darling, you're the only real woman here!

CALONICE: But suppose we abstained as much as you like from . . . what you said — which heaven forbid — would that make peace any more likely to happen?

LYSISTRATA: It very much would, by the Two Goddesses. If we sat there at home in our make-up, and came into their rooms wearing our lawn shifts and nothing else and plucked down below delta-style, and our husbands got all horny and eager for the old spleck-spleck, but we kept away and didn't come to them — they'd make peace fast enough, I know for sure.

CALONICE: But, my dear girl, what if our husbands just ignore us?

LYSISTRATA: In the words of Pherecrates — skin the skinned dog.

CALONICE: Those imitation things are just sheer garbage. And what if they take us and drag us into the bedroom by force?

LYSISTRATA: You should cling to the door.

CALONICE: And if they beat us?

LYSISTRATA: You should submit in the grudgingest way — there's no pleasure in it when it's done by force — and you should vex them generally; and have no fear, they'll tire of it very quickly. For no man is ever going to get any gratification unless it suits the woman that he should.

CALONICE: Well, if that's what you both think, then we agree. [*The others indicate assent.*]

LAMPITO: And *we'll* see to it that *our* menfolk keep the peace with complete honesty and sincerity. But your Athenians — how is one going to persuade that riffraff not to act barmy?

LYSISTRATA: Don't you worry, we'll do our part of the persuading all right.

LAMPITO: Not while your warships still have feet, and while there's that bottomless store of money in the house of your Goddess.[15]

LYSISTRATA: Ah, that's also been thoroughly provided for. We're going to occupy the Acropolis today. The over-age women have instructions to do that: while we get our act together, they're to seize the Acropolis under pretence of making a sacrifice.

LAMPITO: That should be absolutely fine — another good idea of yours.

LYSISTRATA: Well then, Lampito, why don't we bind ourselves together straight away by an oath, so as to make our resolution unbreakable?

LAMPITO: Present us with the oath, then; we are ready to swear.

.   .   .   .

LYSISTRATA: Let one of you, on behalf of all, repeat the exact words that I say, and the rest will swear to them afterwards in confirmation. No man whatever, neither lover nor husband —

CALONICE: No man whatever, neither lover nor husband —

LYSISTRATA: — shall come near me with his cock up. [*Calonice hesitates.*] Say it.

CALONICE: — shall come near me with his cock up. [*Swaying as if about to swoon*] Help, help, Lysistrata, my knees are buckling!

LYSISTRATA: And I will pass my life at home, pure and chaste —

CALONICE [*recovering*]: And I will pass my life at home, pure and chaste —

LYSISTRATA: — in make-up and saffron gown —

CALONICE: — in make-up and saffron gown —

LYSISTRATA: — so that my husband may be greatly inflamed with desire for me —

CALONICE: — so that my husband may be greatly inflamed with desire for me —

LYSISTRATA: — and will never of my free will yield myself to my husband.

CALONICE: — and will never of my free will yield myself to my husband.

LYSISTRATA: And if he force me by force against my will —

CALONICE: And if he force me by force against my will —

LYSISTRATA: — I will submit grudgingly and will not thrust back.

CALONICE: — I will submit grudgingly and will not thrust back.

LYSISTRATA: I will not raise up my Persian slippers ceilingwards.

CALONICE: I will not raise up my Persian slippers ceilingwards.

---

[15]For over twenty years the financial reserves of the Athenian state had been kept on the Acropolis in the west end of the ancient temple of Athena.

LYSISTRATA: I will not stand in the lioness-on-a-cheesegrater position.

CALONICE: I will not stand in the lioness-on-a-cheesegrater position.

LYSISTRATA: If I fulfil all this, may I drink from this cup.

CALONICE: If I fulfil all this, may I drink from this cup.

LYSISTRATA: But if I transgress it, may the cup be filled with water.

CALONICE: But if I transgress it, may the cup be filled with water.

LYSISTRATA [*to the others*]: Do all of you join in swearing this oath?

ALL: We do.

LYSISTRATA: Here, let me consecrate this. [*She is about to drink off the cup.*]

CALONICE [*interposing*]: Only your share, my friend; we want to *be* friends with each other, right from the start.

[*As Lysistrata is about to drink from the cup and pass it round, a women's cry of joy is heard from backstage.*]

LAMPITO: What's that shout for?

LYSISTRATA: It's the very thing I told you about: the women have now seized the Citadel of the Goddess. So now, Lampito, you go and arrange everything at your end, but leave these others here with us as hostages. [*Exit Lampito.*] And for ourselves, let's go inside and join the other women on the Acropolis in barring the doors.

CALONICE: But don't you expect the men to make a united counter-attack on us straight away?

LYSISTRATA: They don't bother me. There are no menaces, no fire, that they can bring against us, strong enough to get these gates open, except on the conditions that we have laid down.

CALONICE: No, by Aphrodite, never! Otherwise it would be for nothing that all we women are called villains whom there's "no getting the better of."

DISCUSSION QUESTIONS

1. According to Aristophanes, how do women in Greece's Golden Age feel about sex? What, if anything, is surprising about Lysistrata's proposal to the group?

2. How does the play reflect the role of women in Greek society? Does the satirical and comedic intent of the playwright affect your interpretation?

3. How does Aristophanes use defined gender roles to make a political statement?

COMPARATIVE QUESTIONS

1. In what ways does the Discus Thrower embody the characteristics of Athenian society celebrated in Thucydides' speech?

2. How might Socrates have reacted to Pericles' description of the role of wealth in Athenian society?

3. In what ways do Pericles' and Euphiletus's views on the relationship between the individual and the state overlap?

4. How did both Socrates and Hippocrates challenge traditional forms of wisdom in Greek society? What was the basis of their reasoning?

5. Both Euphiletus's defense and Aristophanes' comedy suggest that attempts to regulate women's contact with men from outside the family did not always work. Compare the actual women mentioned in the defense with the fictional heroines of the play. What do they have in common? What does Aristophanes exaggerate or make up to raise laughs from his audience and to advance his antiwar position?

From the Classical to the Hellenistic World

400–30 B.C.E.

F ollowing the end of the Peloponnesian War in 404 B.C.E., the Greek city-states fell victim to internal squabbling and disunity as each vied to dominate Greece. The first document elucidates how Macedonian kings seized this opportunity to become masters of the eastern Mediterranean and beyond. Their successors capitalized on this legacy, carving out individual kingdoms from the Macedonian Empire. The result was a mix of Greek and Near Eastern peoples and traditions that became a hallmark of the Hellenistic world. In the second document, we see this world through the eyes of an official working in one of its hubs, Egypt, to keep royal rule running smoothly at the local level. The third document helps us to understand women's roles in this new landscape. Against this backdrop, the once mighty Greek city-states became second-rate powers, prompting many Greek thinkers, including Epicurus (Document 4), to reexamine the role of fate and chance in life. As the final document attests, Hellenistic scientists likewise expanded the boundaries of knowledge with innovative methods and discoveries.

1.
The Conquest of New Lands

Arrian, *The Campaigns of Alexander the Great*
(Fourth Century B.C.E.)

During his reign from 336 to 323 B.C.E., the Macedonian king Alexander the Great forever changed the eastern Mediterranean world. Following his father's lead, Alexander not only secured Macedonia's position as the leading power in Greece, but he also conquered the mighty Persian Empire. This excerpt from the most reliable known

From Arrian, *The Campaigns of Alexander*, trans. Aubrey de Sélincourt (London: Penguin Books, 1971), 360–66.

account of Alexander's Asian campaign, The Campaigns of Alexander *by Arrian of Nicomedia, written in the second century* C.E., *paints a vivid picture of Alexander as a warrior and king. In this passage, he has just returned to Persia in 324* B.C.E. *from his expedition to India, where his exhausted soldiers had forced him to turn back because they wanted to return home. His decision to discharge disabled veterans sparked anger among his Macedonian troops, who feared they were to be replaced by foreigners. Alexander delivered the following speech to chastise them, while glorifying his father's and his own accomplishments.*

"My countrymen, you are sick for home — so be it! I shall make no attempt to check your longing to return. Go whither you will; I shall not hinder you. But, if go you must, there is one thing I would have you understand — what I have done for you, and in what coin you will have repaid me.

"First I will speak of my father Philip, as it is my duty to do. Philip found you a tribe of impoverished vagabonds, most of you dressed in skins, feeding a few sheep on the hills and fighting, feebly enough, to keep them from your neighbors — Thracians and Triballians and Illyrians. He gave you cloaks to wear instead of skins; he brought you down from the hills into the plains; he taught you to fight on equal terms with the enemy on your borders, till you knew that your safety lay not, as once, in your mountain strongholds, but in your own valor. He made you city-dwellers; he brought you law; he civilized you. He rescued you from subjection and slavery, and made you masters of the wild tribes who harried and plundered you; he annexed the greater part of Thrace, and by seizing the best places on the coast opened your country to trade, and enabled you to work your mines without fear of attack.[1] Thessaly, so long your bugbear and your dread, he subjected to your rule, and by humbling the Phocians he made the narrow and difficult path into Greece a broad and easy road.[2] The men of Athens and Thebes, who for years had kept watching for their moment to strike us down, he brought so low — and by this time I myself was working at my father's side[3] that they who once exacted from us either our money or our obedience, now, in their turn, looked to us as the means of their salvation. Passing into the Peloponnese, he settled everything there to his satisfaction, and when he was made supreme commander of all the rest of Greece for the war against Persia, he claimed the glory of it not for himself alone, but for the Macedonian people.

"These services which my father rendered you are, indeed, intrinsically great; yet they are small compared with my own. I inherited from him a handful of gold and silver cups, coin in the treasury worth less than sixty talents and over eight times that amount of debts incurred by him; yet to add to this burden I borrowed a further sum of eight hundred talents, and, marching out from a country too poor to maintain you decently, laid open for you at a blow, and in spite of Persia's naval supremacy, the gates of the Hellespont. My cavalry crushed the *satraps* [governors]

---

[1]The gold and silver mines at Mount Pangaeum near Philippi are said to have brought Philip more than 1,000 talents a year.
[2]In 346 B.C.E.
[3]He refers principally, no doubt, to his part in the battle of Chaeronea in 338 B.C.E.

of Darius, and I added all Ionia and Aeolia, the two Phrygias and Lydia to your empire. Miletus I reduced by siege; the other towns all yielded of their own free will — I took them and gave them you for your profit and enjoyment. The wealth of Egypt and Cyrene, which I shed no blood to win, now flows into your hands; Palestine and the plains of Syria and the Land between the Rivers are now your property; Babylon and Bactria and Susa are yours; you are masters of the gold of Lydia, the treasures of Persia, the wealth of India — yes, and of the sea beyond India, too. You are my captains, my generals, my governors of provinces.

"From all this which I have labored to win for you, what is left for myself except the purple and this crown? I keep nothing for my own; no one can point to treasure of mine apart from all this which you yourselves either possess, or have in safe keeping for your future use. Indeed, what reason have I to keep anything, as I eat the same food and take the same sleep as you do? Ah, but there are epicures among you who, I fancy, eat more luxuriously than I; and this I know, that I wake earlier than you — and watch, that you may sleep.

"Perhaps you will say that, in my position as your commander, I had none of the labors and distress which you had to endure to win for me what I have won. But does any man among you honestly feel that he has suffered more for me than I have suffered for him? Come now — if you are wounded, strip and show your wounds, and I will show mine. There is no part of my body but my back which has not a scar; not a weapon a man may grasp or fling the mark of which I do not carry upon me. I have sword-cuts from close fight; arrows have pierced me, missiles from catapults bruised my flesh; again and again I have been struck by stones or clubs — and all for your sakes: for your glory and your gain. Over every land and sea, across river, mountain, and plain I led you to the world's end, a victorious army. I married as you married, and many of you will have children related by blood to my own. Some of you have owed money — I have paid your debts, never troubling to inquire how they were incurred, and in spite of the fact that you earn good pay and grow rich from the sack of cities. To most of you I have given a circlet of gold as a memorial for ever and ever of your courage and of my regard.[4] And what of those who have died in battle? Their death was noble, their burial illustrious; almost all are commemorated at home by statues of bronze; their parents are held in honor, with all dues of money or service remitted, for under my leadership not a man among you has ever fallen with his back to the enemy.

"And now it was in my mind to dismiss any man no longer fit for active service — all such should return home to be envied and admired. But you all wish to leave me. Go then! And when you reach home, tell them that Alexander your King, who vanquished Persians and Medes and Bactrians and Sacae; who crushed the Uxii, the Arachotians, and the Drangae, and added to his empire Parthia, the Chorasmian waste, and Hyrcania to the Caspian Sea; who crossed the Caucasus beyond the Caspian Gates, and Oxus and Tanais and the Indus, which none but Dionysus had crossed before him, and Hydaspes and Acesines and Hydraotes —

---

[4]Surely an exaggeration.

yes, and Hyphasis too, had you not feared to follow; who by both mouths of the Indus burst into the Great Sea beyond, and traversed the desert of Gedrosia, untrodden before by any army; who made Carmania his own, as his troops swept by, and the country of the Oreitans; who was brought back by you to Susa, when his ships had sailed the ocean from India to Persia — tell them, I say, that you deserted him and left him to the mercy of barbarian men, whom you yourselves had conquered. Such news will indeed assure you praise upon earth and reward in heaven. Out of my sight!"

As he ended, Alexander sprang from the rostrum and hurried into the palace. All that day he neither ate nor washed nor permitted any of his friends to see him. On the following day too he remained closely confined. On the third day he sent for the Persian officers who were in the highest favor and divided among them the command of the various units of the army. Only those whom he designated his kinsmen were now permitted to give him the customary kiss.[5]

On the Macedonians the immediate effect of Alexander's speech was profound. They stood in silence in front of the rostrum. Nobody made a move to follow the King except his closest attendants and the members of his personal guard; the rest, helpless to speak or act, yet unwilling to go away, remained rooted to the spot. But when they were told about the Persians and Mede — how command was being given to Persian officers, foreign troops drafted into Macedonian units, a Persian Corps of Guards called by a Macedonian name, Persian infantry units given the coveted title of Companions, Persian Silver Shields,[6] and Persian mounted Companions, including even a new Royal Squadron, in process of formation — they could contain themselves no longer. Every man of them hurried to the palace; in sign of supplication they flung their arms on the ground before the doors and stood there calling and begging for admission. They offered to give up the ring-leaders of the mutiny and those who had led the cry against the King, and swore they would not stir from the spot day or night unless Alexander took pity on them.

Alexander, the moment he heard of this change of heart, hastened out to meet them, and he was so touched by their groveling repentance and their bitter lamentations that the tears came into his eyes. While they continued to beg for his pity, he stepped forward as if to speak, but was anticipated by one Callines, an officer of the Companions, distinguished both by age and rank. "My lord," he cried, "what hurts us is that you have made Persians your kinsmen — Persians are called Alexander's kinsmen — Persians kiss you. But no Macedonian has yet had a taste of this honor."

"Every man of you," Alexander replied, "I regard as my kinsman, and from now on that is what I shall call you."

Thereupon Callines came up to him and kissed him, and all the others who wished to do so kissed him too. Then they picked up their weapons and returned to their quarters singing the song of victory at the top of their voices.

---

[5]*Kinsman* was an honorific title bestowed by the Persian king on leading Persians.
[6]This is a later name for the Guards (*Hypaspists*).

To mark the restoration of harmony, Alexander offered sacrifice to the gods he was accustomed to honor, and gave a public banquet which he himself attended, sitting among the Macedonians, all of whom were present.[7] Next to them the Persians had their places, and next to the Persians distinguished foreigners of other nations; Alexander and his friends dipped their wine from the same bowl and poured the same libations, following the lead of the Greek seers and the Magi (Persian priests). The chief object of his prayers was that Persians and Macedonians might rule together in harmony as an imperial power. It is said that 9,000 people attended the banquet; they unanimously drank the same toast, and followed it by the paean of victory.[8]

DISCUSSION QUESTIONS

1. According to Alexander, how did Philip II transform Macedonia from a minor kingdom into a great power?

2. What does Alexander reveal about the impact Macedonia's rise to power had on the Greek city-states?

3. Why does Alexander consider his achievements to be even greater than those of his father?

4. Based on Alexander's speech, how would you characterize his method of rule?

2.
Imperial Bureaucracy

Zeno, Egyptian Official, *Records* (259–250 B.C.E.)

Although Alexander the Great's imperial glory was short-lived, it opened the door to a new, more international eastern Mediterranean world. Upon his death in 323 B.C.E., Alexander's army commanders divided his empire into separate kingdoms over which they assumed control. To rule effectively, these new kings and their successors relied on a hierarchical bureaucracy staffed by Greeks and local administrators to oversee local affairs. This document illuminates the busy life of a Greek named Zeno, who was an agent for Apollonius, the financial minister for Ptolemy Philadelphus of Egypt (r. 285–246 B.C.E.). At the time, Egypt was home to both Greeks and indigenous peoples who contributed to a vibrant urban culture and economy. These extracts include instructions from Apollonius, requests for help, a desk diary, and other records of Zeno's daily affairs.

From *Select Papyri*, vol. 1, trans. A. S. Hunt and C. C. Edgar (London and New York: William Heinemann Ltd., 1932), 269–77, 397–99, 409–15.

[7] An evident exaggeration, unless only officers are meant.

[8] This banquet was held to celebrate the reconciliation between Alexander and his Macedonians and (it was hoped) between them and the Persians.

Letter from Hierocles (257 B.C.E.)

Hierocles to Zeno greeting. If you are well, it would be excellent. I too am in good health. You wrote to me about Pyrrhus, telling me to train[1] him if I am quite certain of his success, but if not, to avoid incurring useless expense and distracting him from his studies. Now as for my being certain, the gods should know best, but it seems to Ptolemaeus, as far as a man can tell, that Pyrrhus is much better than those now being trained, though they started long before him, and that in a very short time he will be far ahead of them; moreover he is pursuing his other studies as well; and to speak with the gods' leave, I hope to see you crowned. Make haste to send him a bathing-apron, and if possible let it be of goatskin or, if not, of thin sheepskin, and a tunic and cloak, and the mattress, coverlet and pillows, and the honey. You wrote to me that you were surprised at my not understanding that all these things are subject to toll. I know it, but you are well able to arrange for them to be sent in perfect security.[2] (Addressed) To Zeno. (Docketed) Hierocles about Pyrrhus. Year 29, Xandicus 3, at Memphis.

Letter from Promethion (256 B.C.E.)

Promethion[3] to Zeno greeting. I suffered anxiety when I heard of your long protracted illness, but now I am delighted to hear that you are convalescent and already on the point of recovery. I myself am well. I previously gave your agent Heraclides 150 drachmae in silver from your account, as you wrote to me to do, and he is bringing you now 10 *hins* of perfume in 21 vases which have been sealed with my finger-ring. For though Apollonius wrote to me to buy and give him also 300 wild pomegranate wreaths, I did not manage to give him these at the same time, as they were not ready, but Pa . . . will bring them to him at Naucratis; for they will be finished before the 30th. I have paid the price both of these and of the perfume from your account, as Apollonius wrote. I have also paid a charge of 10 drachmae in copper for the boat in which he is sailing up. And 400 drachmae in silver have been paid to Iatrocles for the papyrus rolls which are being manufactured in Tanis for Apollonius. Take note then that these affairs have been settled thus. And please write yourself if ever you need anything here. Goodbye. Year 29, Choiach 28. (Addressed) To Zeno. (Docketed) Year 29, Peritius 3. Promethion about what he has paid.

Letter from Apollonius the Dioecetes (256 B.C.E.)

Apollonius to Zeno greeting. From the dry wood put on board a boat as many of the thickest logs as possible and send them immediately to Alexandria that we may be able to use them for the festival of Isis. Goodbye. Year 30, Dius 3, Phaophi 23.

---

[1]For competition in the public games.
[2]That is, by using his influence as an agent of the financial minister.
[3]A banker in Mendes.

(Addressed) To Zeno. At once.[4] (Docketed by Zeno) Year 30, Dius 18, Hathur 18. Apollonius about wood for the Isis festival. (Docketed by sender) Wood for the Isis festival.

Letter from Plato (255 b.c.e.)

Plato to Zeno greeting. The father of Demetrius the bearer of this letter happens, it seems, to be residing in the Arsinoite nome,[5] and the lad therefore wishes to find employment there himself. On hearing of your kindly disposition some of his friends asked me to write to you about him, begging you to give him a post in your service. Please then do me a favor and provide some employment for him, whatever you may think suitable, and otherwise look after him, if you find him useful. As a token (of goodwill) I have sent you, from Sosus, 2 artabae[6] of chick-peas bought at 5 drachmae each, and if there are any at Naucratis, I will try to buy you about 20 artabae more and bring them up to you myself. Goodbye. Year 31, Dius 12. (Addressed) To Zeno.

Letter from Artemidorus (252 b.c.e.)

Artemidorus[7] to Zeno greeting. If you are well, it would be excellent. I too am well and Apollonius is in good health and other things are satisfactory. As I write this, we have just arrived in Sidon after escorting the princess[8] to the frontier, and I expect that we shall soon be with you. Now you will do me a favor by taking care of your own health and writing to me if you want anything done that I can do for you. And kindly buy me, so that I may get them when I arrive, 3 metretae[9] of the best honey and 600 artabae of barley for the animals, and pay the cost of them out of the produce of the sesame and croton,[10] and also see to the house in Philadelphia in order that I may find it roofed when I arrive. Try also as best you can to keep watch on the oxen and the pigs and the geese and the rest of the stock there; I shall have a better supply of provisions if you do. Also see to it that the crops are harvested somehow, and if any outlay is required, do not hesitate to pay what is necessary. Goodbye. Year 33, intercalary Peritius 6. (Addressed) To Zeno. To Philadelphia. (Docketed) Year 33, Phamenoth 6. Artemidorus.

---

[4]An admonition to the persons concerned to send the letter immediately.
[5]**nome:** Region. [Ed.]
[6]**artabae:** Baskets. [Ed.]
[7]A physician in the service of the dioecetes.
[8]The princess Berenice, who was escorted to Syria by Apollonius on the occasion of her marriage to Antiochus II.
[9]**metretae:** Jars. [Ed.]
[10]The two oils chiefly used in Egypt at this period were made from sesame and croton (the castor-oil plant), the former for food and the latter for lamps.

Letter from an Invalid (259–257 B.C.E.)

Memorandum to Zeno from Cydippus. If in accordance with the doctors' orders I could have purchased any of the following things in the market, I should not have troubled you; but as it is I have written you a note of what I require, as Apollonius thought I ought to do. So if you have them in store, send me a jar of wine, either Lesbian or Chian, of the very sweetest, and if possible a chous[11] of honey or, if not, as much as you can; and order them to fill me the vessel with salt fish. For both these things they consider to be most needful. And if my health improves and I go abroad to Byzantium, I will bring you back some excellent salt fish. (On the back) Memorandum from Cydippus.

Letter from a House-Painter (c. 255 B.C.E.)

Memorandum to Zeno from Theophilus the . . . About the work in the house of Diotimus: for the portico, [I undertake] to have the cornice painted with a purple border, the upper part of the wall variegated, the lower course like vetch-seed,[12] and the pediment with circular veining, providing myself with all materials, for 30 drachmae. For the dining-room with seven couches, I will do the vault according to the pattern which you saw, and give the lower course an agreeable tint and paint the Lesbian cornice, providing myself with all materials, for 20 drachmae. And for the dining-rooms with five couches, I will paint the cornices, providing myself with all materials, for 3 drachmae. The sum total is 53 drachmae. But if you provide everything, it will come to 30 drachmae. Goodbye.

Zeno's Agenda (c. 250 B.C.E.)

To ask Herodotus about the goat hair. To ask Aminias at how much mina he sold it. The letter to Dioscurides about the boat. To make an agreement with Timaeus about the pigs. To draft the contract with Apollodorus and write to him to hand over. To load the boat with wool. To write to Jason to let Dionysius put the wool on board and take it down the river when cleaned; the fourth part of the Arabian wool; to let him take down the sour wine. To write to Meliton to plant shoots of the *bumastus* vine belonging to Neoptolemus, and to Alcimus to do likewise if he approves. To Theogenes about twelve yokes of bulls. To give Apollodorus and Callippus . . . [f]rom Metrodorus to Athenagoras about the same year's produce. To Theophilus granting a favor and about the state of the work. To write about corn to Iatrokles and Theodorus before the water from the canal. . . .

Zeno's Agenda (c. 250 B.C.E.)

To get the olive kernels. The oil from Heragoras. To buy for the horses 4 strigils, 4 rubbing cloths, 4 scrapers, and for Phatres 1 strigil. To get shoots of the walnut trees. To ascertain the registration of the wine carried down, for which nome it has been registered. To receive Hermon's boy.

---

[11]**chous**: Container. [Ed.]
[12]**vetch-seed**: Pea-colored. [Ed.]

List of Foreign Goods (257 b.c.e.)

Year 29, Xandicus 11, at Hermopolis.[13] We have left behind these articles which Charmus has handed over to Apollodotus: in a basket 5 small bags of nard sealed and 1 small wallet sealed, 1 small wallet, sealed, containing dice of gazelle bone; purple dye in one pillow-case; 1 strip of variegated cloth; 3 half-strips of variegated cloth; 2 strips of white cloth; 4 strips of purple cloth; 3 bags and 1 small bag of frankincense sealed; 3 small bags of myrrh sealed; 1 wallet containing dice of gazelle bone; 1 small wallet of purple dye sealed; 1 small wallet of saffron sealed.

List of Zeno's Clothes (c. 257 b.c.e.)

Zeno's trunk in which are contained: 1 linen wrap, washed; 1 clay-colored cloak, for winter, washed, and 1 worn, 1 for summer, half-worn, 1 natural-colored, for winter, washed, and 1 worn, 1 vetch-colored, for summer, new; 1 white tunic for winter, with sleeves, washed, 1 natural-colored, for winter, with sleeves, worn, 1 natural-colored, for winter, worn, 2 white, for winter, washed, and 1 half-worn, 3 for summer, white, new, 1 unbleached, 1 half-worn; 1 outer garment, white, for winter, washed; 1 coarse mantle; 1 summer garment, white, washed, and 1 half-worn; 1 pair of Sardian pillow-cases; 2 pairs of socks, clay-colored, new, 2 pairs of white, new; 2 girdles, white, new. (Endorsed) From Pisicles, a list of Zeno's clothes.

Discussion Questions

1. If you had to write a job description for Zeno based on these records, what responsibilities would it include?
2. What do Zeno's records reveal about the local economy?
3. What evidence do you find in Zeno's records of cross-cultural influences within the Hellenistic world?

3.
Everyday Life

Funerary Inscriptions and Epitaphs (Fifth–First Centuries b.c.e.)

These inscriptions and epitaphs provide a glimpse of women's place in the classical and Hellenistic worlds as described by family members and admirers after their deaths. The words preserved in this form do not simply mark each woman's passing from this world to the next, but they hold her up as an exemplar of female behavior. As in the past, a woman's identity revolved principally around her roles as daughter, wife, and mother. Yet not all women's lives were confined to domestic duties.

From Mary R. Lefkowitz and Maureen B. Fant, eds., *Women's Life in Greece and Rome*, 2nd ed. (Baltimore: Johns Hopkins University Press, 1992), 16–17, 190, 206, 219, 221–22, 263, 266–67, 274.

[13]Hermopolis Parva in the Delta.

Some were royal attendants, priestesses, and even physicians, whose daily activities extended into the public sphere.

Archedice, Athens, Fifth Century B.C.E.

This dust hides Archedice, daughter of Hippias, the most important man in Greece in his day. But though her father, husband, brothers, and children were tyrants, her mind was never carried away into arrogance.

Aspasia, Chios, c. 400 B.C.E.

Of a worthy wife this is the tomb — here, by the road that throngs with people — of Aspasia, who is dead; in response to her noble disposition Euopides set up this monument for her; she was his consort.

Dionysia, Athens, Fourth Century B.C.E.

It was not clothes, it was not gold that this woman admired during her lifetime; it was her husband and the good sense that she showed in her behavior. But in return for the youth you shared with him, Dionysia, your tomb is adorned by your husband Antiphilus.

Claudia, Rome, Second Century B.C.E.

Friend, I have not much to say; stop and read it. This tomb, which is not fair, is for a fair woman. Her parents gave her the name Claudia. She loved her husband in her heart. She bore two sons, one of whom she left on earth, the other beneath it. She was pleasant to talk with, and she walked with grace. She kept the house and worked in wool. That is all. You may go.

An Accomplished Woman, Sardis, First Century B.C.E.

[An inscription set up by the municipality of Sardis in honor of Menophila, daughter of Hermagenes.] This stone marks a woman of accomplishment and beauty. Who she is the Muses' inscriptions reveal: Menophila. Why she is honored is shown by a carved lily and an alpha, a book and a basket, and with these a wreath. The book shows that you were wise, the wreath that you wore on your head shows that you were a leader; the letter alpha that you were an only child; the basket is a sign of your orderly excellence; the flower shows the prime of your life, which Fate stole away. May the dust lie light on you in death. Alas; your parents are childless; to them you have left tears.

Posilla Senenia, Monteleone Sabino, First Century B.C.E.

Posilla Senenia, daughter of Quartus and Quarta Senenia, freedwoman of Gaius.

    Stranger, stop and, while you are here, read what is written: that a mother was not permitted to enjoy her only daughter, whose life, I believe, was envied by some god.

Since her mother was not allowed to adorn her while she was alive, she does so just the same after death; at the end of her time, [her mother] with this monument honors her whom she loved.

Xenoclea, Piraeus, 360? b.c.e.

Leaving two young girls, Xenoclea, daughter of Nicarchus, lies here dead; she mourned the sad end of her son, Phoenix, who died out at sea when he was eight years old.

There is no one so ignorant of grief, Xenoclea, that he doesn't pity your fate. You left behind two young girls and died of grief for your son, who has a pitiless tomb where he lies in the dark sea.

Handiwork, Athens, after 350 b.c.e.

I worked with my hands; I was a thrifty woman, I, Nicarete who lie here.

A Storeroom Attendant, Cape Zoster, near Athens, 56–55 b.c.e.

[An epitaph by a mother for a daughter who worked for Cleopatra at the royal court of Alexandria.] Her mother, an Athenian woman, raised her to be an attendant of foreign storerooms. She too rushed for her child's sake to come to the palace of the king who had set her over his rich possessions. Yet still she could not bring her daughter back alive. But the daughter has a tomb in Athens instead of on Libyan sand.

Epitaph for a Woman Who Died While Pregnant, Egypt, Second–First Centuries b.c.e.

Dosithea, daughter of ——. Look at these letters on the polished rock. Thallo's son Chaeremon married me in his great house. I die in pain, escaping the pangs of childbirth, leaving the breath of life when I was twenty-five years old; from a disease which he died of before, I succumbed after. I lie here in Schedia. Wayfarers, as you go by, all of you, say: "Beloved Dosithea, stay well, also among the dead."

A Midwife and Physician, Athens, Fourth Century b.c.e.

[The memorial tablet represents two women, one seated, one standing, surrounded by infants of both sexes.] Phanostrate, a midwife and physician, lies here. She caused pain to none, and all lamented her death.

A Nurse, Athens, after 350 b.c.e.

[Epitaph for] Apollodorus the immigrant's daughter, Melitta, a nurse. Here the earth covers Hippostrate's good nurse; and Hippostrate still misses you. "I loved you while you were alive, nurse, I love you still now even beneath the earth and now I shall honor you as long as I live. I know that for you beneath the earth also, if there is reward for the good, honors will come first to you, in the realm of Persephone and of Pluto."

Epitaph for a Priestess, Miletus, Third Century B.C.E.

Bacchae[1] of the City, say, "Farewell you holy priestess." This is what a good woman deserves. She led you to the mountain and carried all the sacred objects and implements, marching in procession before the whole city. Should some stranger ask for her name: Alcmeonis, daughter of Rhodius, who knew her share of the blessings.

DISCUSSION QUESTIONS

1. Judging from these inscriptions and epitaphs, what particular qualities did people admire in women, and why?
2. Scholars have described Greek society at the time as patriarchal. Do the epitaphs and inscriptions support this view?
3. What do the epitaphs and inscriptions reveal about the social and economic standing of the women they describe?

4.
In Pursuit of Happiness

Epicurus, *Letter to a Friend* (Late Third Century B.C.E.)

Born on the island of Samos, Epicurus (c. 341–270 B.C.E.) earned a reputation as an accomplished teacher in Asia Minor that eventually led him to Athens in 306. In the tradition of the schools of philosophy of Plato and Aristotle, the "Garden" of Epicurus attracted a strong following. Although the adjective epicurean *has often been taken to mean the enjoyment of life's pleasures, Epicurus's actual philosophy was based on the pursuit of true, spiritual happiness. In his* Letter to a Friend, *Epicurus explores the meaning of happiness, and concludes that it is based on simple needs and a serene spirit.*

We must consider that of desires some are natural, others empty; that of the natural some are necessary, others not; and that of the necessary some are necessary for happiness, others for bodily comfort, and others for life itself. A right understanding of these facts enables us to direct all choice and avoidance toward securing the health of the body and tranquillity of the soul; this being the final aim of a blessed life. For the aim of all actions is to avoid pain and fear; and when this is once secured for us the tempest of the soul is entirely quelled, since the living animal no longer needs to wander as though in search of something he lacks, hunting for that by which he can fulfill some need of soul or body. We feel a need of pleasure only when we grieve over its absence; when we stop grieving we are in need of pleasure no longer. Pleasure, then, is the beginning and end of the blessed life. For we

From "Letter to Menoecius," in *The Way of Philosophy*, trans. Philip Wheelwright (Upper Saddle River, NJ: Pearson Education, Inc., 1960), 423–25.
[1]**Bacchae**: Women worshipers of Dionysus. [Ed.]

recognize it as a good which is both primary and kindred to us. From pleasure we begin every act of choice and avoidance; and to pleasure we return again, using the feeling as the standard by which to judge every good.

Now since pleasure is the good that is primary and most natural to us, for that very reason we do not seize all pleasures indiscriminately; on the contrary we often pass over many pleasures, when greater discomfort accrues to us as a result of them. Similarly we not infrequently judge pains better than pleasures, when the long endurance of a pain yields us a greater pleasure in the end. Thus every pleasure because of its natural kinship to us is good, yet not every pleasure is to be chosen; just as every pain also is an evil, yet that does not mean that all pains are necessarily to be shunned. It is by a scale of comparison and by the consideration of advantages and disadvantages that we must form our judgment on these matters. On particular occasions we may have reason to treat the good as bad, and the bad as good.

Independence of circumstance we regard as a great good: not because we wish to dispense altogether with external advantages, but in order that, if our possessions are few, we may be content with what we have, sincerely believing that those enjoy luxury most who depend on it least, and that natural wants are easily satisfied if we are willing to forego superfluities. Plain fare yields as much pleasure as a luxurious table, provided the pain of real want is removed; bread and water can give exquisite delight to hungry and thirsty lips. To form the habit of a simple and modest diet, therefore, is the way to health: it enables us to perform the needful employments of life without shrinking, it puts us in better condition to enjoy luxuries when they are offered, and it renders us fearless of fortune.

Accordingly, when we argue that pleasure is the end and aim of life, we do not mean the pleasure of prodigals and sensualists, as some of our ignorant or prejudiced critics persist in mistaking us. We mean the pleasure of being free from pain of body and anxiety of mind. It is not a continual round of drunken debauches and lecherous delights, nor the enjoyment of fish and other delicacies of a wealthy table, which produce a pleasant life; but sober reasoning, searching out the motives of choice and avoidance, and escaping the bondage of opinion, to which the greatest disturbances of spirit are due.

The first step and the greatest good is prudence — a more precious thing than philosophy even, for all the other virtues are sprung from it. By prudence we learn that we can live pleasurably only if we live prudently, honorably, and justly, while contrariwise to live prudently, honorably, and justly guarantees a life that is pleasurable as well. The virtues are by nature bound up with a pleasant life, and a pleasant life is inseparable from them in turn.

Is there any better and wiser man than he who holds reverent beliefs about the gods, is altogether free from the fear of death, and has serenely contemplated the basic tendencies (telê) of natural law? Such a man understands that the limit of good things is easy to attain, and that evils are slight either in duration or in intensity. He laughs at Destiny, which so many accept as all-powerful. Some things, he observes, occur of necessity, others by chance, and still others through our own agency. Necessity is irresponsible, chance is inconstant, but our own actions are free, and it is to them that praise and blame are properly attached. It would be better even to believe the myths about the gods than to submit to the Destiny which the natural philosophers teach. For the old superstitions at least offer some faint hope of placating the gods by worship, but the Necessity of the scientific philosophers is absolutely unyielding. As to chance, the wise man does not deify it as most men do; for if it were divine it would not be without order. Nor will he accept the view that it is a universal cause even though of a wavering kind; for he believes that what chance bestows is not the good and evil that determine a man's blessedness in life, but the starting-points from which each person can arrive at great good or great evil. He esteems the misfortune of the wise above the prosperity of a fool; holding it better that well chosen courses of action should fail than that ill chosen ones should succeed by mere chance.

Meditate on these and like precepts day and night, both privately and with some companion who is of kindred disposition. Thereby shall you never suffer disturbance, waking or asleep, but shall live like a god among men. For a man who lives constantly among immortal blessings is surely more than mortal.

DISCUSSION QUESTIONS

1. According to Epicurus, what is the relationship between pleasure and pain? What is pleasure? Why might someone choose pain over pleasure?

2. What guidelines should a human being follow in making life choices?

3. How could someone best reconcile the fact that destiny, or chance, is beyond his or her control?

5.
Exacting Science

Archimedes, *Letter to Eratosthenes* (Third Century B.C.E.)
and
Marcus Vitruvius Pollio, *Archimedes' "Eureka!" Moment*
(c. 30–20 B.C.E.)

Scientific innovation blossomed during the Hellenistic period. Alexander the Great had ordered the city of Alexandria built, and it became the capital of the Hellenistic kingdom of the Ptolemies. Scientists flocked to the city's royally funded library and research institute, including the mathematician Archimedes of Syracuse (287–212 B.C.E.). Here is where he most likely met the library's director, Eratosthenes of Cyrene (c. 285–194 B.C.E.), a pioneer in mathematical geography. Upon returning home, Archimedes remained in contact with Eratosthenes, thereby promoting the exchange of ideas typical of the intellectual scene at the time. Archimedes included the letter

From *The Works of Archimedes*, ed. T. L. Heath (Mineola, NY: Dover Publications, Inc., 2002), 12–13; and *Vitruvius: Ten Books on Architecture*, trans. Ingrid D. Rowland (New York: Cambridge University Press, 1999), 108.

excerpted below in the preface to his treatise Method. *Discovered in 1906, it is unusual in its focus when compared to works by other classical Greek geometers. As Archimedes writes to Eratosthenes, he did not simply want to present his discoveries as finished products, in this case certain geometric theorems; he wanted to pull back the veil on the steps of analysis he took to arrive at them. The second document recounts a story about Archimedes' thinking in action included in a first-century* b.c.e. *text. For its author, the Roman architect Vitruvius, the tale embodied the wisdom past thinkers had to offer contemporary civilization. Together, the two documents illuminate the thrill of discovery through measurement, observation, and experimentation that helped to lay the foundation of later Western scientific thought.*

Archimedes

Archimedes to Eratosthenes greeting.

I sent you on a former occasion some of the theorems discovered by me, merely writing out the enunciations and inviting you to discover the proofs, which at the moment I did not give. . . .

. . . The proofs then of these theorems I have written in this book and now send to you. Seeing moreover in you, as I say, an earnest student, a man of considerable eminence in philosophy, and an admirer [of mathematical inquiry], I thought fit to write out for you and explain in detail in the same book the peculiarity of a certain method, by which it will be possible for you to get a start to enable you to investigate some of the problems in mathematics by means of mechanics. This procedure is, I am persuaded, no less useful even for the proof of the theorems themselves; for certain things first became clear to me by a mechanical method, although they had to be demonstrated by geometry afterwards because their investigation by the said method did not furnish an actual demonstration. But it is of course easier, when we have previously acquired, by the method, some knowledge of the questions, to supply the proof than it is to find it without any previous knowledge. . . .

Vitruvius

As for Archimedes, although in his limitless wisdom he discovered many wonderful things, nonetheless, of all of them, one in particular, which I shall now describe, seems to convey his boundless ingenuity. It is no surprise that Hieron,[1] after he had obtained immense kingly power in Syracuse, decided, because of the favorable turn of events, to dedicate a votive crown of gold to the immortal gods in a certain shrine. He contracted for the craftsman's wages, and he [himself] weighed out the gold precisely for the contractor. This contractor completed the work with great skill and on schedule; it was approved by the king, and the contractor seemed to have used up the furnished supply of gold. Later, charges were leveled that in the making of the crown a certain amount of gold had been removed and replaced by an equal amount of silver. Hieron, outraged that he should have been shown so

---

[1]**Hieron:** Hieron II was tyrant of Syracuse (270–215 b.c.e.). [Ed.]

little respect, and not knowing by what method he might expose the theft, requested that Archimedes take the matter under consideration on his behalf.

Now Archimedes, once he had charge of this matter, chanced to go to the baths, and there, as he stepped into the tub, he noticed that however much he immersed his body in it, that much water spilled over the sides of the tub. When the reason for this occurrence came clear to him, he did not hesitate, but in a transport of joy he leapt out of the tub, and as he rushed home naked, he let one and all know that he had truly found what he had been looking for — because as he ran he shouted over and over in Greek: "I found it! I found it!" (*Eurêka! Eurêka!*)

On the basis of this discovery he is said to have made two masses whose weight was equal to that of the crown: one of gold and one of silver. When he had done this, he filled a large vessel to the brim with water, into which he sank the mass of silver. Whatever amount of silver was submerged, that much water spilled out. Then, once the mass had been taken out, he poured back the missing amount of water so that it would be level with the brim in the same way as before, using a one-sextarius pitcher [= 1/2 liter] as a measure. From this procedure he discovered that a certain weight of silver corresponded to a certain measure of water. Once he had tried this, then in the same fashion he sank the gold mass into the full vessel, and when he had removed it, replacing the water by the same method, he discovered that not so much of the water had been lost, and less was required to replace it, as much less as a mass of gold will be smaller in body than a mass of silver which has the same weight. After this, once he had filled the vessel yet again, the crown itself was sunk into the water, and he discovered that more water was required to replace the crown than to replace the mass of gold of equal weight, and because there was more water in the crown's place than in the place of the mass of gold, he detected, by deduction, the mixture of silver in the crown and the contractor's flagrant theft.

DISCUSSION QUESTIONS

1. Why does Archimedes think it is valuable to describe his methods of discovery to Eratosthenes rather than just the discoveries themselves? What does he hope Eratosthenes will gain from the description?

2. What do Archimedes' methods suggest about his thinking process? Do you see evidence of this process at work in Vitruvius's account?

3. It was typical of Archimedes to include letters of this type in the introductions to his works. What does this say about the nature of the scientific community in the Hellenistic world?

4. What do these two sources suggest about the role of observation and mechanical methods in Hellenistic science?

COMPARATIVE QUESTIONS

1. How does Alexander the Great define "civilization" in his assessment of his father's and his own accomplishments (Document 1)? In what ways did Hellenistic kingdoms reflect and build on this definition as revealed in the Egyptian records (Document 2)?

2. What are the similarities and differences between Epicurus's views of the human condition and those expressed in the inscriptions and epitaphs?

3. What evidence can you find in these documents of increased interactions between Greek and Near Eastern peoples in the Hellenistic world?

4. In what ways did these interactions shape everyday political, intellectual, and economic life?

CHAPTER 5

The Rise of Rome and Its Republic
753–44 B.C.E.

W hen the Roman republic was founded in 509 B.C.E., few could have foreseen its future as a mighty imperialist state. At the time, Greece was on the threshold of its Golden Age, which was soon followed by Macedonia's meteoric rise to power. Yet throughout this period, the Romans gradually expanded their territories and wealth so that by the end of the second century B.C.E., they controlled most of southern Europe, North Africa, and beyond. Victory came at a price, however, as Roman politicians and military leaders came to value their individual successes more than that of the republic. The documents in this chapter help us chart the republic's development from several different angles. Together, they reveal the pillars of the republic — law, tradition, and communal values — while providing a glimpse of their ultimate demise.

1.
Formalizing Roman Law

The Twelve Tables (451–449 B.C.E.)

Although Rome's elite successfully overthrew the Roman monarchy and established the republic in 509 B.C.E., more challenges lay ahead. For the next two centuries, the city's patricians and the rest of its citizens battled over the course the new government should take and their respective roles in it. Promulgated between 451 and 449 B.C.E., the Twelve Tables were a turning point in this struggle, marking the republic's first step toward establishing a fair system of justice. Surviving in fragments only, this code, the earliest in Roman law, was based largely on existing customs. The following excerpts illuminate not only the social and economic landscape of early Rome, but also the foundation of Roman jurisprudence.

From *Ancient Rome Statutes*, trans. Allan Chester Johnson et al. (Austin: University of Texas Press, 1961), 9–17.

Table I. Proceedings Preliminary to Trial

If the plaintiff summons the defendant to court the defendant shall go. If the defendant does not go the plaintiff shall call a witness thereto. Only then the plaintiff shall seize the defendant.

If the defendant attempts evasion or takes flight the plaintiff shall lay hand on him.

If sickness or age is an impediment he who summons the defendant to court shall grant him a vehicle. If he does not wish he shall not spread a carriage with cushions.

For a freeholder[1] a freeholder shall be surety;[2] for a proletary[3] anyone who wishes shall be surety.

There shall be the same right of bond and of conveyance with the Roman people for a steadfast person and for a person restored to allegiance.[4]

When the parties agree on the matter the magistrate shall announce it.

If they agree not on terms the parties shall state their case before the assembly in the meeting place or before the magistrate in the market place before noon. Both parties being present shall plead the case throughout together.

If one of the parties does not appear the magistrate shall adjudge the case, after noon, in favor of the one present.

If both parties are present sunset shall be the time limit of the proceedings. . . .

Table II. Trial

The penal sum[5] in an action by solemn deposit shall be either 500 asses or 50 asses.[6] . . . It shall be argued by solemn deposit with 500 asses, when the property is valued at 1,000 asses or more, but with 50 asses, when the property is valued at less than 1,000 asses. But if the controversy is about the freedom of a person, although the person may be very valuable, yet the case shall be argued by a solemn deposit of 50 asses. . . .

---

[1] A taxpayer whose fortune is valued at not less than 1,500 asses.

[2] That is, for his appearance at trial.

[3] A "proletary" is a nontaxpayer whose fortune is rated at less than a freeholder's.

[4] This apparently allows the Latin allies who had revolted and later returned into allegiance to enjoy the same rights and to use the same legal formulas in contractual matters and in transferring property as those who had remained loyal.

[5] Each litigant deposited a sum with the court as a kind of "wager on oath" that his cause was right. The defeated party forfeited his deposit to the state. On account of the desire to show special favor to persons illegally held as slaves and claiming their freedom, the law made the deposit for them very low, typically only fifty asses in such cases.

[6] asses: An as was a bronze coin. At the time the Twelve Tables were composed, an as was a one-foot-long bar of copper. It took the form of a coin later, around 269 B.C.E. [Ed.]

Table III. Execution of Judgment

Thirty days shall be allowed by law for payment of confessed debt and for settlement of matters adjudged in court.

After this time the creditor shall have the right of laying hand on the debtor. The creditor shall hale the debtor into court.

Unless the debtor discharges the debt adjudged or unless someone offers surety for him in court the creditor shall take the debtor with him. He shall bind him either with a thong or with fetters of not less than fifteen pounds in weight, or if he wishes he shall bind him with fetters of more than this weight.

If the debtor wishes he shall live on his own means. If he does not live on his own means the creditor who holds him in bonds shall give him a pound of grits daily. If he wishes he shall give him more.

. . . Meanwhile they shall have the right to compromise, and unless they make a compromise the debtors shall be held in bonds for sixty days. During these days they shall be brought to the praetor[7] into the meeting place on three successive market days, and the amount for which they have been judged liable shall be declared publicly. Moreover, on the third market day they shall suffer capital punishment or shall be delivered for sale abroad across the Tiber River.

On the third market day the creditors shall cut shares. If they have cut more or less than their shares it shall be without prejudice.

Table IV. Paternal Power

A notably deformed child shall be killed immediately.

To a father . . . shall be given over a son the power of life and death.

If a father thrice surrenders a son for sale the son shall be free from the father.[8]

To repudiate his wife her husband shall order her . . . to have her own property for herself, shall take the keys, shall expel her.[9]

A child born within ten months of the father's death shall enter into the inheritance. . . .

---

[7]**praetor**: A high elected official. [Ed.]

[8]In the early days of Rome, a Roman father could sell his son into slavery. If the buyer freed the son, the son reentered his father's control (*patria potestas*).

[9]The formula for a valid repudiation of the other by either the husband or the wife is said to have contained the words "have (*or* manage) your own property for yourself." Dissolution of marriage by mutual consent is divorce (*divortium*). In either event, an essential feature is the husband's return of the wife's dowry, if any, whose investment he had controlled during marriage.

Table V. Inheritance and Guardianship

. . . Women, even though they are of full age,[10] because of their levity of mind shall be under guardianship . . . except vestal virgins, who . . . shall be free from guardianship. . . .

The conveyable possessions of a woman who is under guardianship of male agnates[11] shall not be acquired by prescriptive right unless they are transferred by the woman herself with the authorization of her guardian. . . .

According as a person has made bequest regarding his personal property or the guardianship of his estate so shall be the law.

If anyone who has no direct heir dies intestate the nearest male agnate shall have the estate.

If there is not a male agnate the male clansmen shall have the estate.

Persons for whom by will . . . a guardian is not given, for them . . . their male agnates shall be guardians.

If a person is insane authority over him and his personal property shall belong to his male agnates and in default of these to his male clansmen. . . .

If a Roman citizen freedman dies intestate without a direct heir, to his patron shall fall the inheritance . . . from said household . . . into said household. . . .

Table VI. Ownership and Possession

. . . If any woman is unwilling to be subjected in this manner[12] to her husband's marital control she shall absent herself for three successive nights in every year and by this means shall interrupt his prescriptive right of each year.[13] . . .

One shall not take from framework timber fixed in buildings or in vineyards. . . . One shall be permitted neither to remove nor to claim stolen timber fixed in buildings or in vineyards, . . . but against the person who is convicted of having fixed such timber there an action for double damages shall be given. . . .

---

[10]For females "full age" was twenty-five years. According to the law of this period, a woman never has legal independence: if she is not in her father's power (*potestas*), she is dependent on her husband's control (*manus*) or, if unmarried and fatherless, she is subject to her guardian's governance (*tutela*).

[11]**agnates**: Relatives from the father's family. [Ed.]

[12]That is, by prescriptive right (*usus*).

[13]This method, the so-called *ius trinoctii* (right of three nights; that is, the right acquired by an absence of three successive nights), enabled a wife to remain married to her husband and yet neither to come into nor to remain in his marital control. If the prescriptive right has been interrupted for three consecutive nights annually, the time of *usus* must commence afresh because the husband's previous possession is considered to be canceled.

Table VII. Real Property

If a watercourse conducted through a public place does damage to a private person the said person shall have the right to bring an action . . . that security against damage may be given to the owner.

. . . Branches of a tree shall be pruned all around to a height of fifteen feet.

If a tree from a neighbor's farm has been felled by the wind over one's farm, . . . one rightfully can take legal action for that tree to be removed.

. . . It shall be lawful to gather fruit falling upon another's farm. . . .

A slave is ordered in a will to be a free man under this condition: "if he has given 10,000 asses to the heir"; although the slave has been alienated by the heir, yet the slave by giving the said money to the buyer shall enter into his freedom. . . .

Table VIII. Torts or Delicts

. . . If anyone sings or composes an incantation that can cause dishonor or disgrace to another . . . he shall suffer a capital penalty.[14]

If anyone has broken another's limb there shall be retaliation in kind unless he compounds for compensation with him.

. . . If a person breaks a bone of a freeman with hand or by club, he shall undergo a penalty of 300 asses; or of 150 asses, if of a slave.

If one commits an outrage against another the penalty shall be twenty-five asses.

. . . One has broken. . . . One shall make amends.

If a quadruped is said to have caused damage an action shall lie therefore . . . either for surrendering that which did the damage to the aggrieved person . . . or for offering an assessment of the damage.

If fruit from your tree falls onto my farm and if I feed my flock off it by letting the flock onto it . . . no action can lie against me either on the statute concerning pasturage of a flock, because it is not being pastured on your land, or on the statute concerning damage caused by an animal. . . .

If anyone pastures on or cuts by night another's crops obtained by cultivation the penalty for an adult shall be capital punishment and after having been hung up, death as a sacrifice to Ceres. . . . A person below the age of puberty at the praetor's decision shall be scourged and shall be judged as a person either to be surrendered to the plaintiff for damage done or to pay double damages.

Whoever destroys by burning a building or a stack of grain placed beside a house . . . shall be bound, scourged, burned to death, provided that knowingly and consciously he has committed this crime; but if this deed is by accident, that is, by negligence, either he shall repair the damage or if he is unable he shall be corporally punished more lightly.

---

[14]According to one ancient account the infliction of this penalty perhaps may have included clubbing to death.

Whoever fells unjustly another's trees shall pay twenty-five asses for each tree.

If a thief commits a theft by night, if the owner kills the thief, the thief shall be killed lawfully.

By daylight . . . if a thief defends himself with a weapon . . . and the owner shall shout.

In the case of all other . . . thieves caught in the act freemen shall be scourged and shall be adjudged as bondsmen to the person against whom the theft has been committed provided that they have done this by daylight and have not defended themselves with a weapon; slaves caught in the act of theft . . . shall be whipped with scourges and shall be thrown from the rock;[15] but children below the age of puberty shall be scourged at the praetor's decision and the damage done by them shall be repaired. . . .

If a patron defrauds a client he shall be accursed.[16]

Unless he speaks his testimony whoever allows himself to be called as a witness or is a scales-bearer shall be dishonored and incompetent to give or obtain testimony. . . .

If anyone pastures on or cuts stealthily by night . . . another's crops . . . the penalty shall be capital punishment, and, after having been hung up, death as a sacrifice to Ceres, a punishment more severe than in homicide. . . .

Table IX. Public Law

Laws of personal exception shall not be proposed. Laws concerning capital punishment of a citizen shall not be passed . . . except by the Greatest Assembly. . . .

. . . Whoever incites a public enemy or whoever betrays a citizen to a public enemy shall be punished capitally.

For anyone whomsoever to be put to death without a trial and unconvicted . . . is forbidden.

Table X. Sacred Law

A dead person shall not be buried or burned in the city.[17] . . .

. . . Expenses of a funeral shall be limited to three mourners wearing veils and one mourner wearing an inexpensive purple tunic and ten flutists. . . .

Women shall not tear their cheeks or shall not make a sorrowful outcry on account of a funeral.

A dead person's bones shall not be collected that one may make a second funeral.

An exception is for death in battle and on foreign soil. . . .

---

[15]A southern spur of the Capitoline Hill, which overlooks the Forum.

[16]That is, declared forfeited to the lower gods and liable to be slain by anyone with impunity.

[17]Inhumation on a large scale and in a crowded community not only was insanitary but also took too much space. Cremation could involve hazards from fire.

Table XI. Supplementary Laws

. . . There shall not be intermarriage between plebeians and patricians.

Table XII. Supplementary Laws

It is forbidden to dedicate for consecrated use a thing concerning whose owner-ship there is a controversy; otherwise a penalty of double the value involved shall be suffered. . . .

DISCUSSION QUESTIONS

1. What are the principal concerns expressed in this code?
2. What do these concerns suggest about Roman society at the time?
3. In what ways did these laws represent a triumph for the plebeian class?

2.
Artistic Influences

Etruscan Statuette of a Rider (c. 434–400 B.C.E.)
and
Roman Bust of Lucius Junius Brutus (c. 300 B.C.E.)

Within two decades of its foundation, the Roman republic relied on an aggressive policy of territorial expansion in Italy and abroad to enhance its wealth and power. Unlike the practice of Greek city-states, the Romans absorbed conquered peoples into their population as citizens or allies. In the process, they were also exposed to new forms of art, literature, and language, which helped to shape Rome's own cultural development. The Etruscans were an especially important cross-cultural influence, as the two images that follow suggest. The first displays a bronze statuette of a male rider, dating from c. 434–400 B.C.E. A wealthy and urbanized people, the Etruscans were fine craftsmen as well as avid importers of luxury goods from throughout the Mediterranean, including Greece. The second, a bust thought to be of Lucius Junius Brutus, one of the founders of the republic, dates from c. 300 B.C.E., after the Roman conquest of Etruscan territory.

From Detroit Institute of Arts; and Capitoline Museums (Palazzo dei Conservatori).

Detroit Institute of Arts, USA/City of Detroit Purchase/The Bridgeman Art Library

Scala/Art Resource, NY

DISCUSSION QUESTIONS

1. How would you describe the facial features of the Etruscan rider? How do they compare to those of the bust of Brutus?

2. In choosing to portray human faces in this way, what emotions do you think the sculptors sought to provoke within the viewer?

3. Unlike the Etruscan statuette, the Roman bust probably depicts a known individual. How do you think this fact may have influenced the sculptor's design and why?

3.
Status and Discrimination

Roman Women Demonstrate against the
Oppian Law (195 b.c.e.)

Women in ancient Rome were most valued as wives and mothers, yet sometimes they stepped outside the boundaries of family life to make their voices heard. In his History of Rome, the Roman historian Livy (59 b.c.e.–17 c.e.) reconstructs a heated debate that erupted on one such occasion. In 195 b.c.e., upper-class women from the city and its environs joined together to demonstrate publicly against the Oppian law, which had been passed during wartime and restricted the amount of finery women could wear and their use of carriages in an effort to reduce friction between rich and poor. Their demand for the law's repeal so that they could once again display their elite status sparked both disdain and sympathy among various leaders, to whom they appealed for support. Each camp, represented here by the consul Cato and the tribune Valerius, claimed to have tradition on its side.*

Amid the anxieties of great wars, either scarce finished or soon to come, an incident occurred, trivial to relate, but which, by reason of the passions it aroused, developed into a violent contention. Marcus Fundanius and Lucius Valerius, tribunes of the people, proposed to the assembly the abrogation of the Oppian law. The tribune Gaius Oppius had carried this law in the heat of the Punic War, in the consulship of Quintus Fabius and Tiberius Sempronius, that no woman should possess more than half an ounce of gold or wear a parti-coloured garment or ride in a carriage in the City or in a town within a mile thereof, except on the occasion of a religious festival. The tribunes Marcus and Publius Iunius Brutus were supporting the Oppian law, and averred that they would not permit its repeal; many distinguished men came forward to speak for and against it; the Capitoline was filled with crowds of supporters and opponents of the bill. The matrons could not be kept at home by advice or modesty or their husbands' orders, but blocked all the streets and approaches to the Forum, begging the men as they came down to the Forum that, in the prosperous condition of the state, when the private fortunes of all men were daily increasing, they should allow the women too to have their former distinctions restored. The crowd of women grew larger day by day; for they were now coming in from the towns and rural districts. Soon they dared even to approach and appeal to the consuls, the praetors, and the other officials, but one consul, at least, they found adamant, Marcus Porcius Cato, who spoke thus in favor of the law whose repeal was being urged.

"If each of us, citizens, had determined to assert his rights and dignity as a husband with respect to his own spouse, we should have less trouble with the sex as a whole; as it is, our liberty, destroyed at home by female violence, even here in

---

From Livy, *History of Rome*, vol. 9, trans. Evan T. Sage (Cambridge, MA: Harvard University Press, 1961), 413–21, 425–39.

the Forum is crushed and trodden underfoot, and because we have not kept them individually under control, we dread them collectively. . . .

"For myself, I could not conceal my blushes a while ago, when I had to make my way to the Forum through a crowd of women. Had not respect for the dignity and modesty of some individuals among them rather than of the sex as a whole kept me silent, lest they should seem to have been rebuked by a consul, I should have said, 'What sort of practice is this, of running out into the streets and blocking the roads and speaking to other women's husbands? Could you not have made the same requests, each of your own husband, at home? Or are you more attractive outside and to other women's husbands than to your own? And yet, not even at home, if modesty would keep matrons within the limits of their proper rights, did it become you to concern yourselves with the question of what laws should be adopted in this place or repealed.' Our ancestors permitted no woman to conduct even personal business without a guardian to intervene in her behalf;[1] they wished them to be under the control of fathers, brothers, husbands; we (Heaven help us!) allow them now even to interfere in public affairs, yes, and to visit the Forum and our informal and formal sessions. What else are they doing now on the streets and at the corners except urging the bill of the tribunes and voting for the repeal of the law? Give loose rein to their uncontrollable nature and to this untamed creature and expect that they will themselves set bounds to their license; unless you act, this is the least of the things enjoined upon women by custom or law and to which they submit with a feeling of injustice. It is complete liberty or, rather, if we wish to speak the truth, complete license that they desire.

"If they win in this, what will they not attempt? Review all the laws with which your forefathers restrained their license and made them subject to their husbands; even with all these bonds you can scarcely control them. What of this? If you suffer them to seize these bonds one by one and wrench themselves free and finally to be placed on a parity with their husbands, do you think that you will be able to endure them? The moment they begin to be your equals, they will be your superiors. . . . No law is entirely convenient for everyone; this alone is asked, whether it is good for the majority and on the whole. If every law which harms anyone in his private affairs is to be repealed and discarded, what good will it do for all the citizens to pass laws which those at whom they are aimed will at once annul? . . . What pretext, respectable even to mention, is now given for this insurrection of the women? 'That we may glitter with gold and purple,' says one, 'that we may ride in carriages on holidays and ordinary days, that we may be borne through the city as if in triumph over the conquered and vanquished law and over the votes which we have captured and wrested from you; that there may be no limits to our spending and our luxury.' . . .

"She who can buy from her own purse will buy; she who cannot will beg her husband. Poor wretch that husband, both he who yields and he who yields not,

---

[1] A woman was never independent and was not a person in the legal sense. If she was not under the power of a father or of a husband, a *tutor* was appointed to act for her in legal matters.

since what he will not himself give he will see given by another man. Now they publicly address other women's husbands, and, what is more serious, they beg for a law and votes, and from sundry men they get what they ask. In matters affecting yourself, your property, your children, you, Sir, can be importuned; once the law has ceased to set a limit to your wife's expenditures you will never set it yourself. Do not think, citizens, that the situation which existed before the law was passed will ever return. It is safer for a criminal to go unaccused than to be acquitted; and luxury, left undisturbed, would have been more endurable then than it will be now, when it has been, like a wild beast, first rendered angry by its very fetters and then let loose. My opinion is that the Oppian law should on no account be repealed; whatever is your decision, I pray that all the gods may prosper it."

After this the tribunes of the people who had declared that they would veto the bill spoke briefly to the same effect, and then Lucius Valerius argued thus for the measure which he had proposed: . . . "Now, since that most influential man, the consul Marcus Porcius, has attacked our proposal not only with his authority, which unexpressed would have had enough of weight, but also in a long and carefully-prepared speech, it is necessary to make a brief reply. And yet he used up more words in reproving the matrons than he did in opposing our bill, and, in fact, left it in doubt whether the conduct for which he rebuked the matrons was spontaneous or inspired by us. I propose to defend the measure rather than ourselves, at whom the consul directed his insinuations, more to have something to say than to make a serious charge. This gathering of women he called a sedition and sometimes 'a female secession,' because the matrons, in the streets, had requested you to repeal, in a time of peace and in a rich and prosperous commonwealth, a law that was passed against them in the trying days of a war. . . .

"What new thing, pray, have the matrons done in coming out into the streets in crowds in a case that concerned them? Have they never before this moment appeared in public? Let me unroll your own *Origines* against you.[2] Hear how often they have done it and always, indeed, for the general good. . . . These cases, you say, are different. It is not my purpose to prove them similar; it suffices if I prove that this is nothing new. But what no one wonders that all, men and women alike, have done in matters that concern them, do we wonder what the women have done in a case peculiarly their own? What now have they done? We have proud ears, upon my word, if, although masters do not scorn to hear the petitions of slaves, we complain that we are appealed to by respectable women. . . .

"Laws passed in time of peace, war frequently annuls, and peace those passed in times of war, just as in handling a ship some means are useful in fair weather and others in a storm. Since they are so distinguished by nature, to which class, I ask, does the law which we are trying to repeal seem to belong? Well? Is it an ancient regal law, born with the City itself, or, what is next to that, one inscribed on the twelve tables by the decemvirs appointed to codify the law? Is it a law without

---

[2]Although Valerius pretends to quote from Cato's own historical work *Origines*, which discussed early Roman history, the work had not actually been written at the time of the feminist agitation. The scroll form of the ancient book explains the choice of the verb *revolvam*.

which our ancestors held that a matron's virtue could not be preserved, and which we too must fear to repeal lest along with it we repeal the modesty and purity of our women? Who is there, then, who does not know that this is a new law, passed twenty years ago, in the consulship of Quintus Fabius and Tiberius Sempronius? Since for so many years our matrons lived virtuous lives without it, what danger is there that when it is repealed they will rush into riotous luxury? . . .

"Who fails to see that the poverty and distress of the state wrote that law, since all private property had to be diverted to public use, and that the law was to remain in force so long as the cause of its enactment lasted?[3]

"All other orders, all men, will feel the change for the better in the state; shall our wives alone get no enjoyment from national peace and tranquillity? . . . By Hercules, there is mourning and anger among all when they see the wives of allies of the Latin confederacy permitted the ornaments which are refused to them, when they see them decked out in gold and purple, when they see them riding through the city, and themselves following on foot, as if dominion resided in the Latin towns and not in Rome. A thing like this would hurt the feelings even of men: what do you think is its effect upon weak women, whom even little things disturb? No offices, no priesthoods, no triumphs, no decorations, no gifts, no spoils of war can come to them; elegance of appearance, adornment, apparel — these are the woman's badges of honor; in these they rejoice and take delight; these our ancestors called the woman's world. What else do they lay aside in times of mourning than purple and jewelery? What do they put on when they have finished their time of mourning? What do they add save more splendid jewels in times of congratulations and thanksgiving? Of course, if you repeal the Oppian law, you will have no authority if you wish to forbid any of these things which now the law forbids; daughters, wives, even sisters of some will be less under control — never while their males survive is feminine slavery shaken off; and even they abhor the freedom which loss of husbands and fathers gives.[4] They prefer to have their finery under your control and not the law's; you too should keep them in control and guardianship and not in slavery, and should prefer the name of father or husband to that of master." . . .

When these speeches against and for the bill had been delivered, the next day an even greater crowd of women appeared in public, and all of them in a body beset the doors of the Bruti, who were vetoing their colleagues' proposal, and they did not desist until the threat of veto was withdrawn by the tribunes. After that there was no question that all the tribes would vote to repeal the law. The law was repealed twenty years after it was passed.

---

[3]Valerius argues that the Oppian law was merely one of a series of emergency measures by which all elements in the state were affected. To leave this one law in force would mean continued discrimination against only women, after the other methods had been abandoned. [4]Under the stricter Roman law, a woman was throughout life under the *potestas* of her father or his representative or the *manus* of her husband. Valerius makes the point that this domestic authority will be resumed in full with the repeal of the law, and that the same restrictions that the law provided can be enforced if desired.

DISCUSSION QUESTIONS

1. Why did Cato object to repealing the Oppian law? What was the basis of his objections?

2. How did Valerius counter Cato's assertions? What evidence did he use?

3. What do both men reveal about contemporary attitudes toward women and their place in the republic?

4. What does this excerpt show about the republic's government?

4.
"Cultivating Justice and Piety"

Cicero, *On the Commonwealth* (54 B.C.E.)

During his illustrious public career in Rome, Marcus Tullius Cicero (106–43 B.C.E.) was a lawyer, statesman, author, and orator. In each role, he displayed a keen intelligence, fierce patriotism, and high moral standards. This excerpt is from the last chapter of his treatise On the Commonwealth *(54–51 B.C.E.), written at a time when Rome was rife with political and social conflicts. In this excerpt, Cicero uses an imaginary conversation between two military heroes from the Punic Wars — Publius Cornelius Scipio Africanus (236–183 B.C.E.) and his adopted grandson, Publius Cornelius Scipio Aemilianus Africanus the Younger (185–129 B.C.E.) — to highlight the moral values and sense of destiny that he considered to be at the heart of the republic's greatness. Set in 149 B.C.E., the story begins with Scipio Africanus speaking to Publius Scipio the Younger in a dream.*

When I recognized him, I shuddered; but he said, "Stay calm and don't be afraid, Scipio, and remember what I tell you."

"Do you see that city, which I forced to obey the Roman people but which now renews its earlier wars and is incapable of remaining peaceful?" (He was pointing at Carthage from a spot high up and filled with stars, that was bright and glorious.) "You are coming to besiege it now as little more than a simple soldier, but within two years you will destroy it as consul, and you will receive on your own account the name which you have already inherited from me. But after you have destroyed Carthage, have celebrated a triumph, and have been censor, and after you have as an ambassador visited Egypt, Syria, Asia, and Greece, you will be elected consul for the second time in your absence and you will bring to a conclusion a major war by destroying Numantia. But after you ride up the Capitol in your triumphal chariot, you will encounter the commonwealth in a state of disorder because of the plans of my grandson.[1] At this point, Africanus, you will have to display to your

---

From Cicero, *On the Commonwealth and On the Laws*, ed. James E. G. Zetzel (Cambridge: Cambridge University Press, 1999), 95–102.

[1]Tiberius Gracchus, the son of Africanus' daughter Cornelia.

country the brilliance of your mind and talent and judgment. But I see at this point a double path of fate: when your span of years has traversed seven times eight turns and returns of the sun, . . . the whole state will turn to you alone and to your name: the senate, all upstanding citizens, the allies, and the Latins will look at you; you will be the one person on whom the safety of the state rests. To be brief: you will have to restore the commonwealth as dictator.[2] . . .

"But so that you may be all the more eager, Africanus, to protect the commonwealth, know this: for all those who have saved, aided, or increased the fatherland there is a specific place set aside in the sky where they may enjoy eternity in blessedness. There is nothing that can happen on earth that is more pleasing to that leading god who rules the whole world than those councils and assemblages of men associated through law which are called states; the guides and preservers of these have set out from here, and here they return."

At this point, even though I was terrified not so much by the fear of death as of treachery on the part of my own people, I still asked him whether he was alive, along with my father Paullus and the others whom we think of as dead. "Yes indeed," he said, "these people are alive; they have escaped from the chains of the body as if from a prison, and what is called life among you is in fact death. Don't you see your father Paullus approaching you?" And when I saw him, I wept heavily, but he embraced me and kissed me and told me not to weep.

As soon as I could quell my tears and began to be able to speak, I said: "I ask you, best and most sacred of fathers, since this is life, as Africanus tells me, why am I delaying on earth? Why don't I hurry to come here to you?"

"That isn't the way things are," he said. "Unless the god, whose precinct is all that you behold, frees you from the guardianship of your body, you have no access to this place.[3] Men are created under these terms, that they are to look after that globe which you see in the middle of this precinct, which is called earth; and they are given a soul from those eternal fires which you call constellations and stars, which are spherical globes endowed with divine minds and accomplish their rotations and revolutions with amazing speed. And so, Publius, both you and all pious people must keep your soul in the guardianship of the body, and you must not depart from human life without the order of him who gave you your soul: you must not seem to run away from the human duty assigned by the god. But, Scipio, you should be like your grandfather here and like me your father in cultivating justice and piety; it is important in relation to your parents and family, but most important in relation to your fatherland. That way of life is the way to the heavens and to this gathering of those who have ceased to live and after having been released from the body now inhabit the place you see" (it was a bright circle shining among the stars with a most radiant whiteness), "which you have learned from

---

[2]The dictatorship never happened (because of Scipio's death), and it is probably C.'s invention that it was even contemplated in 129: there had been no dictatorship for many years and was to be none again until Sulla seized power more than 40 years later.
[3]. . . "Guardianship of your body" means both that you are in charge of looking after your body and that your body is your prison guard.

the Greeks to name the Milky Way." And from that point, as I studied everything, it all seemed to me glorious and marvelous. There were stars which we never see from this place, and their size was such as we have never suspected; the smallest one was the one furthest from the heavens and closest to earth and shone with borrowed light.[4] The globes of the stars easily surpassed the size of the earth, and earth itself now seemed so small to me that I was ashamed of our empire, which touches only a little speck of it. . . .

. . . Then Africanus said: "I realize that you are still looking at the home and dwelling of men; but if it seems to you as small as in fact it is, you must always look at these heavenly bodies and scorn what is human. What fame can you achieve in what men say, or what glory can you achieve that is worth seeking? You see that humans inhabit small and scattered portions of the earth, and that huge emptiness separates the blotches of human habitation. The people who inhabit the earth are not only so broken up that nothing can pass from one group of them to another, but some of them live across from you, others below you, and some directly opposite you on the earth; and it is clear that you can expect no glory among them. . . .

"Thus, even if you lose hope of returning to this place, where all things exist for great and outstanding men, still — what is that human glory really worth which can last scarcely a fraction of a single year? Therefore look on high if you wish; contemplate this dwelling and eternal home; and do not give yourself to the words of the mob, and do not place your hopes in human rewards: virtue itself by its own allurements should draw you towards true honor. Let others worry about what they say about you — and they will say things in any case. But everything they say is bounded by the narrow limits of the area, as you see, and it is never eternal about anyone, and it is overwhelmed by the deaths of men and extinguished by the forgetfulness of future generations."

After he had said this, I replied: "For my part, Africanus, if in fact there is a kind of path to the heavens for those who have deserved well of their fatherland, even if through following your footsteps and those of my father from my childhood I have not fallen short of your glory, still now, when I see such a prize set before me, I will struggle all the more vigorously."

And he answered me: "Keep at it; and know this: it is not you that is mortal but your body. You are not what your physical shape reveals, but each person is his mind, not the body that a finger can point at. Know then that you are a god, as surely as a god is someone who is alert, who feels, who remembers, who looks ahead, who rules and guides and moves the body of which he is in command just as that leading god does for the universe. And just as the eternal god moves the universe, which is partly mortal, so too does the eternal soul move the fragile body . . . Use your soul in the best activities! And the best concerns are those that involve the safety of the fatherland; the soul which is aroused and exercised by them will fly more swiftly to this, its dwelling and home. It will do so all the more swiftly if even when it is enclosed in the body it projects outward and by contemplating those things that are outside it draws itself as much as possible from the body. The

---

[4]The moon.

souls of men who have surrendered themselves to the pleasures of the body and have made themselves into the servants of those pleasures, and at the urging of desires that are directed by pleasure have broken the laws of gods and men — those souls, when they have departed from the body, circle around the earth and only after having been harried for many generations do they return to this place."

He departed, and I awoke.

DISCUSSION QUESTIONS

1. Based on this excerpt, what social and political values did Cicero consider essential to leading a good life on earth and gaining eternal life in the hereafter?

2. According to Cicero, how were these values being undermined, and with what consequences?

3. What does this story suggest about the Romans' view of the world and their place in it?

5.
Failure and Factionalism

The Gracchan Reforms (133 B.C.E.)

By the second century B.C.E., decades of war had exacted an economic toll on the Roman republic. Despite the vast territories and riches of the elite, many Roman citizens struggled to survive, especially veterans who had been displaced from their farms. In 133 B.C.E., the official newly elected by the plebs to protect their rights, Tiberius Gracchus (d. 133 B.C.E.), initiated a reform program to relieve the people's plight, described here by his biographer, Plutarch (c. 50–120 C.E.). As Plutarch vividly recounts, Tiberius's senatorial colleagues vehemently opposed him and viewed his efforts as a threat to their elite status and wealth. Tiberius paid for his reform initiative with his life, and thereby opened a new and violent chapter in Roman politics. Henceforth, Roman citizens became increasingly more polarized, which set the stage for civil war.

But his brother Gaius has left it to us in writing, that when Tiberius went through Tuscany to Numantia, and found the country almost depopulated, there being hardly any free peasants or shepherds, but for the most part only barbarian, imported slaves, he then first conceived the course of policy which in the sequel proved so fatal to his family. Though it is also most certain that the people themselves chiefly excited his zeal and determination in the prosecution of it, by setting up writings upon the porches, walls, and monuments, calling upon him to reinstate the poor citizens in their former possessions.

However, he did not draw up his law without the advice and assistance of those citizens that were then most eminent for their virtue and authority; amongst whom were Crassus, the high-priest, Mucius Scaevola, the lawyer, who at that time

From *Plutarch's Lives*, vol. 4, rev. trans. A. H. Clough (Boston: Little, Brown, 1909), 514–21.

was consul, and Claudius Appius, his father-in-law. Never did any law appear more moderate and gentle, especially being enacted against such great oppression and avarice. For they who ought to have been severely punished for transgressing the former laws, and should at least have lost all their titles to such lands which they had unjustly usurped, were notwithstanding to receive a price for quitting their unlawful claims, and giving up their lands to those fit owners who stood in need of help. But though this reformation was managed with so much tenderness, that, all the former transactions being passed over, the people were only thankful to prevent abuses of the like nature for the future, yet, on the other hand, the moneyed men, and those of great estates, were exasperated, through their covetous feelings against the law itself, and against the law giver, through anger and party spirit. They therefore endeavored to seduce the people, declaring that Tiberius was designing a general redivision of lands, to overthrow the government, and put all things into confusion.

But they had no success. For Tiberius, maintaining an honorable and just cause, and possessed of eloquence sufficient to have made a less creditable action appear plausible, was no safe or easy antagonist, when, with the people crowding around the hustings, he took his place, and spoke in behalf of the poor. "The savage beasts," said he, "in Italy, have their particular dens, they have their places of repose and refuge; but the men who bear arms, and expose their lives for the safety of their country, enjoy in the mean time nothing more in it but the air and light; and having no houses or settlements of their own, are constrained to wander from place to place with their wives and children." He told them that the commanders were guilty of a ridiculous error, when, at the head of their armies, they exhorted the common soldiers to fight for their sepulchres and altars; when not any amongst so many Romans is possessed of either altar or monument, neither have they any houses of their own, or hearths of their ancestors to defend. They fought indeed, and were slain, but it was to maintain the luxury and the wealth of other men. They were styled the masters of the world, but in the mean time had not one foot of ground which they could call their own. An harangue of this nature, spoken to an enthusiastic and sympathizing audience, by a person of commanding spirit and genuine feeling, no adversaries at that time were competent to oppose. Forbearing, therefore, all discussion and debate, they addressed themselves to Marcus Octavius, his fellow-tribune, who, being a young man of a steady, orderly character, and an intimate friend of Tiberius, upon this account declined at first the task of opposing him; but at length, over persuaded with the repeated importunities of numerous considerable persons, he was prevailed upon to do so, and hindered the passing of the law; it being the rule that any tribune has a power to hinder an act, and that all the rest can effect nothing, if only one of them dissents. . . .

When the day appointed was come, and the people summoned to give their votes, the rich men seized upon the voting urns, and carried them away by force; thus all things were in confusion. . . .

But when the senate assembled, and could not bring the business to any result, through the prevalence of the rich faction, he [Tiberius] then was driven to a course neither legal nor fair, and proposed to deprive Octavius of his tribuneship, it being impossible for him in any other way to get the law brought to the vote. . . .

He referred the whole matter to the people, calling on them to vote at once, whether Octavius should be deposed or not; and when seventeen of the thirty-five tribes had already voted against him, and there wanted only the votes of one tribe more for his final deprivation, Tiberius put a short stop to the proceedings, and once more renewed his importunities; he embraced and kissed him before all the assembly, begging, with all the earnestness imaginable, that he would neither suffer himself to incur the dishonor, nor him to be reputed the author and promoter of so odious a measure. Octavius, we are told, did seem a little softened and moved with these entreaties; his eyes filled with tears, and he continued silent for a considerable time. But presently looking towards the rich men and proprietors of estates, who stood gathered in a body together, partly for shame, and partly for fear of disgracing himself with them, he boldly bade Tiberius use any severity he pleased. The law for his deprivation being thus voted, Tiberius ordered one of his servants, whom he had made a freeman, to remove Octavius from the rostra, employing his own domestic freed servants in the stead of the public officers. And it made the action seem all the sadder, that Octavius was dragged out in such an ignominious manner. The people immediately assaulted him, whilst the rich men ran in to his assistance. Octavius, with some difficulty, was snatched away, and safely conveyed out of the crowd; though a trusty servant of his, who had placed himself in front of his master that he might assist his escape, in keeping off the multitude, had his eyes struck out, much to the displeasure of Tiberius, who ran with all haste, when he perceived the disturbance, to appease the rioters.

This being done, the law concerning the lands was ratified and confirmed, and three commissioners were appointed, to make a survey of the grounds and see the same equally divided. These were Tiberius himself, Claudius Appius, his father-in-law, and his brother, Caius Gracchus, who at this time was not at Rome, but in the army under the command of Scipio Africanus before Numantia. These things were transacted by Tiberius without any disturbance, none daring to offer any resistance to him. . . .

About this time, king Attalus, surnamed Philometor, died, and Eudemus, a Pergamenian, brought his last will to Rome, by which he had made the Roman people his heirs. Tiberius, to please the people, immediately proposed making a law, that all the money which Attalus left, should be distributed amongst such poor citizens as were to be sharers of the public lands, for the better enabling them to proceed in stocking and cultivating their ground; and as for the cities that were in the territories of Attalus, he declared that the disposal of them did not at all belong to the senate, but to the people, and that he himself would ask their pleasure herein. By this he offended the senate more than ever he had done before.

DISCUSSION QUESTIONS

1. According to Plutarch, what specific factors prompted Tiberius to take action in the people's favor?
2. In his address to the crowd, how does Tiberius characterize his opponents, and why?
3. As portrayed by Plutarch, what fundamental Roman values did Tiberius embody?

6.
Toward Empire

Julius Caesar, *The Gallic War* (52 B.C.E.)

The violent failure of the Gracchan reforms marked the end of political cooperation among the Roman elite and, in the process, opened the door for a new kind of leader in the republic — the general-politician — who used his own troops to gain wealth and power. After securing a special command in Gaul, Julius Caesar (100–44 B.C.E.) exhibited just such a strategy through a combination of military genius and political savvy. Between 58 and 50 B.C.E., he and his army pushed past Rome's northwest frontier, conquering much of modern-day France along the way. His success sparked a general rebellion among the peoples of central Gaul in 52 B.C.E., led by the tribal chief Vercingetorix (d. 46 B.C.E.). Caesar described the revolt and its climax at the fortress of Alesia in The Gallic War, *excerpted below. In his account, he provides a glimpse of the realities of warfare and, at the same time, of how he won loyalty both at home and abroad. He used this loyalty as leverage in the civil war brewing in Rome, which ultimately destroyed the republic.*

. . . Now all his cavalry had fled, Vercingetorix withdrew his infantry force, which he had stationed in front of the three camps, and immediately began the march to Alesia, which is a town of the Mandubii. He issued orders for the baggage to be fetched quickly from the camps and to follow on behind. Caesar had his army's baggage taken to the nearest high ground and left two legions behind to guard it. He pursued Vercingetorix as long as the light lasted and killed about 3,000 of the enemy rearguard. The following day he pitched camp near Alesia. He reconnoitered the city's position and provoked panic in the enemy; then, after encouraging the soldiers for the task they faced, he set about the work of circumvallation.[1]

The actual stronghold of Alesia[2] was in an extremely lofty position on top of a hill, apparently impregnable except by means of a siege. On two sides the foot of this hill was washed by rivers, and for about three miles there stretched a plain in front of the town. Close by in every other direction more hills of equal height girded the town. Beneath the wall, where the hill faced east, the Gallic forces filled the entire space: they had constructed a ditch and a six-foot wall. The length of the siege-works which the Romans had started reached ten miles. Camps had been pitched at suitable locations and twenty-three forts built along the line. These forts were garrisoned in the daytime, to guard against unexpected sorties; at night sentries and reinforced patrols kept watch there. . . .

From Julius Caesar, *The Gallic War*, trans. Carolyn Hammond (New York and Oxford: Oxford University Press, 1996), 181, 183–84, 188–89, 191–94, 241–42.

[1]The construction of a fort for mounting weapons by a besieging army. The scale of the circumvallation at Alesia was so astonishing as to become the classic proof of Caesar's mastery of the art of generalship and command.

[2]The size of the forces on both sides is disputed: 50,000 has been suggested for Caesar's entire force, both cavalry and infantry, and 80,000 for the Gallic force inside Alesia.

Vercingetorix now decided to send all his cavalry away by night before the Romans completed their siege-works. As they left, he told each of them to go to his own people and muster for battle all the men of an age to bear arms. He described the services he had done them and called upon them to take thought for his safety, and not to abandon him to the enemy's torments after he had done so much to secure the liberty of all. . . .

All these arrangements were relayed to Caesar by deserters and prisoners. He then decided to set up the following types of fortification. He had a twenty-foot-wide ditch dug, with vertical sides, so that the bottom of the ditch was as wide as its edges at the top. He fixed the position of all the other fortifications 400 paces back from the ditch, with the intention of preventing an unexpected or night-time onslaught on them by the enemy army, and of stopping the enemy aiming missiles at our men while they were busy on the siege-works; for the area he had enclosed was necessarily of considerable size, and it would be difficult to encircle the entire site with a cordon of soldiers. At this distance away, then, he extended two more ditches, of the same depth but fifteen feet across; he filled the inner one (which was on low-lying ground in the plain) with water diverted from the river. Behind them he constructed an earthwork with a rampart on top, twelve feet high; to this he attached a parapet and battlements, with large pointed stakes projecting at the joints where the parapet attached to the earthwork. This would slow down an enemy ascent. He placed towers all round the siege-works at intervals of eighty feet. . . .

Meanwhile Commius[3] and the other leaders entrusted with the supreme command reached Alesia with all their forces. They occupied a hill outside, less than a mile from our fortifications, and took up position there. The next day they brought their cavalry out of camp and filled the whole of the plain which we described earlier as being three miles across. They withdrew their infantry force a short distance and halted it on high ground. From the town of Alesia there was a clear view on to the plain. . . .

Vercingetorix saw his men from the citadel of Alesia and marched out of the town, taking the wicker hurdles, poles, shelters, siege-hooks, and the rest of the equipment he had had made ready for the sortie. At one and the same moment there was fighting on every side, and every expedient was put to the test. Wherever a hint of weakness appeared, there they flocked to the attack. The Roman force was strung out along its extensive fortifications and found rallying to the defense difficult in many places. The shouting which arose behind them was effective in frightening our men as they fought, for they realized that the risk to themselves depended on the courage shown by others: after all, it is usually the case that what is unseen is more effective in disturbing men's minds.

Caesar took over a suitable spot and found out what was happening in every quarter; he sent help to those who were in difficulties. Both sides realized that this was the very moment for putting their utmost effort into the fight — the Gauls must despair of saving themselves unless they broke through the Roman defenses,

---

[3]Before the uprising in Gaul, Commius had been an ally of Caesar's in Britain; in return, Caesar had made him King of the Atrebates. [Ed.]

and the Romans, if they held firm, were looking forward to the end of all their labors. . . . The unfavorable downward slope of the site played a crucial part. Some of the enemy threw missiles, others formed a "tortoise" and moved up close; exhausted troops were continually being replaced by fresh. They all threw earth on to the defenses, which gave the Gauls a means of ascent as well as covering over the devices which the Romans had hidden in the ground. Our men were now running out of weapons and of strength.

When he realized what was happening Caesar sent Labienus with six cohorts to help the men in trouble. He told him that if it was impossible to hold his ground he should withdraw his forces and then launch a counter-attack — but this was only to be done in an emergency. Caesar then approached the rest of the men in person, and urged them not to give up the struggle. He explained how the fruits of all their previous battles depended on that day, that hour. Inside the Roman lines the enemy abandoned hope of success on the level ground because of the size of the defenses; so they tried to climb one of the steep ascents to take it, and had all the equipment they had prepared conveyed there. A hail of missiles from the defenders on the towers scattered them, but they filled in the ditches with earth and hurdles, and started to tear down the rampart and parapet with grappling-hooks.

Caesar sent first the young Brutus[4] with some cohorts, then his legate Gaius Fabius with more. Finally, when the fighting grew more fierce, he came in person, leading fresh troops for reinforcements. The battle was renewed and the enemy forced back. Then Caesar made for the place where he had sent Labienus. He withdrew four cohorts from the nearest fort and ordered one section of the cavalry to follow him, the rest to move round the outer defenses and attack the enemy from the rear. Once Labienus had found that neither earthworks nor ditches could stand up to the enemy attack, he gathered eleven cohorts, which happened to be available after their withdrawal from the nearby guardposts. He then sent word to Caesar of what he thought needed to be done.

Caesar hurried to join in the fighting. The conspicuous color of the cloak[5] he habitually wore in battle proclaimed his arrival. Because the downward slopes were in clear view from the heights above, the enemy spotted the cavalry squadrons and cohorts he had ordered to follow him and joined battle. A shout went up from both sides, and was answered by another from the rampart and defense-works. Our men threw their spears, then fought with swords. Suddenly the cavalry was glimpsed in the rear: more cohorts were advancing. The enemy turned tail and the cavalry charged them as they fled. Massive slaughter followed. . . . Those in the town viewed the slaughter and the flight of their comrades: abandoning hope, they withdrew their forces from the defenses.

As soon as the news broke, the Gauls fled from their camp. If our men had not been exhausted after numerous relief efforts and all the struggles of the day they

---

[4]Decimus Junius Brutus Albinus commanded Caesar's fleet against the Veneti in 56 b.c.e. and later at Massilia in 49 b.c.e., following which he was made governor of Transalpine Gaul. He was also one of Caesar's assassins.

[5]A reference to the scarlet cloak worn by the *imperator*.

would have been able to wipe out the entire enemy army. The cavalry was sent out at around midnight and caught up with the enemy rearguard. Many of the enemy were taken and killed, and the rest fled to their home states.

The following day Vercingetorix called a council and argued that he had undertaken this war not in his own interests but for the liberty of all. Since they were forced to yield to fortune, he went on, he was putting himself in their hands, ready for either outcome, whether they wanted to make reparation to the Romans by putting him to death, or to hand him over alive.

They sent envoys to Caesar to discuss these options, and he ordered them to give up their weapons and bring out the ringleaders. Then he took his seat within the fortifications in front of his camp, and the ringleaders were brought to him there. Vercingetorix was handed over, and weapons were thrown down. Caesar had the Aedui and Arverni kept back, in case he could use them to win back their states' allegiance, and the rest of the prisoners he shared out as booty, one apiece, to his entire army.

Once this business was settled he set out for the territory of the Aedui and won back their nation. The Arvernian envoys who had been sent there pledged to carry out whatever he told them to do.

DISCUSSION QUESTIONS

1. What does Caesar's description of the siege of Alesia reveal about the technology of war at the time? How did Caesar use this technology to his advantage?

2. What does Caesar's portrait of Vercingetorix suggest about Roman attitudes toward non-Romans?

3. Although Caesar wrote *The Gallic War* to describe his own deeds, he uses "he" (the third person) instead of "I" (the first person) in telling his story. Why do you think he made this choice? Does his use of the third person give you more confidence, or less, in the truth of his account?

4. In writing this account, how do you think Caesar intended to shape his public image and why?

COMPARATIVE QUESTIONS

1. Although the Roman republic was not a democracy, its nonelite citizens were an important political force. What evidence can you find in *Roman Women Demonstrate against the Oppian Law* and *The Gracchan Reforms* to support this claim?

2. How do the documents in this chapter lend support to the argument that the importance of law was a basic Roman value?

3. What do both Plutarch and Caesar reveal about the ways in which war shaped Roman society and politics?

4. Imagine that the sculptor of the Roman bust was designing a statue of Caesar. Based on Caesar's self-portrait in *The Gallic War* of his actions during the climax of the siege of Alesia, what features do you think the sculptor would include and why?

CHAPTER 6

The Creation of the Roman Empire
44 B.C.E.–284 C.E.

The civil wars sparked by the assassination of Julius Caesar in 44 B.C.E. may have marked the death of the Roman republic, but they also signaled the birth of the Roman Empire. Through masterful political and military maneuvering, Caesar's heir Octavian (63 B.C.E.–14 C.E.) emerged from the wars as Rome's undisputed leader. In recognition of this fact, in 27 C.E., the Senate granted him special powers and a new title, Augustus ("divinely favored"). He thereupon forged a new system of government that laid the foundations for two hundred years of peace and prosperity. The documents in this chapter bring the empire to life from a variety of perspectives — from Virgil's epic poem praising the glory of Rome to everyday people living under Roman rule. The final two documents cast light on the Roman religious landscape; inevitably it, too, would be swept up in currents of change as a new religion, Christianity, emerged to compete with traditional beliefs and practices.

1.
An Empire Foretold

Virgil, *The Aeneid* (First Century B.C.E.)

When Augustus assumed power in 27 B.C.E., he did not cast himself as an innovator. Well aware of Romans' reverence for tradition, he used republican customs to cloak his creation of a new political system anchored in the power of its "first man," the emperor. Despite the misgivings some Romans had with this transformation, they enjoyed a period of unrivaled prosperity and stability. During Augustus's reign, artists and writers celebrated Rome's glory and superiority. One of the emperor's favorites was the poet Virgil (70–19 B.C.E.), who regularly shared his work with Augustus.

From Virgil, *The Aeneid*, trans. Robert Fagles (New York: Penguin Group, 2006), 205–10.

Inspired by Homer, Virgil composed an epic poem about the origins of Rome, The Aeneid. He died before finishing it to his satisfaction and, in his will, requested that it be destroyed. Augustus intervened, however, thereby preserving The Aeneid for posterity. The poem recounts the story of the legendary founder of Rome, the Trojan Aeneas. The first six books focus on his travels to Italy from Troy; as in The Odyssey, the hero's voyage takes longer than expected due to a variety of mishaps and diversions along the way. These include a visit to the Underworld, as described in the excerpt below. Guided by the Sibyl, here Aeneas meets his dead father, Anchises, who shows him a pageant of the spirits of the great Romans to come, who will establish the empire and peace throughout the world.

Now father Anchises, deep in a valley's green recess,
was passing among the souls secluded there, reviewing them,
eagerly, on their way to the world of light above. By chance
he was counting over his own people, all his cherished heirs,
their fame and their fates, their values, acts of valor.
When he saw Aeneas striding toward him over the fields,
he reached out both his hands as his spirit lifted,
tears ran down his cheeks, a cry broke from his lips:
"You've come at last? Has the love your father hoped for
mastered the hardship of the journey? Let me look at your face,
my son, exchange some words, and hear your familiar voice.
So I dreamed, I knew you'd come, I counted the moments —
my longing has not betrayed me.
Over what lands, what seas have you been driven,
buffeted by what perils into my open arms, my son?
How I feared the realm of Libya might well do you harm!"

    "Your ghost, my father," he replied, "your grieving ghost,
so often it came and urged me to your threshold!
My ships are lying moored in the Tuscan sea.
Let me clasp your hand, my father, let me —
I beg you, don't withdraw from my embrace!"

    So Aeneas pleaded, his face streaming tears.
Three times he tried to fling his arms around his neck,
three times he embraced — nothing . . . the phantom
sifting through his fingers,
light as wind, quick as a dream in flight.

    And now Aeneas sees in the valley's depths
a sheltered grove and rustling wooded brakes
and the Lethe[1] flowing past the homes of peace.

---

[1]**Lethe:** One of the major rivers in the Underworld. [Ed.]

Around it hovered numberless races, nations of souls
like bees in meadowlands on a cloudless summer day
that settle on flowers, riots of color, swarming round
the lilies' lustrous sheen, and the whole field comes alive
with a humming murmur. Struck by the sudden sight,
Aeneas, all unknowing, wonders aloud, and asks:
"What is the river over there? And who are they
who crowd the banks in such a growing throng?"

     His father Anchises answers: "They are the spirits
owed a second body by the Fates. They drink deep
of the river Lethe's currents there, long drafts
that will set them free of cares, oblivious forever.
How long I have yearned to tell you, show them to you,
face-to-face, yes, as I count the tally out
of all my children's children. So all the more
you can rejoice with me in Italy, found at last." . . .

     Anchises, silent a moment, drawing his son and Sibyl
with him into the midst of the vast murmuring throng,
took his stand on a rise of ground where he could scan
the long column marching toward him, soul by soul,
and recognize their features as they neared.
                       "So come,
the glory that will follow the sons of Troy through time,
your children born of Italian stock who wait for life,
bright souls, future heirs of our name and our renown:
I will reveal them all and tell you of your fate. . . .

                       "Here,
a son of Mars, his grandsire Numitor's comrade — Romulus,
bred from Assaracus' blood by his mother, Ilia.
See how the twin plumes stand joined on his helmet?
And the Father of Gods himself already marks him out
with his own bolts of honor. Under his auspices, watch,
my son, our brilliant Rome will extend her empire far
and wide as the earth, her spirit high as Olympus.
Within her single wall she will gird her seven hills,
blest in her breed of men: like the Berecynthian Mother
crowned with her turrets, riding her victor's chariot
through the Phrygian cities, glad in her brood of gods,
embracing a hundred grandsons. All dwell in the heavens,
all command the heights.

                  "Now turn your eyes this way
and behold these people, your own Roman people.

Here is Caesar and all the line of Iulus
soon to venture under the sky's great arch.
Here is the man, he's here! Time and again
you've heard his coming promised — Caesar Augustus!
Son of a god, he will bring back the Age of Gold
to the Latian fields where Saturn once held sway,
expand his empire past the Garamants and the Indians
to a land beyond the stars, beyond the wheel of the year,
the course of the sun itself, where Atlas bears the skies
and turns on his shoulder the heavens studded with flaming stars.
Even now the Caspian and Maeotic kingdoms quake at his coming,
oracles sound the alarm and the seven mouths of the Nile
churn with fear. Not even Hercules[2] himself could cross
such a vast expanse of earth, though it's true he shot
the stag with its brazen hoofs, and brought peace
to the ravaged woods of Erymanthus, terrorized
the Hydra of Lerna with his bow. Not even Bacchus[3]
in all his glory, driving his team with vines for reins
and lashing his tigers down from Nysa's soaring ridge.
Do we still flinch from turning our valor into deeds?
Or fear to make our home on Western soil? . . .

    "Others, I have no doubt,
will forge the bronze to breathe with suppler lines,
draw from the block of marble features quick with life,
plead their cases better, chart with their rods the stars
that climb the sky and foretell the times they rise.
But you, Roman, remember, rule with all your power
the peoples of the earth — these will be your arts:
to put your stamp on the works and ways of peace,
to spare the defeated, break the proud in war."

Discussion Questions

1. What does the pageant of souls suggest about the values Romans believed fueled the empire's success?

2. How does Virgil describe Augustus? What does this description reveal about his understanding of the emperor's particular place in Roman history?

3. In the final verses of this passage, Anchises distinguishes between Roman "arts" and those of "Others" — an implicit reference to the Greeks. What are the differences? Do you think there is a broader message here about Roman imperialism?

---

[2]**Hercules:** The son of Zeus. [Ed.]
[3]**Bacchus:** The god of wine, the vine, and ecstasy. [Ed.]

2.
An Urban Empire
Notices and Graffiti Describe Life in Pompeii
(First Century c.e.)

Among the remarkable features of the Roman Empire was its immense expanse and the many cities, both new and old, that dotted its landscape. The following messages, graffiti, and election notices from the Roman municipality of Pompeii illuminate the hustle and bustle of urban life in the first century of the empire. Located at the foot of Mount Vesuvius in southern Italy, Pompeii at the time was a thriving commercial city, with a fashionable resort nearby. In 79 c.e., Mount Vesuvius erupted, burying the city in cinders and ash. Although the local population was destroyed or fled, remarkably, the city's buildings were preserved, as were hundreds of announcements painted in red on whitewashed walls, along with the scribbles of passersby. Here we see many facets of people's daily lives within the empire, from political appeals to lovesick lamentations.

In the Arrius Pollio block owned by Gnaeus Alleius Nigidius Maius, to let from the fifteenth of next July, shops with their stalls, high-class second-story apartments, and a house. Prospective lessees may apply to Primus, slave of Gnaeus Alleius Nigidius Maius.

On the property owned by Julia Felix, daughter of Spurius, to let from the thirteenth of next August to the thirteenth of the sixth August hence, or five consecutive years, the elite Venus Baths, shops, stalls, and second-story apartments. Interested parties may apply to the lessor in the matter.

The fruit dealers together with Helvius Vestalis unanimously urge the election of Marcus Holconius Priscus as duovir[1] with judicial power.

The goldsmiths unanimously urge the election of Gaius Cuspius Pansa as aedile.[2]

I ask you to elect Gaius Julius Polybius aedile. He gets good bread [for us].

The muleteers urge the election of Gaius Julius Polybius as duovir.

The worshippers of Isis unanimously urge the election of Gnaeus Helvius Sabinus as aedile.

Proculus, make Sabinus aedile and he will do as much for you.

From Naphtali Lewis and Meyer Reinhold, eds., *Roman Civilization: Selected Readings*, 3rd ed., vol. 2 (New York: Columbia University Press, 1990), 126–27, 237–38, 276–78.

[1]**duovir**: One of two chief magistrates of Roman municipalities. [Ed.]
[2]**aedile**: A municipal administrator. [Ed.]

His neighbors urge you to elect Lucius Statius Receptus duovir with judicial power; he is worthy. Aemilius Celer, a neighbor, wrote this. May you take sick if you maliciously erase this!

Satia and Petronia support and ask you to elect Marcus Casellius and Lucius Albucius aediles. May we always have such citizens in our colony!

I ask you to elect Epidius Sabinus duovir with judicial power. He is worthy, a defender of the colony, and in the opinion of the respected judge Suedius Clemens and by agreement of the council, because of his services and uprightness, worthy of the municipality. Elect him!

If upright living is considered any recommendation, Lucretius Fronto is well worthy of the office.

Genialis urges the election of Bruttius Balbus as duovir. He will protect the treasury.

I ask you to elect Marcus Cerrinius Vatia to the aedileship. All the late drinkers support him. Florus and Fructus wrote this.

The petty thieves support Vatia for the aedileship.

I ask you to elect Aulus Vettius Firmus aedile. He is worthy of the municipality. I ask you to elect him, ballplayers. Elect him!

I wonder, O wall, that you have not fallen in ruins from supporting the stupidities of so many scribblers.[3]

Twenty pairs of gladiators of Decimus Lucretius Satrius Valens, life-time flamen[4] of Nero son of Caesar Augustus, and ten pairs of gladiators of Decimus Lucretius Valens, his son, will fight at Pompeii on April 8, 9, 10, 11, 12. There will be a full card of wild beast combats, and awnings [for the spectators]. Aemilius Celer [painted this sign], all alone in the moonlight.

Market days: Saturday in Pompeii, Sunday in Nuceria, Monday in Atella, Tuesday in Nola, Wednesday in Cumae, Thursday in Puteoli, Friday in Rome.

6th: cheese 1, bread 8, oil 3, wine 3[5]
7th: bread 8, oil 5, onions 5, bowl 1, bread for the slave[?] 2, wine 2

---

[3]Unlike the others, this inscription is a *graffito*, scratched on the wall.
[4]**flamen**: A priest. [Ed.]
[5]The initial number is the day of the month, the numbers following the items of food indicate expenditures in asses, except where *denarii* are specified. A *denarius* was a Roman silver coin originally valued at ten, and later sixteen, asses. It was the equivalent of the Greek drachma. [Ed.]

8th: bread 8, bread for the slave[?] 4, grits 3
9th: wine for the winner 1 *denarius*, bread 8, wine 2, cheese 2
10th: . . . 1 *denarius*, bread 2, for women 8, wheat 1 *denarius*, cucumber 1,
    dates 1, incense 1, cheese 2, sausage 1, soft cheese 4, oil 7

Pleasure says: "You can get a drink here for an *as*, a better drink for two, Falernian[6] for four.

A copper pot is missing from this shop. 65 sesterces reward if anybody brings it back, 20 sesterces if he reveals the thief so we can get our property back.

The weaver Successus loves the innkeeper's slave girl, Iris by name. She doesn't care for him, but he begs her to take pity on him. Written by his rival. So long.
    [Answer by the rival:] Just because you're bursting with envy, don't pick on a handsomer man, a lady-killer and a gallant.
    [Answer by the first writer:] There's nothing more to say or write. You love Iris, who doesn't care for you.

Take your lewd looks and flirting eyes off another man's wife, and show some decency on your face!

Anybody in love, come here. I want to break Venus's ribs with a club and cripple the goddess' loins. If she can pierce my tender breast, why can't I break her head with a club?
    I write at Love's dictation and Cupid's instruction;
    But damn it! I don't want to be a god without you.

[A prostitute's sign:] I am yours for two *asses* cash.

Discussion Questions

1. Based on these messages and notices, how would you describe life in Pompeii? What did the city look like?

2. What are some of the things people did for a living?

3. What do the election announcements reveal about the residents' political expectations and their role in local politics?

---

[6]One of the prized wines of the Italian countryside (named after a district in Campania), best known from the poems of Horace that sing its praises.

3.
New Influences to the North
Tacitus, *Germania* (c. 98 c.e.)

The historian Tacitus (c. 56–120) was a shrewd observer and scathing critic of impe-rial rule, often contrasting the reportedly superior lives and morals of foreign peoples with those of Romans. Alongside his major historical writings, his works include a short treatise describing the Germanic peoples in the Rhineland. Drawing on ear-lier descriptions, he paints a compelling picture of the public and private life of the Germanic tribes, who at the time lived outside of Roman rule. Although Tacitus's account was perhaps idealized because of his dissatisfaction with contemporary Roman society — in his view, the Roman emperor was too high-handed and Roman citizens too decadent — his description offers information about the early Germans found in no other contemporary literary source.

Germany and Its Tribes

The Inhabitants. Origin of the Name "Germany"

The Germans themselves I should regard as aboriginal, and not mixed at all with other races through immigration or intercourse. For, in former times, it was not by land but on shipboard that those who sought to emigrate would arrive; and the boundless and, so to speak, hostile ocean beyond us, is seldom entered by a sail from our world. And, beside the perils of rough and unknown seas, who would leave Asia, or Africa, or Italy for Germany, with its wild country, its inclement skies, its sullen manners and aspect, unless indeed it were his home? . . .

Physical Characteristics

For my own part, I agree with those who think that the tribes of Germany are free from all taint of intermarriages with foreign nations, and that they appear as a dis-tinct, unmixed race, like none but themselves. Hence, too, the same physical pecu-liarities throughout so vast a population. All have fierce blue eyes, red hair, huge frames, fit only for a sudden exertion. They are less able to bear laborious work. Heat and thirst they cannot in the least endure; to cold and hunger their climate and their soil inure them. . . .

Government. Influence of Women

They choose their kings by birth, their generals for merit. These kings have not unlimited or arbitrary power, and the generals do more by example than by authority. If they are energetic, if they are conspicuous, if they fight in the front, they lead because they are admired. But to reprimand, to imprison, even to flog, is

From *The Agricola and Germany of Tacitus*, trans. Alfred John Church and William Jackson Brodribb (London: Macmillan, 1885), 87–90, 92–101.

permitted to the priests alone, and that not as a punishment, or at the general's bidding, but, as it were, by the mandate of the god whom they believe to inspire the
warrior. They also carry with them into battle certain figures and images taken
from their sacred groves. And what most stimulates their courage is, that their
squadrons or battalions, instead of being formed by chance or by a fortuitous gathering, are composed of families and clans. Close by them, too, are those dearest
to them, so that they hear the shrieks of women, the cries of infants. *They* are to
every man the most sacred witnesses of his bravery — *they* are his most generous
applauders. The soldier brings his wounds to mother and wife, who shrink not
from counting or even demanding them and who administer both food and
encouragement to the combatants. . . .

Councils

About minor matters the chiefs deliberate, about the more important the whole
tribe. Yet even when the final decision rests with the people, the affair is always
thoroughly discussed by the chiefs. They assemble, except in the case of a sudden
emergency, on certain fixed days, either at new or at full moon; for this they consider the most auspicious season for the transaction of business. . . . When the
multitude think proper, they sit down armed. Silence is proclaimed by the priests,
who have on these occasions the right of keeping order. Then the king or the chief,
according to age, birth, distinction in war, or eloquence, is heard, more because he
has influence to persuade than because he has power to command. If his sentiments displease them, they reject them with murmurs; if they are satisfied, they
brandish their spears. . . .

Training of the Youth

They transact no public or private business without being armed. It is not, however, usual for anyone to wear arms till the state has recognized his power to use
them. Then in the presence of the council one of the chiefs, or the young man's
father, or some kinsman, equips him with a shield and a spear. These arms are
what the "toga" is with us, the first honor with which youth is invested. Up to this
time he is regarded as a member of a household, afterwards as a member of the
commonwealth. Very noble birth or great services rendered by the father secure
for lads the rank of a chief; such lads attach themselves to men of mature strength
and of long approved valor. It is no shame to be seen among a chief's followers.
Even in his escort there are gradations of rank, dependent on the choice of the
man to whom they are attached. These followers vie keenly with each other as to
who shall rank first with his chief, the chiefs as to who shall have the most numerous and the bravest followers. It is an honor as well as a source of strength to be
thus always surrounded by a large body of picked youths; it is an ornament in
peace and a defense in war. And not only in his own tribe but also in the neighboring states it is the renown and glory of a chief to be distinguished for the number
and valor of his followers, for such a man is courted by embassies, is honored with
presents, and the very prestige of his name often settles a war. . . .

Habits in Time of Peace

Whenever they are not fighting, they pass much of their time in the chase, and still more in idleness, giving themselves up to sleep and to feasting, the bravest and the most warlike doing nothing, and surrendering the management of the household, of the home, and of the land, to the women, the old men, and all the weakest members of the family. They themselves lie buried in sloth, a strange combination in their nature that the same men should be so fond of idleness, so averse to peace. . . .

Arrangement of Their Towns. Subterranean Dwellings

It is well known that the nations of Germany have no cities, and that they do not even tolerate closely contiguous dwellings. They live scattered and apart, just as a spring, a meadow, or a wood has attracted them. Their villages they do not arrange in our fashion, with the buildings connected and joined together, but every person surrounds his dwelling with an open space, either as a precaution against the disasters of fire, or because they do not know how to build. No use is made by them of stone or tile; they employ timber for all purposes, rude masses without ornament or attractiveness. Some parts of their buildings they stain more carefully with a clay so clear and bright that it resembles painting, or a colored design. . . .

Dress

They all wrap themselves in a cloak which is fastened with a clasp, or, if this is not forthcoming, with a thorn, leaving the rest of their persons bare. They pass whole days on the hearth by the fire. The wealthiest are distinguished by a dress which is not flowing, like that of the Sarmatæ and Parthi, but is tight, and exhibits each limb. They also wear the skins of wild beasts; the tribes on the Rhine and Danube in a careless fashion, those of the interior with more elegance, as not obtaining other clothing by commerce. These select certain animals, the hides of which they strip off and vary them with the spotted skins of beasts, the produce of the outer ocean, and of seas unknown to us. The women have the same dress as the men, except that they generally wrap themselves in linen garments, which they embroider with purple, and do not lengthen out the upper part of their clothing into sleeves. The upper and lower arm is thus bare, and the nearest part of the bosom is also exposed.

Marriage Laws

Their marriage code, however, is strict, and indeed no part of their manners is more praiseworthy. Almost alone among barbarians they are content with one wife, except a very few among them, and these not from sensuality, but because their noble birth procures for them many offers of alliance. The wife does not bring a dower to the husband, but the husband to the wife. The parents and relatives are present, and pass judgment on the marriage-gifts, gifts not meant to suit a woman's taste, nor such as a bride would deck herself with, but oxen, a caparisoned steed, a shield, a lance, and a sword. With these presents the wife is espoused, and she herself in her turn brings her husband a gift of arms. This they count their strongest bond of union, these their sacred mysteries, these their gods of marriage. Lest the woman should think herself to stand apart from aspirations after noble deeds and from the perils of war, she is reminded by the ceremony which inaugurates marriage that she is her husband's partner in toil and danger, destined to suffer and to dare with him alike both in peace and in war. The yoked oxen, the harnessed steed, the gift of arms, proclaim this fact. She must live and die with the feeling that she is receiving what she must hand down to her children neither tarnished nor depreciated, what future daughters-in-law may receive, and may be so passed on to her grandchildren.

DISCUSSION QUESTIONS

1. How does Tacitus portray the German tribes' way of life? What aspects does he admire? What aspects does he criticize?

2. What message do you think Tacitus was trying to convey to his audience in his assessment of the strengths and weaknesses of Germanic society?

3. What role did women play in Germanic society? What was their relationship with men? Why do you think that Tacitus singled out this topic in particular for elaboration?

4.
The Making of a New Religion

Paul of Tarsus, *Letter to the Galatians* (First Century c.e.)

Despite their immense power, Roman emperors faced various threats as they strove to maintain stability across the broad expanse of the empire. Palestine was especially troubled due to increasingly harsh Roman rule there. Jews were resentful of Roman authority in their homeland and many agitated for change. Jesus was among them, calling his fellow Jews to prepare for God's kingdom. Paul of Tarsus (c. 10–65 c.e.), a Jew and a Roman citizen, actively persecuted Jesus's followers for distorting the Jewish faith. Paul was transformed, however, by a revelation calling him to follow Jesus as the Messiah; he thereupon devoted his life to spreading Jesus's teachings to both non-Jews and Jews throughout Asia Minor. Thirteen letters are attributed to him in the writings that came to comprise the New Testament. Below is an excerpt from his letter to a fledgling community of converts in Galatia, who were embroiled in a crisis over whether non-Jewish converts to Christianity needed to keep the Jewish law. Paul reacted passionately to the situation by setting forth key principles that came to define Christianity as a distinct religion.

From *The Jerusalem Bible: Reader's Edition*, ed. Alexander Jones (New York: Doubleday, 1966), 240–44.

Address

From Paul to the churches of Galatia, and from all the brothers who are here with me, an apostle who does not owe his authority to men or his appointment to any human being but who has been appointed by Jesus Christ and by God the Father who raised Jesus from the dead. We wish you the grace and peace of God our Father and of the Lord Jesus Christ, who in order to rescue us from this present wicked world sacrificed himself for our sins, in accordance with the will of God our Father, to whom be glory for ever and ever. Amen. . . .

The Good News as Proclaimed by Paul

"Though we were born Jews and not pagan sinners, we acknowledge that what makes a man righteous is not obedience to the Law, but faith in Jesus Christ. We had to become believers in Christ Jesus no less than you had, and now we hold that faith in Christ rather than fidelity to the Law is what justifies us, and that *no one can be justified*[1] by keeping the Law. Now if we were to admit that the result of looking to Christ to justify us is to make us sinners like the rest, it would follow that Christ had induced us to sin, which would be absurd. If I were to return to a position I had already abandoned, I should be admitting I had done something wrong. In other words, through the Law I am dead to the Law, so that now I can live for God. I have been crucified with Christ, and I live now not with my own life but with the life of Christ who lives in me. The life I now live in this body I live in faith: faith in the Son of God who loved me and who sacrificed himself for my sake. I cannot bring myself to give up God's gift: if the Law can justify us, there is no point in the death of Christ."

Justification by Faith

Are you people in Galatia mad? Has someone put a spell on you, in spite of the plain explanation you have had of the crucifixion of Jesus Christ? Let me ask you one question: was it because you practised the Law that you received the spirit, or because you believed what was preached to you? Are you foolish enough to end in outward observances what you began in the Spirit? Have all the favours you received been wasted? And if this were so, they would most certainly have been wasted. Does God give you the Spirit so freely and work miracles among you because you practise the Law or because you believed what was preached to you?

Take Abraham for example: *he put his faith in God, and this faith was considered as justifying him.*[2] Don't you see that it is those who rely on faith who are the sons of Abraham? Scripture foresaw that God was going to use faith to justify the pagans, and proclaimed the Good News long ago when Abraham was told: *In you all the pagans will be blessed.*[3] Those therefore who rely on faith receive the same blessing as Abraham, the man of faith. . . .

---

[1]Ps 143:2.
[2]Gn 15:6.
[3]Gn 12:3.

The Purpose of the Law

What then was the purpose of adding the Law? This was done to specify crimes, until the posterity came to whom the promise was addressed. The Law was promulgated by angels,[4] assisted by an intermediary. Now there can only be an intermediary between two parties, yet God is one. Does this mean that there is opposition between the Law and the promises of God? Of course not. We could have been justified by the Law if the Law we were given had been capable of giving life, but it is not: scripture makes no exceptions when it says that sin is master everywhere. In this way the promise can only be given through faith in Jesus Christ and can only be given to those who have this faith.

The Coming of faith

Before faith came, we were allowed no freedom by the Law; we were being looked after till faith was revealed. The Law was to be our guardian until the Christ came and we could be justified by faith. Now that that time has come we are no longer under that guardian, and you are, all of you, sons of God through faith in Christ Jesus. All baptised in Christ, you have all clothed yourselves in Christ, and there are no more distinctions between Jew and Greek, slave and free, male and female, but all of you are one in Christ Jesus. Merely by belonging to Christ you are the posterity of Abraham, the heirs he was promised. . . .

Christian Liberty

When Christ freed us, he meant us to remain free. Stand firm, therefore, and do not submit again to the yoke of slavery. It is I, Paul, who tell you this: if you allow yourselves to be circumcised, Christ will be of no benefit to you at all. With all solemnity I repeat my warning: Everyone who accepts circumcision is obliged to keep the whole Law. But if you do look to the Law to make you justified, then you have separated yourselves from Christ, and have fallen from grace. Christians are told by the Spirit to look to faith for those rewards that righteousness hopes for, since in Christ Jesus whether you are circumcised or not makes no difference — what matters is faith that makes its power felt through love. . . .

Liberty and Charity

My brothers, you were called, as you know, to liberty; but be careful, or this liberty will provide an opening for self-indulgence. Serve one another, rather, in works of love, since the whole of the Law is summarised in a single command: *Love your neighbour as yourself*.[5] If you go snapping at each other and tearing each other to pieces, you had better watch or you will destroy the whole community.

---

[4]In Jewish tradition angels were present at Sinai; the "intermediary" is Moses.
[5]Lv 19:18.

DISCUSSION QUESTIONS

1. Why was the role of Jewish law in Christian beliefs and practices a source of conflict among converts?

2. How does Paul address this conflict? What does he mean when he asserts that justification is based on faith in Jesus Christ, and not in the works of the law?

3. What does this letter suggest about the process by which Christians forged their own distinct identity in the years immediately following Christ's death?

5.
The Cult of Isis

Apuleius, *The Golden Ass* (c. 170 c.e.)

Even as Christianity gained new adherents in the Roman Empire, the vast majority of people remained firmly attached to traditional polytheism. The cult of the goddess Isis was among the most popular at the time. It had its origins in Egypt and spread from there throughout the Mediterranean world — note that followers of Isis were among the many residents who scribbled messages on Pompeii's walls (see Document 2 in this chapter). The Roman author Apuleius (c. 125–170 c.e.) included an emotional and detailed account of Isis worship in the final section of The Golden Ass, *the only complete Latin novel to have survived from this period. In the novel, Lucius, the protagonist, suffers a variety of mishaps due to his fascination with magic. After watching a witch transform herself into a bird, he tried the magic on himself. Yet the experiment went horribly wrong, and he turned himself into a donkey instead. Longing to return to human form, he prays to Isis to rescue him from his troubles. She responds to his prayers as his savior, telling him he has to live a moral life to earn her protection.*

A sudden fear aroused me at about the first watch of the night. At that moment I beheld the full moon rising from the sea-waves, and gleaming with special brightness. In my enjoyment of the hushed isolation of the shadowy night, I became aware that the supreme goddess wielded her power with exceeding majesty, that human affairs were controlled wholly by her providence, that the world of cattle and wild beasts and even things inanimate were lent vigour by the divine impulse of her light and power; that the bodies of earth, sea, and sky now increased at her waxing, and now diminished in deference to her waning. It seemed that Fate had now had her fill of my grievous misfortunes, and was offering hope of deliverance, however delayed. So I decided to address a prayer to the venerable image of the goddess appearing before my eyes. I hastily shook off my torpid drowsiness, and sprang up, exultant and eager. I was keen to purify myself at once, so I bathed

From Apuleius, *The Golden Ass*, trans. P. G. Walsh (New York: Oxford University Press, 1994), 218–22.

myself in the sea-waters. . . . Then with tears in my eyes I addressed this prayer to the supremely powerful goddess:

". . . You wander through diverse groves, and are appeased by varying rites. With this feminine light of yours you brighten every city and nourish the luxuriant seeds with your moist fire, bestowing your light intermittently according to the wandering paths of the sun. But by whatever name or rite or image it is right to invoke you, come to my aid at this time of extreme privation, lend stability to my disintegrating fortunes, grant respite and peace to the harsh afflictions which I have endured. Let this be the full measure of my toils and hazards; rid me of this grisly, four-footed form. Restore me to the sight of my kin; make me again the Lucius that I was. But if I have offended some deity who continues to oppress me with implacable savagery, at least allow me to die, since I cannot continue to live."

These were the prayers which I poured out, supporting them with cries of lamentation. But then sleep enveloped and overpowered my wasting spirit as I lay on that couch of sand. But scarcely had I closed my eyes when suddenly from the midst of the sea a divine figure arose, revealing features worthy of veneration even by the gods. Then gradually the gleaming form seemed to stand before me in full figure as she shook off the sea-water. I shall try to acquaint you too with the detail of her wondrous appearance, if only the poverty of human speech grants me powers of description, or the deity herself endows me with a rich feast of eloquent utterance.

To begin with, she had a full head of hair which hung down, gradually curling as it spread loosely and flowed gently over her divine neck. Her lofty head was encircled by a garland interwoven with diverse blossoms, at the centre of which above her brow was a flat disk resembling a mirror, or rather the orb of the moon, which emitted a glittering light. The crown was held in place by coils of rearing snakes on right and left, and it was adorned above with waving ears of corn. She wore a multicoloured dress woven from fine linen, one part of which shone radiantly white, a second glowed yellow with saffron blossom, and a third blazed rosy red. But what riveted my eyes above all else was her jet-black cloak, which gleamed with a dark sheen as it enveloped her. It ran beneath her right arm across to her left shoulder, its fringe partially descending in the form of a knot. The garment hung down in layers of successive folds, its lower edge gracefully undulating with tasselled fringes.

Stars glittered here and there along its woven border and on its flat surface, and in their midst a full moon exhaled fiery flames. Wherever the hem of that magnificent cloak billowed out, a garland composed of every flower and every fruit was inseparably attached to it. The goddess's appurtenances were extremely diverse. In her right hand she carried a bronze rattle; it consisted of a narrow metal strip curved like a belt, through the middle of which were passed a few rods; when she shook the rattle vigorously three times with her arm, the rods gave out a shrill sound. From her left hand dangled a boat-shaped vessel, on the handle of which was the figure of a serpent in relief, rearing high its head and swelling its broad neck. Her feet, divinely white, were shod in sandals fashioned from the leaves of the palm of victory. Such, then, was the appearance of the mighty goddess. She breathed forth the fertile fragrance of Arabia as she deigned to address me in words divine:

"Here I am, Lucius, roused by your prayers. I am the mother of the world of nature, mistress of all the elements, first-born in this realm of time. I am the loftiest of deities, queen of departed spirits, foremost of heavenly dwellers, the single embodiment of all gods and goddesses. I order with my nod the luminous heights of heaven, the healthy sea-breezes, the sad silences of the infernal dwellers. The whole world worships this single godhead under a variety of shapes and liturgies and titles. . . . But the peoples on whom the rising sun-god shines with his first rays — eastern and western Ethiopians, and the Egyptians who flourish with their time-honoured learning — worship me with the liturgy that is my own, and call me by my true name, which is queen Isis.

"I am here out of pity for your misfortunes; I am here to lend you kindly support. End now your weeping, abandon your lamentation, set aside your grief, for through my providence your day of salvation is now dawning. So pay careful attention to my commands. The day to be born of this night has been dedicated to me in religious observance from time immemorial. Now that the storms of winter are stilled, and the tempestuous waves of the ocean are calmed, the sea is now safe for shipping, and my priests entrust to it a newly built vessel dedicated as the first fruits of our journeys by sea. You are to await this rite with an untroubled and reverent mind. . . .

"What you must carefully remember and keep ever locked deep in your heart is that the remaining course of your life until the moment of your last breath is pledged to me, for it is only right that all your future days should be devoted to the one whose kindness has restored you to the company of men. Your future life will be blessed, and under my protection will bring you fame; and when you have lived out your life's span and you journey to the realm of the dead, even there in the hemisphere beneath the earth you will constantly adore me, for I shall be gracious to you. You will dwell in the Elysian fields,[1] while I, whom you now behold, shine brightly in the darkness of Acheron[2] and reign in the inner Stygian depths. But if you deserve to win my divine approval by diligent service, you will come to know that I alone can prolong your life even here on earth beyond the years appointed by your destiny."

DISCUSSION QUESTIONS

1. Why does Lucius pray to Isis as opposed to other gods? How does she respond?

2. Based on this sequence of events, how would you describe Isis? What does she look like? What are her powers?

3. What does Apuleius suggest about the basis of Isis's popularity? Why do you think people were attracted to her cult?

---

[1]**Elysian fields:** Where the fortunate lived in the Underworld.
[2]**Acheron:** A river in the Underworld.

Comparative Questions

1. As portrayed by Virgil, what was the basis of Rome's success as an imperial power? How had perceptions of Roman rule changed by the time Tacitus was writing?

2. What features of Roman life does the graffiti from Pompeii bring to light? How do these features compare to those of the Germanic peoples described by Tacitus?

3. Compare Paul's letter to the section on Isis from Apuleius's novel. What similarities and/or differences do you see in their respective religious beliefs?

4. What attitudes do you think Virgil, Paul, and Apuleius hoped to inspire in their audiences regarding Augustus, Jesus, and Isis respectively? What reward or "promise" does each of these glorified figures have to offer his or her followers? Do you think these attitudes could be in conflict?

The Transformation of the Roman Empire
284–600 C.E.

T he Roman Empire had faced many challenges since its formation at the end of the first century B.C.E., but by the fourth century C.E., the forces of change proved too powerful to resist, as the documents in this chapter attest. Christianity was spreading far and wide, even gaining the allegiance of the emperor Constantine (r. 306–337 C.E.). In the process, Christians also attempted to define doctrine and combat heresy in the Nicene Creed; it did not, however, end controversies. Although polytheism persisted, over the course of the fourth century Christianity gained the upper hand by calling on its followers to surrender themselves to God in both body and will. The success of this message permanently transformed Roman culture and society. At the same time, waves of Germanic peoples penetrated the empire's borders and migrated westward, eventually establishing their own kingdoms that replaced imperial government. These new regimes became the heirs of Roman civilization in the West, setting the stage for the development of medieval Europe, whereas in the East the imperial legacy lived on in the Byzantine Empire.

1.
The Establishment of Roman Christian Doctrine
Arius, *Letter to Alexander, Bishop of Alexandria* (c. 320 C.E.)
and
The Nicene Creed (325 C.E.)

Although Emperor Constantine (288–337 C.E.) had made Christianity a legal religion in the Roman Empire in 313 C.E., major controversies about doctrine and belief

From J. Stevenson, *A New Eusebius: Documents Illustrating the History of the Church to AD 337*, rev. ed. (London: SPCK, 1987), 326–27; and Patrick V. Reid, *Readings in Western Religious Thought: The Ancient World* (New York: Paulist Press, 1987), 376.

continued to rage. Arius (c. 260–336 C.E.), a priest and theologian of Alexandria, posed the most serious challenge to the developing church. Setting forth the belief that the Father and Son could not both be uncreated, Arius insisted that Jesus Christ was not God in the same manner as God the Father. He defended his views in the letter that follows, written circa 320 to the bishop of Alexandria after Arius's condemnation by the Synod of Egypt. As the doctrine of Arianism swept through the empire, sparking anger among many Christians, Constantine called the Council of Nicaea (325 C.E.) to resolve the issue. Two hundred to three hundred bishops attended the council, at which Arius was allowed to explain his position. It was rejected, and the council formulated a creed — one that is still used in slightly different forms in most Western Christian churches. Despite the creed's widespread acceptance, Arianism continued to spread and divide the church.

Letter of Arius to Alexander, Bishop of Alexandria

To our blessed Pope[1] and Bishop Alexander, the Presbyters and Deacons send greeting in the Lord.

Our faith from our forefathers, which we have learned also from thee, Blessed Pope, is this: We acknowledge One God, alone unbegotten, alone everlasting, alone unbegun, alone true, *alone having immortality*, alone wise, alone good, alone sovereign; judge, governor, and administrator of all, unalterable and unchangeable, just and good, God of Law and Prophets and New Testament; who begat an Only-begotten Son before eternal times, through whom he has made both the ages and the universe; and begat him not in semblance, but in truth: and that he made him subsist at his own will, unalterable and unchangeable; perfect creature of God, . . . created before times and before ages, and gaining life and being and his glories from the Father, who gave real existence to those together with him. For the Father did not, in giving to him the inheritance of all things, deprive himself of what he has ingenerately in himself; for he is the Fountain of all things. Thus there are three Subsistences. And God, being the cause of all things, is unbegun and altogether sole but the Son being begotten apart from time by the Father, and being created and found before ages, was not before his generation; but, being begotten apart from time before all things, alone was made to subsist by the Father. For he is not eternal or co-eternal or co-unoriginate with the Father, nor has he his being together with the Father, as some speak of relations, introducing two ingenerate beginnings, but God is before all things as being Monad and Beginning of all.

The Nicene Creed

We believe in one God, the Father Almighty, Maker of all things visible and invisible; and in one Lord Jesus Christ, the Son of God, the only-begotten of his Father, of the substance of the Father, God of God, Light of Light, very God of very God, begotten, not made, being of one substance with the Father. By whom all things

---

[1]Pope, a title of respect for distinguished churchmen.

were made, both which be in heaven and in earth. Who for us men and for our salvation came down [from heaven] and was incarnate and was made man. He suffered and the third day he rose again, and ascended into heaven. And he shall come again to judge both the quick and the dead.

And [we believe] in the Holy Ghost.

And whosoever shall say that there was a time when the Son of God was not, or that before he was begotten he was not, or that he was made of things that were not, or that he is of a different substance or essence [from the Father] or that he is a creature, or subject to change or conversion — all that so say, the Catholic and Apostolic Church anathematizes them.

DISCUSSION QUESTIONS

1. What does Arius mean that Jesus is "not eternal or co-eternal or co-unoriginate with the Father"? How is this statement central to his and his followers' faith?

2. How does the Nicene Creed refute the Arian position while defining essential doctrinal beliefs about Christianity?

3. By defining "correct belief," how does the church put into place a mechanism for dealing with heresy?

4. How does the Nicene Creed illustrate the changes in the church as it grew from relatively small, illegal communities into a major hierarchical institution?

2.
The Struggle of Conversion

Augustine of Hippo, *Confessions* (c. 397 c.e.)

The establishment of a church hierarchy and uniform doctrine was not the only force driving the Christianization of the Roman Empire. It also depended on individuals abandoning tradition to embrace Christ. Augustine of Hippo reveals in his auto-biographical work, Confessions, *that this choice was not always easy no matter how strong Christianity's appeal was in the wake of Constantine's conversion. Although Augustine eventually became both a bishop and a renowned theologian, his path there was arduous. Born to a Christian mother and pagan father in North Africa, Augustine was smart and eager to move up in the world. While pursuing his studies and a teaching career, he scoffed at the Christian scriptures, convinced that true wisdom lay elsewhere. He was also swept up in his own desire for fame, wealth, and sensual pleasure. Yet he struggled to break free from his sinful habits, which he considered to be obstacles to living a Christian life. As he recounts in this excerpt from* Confessions, *his struggles came to a climax while he was living in Milan. The setting of the scene below is his house, where he lived with several companions, including Alypius. A visitor has just finished telling them a story about two Roman officials*

From Saint Augustine, *Confessions*, trans. R. S. Pine-Coffin (London: Penguin Books, 1961), 170–71, 173, 175–78.

who abandoned their careers to serve Christ. The story gnaws at Augustine's conscience, and he retreats into the adjacent garden in a state of emotional turmoil. It is here that he finally receives the grace needed to devote himself to the Christian faith.

There was a small garden attached to the house where we lodged. We were free to make use of it as well as the rest of the house because our host, the owner of the house, did not live there. I now found myself driven by the tumult in my breast to take refuge in this garden, where no one could interrupt that fierce struggle, in which I was my own contestant, until it came to its conclusion. What the conclusion was to be you knew, O Lord, but I did not. Meanwhile I was beside myself with madness that would bring me sanity. I was dying a death that would bring me life. I knew the evil that was in me, but the good that was soon to be born in me I did not know. So I went out into the garden and Alypius followed at my heels. His presence was no intrusion on my solitude, and how could he leave me in that state? We sat down as far as possible from the house. I was frantic, overcome by violent anger with myself for not accepting your will and entering into your covenant. Yet in my bones I knew that this was what I ought to do. In my heart of hearts I praised it to the skies. And to reach this goal I needed no chariot or ship. I need not even walk as far as I had come from the house to the place where we sat, for to make the journey, and to arrive safely, no more was required than an act of will. But it must be a resolute and whole-hearted act of the will, not some lame wish which I kept turning over and over in my mind, so that it had to wrestle with itself, part of it trying to rise, part falling to the ground. . . .

When I was trying to reach a decision about serving the Lord my God, as I had long intended to do, it was I who willed to take this course and again it was I who willed not to take it. It was I and I alone. But I neither willed to do it nor refused to do it with my full will. So I was at odds with myself. . . .

Yet I did not fall back into my old state. I stood on the brink of resolution, waiting to take fresh breath. I tried again and came a little nearer to my goal, and then a little nearer still, so that I could almost reach out and grasp it. But I did not reach it. I could not reach out to it or grasp it, because I held back from the step by which I should die to death and become alive to life. My lower instincts, which had taken firm hold of me, were stronger than the higher, which were untried. And the closer I came to the moment which was to mark the great change in me, the more I shrank from it in horror. But it did not drive me back or turn me from my purpose: it merely left me hanging in suspense.

I was held back by mere trifles, the most paltry inanities, all my old attachments. They plucked at my garment of flesh and whispered, "Are you going to dismiss us? From this moment we shall never be with you again, for ever and ever. From this moment you will never again be allowed to do this thing or that, for evermore." What was it, my God, that they meant when they whispered "this thing or that"? Things so sordid and so shameful that I beg you in your mercy to keep the soul of your servant free from them! . . .

I probed the hidden depths of my soul and wrung its pitiful secrets from it, and when I mustered them all before the eyes of my heart, a great storm broke within me, bringing with it a great deluge of tears. I stood up and left Alypius so that I might weep and cry to my heart's content, for it occurred to me that tears were best shed in solitude. I moved away far enough to avoid being embarrassed even by his presence. He must have realized what my feelings were, for I suppose I had said something and he had known from the sound of my voice that I was ready to burst into tears. So I stood up and left him where we had been sitting, utterly bewildered. Somehow I flung myself down beneath a fig tree and gave way to the tears which now streamed from my eyes, the sacrifice that is acceptable to you.[1] I had much to say to you, my God, not in these very words but in this strain: *Lord, will you never be content?*[2] *Must we always taste your vengeance? Forget the long record of our sins.*[3] For I felt that I was still the captive of my sins and in my misery I kept crying "How long shall I go on saying 'tomorrow, tomorrow'? Why not now? Why not make an end of my ugly sins at this moment?"

I was asking myself these questions, weeping all the while with the most bitter sorrow in my heart, when all at once I heard the sing-song voice of a child in a nearby house. Whether it was the voice of a boy or a girl I cannot say, but again and again it repeated the refrain "Take it and read, take it and read." At this I looked up, thinking hard whether there was any kind of game in which children used to chant words like these, but I could not remember ever hearing them before. I stemmed my flood of tears and stood up, telling myself that this could only be a divine command to open my book of Scripture and read the first passage on which my eyes should fall. . . .

So I hurried back to the place where Alypius was sitting, for when I stood up to move away I had put down the book containing Paul's Epistles. I seized it and opened it, and in silence I read the first passage on which my eyes fell: *Not in revelling and drunkenness, not in lust and wantonness, not in quarrels and rivalries. Rather, arm yourselves with the Lord Jesus Christ; spend no more thought on nature and nature's appetites.*[4] I had no wish to read more and no need to do so. For in an instant, as I came to the end of the sentence, it was as though the light of confidence flooded into my heart and all the darkness of doubt was dispelled.

DISCUSSION QUESTIONS

1. Why is it so difficult for Augustine to make a decision about embracing the Christian faith? Why is he so at odds with himself?

2. How does his choice of language convey the depth of his emotion as he struggles with this decision?

3. What triggers Augustine's conversion? Why do you think he includes this account in his *Confessions*, which he wrote more than a decade after the events he describes?

---

[1]See Ps. 50:19 (51:17).
[2]Ps. 6:4 (6:3).
[3]Ps. 78:5, 8 (79:5, 8).
[4]Rom. 13:13, 14. Saint Augustine does not quote the whole passage, which begins "*Let us pass our time honourably, as by the light of day, not in revelling and drunkenness,*" etc.

3.
The Development of Monasticism
Benedict of Nursia, *The Rule of Saint Benedict* (c. 540 c.e.)

The rise of monasticism was another important vehicle for religious change in the Roman Empire. Individual monks first appeared in third-century Egypt, where they rejected the everyday world and its comforts in pursuit of holiness. By the next century, communities of monks formed in the region and their example spread to other parts of the empire. Discipline and communal self-sufficiency were hallmarks of life within monasteries, often resulting in harsh living conditions for members. Benedict of Nursia (c. 480–553) sought to balance the ascetic ideal with his own understanding of monks' spiritual and physical needs. The result was a code of conduct, called the Benedictine rule, which became the basis of monasticism in the West. The Rule prescribed a regime centered on prayer, scriptural readings, and manual labor. A head monk, known as the abbot, was to oversee the community according to the Rule's instructions. As the excerpts here reveal, at the heart of these instructions was the goal of instilling obedience and humility within every monk; only then could a monastic community achieve its ultimate spiritual mission, salvation and service to God.

Prologue

Listen carefully, my son, to the master's instructions, and attend to them with the ear of your heart. This is advice from a father who loves you; welcome it, and faithfully put it into practice. The labor of obedience will bring you back to him from whom you had drifted through the sloth of disobedience. This message of mine is for you, then, if you are ready to give up your own will, once and for all, and armed with the strong and noble weapons of obedience to do battle for the true King, Christ the Lord.

First of all, every time you begin a good work, you must pray to him most earnestly to bring it to perfection. In his goodness, he has already counted us as his sons, and therefore we should never grieve him by our evil actions. With his good gifts which are in us, we must obey him at all times that he may never become the angry father who disinherits his sons, nor the dread lord, enraged by our sins, who punishes us forever as worthless servants for refusing to follow him to glory. . . .

Clothed then with faith and the performance of good works, let us set out on this way, with the Gospel for our guide, that we may deserve to see him *who has called* us *to his kingdom* (1 Thess 2:12).

If we wish to dwell in the tent of this kingdom, we will never arrive unless we run there by doing good deeds. But let us ask the Lord with the Prophet: *Who will dwell in your tent, O Lord, who will find rest upon your holy mountain?* (Ps 14[15]:1) After this question, brothers, let us listen well to what the Lord says in reply, for he

From *The Rule of St. Benedict*, ed. Timothy Fry (Collegeville, MN: The Liturgical Press, 1981), 157, 159, 161, 163, 165, 167, 181, 183, 185, 187, 189.

shows us the way to his tent. *One who walks without blemish*, he says, *and is just in all his dealings; who speaks the truth from his heart and has not practiced deceit with his tongue; who has not wronged a fellowman in any way, nor listened to slanders against his neighbor* (Ps 14[15]:2–3). . . .

Brothers, now that we have asked the Lord who will dwell in his tent, we have heard the instruction for dwelling in it, but only if we fulfill the obligations of those who live there. We must, then, prepare our hearts and bodies for the battle of holy obedience to his instructions. What is not possible to us by nature, let us ask the Lord to supply by the help of his grace. If we wish to reach eternal life, even as we avoid the torments of hell, then — while there is still time, while we are in this body and have time to accomplish all these things by the light of life — we must run and do now what will profit us forever.

Therefore we intend to establish a school for the Lord's service. In drawing up its regulations, we hope to set down nothing harsh, nothing burdensome. The good of all concerned, however, may prompt us to a little strictness in order to amend faults and to safeguard love. Do not be daunted immediately by fear and run away from the road that leads to salvation. It is bound to be narrow at the outset. But as we progress in this way of life and in faith, we shall run on the path of God's commandments, our hearts overflowing with the inexpressible delight of love. Never swerving from his instructions, then, but faithfully observing his teaching in the monastery until death, we shall through patience share in the sufferings of Christ that we may deserve also to share in his kingdom. Amen.

Chapter 4. The Tools for Good Works

Your way of acting should be different from the world's way; the love of Christ must come before all else. You are not to act in anger or nurse a grudge. Rid your heart of all deceit. Never give a hollow greeting of peace or turn away when someone needs your love. Bind yourself to no oath lest it prove false, but speak the truth with heart and tongue. . . .

Place your hope in God alone. If you notice something good in yourself, give credit to God, not to yourself, but be certain that the evil you commit is always your own and yours to acknowledge.

Live in fear of judgment day and have a great horror of hell. Yearn for everlasting life with holy desire. Day by day remind yourself that you are going to die. Hour by hour keep careful watch over all you do, aware that God's gaze is upon you, wherever you may be. As soon as wrongful thoughts come into your heart, dash them against Christ and disclose them to your spiritual father. Guard your lips from harmful or deceptive speech. Prefer moderation in speech and speak no foolish chatter, nothing just to provoke laughter; do not love immoderate or boisterous laughter.

Listen readily to holy reading, and devote yourself often to prayer. Every day with tears and sights confess your past sins to God in prayer and change from these evil ways in the future. . . .

Do not aspire to be called holy before you really are, but first be holy that you may more truly be called so. Live by God's commandments every day; treasure chastity, harbor neither hatred nor jealousy of anyone, and do nothing out of envy. Do not love quarreling; shun arrogance. Respect the elders and love the young. Pray for your enemies out of love for Christ. If you have a dispute with someone, make peace with him before the sun goes down.

And finally, never lose hope in God's mercy.

These, then, are the tools of the spiritual craft. . . .

The workshop where we are to toil faithfully at all these tasks is the enclosure of the monastery and stability in the community.

Chapter 5. Obedience

The first step of humility is unhesitating obedience, which comes naturally to those who cherish Christ above all. Because of the holy service they have professed, or because of dread of hell and for the glory of everlasting life, they carry out the superior's order as promptly as if the command came from God himself. . . . Such people as these immediately put aside their own concerns, abandon their own will, and lay down whatever they have in hand, leaving it unfinished. With the ready step of obedience, they follow the voice of authority in their actions. Almost at the same moment, then, as the master gives the instruction the disciple quickly puts it into practice in the fear of God; and both actions together are swiftly completed as one.

It is love that impels them to pursue everlasting life; therefore, they are eager to take the narrow road of which the Lord says: *Narrow is the road that leads to life* (Matt 7:14). They no longer live by their own judgment, giving in to their whims and appetites; rather they walk according to another's decisions and directions, choosing to live in monasteries and to have an abbot over them. . . .

This very obedience, however, will be acceptable to God and agreeable to men only if compliance with what is commanded is not cringing or sluggish or half-hearted, but free from any grumbling or any reaction of unwillingness. For the obedience shown to superiors is given to God, as he himself said: *Whoever listens to you, listens to me* (Luke 10:16). Furthermore, the disciples' obedience must be given gladly, for *God loves a cheerful giver* (2 Cor 9:7). If a disciple obeys grudgingly and grumbles, not only aloud but also in his heart, then, even though he carries out the order, his action will not be accepted with favor by God, who sees that he is grumbling in his heart. He will have no reward for service of this kind; on the contrary, he will incur punishment for grumbling, unless he changes for the better and makes amends.

Discussion Questions

1. How would you describe Benedict's tone in the Prologue? What does this suggest about his overall goal in composing his *Rule*?

2. As explained here, what general religious principles and goals were supposed to guide the monks' lives and why?

3. Why does Benedict place such a strong emphasis on humility? Why did he consider it to be so important to doing God's work?

4.
Germanic Law in the Roman Empire

The Burgundian Code (c. 475–525 c.e.)

The migration of Germanic tribes into the West changed imperial politics and society just as profoundly as Christianity did. Members of these tribes gradually formed independent kingdoms based on a mixture of their own and Roman traditions, which soon superseded Roman provincial government. Law codes established by Germanic leaders from the fifth century on were a crucial component of their state-building efforts. Rome provided a powerful precedent in this regard, with its emphasis on written law as both the basis of social order and a manifestation of state authority. These excerpts are drawn from one of the most comprehensive early Germanic law codes, the Burgundian Code, compiled by the kings of the Burgundians, an East Germanic tribe, in the late fifth and early sixth centuries. At this time, they ruled over a large kingdom encompassing much of the former Roman province of Gaul. Early Frankish and Anglo-Saxon societies that were developing during this period were plagued by feuds that undermined political authority and perpetuated increasing cycles of violence. In an effort to curb personal vendettas and increase stability, many rulers established law codes based on wergeld *("man money") that set fines based on the type of crime and a person's value in that society.*

First Constitution

In the name of God in the second year of the reign of our lord the most glorious king Gundobad, this book concerning laws past and present, and to be preserved throughout all future time, has been issued on the fourth day before the Kalends of April (March 29) at Lyons. . . .

For the love of justice, through which God is pleased and the power of earthly kingdoms acquired, we have obtained the consent of our counts (*comites*) and leaders (*proceres*), and have desired to establish such laws that the integrity and equity of those judging may exclude all rewards and corruptions from themselves.

Therefore all administrators (*administrantes*) and judges must judge from the present time on between Burgundians and Romans according to our laws which have been set forth and corrected by a common method, to the end that no one may hope or presume to receive anything by way of reward or emolument from any party as the result of the suits or decisions; but let him whose case is deserving obtain justice and let the integrity of the judge alone suffice to accomplish this. . . .

Therefore let all nobles (*obtimates*), counsellors (*consiliarii*), bailiffs (*domestici*), mayors of our palace (*maiores domus nostrae*), chancellors (*cancellarii*), counts (*comites*) of the cities or villages, Burgundian as well as Roman, and all appointed judges and military judges (*judices militantes*) know that nothing can be accepted

From *The Burgundian Code*, trans. Katherine Fischer Drew (Philadelphia: University of Pennsylvania Press, 1972), 17–24, 30–33, 40–47.

in connection with those suits which have been acted upon or decided, and that nothing can be sought in the name of promise or reward from those litigating; nor can the parties (to the suit) be compelled by the judge to make a payment in order that they may receive anything (from their suit). . . .

Indeed if any judge, barbarian as well as Roman, shall not render decisions according to those provisions which the laws contain because he has been prevented by ignorance or negligence, and he has been diverted from justice for this reason, let him know that he must pay thirty solidi[1] and that the case must be judged again on behalf of the aggrieved parties. . . .

Of Murders

If anyone presumes with boldness or rashness bent on injury to kill a native freeman of our people of any nation or a servant of the king, in any case a man of barbarian tribe, let him make restitution for the committed crime not otherwise than by the shedding of his own blood.

We decree that this rule be added to the law by a reasonable provision, that if violence shall have been done by anyone to any person, so that he is injured by blows of lashes or by wounds, and if he pursues his persecutor and overcome by grief and indignation kills him, proof of the deed shall be afforded by the act itself or by suitable witnesses who can be believed. Then the guilty party shall be compelled to pay to the relatives of the person killed half his wergeld according to the status of the person: that is, if he shall have killed a noble of the highest class (*optimas nobilis*), we decree that the payment be set at one hundred fifty solidi, i.e., half his wergeld; if a person of middle class (*mediocris*), one hundred solidi; if a person of the lowest class (*minor persona*), seventy-five solidi.

If a slave unknown to his master presumes to kill a native freeman, let the slave be handed over to death, and let the master not be made liable for damages.

If the master knows of the deed, let both be handed over to death.

If the slave himself flees (*defuerit*) after the deed, let his master be compelled to pay thirty solidi to the relatives of the man killed for the value (wergeld) of the slave.

Similarly in the case of royal slaves, in accordance with the status of such persons, let the same condition about murderers be observed.

In such cases let all know this must be observed carefully, that the relatives of the man killed must recognize that no one can be pursued except the killer; because just as we have ordered the criminals to be destroyed, so we will suffer the innocent to sustain no injury. . . .

Let Burgundians and Romans Be Held under the Same Condition in the Matter of Killing Slaves

If anyone kills a slave, barbarian by birth, a trained (select) house servant or messenger, let him compound sixty solidi; moreover, let the amount of the fine be

---

[1] **solidi:** A gold coin. [Ed.]

twelve solidi. If anyone kills another's slave, Roman or barbarian, either plough-man or swineherd, let him pay thirty solidi.

Whoever kills a skilled goldsmith, let him pay two hundred solidi.

Whoever kills a silversmith, let him pay one hundred solidi.

Whoever kills a blacksmith, let him pay fifty solidi.

Whoever kills a carpenter, let him pay forty solidi. . . .

Of the Stealing of Girls

If anyone shall steal a girl, let him be compelled to pay the price set for such a girl ninefold, and let him pay a fine to the amount of twelve solidi.

If a girl who has been seized returns uncorrupted to her parents, let the abduc-tor compound six times the wergeld of the girl; moreover, let the fine be set at twelve solidi.

But if the abductor does not have the means to make the above-mentioned payment, let him be given over to the parents of the girl that they may have the power of doing to him whatever they choose.

If indeed, the girl seeks the man of her own will and comes to his house, and he has intercourse with her, let him pay her marriage price threefold; if more-over, she returns uncorrupted to her home, let her return with all blame removed from him.

If indeed a Roman girl, without the consent or knowledge of her parents, unites in marriage with a Burgundian, let her know she will have none of the prop-erty of her parents. . . .

Of Succession

Among Burgundians we wish it to be observed that if anyone does not leave a son, let a daughter succeed to the inheritance of the father and mother in place of the son.

If by chance the dead leave neither son nor daughter, let the inheritance go to the sisters or nearest relatives.

It is pleasing that it be contained in the present law that if a woman having a husband dies without children, the husband of the dead wife may not demand back the marriage price (*pretium*) which had been given for her.

Likewise, let neither the woman nor the relatives of the woman seek back that which a woman pays when she comes to her husband if the husband dies without children.

Concerning those women who are vowed to God and remain in chastity, we order that if they have two brothers they receive a third portion of the inheritance of the father, that is, of that land which the father, possessing by the right of *sors* (allotment), left at the time of his death. Likewise, if she has four or five brothers, let her receive the portion due to her.

If moreover she has but one brother, let not a half, but a third part go to her on the condition that, after the death of her who is a woman and a nun, whatever she possesses in usufruct from her father's property shall go to the nearest relatives, and she will have no power of transferring anything therefrom, unless perhaps from her mother's goods, that is, from her clothing or things of the cell (*rescellulae*), or what she has acquired by her own labor.

We decree that this should be observed only by those whose fathers have not given them portions; but if they shall have received from their father a place where they can live, let them have full freedom of disposing of it at their will. . . .

Of Burgundian Women Entering a Second or Third Marriage

If any Burgundian woman, as is the custom, enters a second or third marriage after the death of her husband, and she has children by each husband, let her possess the marriage gift (*donatio nuptialis*) in usufruct while she lives; after her death, let what his father gave her be given to each son, with the further provision that the mother has the power neither of giving, selling, or transferring any of the things which she received in the marriage gift.

If by chance the woman has no children, after her death let her relatives receive half of whatever has come to her by way of marriage gift, and let the relatives of the dead husband who was the donor receive half.

But if perchance children shall have been born and they shall have died after the death of their father, we command that the inheritance of the husband or children belong wholly to the mother. Moreover, after the death of the mother, we decree that what she holds in usufruct by inheritance from her children shall belong to the legal heirs of her children. Also we command that she protect the property of her children dying intestate.

If any son has given his mother something by will or by gift, let the mother have the power of doing whatever she wishes therewith; if she dies intestate, let the relatives of the woman claim the inheritance as their possession.

If any Burgundian has sons (children?) to whom he has given their portions, let him have the power of giving or selling that which he has reserved for himself to whomever he wishes. . . .

Of Knocking Out Teeth

If anyone by chance strikes out the teeth of a Burgundian of the highest class, or of a Roman noble, let him be compelled to pay fifteen solidi.

For middle-class freeborn people, either Burgundian or Roman, if a tooth is knocked out, let composition be made in the sum of ten solidi.

For persons of the lowest class, five solidi.

If a slave voluntarily strikes out the tooth of a native freeman, let him be condemned to have a hand cut off; if the loss which has been set forth above has been committed by accident, let him pay the price for the tooth according to the status of the person.

If any native freeman strikes out the tooth of a freedman, let him pay him three solidi. If he strikes out the tooth of another's slave, let him pay two solidi to him to whom the slave belongs. . . .

Of Injuries Which Are Suffered by Women

If any native freewoman has her hair cut off and is humiliated without cause (when innocent) by any native freeman in her home or on the road, and this can be proved with witnesses, let the doer of the deed pay her twelve solidi, and let the amount of the fine be twelve solidi.

If this was done to a freedwoman, let him pay her six solidi.

If this was done to a maidservant, let him pay her three solidi, and let the amount of the fine be three solidi.

If this injury (shame, disgrace) is inflicted by a slave on a native freewoman, let him receive two hundred blows; if a freedwoman, let him receive a hundred blows; if a maidservant, let him receive seventy-five blows.

If indeed the woman whose injury we have ordered to be punished in this manner commits fornication voluntarily (i.e., if she yields), let nothing be sought for the injury suffered.

Of Divorces

If any woman leaves (puts aside) her husband to whom she is legally married, let her be smothered in mire.

If anyone wishes to put away his wife without cause, let him give her another payment such as he gave for her marriage price, and let the amount of the fine be twelve solidi.

If by chance a man wishes to put away his wife, and is able to prove one of these three crimes against her, that is, adultery, witchcraft, or violation of graves, let him have full right to put her away: and let the judge pronounce the sentence of the law against her, just as should be done against criminals.

But if she admits none of these three crimes, let no man be permitted to put away his wife for any other crime. But if he chooses, he may go away from the home, leaving all household property behind, and his wife with their children may possess the property of her husband.

Of the Punishment of Slaves Who Commit a Criminal Assault on Freeborn Women

If any slave does violence to a native freewoman, and if she complains and is clearly able to prove this, let the slave be killed for the crime committed.

If indeed a native free girl unites voluntarily with a slave, we order both to be killed.

But if the relatives of the girl do not wish to punish their own relative, let the girl be deprived of her free status and delivered into servitude to the king.

DISCUSSION QUESTIONS

1. What do these laws reveal about the social and political structure of the Burgundian kingdom? For example, do the laws place the same value on all social groups?

2. What does the code reveal about Burgundian women and family life?

3. Historians regard the interaction between Germanic and Roman peoples as a key component of the process by which Germanic kingdoms replaced imperial government in western Europe. What evidence of such interaction can you find in this document?

5.
Emergence of Byzantium
Procopius, *Secret History* (550 c.e.)

The emperors of the eastern Roman provinces successfully resisted the tides of change that engulfed the West. In the process, they forged a new empire, Byzantium. Emperor Justinian (r. 527–565 c.e.) played a pivotal role in shaping Byzantium's emerging identity as a bastion of Roman imperial glory and civilization. Byzantine historian and courtier Procopius of Caesarea (c. 490/510–560s c.e.) provides unrivaled information about Justinian's rule, including two official histories presenting the emperor's legal, military, and architectural accomplishments as expressions of his strong leadership and divine favor. Procopius also wrote a Secret History, *excerpted below, which likewise described the achievements of Justinian and his wife, Theodora (c. 500–548 c.e.). The book casts them in a highly unfavorable light, however, so much so that it was not published until after Procopius's death out of fear of reprisal for its contents.*

Character and Appearance of Justinian

I think this is as good a time as any to describe the personal appearance of the man. Now in physique he was neither tall nor short, but of average height; not thin, but moderately plump; his face was round, and not bad looking, for he had good color, even when he fasted for two days. . . .

Now such was Justinian in appearance; but his character was something I could not fully describe. For he was at once villainous and amenable; as people say colloquially, a moron. He was never truthful with anyone, but always guileful in what he said and did, yet easily hoodwinked by any who wanted to deceive him. His nature was an unnatural mixture of folly and wickedness. What in olden times a peripatetic philosopher said was also true of him, that opposite qualities combine in a man as in the mixing of colors. I will try to portray him, however, insofar as I can fathom his complexity.

This Emperor, then, was deceitful, devious, false, hypocritical, two-faced, cruel, skilled in dissembling his thought, never moved to tears by either joy or pain, though he could summon them artfully at will when the occasion demanded, a liar always, not only offhand, but in writing, and when he swore sacred oaths to

From Procopius, *Secret History*, trans. Richard Atwater (Ann Arbor: University of Michigan, 1961), 40–44, 55, 58, 60, 75–76.

his subjects in their very hearing. Then he would immediately break his agreements and pledges, like the vilest of slaves, whom indeed only the fear of torture drives to confess their perjury. A faithless friend, he was a treacherous enemy, insane for murder and plunder, quarrelsome and revolutionary, easily led to anything evil, but never willing to listen to good counsel, quick to plan mischief and carry it out, but finding even the hearing of anything good distasteful to his ears.

How could anyone put Justinian's ways into words? These and many even worse vices were disclosed in him as in no other mortal: nature seemed to have taken the wickedness of all other men combined and planted it in this man's soul. And besides this, he was too prone to listen to accusations; and too quick to punish. For he decided such cases without full examination, naming the punishment when he had heard only the accuser's side of the matter. Without hesitation he wrote decrees for the plundering of countries, sacking of cities, and slavery of whole nations, for no cause whatever. So that if one wished to take all the calamities which had befallen the Romans before this time and weigh them against his crimes, I think it would be found that more men had been murdered by this single man than in all previous history.

He had no scruples about appropriating other people's property, and did not even think any excuse necessary, legal or illegal, for confiscating what did not belong to him. And when it was his, he was more than ready to squander it in insane display, or give it as an unnecessary bribe to the barbarians. In short, he neither held on to any money himself nor let anyone else keep any: as if his reason were not avarice, but jealousy of those who had riches. Driving all wealth from the country of the Romans in this manner, he became the cause of universal poverty.

Now this was the character of Justinian, so far as I can portray it. . . .

How the Defender of the Faith Ruined His Subjects

As soon as Justinian came into power he turned everything upside down. Whatever had before been forbidden by law he now introduced into the government, while he revoked all established customs: as if he had been given the robes of an Emperor on the condition he would turn everything topsy-turvy. Existing offices he abolished, and invented new ones for the management of public affairs. He did the same thing to the laws and to the regulations of the army; and his reason was not any improvement of justice or any advantage, but simply that everything might be new and named after himself. And whatever was beyond his power to abolish, he renamed after himself anyway.

Of the plundering of property or the murder of men, no weariness ever overtook him. As soon as he had looted all the houses of the wealthy, he looked around for others; meanwhile throwing away the spoils of his previous robberies in subsidies to barbarians or senseless building extravagances. And when he had ruined perhaps myriads in this mad looting, he immediately sat down to plan how he could do likewise to others in even greater number. . . .

Moreover, while he was encouraging civil strife and frontier warfare to confound the Romans, with only one thought in his mind, that the earth should run red with human blood and he might acquire more and more booty, he invented a new means of murdering his subjects. Now among the Christians in the entire Roman Empire, there are many with dissenting doctrines, which are called heresies by the established church: such as those of the Montanists and Sabbatians, and whatever others cause the minds of men to wander from the true path. All of these beliefs he ordered to be abolished, and their place taken by the orthodox dogma: threatening, among the punishments for disobedience, loss of the heretic's right to will property to his children or other relatives.

After this he passed a law prohibiting pederasty:[1] a law pointed not at offenses committed after this decree, but at those who could be convicted of having practiced the vice in the past. The conduct of the prosecution was utterly illegal. Sentence was passed when there was no accuser: the word of one man or boy, and that perhaps a slave, compelled against his will to bear witness against his owner, was defined as sufficient evidence. Those who were convicted were castrated and then exhibited in a public parade. . . .

How All Roman Citizens Became Slaves

Theodora too unceasingly hardened her heart in the practice of inhumanity. What she did, was never to please or obey anyone else; what she willed, she performed of her own accord and with all her might: and no one dared to intercede for any who fell in her way. For neither length of time, fullness of punishment, artifice of prayer, nor threat of death, whose vengeance sent by Heaven is feared by all mankind, could persuade her to abate her wrath. Indeed, no one ever saw Theodora reconciled to any one who had offended her, either while he lived or after he had departed this earth. Instead, the son of the dead would inherit the enmity of the Empress, together with the rest of his father's estate: and he in turn bequeathed it to the third generation. For her spirit was over ready to be kindled to the destruction of men, while cure for her fever there was none.

To her body she gave greater care than was necessary, if less than she thought desirable. For early she entered the bath and late she left it; and having bathed, went to breakfast. After breakfast she rested. At dinner and supper she partook of every kind of food and drink; and many hours she devoted to sleep, by day till nightfall, by night till the rising sun. Though she wasted her hours thus intemperately, what time of the day remained she deemed ample for managing the Roman Empire.

And if the Emperor intrusted any business to anyone without consulting her, the result of the affair for that officer would be his early and violent removal from favor and a most shameful death.

It was easy for Justinian to look after everything, not only because of his calmness of temper, but because he hardly ever slept, as I have said, and because he was not chary with his audiences. For great opportunity was given to people, however, obscure and unknown, not only to be admitted to the tyrant's presence, but to converse with him, and in private.

---

[1]**pederasty:** Male homosexual relations. [Ed.]

But to the Queen's presence even the highest officials could not enter without great delay and trouble; like slaves they had to wait all day in a small and stuffy antechamber, for to absent himself was a risk no official dared to take. So they stood there on their tiptoes, each straining to keep his face above his neighbor's, so that eunuchs, as they came out from the audience room, would see them. Some would be called, perhaps, after several days; and when they did enter to her presence in great fear, they were quickly dismissed as soon as they had made obeisance and kissed her feet. For to speak or make any request, unless she commanded, was not permitted.

Not civility, but servility was the rule, and Theodora was the slave driver. So far had Roman society been corrupted, between the false geniality of the tyrant and the harsh implacability of his consort. For his smile was not to be trusted, and against her frown nothing could be done. There was this superficial difference between them in attitude and manner; but in avarice, bloodthirstiness, and dissimulation they utterly agreed. They were both liars of the first water.

DISCUSSION QUESTIONS

1. What might have been Procopius's goals in writing this book?
2. How does Procopius's animosity toward Justinian and Theodora shape his account of their reign? Does this mean we cannot trust it as a historical source?
3. Do you see any evidence embedded within Procopius's attacks that may explain the reasons for Justinian's short-term success at reuniting the empire and enhancing imperial rule and its long-term costs?

COMPARATIVE QUESTIONS

1. When viewed together, what do the documents in this chapter reveal about the spread and institutional development of Christianity in the Roman Empire between the fourth and sixth centuries? How do these documents illuminate the interplay between politics and religion?
2. Do you see any similarities between Augustine's and Benedict's understandings of what constituted a holy life? What appeal do you think their views may have had?
3. According to Procopius, Justinian's decisions defined law and were a bulwark of his authority. In what ways does the Burgundian Code reflect a similar attitude toward the function of law in government and society?
4. The Nicene Creed was one of the earliest efforts to unify Christianity doctrinally. Based on the later documents in this chapter, how well did it work in the hundred years that followed?

The Heirs of Rome: Islam, Byzantium, and Europe

600–750

The seventh and eighth centuries marked the beginning of a new era in Western civilization — the Middle Ages. By this time, the Roman Empire had fragmented into three different worlds: Muslim, Byzantine, and western European. Even so, these worlds were all rooted in Hellenistic and Roman traditions, which each region adapted to its own interests and circumstances. The sources in this chapter reveal different dimensions of this process, beginning with Islam. The first document illuminates some of the fundamental beliefs uniting the Islamic community as recorded in the Muslim holy book, the Qur'an. Islamic warriors rapidly expanded the boundaries of the Muslim world, which brought both change and continuity to everyday life in their newly conquered lands, as the second document reveals. The third document describes facets of religious and social life in the provinces of the Byzantine Empire on the eve of the Muslim invasion. Although the western kingdoms shared a common Roman heritage with Byzantium, their development followed a different course as various barbarian peoples built new societies and cultures. The fourth and fifth documents bring this development to life while illustrating the importance of women in the westward spread of Christianity and the personal values that were increasingly seen as desirable.

1.

The Foundations of Islam

Qur'an, Suras 1, 53, 98 (c. 610–632)

The remarkable rise of Islam during the seventh century had far-reaching consequences. Muhammad (c. 570–632), a merchant-turned-holy man from the Arabian city of Mecca, founded the new faith based on what he believed were direct revela-

From *Approaching the Qur'an: The Early Revelations*, trans. Michael Sells (Ashland, OR: White Cloud Press, 1999), 35, 42, 44, 47, 104–6.

tions from God, which he first received around 610. The messages continued until his death and soon thereafter were written down and compiled into what became the Qur'an, the holy book of Islam. Comprising 114 hymnic chapters (suras), the Qur'an begins with the Fatihah ("opening"), which emphasizes God's oneness and the believer's recourse to God alone. The "road straight" is the path of right worship. The first eighteen verses of the Star, among the earliest of Muhammad's revelations, explicitly reveal his position in the divine plan, casting him as God's companion and servant. The final selection, the Testament, represents the later period of Muhammad's prophecy when he and his followers confronted the challenges posed by people who resisted the new religion.

1 The Opening

In the name of God
    the Compassionate the Caring
Praise be to God
    lord sustainer of the worlds
the Compassionate the Caring
master of the day of reckoning[1]
To you we turn to worship
    and to you we turn in time of need
Guide us along the road straight
the road of those to whom you are giving
    not those with anger upon them
    not those who have lost the way

53:1–18 The Star

In the Name of God the Compassionate the Caring

By the star as it falls
Your companion[2] has not lost his way nor is he
    deluded
He does not speak out of desire
This is a revelation
taught him by one of great power
and strength that stretched out over
while on the highest horizon —

---

[1] The word translated here as *reckoning (dīn)* is related to a number of terms for borrowing and payment of debt, as well as to terms for religion and faith. The word for *day (yawm)* also can be a more general term for any length of time or a moment in time. The term has been translated as "day of judgment" and "day of accounting." But it also has an implication similar to the "moment of truth" — that is, a time of indeterminate duration in which each soul will encounter the fundamental reality that normal consciousness masks.
[2] "Your companion" is interpreted as Muhammad.

then drew near and came down
two bows' lengths or nearer
He revealed to his servant what he revealed
The heart did not lie in what it saw
Will you then dispute with him his vision?

He saw it[3] descending another time
at the lote[4] tree of the furthest limit
There was the garden of sanctuary
when something came down over the
    lote tree, enfolding
His gaze did not turn aside nor go too far
He had seen the signs of his lord, great signs

98 The Testament

In the Name of God the Compassionate the Caring

Those who denied the faith —
    from the peoples of the book[5]
    or the idolators —
    could not stop calling it a lie
    until they received the testament

A messenger of God
    reciting pages that are pure

Of scripture that are sure

Those who were given the book
    were not divided one against the other
    until they received the testament

And all they were commanded
    was to worship God sincerely
    affirm oneness, perform the prayer
    and give a share of what they have
    That is the religion of the sure

---

[3]When the Qur'an states "He saw it descending another time," the antecedent of the pronoun (*hu*, it/him) is unstated, and thus the referent of the "it" is not determinable from the passage. The identity of the referent became a matter of controversy, with the debate centering upon whether or not the deity can be seen in this world. Those for whom the vision of God can only occur in the afterlife tend to interpret the it/he as referring to the messengerangel Gabriel.

[4]**lote**: A thorny tree with edible fruit; it is also known as Christ-thorn. [Ed.]

[5]Those with written scriptures named in other passages of the Qur'an as the Jews, Christians, and Sabeans (the exact identity of whom has been a matter of controversy).

Those who deny the faith —
    from the peoples of the book
    or the idolators —
    are in Jahannam's fire
    eternal there
    They are the worst of creation

Those who keep the faith
    and perform the prayer
    they are the best of creation

As recompense for them with their lord —
    gardens of Eden
    waters flowing underground
    eternal there forever

    God be pleased in them
    and they in God

    That is for those who hold their lord in awe

DISCUSSION QUESTIONS

1. What do these excerpts reveal about the fundamental beliefs and practices of Islam?

2. How does the Star portray Muhammad? What does this portrait reveal about his role in Islam?

3. The rejection of Islam by many Jews and Christians ("peoples of the book") in Arabia surprised and disappointed Muhammad since he brought his message in the name of the tradition of Abraham, Moses, and Jesus. How does the Testament give expression to these feelings and, at the same time, defend the truth of Muhammad's revelations?

4. Do you see any differences in the concept of religion presented in the Opening and the Testament?

2.

Jihad and Jizya

Islamic Terms of Peace (633–643)

Despite facing some resistance, Muhammad's revelations soon gained widespread adherence across the Arabian peninsula. Together his converts formed a community united by the worship of God, expressed not only in individual prayer but also in the

From Bernard Lewis, ed., *Islam from the Prophet Muhammad to the Capture of Constantinople*, vol. 1 (New York: Walker & Co., 1974), 234–36, 238–40.

collective duty to "strive" (jihad) against unbelievers, often in war. War was thus a central component of Islam, and by the eighth century Islamic warriors had conquered all of Persia and much of the Byzantine Empire. These letters dictate the terms of peace to conquered communities and illuminate the Muslims' method of conquest and rule in the decade following Muhammad's death. In exchange for the payment of a special tax (jizya), non-Muslim subjects were allowed to live much as they had before. Consequently, Islam became not the destroyer of Hellenistic and Roman traditions, but rather their heir.

Bānqiyā and Basmā (633)

In the name of God, the Merciful and the Compassionate.

This is a letter from Khālid ibn al-Walīd to Ṣalūba ibn Nasṭūnā and his people.

I have made a pact with you for *jizya* and defense for every fit man, for both Bānqiyā and Basmā, for 10,000 dinars, excluding coins with holes punched in them, the wealthy according to the measure of his wealth, the poor according to the measure of his poverty, payable annually. You have been made head of your people and your people are content with you. I, therefore, and the Muslims who are with me, accept you, and I [? you] and your people are content. You have protection [*dhimma*] and defense. If we defend you, the *jizya* is due to us; if we do not, it is not, until we do defend you.

Witnessed by Hishām ibn al-Walīd, al-Qa 'qā 'ibn 'Amr, Jarīr ibn 'Abdallāh al-Ḥimyarī and Ḥanẓala ibn al-Rabī'.

Written in the year 12, in Safar [April–May 633].

Jerusalem (636)

In the name of God the Merciful and the Compassionate.

This is the safe-conduct accorded by the servant of God 'Umar, the Commander of the Faithful, to the people of Aelia [Jerusalem].

He accords them safe-conduct for their persons, their property, their churches, their crosses, their sound and their sick, and the rest of their worship.

Their churches shall neither be used as dwellings nor destroyed. They shall not suffer any impairment, nor shall their dependencies, their crosses, nor any of their property.

No constraint shall be exercised against them in religion nor shall any harm be done to any among them.

No Jew shall live with them in Aelia.

The people of Aelia must pay the *jizya* in the same way as the people of other cities.

They must expel the Romans and the brigands [?] from the city. Those who leave shall have safe-conduct for their persons and property until they reach safety. Those who stay shall have safe-conduct and must pay the *jizya* like the people of Aelia.

Those of the people of Aelia who wish to remove their persons and effects and depart with the Romans and abandon their churches and their crosses shall have safe-conduct for their persons, their churches, and their crosses, until they reach safety.

The country people who were already in the city before the killing of so-and-so may, as they wish, remain and pay the *jizya* the same way as the people of Aelia or leave with the Romans or return to their families. Nothing shall be taken from them until they have gathered their harvest.

This document is placed under the surety of God and the protection [*dhimma*] of the Prophet, the Caliphs and the believers, on condition that the inhabitants of Aelia pay the *jizya* that is due from them.

Witnessed by Khālid ibn al-Walīd, ʿAmr ibn al-ʾĀṣ, ʿAbd al-Raḥmān ibn ʿAwf, Muʿāwiya ibn Abī Sufyān, the last of whom wrote this document in the year 15 [636].

Jurjān (639)

In the name of God, the Merciful and the Compassionate.

This is a letter from Suwayd ibn Muqarrin to Ruzbān Ṣūl ibn Ruzbān, the inhabitants of Dihistān, and the rest of the inhabitants of Jurjān.

You have protection and we must enforce it on the condition that you pay the *jizya* every year, according to your capacity, for every adult male. If we seek help from any of you, the help counts as his *jizya* in place of the payment. They have safe-conduct for themselves, their property, their religions, and their laws. There will be no change in what is due to them as long as they pay and guide the wayfarer and show good will and lodge the Muslims and do not spy or betray. Whoever stays with them shall have the same terms as they have, and whoever goes forth has safe-conduct until he reaches a place of safety, provided that if anyone insults a Muslim he is severely punished, and if he strikes a Muslim, his blood is lawful.

Witnessed by Sawād ibn Quṭba, Hind ibn ʿAmr, Simāk ibn Makhrama, and ʿUtayba ibn al-Naḥḥās.

Written in the year 18 [639].

DISCUSSION QUESTIONS

1. Aside from the payment of a poll tax, what were some of the obligations Muslims imposed on their non-Muslim subjects?

2. What did the conquered people receive in exchange for the fulfillment of these obligations?

3. What does this system of exchange suggest about Muslim attitudes toward nonbelievers?

3.
Byzantine Life

The Life of St. Theodore of Sykeon (Early Seventh Century)

Although Emperor Justinian (r. 527–565) had worked to revive the old Roman Empire, by 600 the eastern half began to change into something new, Byzantium. An emperor continued to rule from Constantinople but his reach was smaller; the empire had shrunk in size and its cities had decayed. Against this backdrop, rural life assumed greater importance as the backbone of Byzantine society. Free and semi-free peasant farmers grew food and herded cattle on small plots of land across the countryside. As the excerpt below from The Life of St. Theodore of Sykeon *reveals, among peasants' most frequent social contacts were monks in the local monasteries dotting the landscape. St. Theodore (c. 550–613) was a monk and bishop who lived in central Anatolia (modern Turkey). He gained a great following as a holy man and healer among the communities located on or near the Roman imperial road linking Constantinople to the eastern frontier of the empire. One of his disciples composed the* Life *in the early seventh century to honor Theodore's memory and to uphold him as a model of Christian virtue. In the process, the author also paints among the best pictures known to us of provincial life during this period, particularly villagers' deeply held belief in the omnipresent power of divine and demonic forces in the everyday world.*

After the Saint had returned to his monastery, it happened that he fell so ill of a desperate sickness that he saw the holy angels coming down upon him; and he began to weep and to be sorely troubled. Now above him there stood an icon of the wonder-working saints Cosmas and Damian. These saints were seen by him looking just as they did in that sacred icon and they came close to him, as doctors usually do; they felt his pulse and said to each other that he was in a desperate state as his strength had failed and the angels had come down from heaven to him. And they began to question him saying, "Why are you weeping and are sore troubled, brother?" He answered them, "Because I am unrepentant, sirs, and also because of this little flock which is only newly-instructed and is not yet established and requires much care." They asked him, "Would you wish us to go and plead for you that you may be allowed to live for a while?" He answered, "If you do this, you would do me a great service, by gaining for me time for repentance and you shall win the reward of my repentance and my work from henceforth." Then the saints turned to the angels and besought them to grant him yet a little time while they went to implore the King on his behalf. They agreed to wait. So the saints departed and entreated on his behalf the heavenly King, the Lord of life and death, Christ our God, Who granted unto Hezekiah the King an addition unto his life of fifteen years.[1] They obtained their request and came back to the Saint bringing with them

---

From *Three Byzantine Saints*, trans. Elizabeth Dawes and Norman H. Baynes (Oxford: Basil Blackwell, 1948), 115–20.

[1] 2 Kings xx. 6.

a very tall young man, like in appearance to the angels that were there, though differing from them greatly in glory. He said to the holy angels, "Depart from him, for supplication has been made for him to the Lord of all and King of glory, and He has consented that he should remain for a while in the flesh." Straightway both they and the young man disappeared from his sight, going up to heaven. But the Saints, Cosmas and Damian, said to the Saint, "Rise up brother, and look to thyself and to thy flock; for our merciful Master who readily yields to supplication has received our petition on your behalf and grants you life to labor for 'the meat which perisheth not, but endureth to everlasting life'[2] and to care for many souls." With these words they, too, vanished.

Theodore immediately regained his health and strength; the sickness left him and glorifying God he resumed his life of abstinence and the regular recital of the psalms with still greater zeal and diligence.

Through the grace bestowed on him by God Theodore continued to work many miracles against every kind of illness and weakness, but especially did he make supplications to God for aid against unclean spirits; hence, if he merely rebuked them, or even sent them a threat through another, they would immediately come out of people. Some persons were so profoundly impressed by these miracles that they left their homes, journeyed to him, and entering upon a life of contemplation joined the monastery; others again who had obtained healing would not leave him but stayed with him, giving him such service as he needed. . . .

In the village of Buzaea, which belonged to the city of Kratianae, the inhabitants wanted to build a bridge over the torrent which ran through it, as the latter often became swollen by many streams and could not be crossed. They hired workmen and when the work had almost reached completion and only a few stone slabs were still needed to finish it the workmen at the Devil's instigation went to a certain hill not far off and dug out some slabs from it on the excuse, as some said, that they were needed for their work; but the majority said that they had stolen away a treasure that was hidden there. Then there issued from the place where they had dug for the stones a host of unclean spirits; some of them entered into sundry men and women of the village and afflicted them savagely, others again brought illnesses upon the remaining inhabitants, while yet others hung about the roads and the neighborhood and did injury to beasts and travelers; hence great misery arose in the village and despair at the misfortunes in their homes and in the countryside. Then they bethought themselves of Theodore, the servant of God, and by prayers in his name they tried to exorcize the unclean spirits when they showed signs of activity, and they found that the spirits showed no little fear when his name was uttered over them, and became docile and were reduced to subjection. With all speed, therefore, they made for the monastery and by dint of many supplications they persuaded him to come with them. When Theodore drew nigh to the village the spirits which were afflicting men felt his presence and met him howling out

---

[2]John vi. 27.

these words: "Oh violence! Why have you come here, you iron-eater, why have you quitted Galatia and come into Gordiane? There was no need for you to cross the frontier. We know why you have come, but we shall not obey you as did the demons of Galatia; for we are much tougher than they and not milder." When he rebuked them they at once held their peace. On the morrow all the inhabitants were gathered together, and those possessed by evil spirits surrounded the Saint who had ordered a procession of supplication to be formed which went right round the village and came to the hill from which they said the demons had come out. Then he tortured them by the divine grace of Christ and by the sign of the holy Cross and by beatings on his chest, and after offering up prayers for a long time he bade them come out of the people and return to their own abode. They uttered loud shouts and tore the garments which covered the sufferers and threw them down at his feet and then came out of them. But one very wicked spirit which was in a woman resisted and would not come out. Then the Saint caught hold of the woman's hair and shook her violently and rebuked the spirit by the sign of the Cross and by prayer to God and finally said, "I will not give way to you nor will I leave this spot until you come out of her!" Then the spirit began to shriek and say, "Oh violence, you are burning me, iron-eater! I am coming out, I will not resist you, only give us something that you are wearing." The Saint loosed a sandal from his foot and threw it into the hole in the hill whence they had entered into people and straightway the spirit hurled the woman down at the feet of the Saint and came out of her.

Then the Saint halted again and prayed to the Lord that He would drive together all the spirits, which were still remaining in the neighborhood and in the roads to the injury of travelers, and would shut them up once more in the place from which they came out. And through the grace of God they were all collected, and to some who saw them they looked like flying blue-bottles or hares or dormice, and they entered into the place where the stones had been dug out, which the Saint then sealed with prayer and the sign of the Cross, and bade the men fill up the hole and restore it as it was before. He then led the procession back to the village, and from that time on that place and the inhabitants of the village and all the neighborhood remained safe from harm to the glory of Christ our God, the prime author of healings.

And the Saint returned and came to his monastery.

DISCUSSION QUESTIONS

1. What role do icons play in Theodore's recovery? What does this reveal about the place of icons in Byzantine religious devotion?

2. Why did the villagers of Buzaea seek Theodore's help? What was the source of his power?

3. What does the *Life* reveal about Byzantine notions of sanctity? Why did Theodore command such prestige among local residents?

4.
A Noblewoman's Life

The Life of Lady Balthild, Queen of the Franks
(Late Seventh Century)

With the collapse of imperial government in the West in the fifth and sixth centuries, the kings from the Frankish royal dynasty, the Merovingians, came to dominate Roman Gaul. Their queens also wielded power, as The Life of Lady Balthild *demonstrates. Lady Balthild (d. c. 680) was an Anglo-Saxon captive sold as a slave to the mayor of the palace in the Frankish kingdom of Neustria. He eventually offered her in marriage to King Clovis II (r. 638–657). On the king's death in 657, Lady Balthild acted as regent until her eldest son came of age in 663 or 664. She thereupon retired from court to a monastery. Although the author is unknown, his or her intent is clear: to hold Lady Balthild up as a model of Christian piety. Religious motives aside, the book illuminates women's place in court life as well as the growing influence of Christianity in Merovingian culture.*

Here Begins the Life of Blessed Queen Balthild

Blessed be the Lord, *who wishes all men to be saved and to come to the recognition of truth,*[1] and *who causes them to will and to complete all in all.*[2] And therefore His praise must be deservedly sung first in the merits and miracles of the saints, He *who makes great men out of those of low station, indeed, He who raises the poor man out of the dunghill and makes him to sit with the princes of His people,*[3] just as He has raised the present great and venerable woman, Lady Balthild, the queen. Divine providence called her from lands across the sea[4] and this precious and best pearl of God arrived here, having been sold at a low price. She was acquired by the late Erchinoald,[5] the leader of the Franks and a man of illustrious standing, in whose service she dwelt as an adolescent most honorably so that her admirable and pious religious way of life pleased both the leader and all his servants. She was indeed kind in her heart, *temperate and prudent*[6] in her whole character, and provident. She contrived evil against no one. She was neither frivolous in her fine expression nor presumptuous in speaking, but most honorable in all her acts. And although

---

From Paul Fouracre and Richard A. Gerberding, eds., *Late Merovingian France: History and Hagiography, 640–720* (Manchester and New York: Manchester University Press, 1996), 119–27, 131–32.

[1]I Timothy 2:4.
[2]This seems to be a combination of Philippians 2:13 and I Corinthians 12:6. See also Ephesians 1:23.
[3]I Kings 2:8; Psalms 112:7–8.
[4]England.
[5]Neustrian mayor from 641 to about 659.
[6]I Timothy 3:11.

she was from the race of the Saxons, the form of her body was pleasing, very slender, and beautiful to see. Her expression was cheerful and her gait dignified. And, since she was thus, *she was exceedingly pleasing to the prince and she found favor in his eyes.*[7] He engaged her to serve him the goblets in his chamber, and as a most honorable cupbearer she stood quite often present in his service. Nonetheless, from the favor of her position she derived no haughtiness but, based in humility, was loving and obedient to all her equals. With fitting honor she so served her seniors that she removed the shoes from their feet and washed and dried them. She fetched water for washing and promptly prepared their clothes. And she performed this service for them without muttering and with a good and pious heart.

. . .

And from her noble way of life, greatest praise and love among her companions accrued to her, and she earned such a favorable reputation that, when the wife of the above-mentioned prince Erchinoald died, he decided to join the most honorable virgin, Balthild, to himself in the matrimonial bed. And, having learned this thing, she secretly and earnestly withdrew herself from his sight. And when she was called to the bedchamber of the prince, she hid herself in an out-of-the-way corner and threw cheap rags over herself so that no one would have thought anyone to be hiding there. Indeed, she was then still a shrewd and prudent virgin fleeing empty high positions and seeking humility. She tried, as she was able, to avoid human marriage so that she might deserve to come to her spiritual and heavenly groom. But indeed, beyond doubt, it was accomplished by divine providence that the prince did not find her, whom he sought, and then joined another matron to himself in marriage. And then the girl Balthild was finally found so that, by the true will of God who had shunned the nuptials of the prince, she would later have Clovis,[8] son of the late King Dagobert,[9] in marriage so that He could thus raise her to a higher station through the merit of her humility. And in this station divine dispensation decided to honor her so that, seeing that she had refused a follower of the king, she might obtain union with the king and, from her, royal progeny might come forth.[10] And this has now come to pass, as it is obvious to everyone that the royal offspring reigning now is hers.

. . .

But as she had the grace of prudence conferred upon her by God, with watchful eagerness she obeyed the king as her lord, and to the princes she showed herself a mother, to the priests as a daughter, and to the young and the adolescents as the best possible nurse. And she was friendly to all, loving the priests as fathers, the monks as brothers, the poor as a faithful nurse does, and giving to each generous

---

[7]Ester 7:3, 2:4 and 9, and 5:8. Ester was also a royal spouse of low origins.
[8]Clovis II, king of Neustria (638–57).
[9]Dagobert I, king of Austrasia (623–33) and Neustria (629–38).
[10]That is, Clothar III, king of Neustria (657–73); Childeric II, king of Austrasia (657–75) and Neustria (673–75); and Theuderic III, king of Neustria (673 and 675–90).

alms. She preserved the honor of the princes and kept their fitting counsel, always exhorting the young to religious studies and humbly and steadfastly petitioning the king for the churches and the poor. While still in secular dress, she desired to serve Christ; she prayed daily, tearfully commending herself to Christ, the heavenly king. And the pious king [Clovis], taking care of her faith and devotion, gave his faithful servant, Abbot Genesius, to her as support, and through his hands she served the priests and the poor, fed the hungry, clothed the naked with garments, and conscientiously arranged the burial of the dead. Through him she sent most generous alms of gold and silver to the monasteries of men and women. . . .

. . .

What more is there to say? At God's command, her husband, King Clovis, went forth from his body, leaving a lineage of sons with their mother. In his place after him, his son, the late King Clothar,[11] took the throne of the Franks and then also with the excellent princes, Chrodbert, bishop of Paris, Lord Audoin, and Ebroin, mayor of the palace, along with the other great magnates and very many of the rest.[12] And, indeed, the kingdom of the Franks was maintained in peace. Then indeed, a little while ago, the Austrasians peacefully received her son Childeric[13] as king in Austrasia by the arrangement of Lady Balthild and, indeed, through the advice of the great magnates. But the Burgundians and the Neustrians were united. And we believe that, with God guiding, and in accordance with the great faith of Lady Balthild, these three kingdoms kept the harmony of peace among themselves.

. . .

At that time it happened that the heresy of simony stained the Church of God with its depraved practice in which they received the rank of bishop by paying a price for it. By the will of God [acting] through her, and at the urging of the good priests, the above-mentioned Lady Balthild stopped this impious evil so that no one would set a price on the taking of holy orders. Through her, the Lord also arranged for another very evil and impious practice to cease, one in which many men were more eager to kill their offspring than to provide for them in order to avoid the royal exactions which were inflicted upon them by custom, and from which they incurred a very heavy loss of property. This the lady prohibited for her own salvation so that no one presumed to do it. Because of this deed, truly a great reward awaits her.

. . .

Who, then, is able to say how many and how great were the sources of income, the entire farms and the large forests she gave up by donating them to the establishments of religious men in order to construct cells or monasteries? And she also

---

[11]Clothar III, king of Neustria, r. 657–73.
[12]Note how the author shows the broad base of the king's aristocratic support. This is the explanation for the peace in the realm.
[13]Childeric II, king of Austrasia 657–75 and of Neustria 673–75.

built as God's own and private houses a huge nunnery for women consecrated by God at Chelles, near Paris where she placed the religious handmaiden of God, the girl Bertila, in the position of the first mother. And in this place the venerable Lady Balthild in turn decided to dwell under the pure rule of religion and to rest in peace. And in truth she fulfilled this with a devoted will. . . .

. . .

Indeed, what else? To the religious man, Lord Filibert, at Jumièges, in order to build that monastery, she conceded both a large forest from the fisc where this monastery of brothers is located, and many gifts and pastures from the royal fisc.[14] Indeed, how many things, both a large villa and many talents of silver and gold, [did she concede] to Lord Laigobert for the monastery at Cobion?[15] Even her own royal belt, with which she was girded, she devotedly took from her holy loins and gave to the brothers in alms. All this she gave with a kind and joyous heart, for as Scripture says, *God loves the cheerful giver.*[16] Likewise, to both Saint-Wandrille[17] and Logium[18] she conceded much property. Indeed, how many things, both many large entire villas and innumerable sums of money, did she give to Luxeuil and to the other monasteries in Burgundy? What [did she give] to the monastery at Jouarre, whence she summoned the holy virgins with the above-mentioned Lady Bertila to her own monastery at Chelles? How many gifts of fields and how much money did she concede to that place? Likewise, she often gave large gifts to the monastery of Faremoutier. Near the city of Paris she conferred many large villas to the basilicas of the saints and to the monasteries, and she enriched them with many gifts. What more is there? As we said, we are not able to relate every one, not even with difficulty the half of them, and certainly all her good acts cannot be told by us. . . .

. . .

It was, however, her holy vow that she ought to dwell in the monastery of religious women which we mentioned above, that is, at Chelles, which she herself built. . . .

. . .

Indeed, with a most pious affection she loved her sisters as her own daughters, she obeyed their holy abbess as her mother, and rendered service to them as the lowest of handmaidens out of holy desire, just as [she had done] when she still ruled the royal palace and often visited her holy monastery. So strongly did she exhibit the example of great humility that she even served her sisters in the kitchen, and

---

[14]The fisc was the great body of land the Merovingian kings inherited from their Roman predecessors or took by right of royal conquest. One of the reasons given for the weakening of the dynasty was the diminution of the fisc through concessions such as the one mentioned here to the point where the royal house lost its economic base.

[15]Saint-Moutiers-au-Perbe (Orne).

[16]II Corinthians 9:7.

[17]Today, Saint-Wandrille-Rançon.

[18]Logium was a monastery for women in that part of Neustria which is now Normandy.

the lowest acts of cleaning, even the latrines, she herself did. All this she undertook with joy and a cheerful heart, in such humble service for Christ. For who would believe that the height of such power would serve in such lowly things if her most abundant and great love of Christ had not demanded it of her in every way? . . .

. . .

Indeed, we recall that other queens in the kingdom of the Franks have been noble and worshippers of God: Clothild, queen of the late King Clovis of old[19] and niece of King Gundobad,[20] who, by her holy exhortations, led both her very brave and pagan husband and many of the Frankish nobles to Christianity and brought them to the Catholic faith. She also was the first to construct the churches in honor of St. Peter at Paris and St. George in the little monastery for virgins at Chelles, and she founded many others in honor of the saints in order to store up her reward, and she enriched them with many gifts. The same is said of Ultrogoda, queen of the most Christian King Childebert,[21] because she was a comforter of the poor and a helper of the servants of God and of monks. And [it is said] also of Queen Radegund, truly a most faithful handmaiden of God, queen of the late elder King Clothar,[22] whom the grace of the Holy Spirit had so inflamed that she left her husband while he was still alive and consecrated herself to the Lord Christ under the holy veil, and, with Christ as her spouse, accomplished many good things. . . .

But it is pleasing, nevertheless, to consider this about her whom it here concerns: the Lady Balthild. Her many good deeds were accomplished in our times, and that these things were done by her herself we have learned in the best manner. Concerning these things, we have here commemorated a few out of the many, and we do not think her to be the inferior in merits of those earlier [queens]; rather we know her to have outdone them in holy striving. After the many good things which she did before her evangelical perfection, she gave herself over to voluntary holy obedience and as a true nun she happily completed her blessed life under complete religious practice. Her holy death and her holy rites are celebrated on 30 January, and, having been interred, she rests in peace in her monastery at Chelles. Truly she reigns in glory with Christ in heaven in everlasting joy, not unmindful, we believe, of her own faithful friends.

DISCUSSION QUESTIONS

1. Why does the author think that Lady Balthild's life is exemplary?

2. To whom do you think the author directed his or her message, and why?

3. What does this source suggest about women's role in Merovingian politics and the relationship between this role and Christian values?

---

[19]Clovis I (481–511).
[20]King of the Burgundians.
[21]Childebert I (511–58).
[22]Clothar I (511–61).

5.
Roman Christian Missions
Pope Gregory the Great, *Letters* (598–601)

Although Britain stood on the periphery of the empire, it, too, could not escape the turmoil of the late imperial period. After the Roman army was recalled to Italy, the Anglo-Saxons invaded the island in the 440s and replaced local traditions, including Christianity, with their own. In due course, however, Christianity was reintroduced from a variety of directions, of which Italy was among the most important. From here Pope Gregory I (r. 590–604) dispatched two groups of missionaries to establish Roman-style Christianity in England. The first group, sent in 595, was led by Augustine and the second was sent in 601 by Mellitus; both were monks from Rome. In these letters, Gregory describes the mission's initial progress and then offers strategies for furthering its success. He points not only to the pope's growing influence in the West but also to the interaction between Roman and non-Roman customs.

To Eulogius, Bishop of Alexandria

Gregory to Eulogius, &c.

Our common son, the bearer of these presents, when he brought the letters of your Holiness found me sick, and has left me sick; whence it has ensued that the scanty water of my brief epistle has been hardly able to exude to the large fountain of your Blessedness. But it was a heavenly boon that, while in a state of bodily pain, I received the letter of your Holiness to lift me up with joy for the instruction of the heretics of the city of Alexandria, and the concord of the faithful, to such an extent that the very joy of my mind moderated the severity of my suffering. And indeed we rejoice with new exultation to hear of your good doings, though at the same time we by no means suppose that it is a new thing for you to act thus perfectly. For that the people of holy Church increases, that spiritual crops of corn for the heavenly garner are multiplied, we never doubted that this was from the grace of Almighty God which flowed largely to you, most blessed ones. . . .

But, since in the good things you do I know that you also rejoice with others, I make you a return for your favor, and announce things not unlike yours; for while the nation of the Angli, placed in a corner of the world, remained up to this time misbelieving in the worship of stocks and stones, I determined, through the aid of your prayers for me, to send to it, God granting it, a monk of my monastery for the purpose of preaching. And he, having with my leave been made bishop by the bishops of Germany, proceeded, with their aid also, to the end of the world to the aforesaid nation; and already letters have reached us telling us of his safety and

From *A Select Library of Nicene and Post-Nicene Fathers of the Christian Church*, 2nd ser., vols. 12 and 13 (New York: Christian Literature Co., 1895 and 1898), 12:240, 13:84–85.

his work; to the effect that he and those that have been sent with him are resplendent with such great miracles in the said nation that they seem to imitate the powers of the apostles in the signs which they display. Moreover, at the solemnity of the Lord's Nativity which occurred in this first indiction, more than ten thousand Angli are reported to have been baptized by the same our brother and fellow-bishop. This have I told you, that you may know what you are effecting among the people of Alexandria by speaking, and what in the ends of the world by praying. For your prayers are in the place where you are not, while your holy operations are shewn in the place where you are.

To Mellitus, Abbot

Gregory to Mellitus, Abbot in France.

Since the departure of our congregation, which is with thee, we have been in a state of great suspense from having heard nothing of the success of your journey. But when Almighty God shall have brought you to our most reverend brother the bishop Augustine, tell him that I have long been considering with myself about the case of the Angli; to wit, that the temples of idols in that nation should not be destroyed, but that the idols themselves that are in them should be. Let blessed water be prepared, and sprinkled in these temples, and altars constructed, and relics deposited, since, if these same temples are well built, it is needful that they should be transferred from the worship of idols to the service of the true God; that, when the people themselves see that these temples are not destroyed, they may put away error from their heart, and, knowing and adoring the true God, may have recourse with the more familiarity to the places they have been accustomed to. And, since they are wont to kill many oxen in sacrifice to demons, they should have also some solemnity of this kind in a changed form, so that on the day of dedication, or on the anniversaries of the holy martyrs whose relics are deposited there, they may make for themselves tents of the branches of trees around these temples that have been changed into churches, and celebrate the solemnity with religious feasts. Nor let them any longer sacrifice animals to the devil, but slay animals to the praise of God for their own eating, and return thanks to the Giver of all for their fullness, so that, while some joys are reserved to them outwardly, they may be able the more easily to incline their minds to inward joys. For it is undoubtedly impossible to cut away everything at once from hard hearts, since one who strives to ascend to the highest place must needs rise by steps or paces, and not by leaps. Thus to the people of Israel in Egypt the Lord did indeed make Himself known; but still He reserved to them in His own worship the use of the sacrifices which they were accustomed to offer to the devil, enjoining them to immolate animals in sacrifice to Himself; to the end that, their hearts being changed, they should omit some things in the sacrifice and retain others, so that, though the animals were the same as what they had been accustomed to offer, nevertheless, as they immolated them to God and not to idols, they should be no longer the same sacrifices. This then it is necessary for thy Love to say to our aforesaid brother, that he, being now in that country, may consider well how he should arrange all things.

Discussion Questions

1. Earlier in his papacy, Gregory had advised the destruction of pagan temples. How does Gregory reverse this decision in his letter to Mellitus, and why?

2. What does Gregory's change of approach suggest about the ways in which Latin Christianity adapted to non-Roman cultures?

3. Historians often refer to Gregory I as the "father of the medieval papacy" because of the role he played in transforming the papacy into the moral and spiritual head of the West. What evidence can you find in these letters to support this view?

Comparative Questions

1. Based on these documents, in what ways did the Muslim, Byzantine, and western European worlds both perpetuate and diverge from the legacy of Rome?

2. What do these documents suggest about the relationship between religious beliefs and politics in both Christian and Islamic cultures during this period?

3. In his letter to Mellitus, Gregory I recommends adapting Christian practices to local customs. How did this strategy differ from the Muslims' approach to other traditions?

4. What similarities and differences do you see in the religious beliefs and principles enunciated in suras 1, 53, and 98 of the Qur'an, the *Life of St. Theodore*, and the *Life of Lady Balthild*?

CHAPTER

9

From Centralization to Fragmentation

750–1050

B etween 750 and 1050, competing forces of unity and fragmentation shaped the development of western Europe, Byzantium, and Islam, as the following documents reveal. The Carolingian king Charlemagne (r. 768–814) forged a vast kingdom, the scope of which had not been seen since Roman times. His success was based not simply on military victory but also on his ability to administer effectively the diverse regions under his rule (Document 1). Although the division of Charlemagne's empire in 843 opened the door to local rule, his legacy endured and enhanced Europe's distinctiveness from Byzantium (Document 2). By that time, the Byzantine emperors had regained much of their lost luster through military victory and a cultural revival (Document 3). Against this backdrop, the Islamic world continued to forge a unified sense of identity even as it fragmented into smaller political units (Documents 4 and 5). With Charlemagne's empire long gone, western Europe underwent its own political and social changes. Independent lords assumed control over many regions, relying on local networks of support and allegiance rather than the king for power (Document 6).

1.
The Rule of Charlemagne

General Capitulary for the Missi (802)

Although the Merovingians forged a powerful political polity on the demise of Roman provincial government, their success paled in comparison to that of the Carolingians, who deposed them in 751. By the 790s, the most famous Carolingian king,

From Dana Carleton Munro, ed., *Translations and Reprints from the Original Sources of European History*, vol. 6 (Philadelphia: University of Pennsylvania Press, 1898), 16–19, 23–24, 26–27.

Charlemagne (r. 768–814), had built an empire across Europe, using imperial Rome as a model. He was crowned emperor in 800 by Pope Leo III (r. 795–816), which further exalted his power. To centralize his rule, Charlemagne dispatched officials, or missi, *annually to every part of the empire to review local affairs and enforce royal legislation. The following document, known as a* capitulary, *provided basic guidelines for these annual visits. Composed of regulatory articles, capitularies were typically compiled at general assemblies convened by Charlemagne to discuss important issues with his magnates. These excerpts illuminate the forces binding the empire together as well as those that ultimately broke it apart.*

First chapter. Concerning the embassy sent out by the lord emperor. Therefore, the most serene and most Christian lord emperor Charles has chosen from his nobles the wisest and most prudent men, both archbishops and some of the other bishops also, and venerable abbots and pious laymen, and has sent them throughout his whole kingdom, and through them by all the following chapters has allowed men to live in accordance with the correct law. Moreover, where anything which is not right and just has been enacted in the law, he has ordered them to inquire into this most diligently and to inform him of it; he desires, God granting, to reform it. And let no one, through his cleverness or astuteness, dare to oppose or thwart the written law, as many are wont to do, or the judicial sentence passed upon him, or to do injury to the churches of God or the poor or the widows or the wards or any Christian. But all shall live entirely in accordance with God's precept, justly and under a just rule, and each one shall be admonished to live in harmony with his fellows in his business or profession; the canonical clergy ought to observe in every respect a canonical life without heeding base gain, nuns ought to keep diligent watch over their lives, laymen and the secular clergy ought rightly to observe their laws without malicious fraud, and all ought to live in mutual charity and perfect peace. And let the *missi* themselves make a diligent investigation whenever any man claims that an injustice has been done to him by any one, just as they desire to deserve the grace of omnipotent God and to keep their fidelity promised to Him, so that entirely in all cases everywhere, in accordance with the will and fear of God, they shall administer the law fully and justly in the case of the holy churches of God and of the poor, of wards and widows and of the whole people. And if there shall be anything of such a nature that they, together with the provincial courts, are not able of themselves to correct it and to do justice concerning it, they shall, without any ambiguity, refer this, together with their reports, to the judgment of the emperor; and the straight path of justice shall not be impeded by any one on account of flattery or gifts from any one, or on account of any relationship, or from fear of the powerful.

Concerning the fidelity to be promised to the lord emperor. And he commanded that every man in his whole kingdom, whether ecclesiastic or layman, and each one according to his vow and occupation, should now promise to him as emperor the fidelity which he had previously promised to him as king; and all of those who had not yet made that promise should do likewise, down to those who were twelve years old. And that it shall be announced to all in public, so that each one might know, how great and how many things are comprehended in that oath;

not merely, as many have thought hitherto, fidelity to the lord emperor as regards his life, and not introducing any enemy into his kingdom out of enmity, and not consenting to or concealing another's faithlessness to him; but that all may know that this oath contains in itself this meaning:

First, that each one voluntarily shall strive, in accordance with his knowledge and ability, to live wholly in the holy service of God in accordance with the precept of God and in accordance with his own promise, because the lord emperor is unable to give to all individually the necessary care and discipline.

Secondly, that no man, either through perjury or any other wile or fraud, on account of the flattery or gift of any one, shall refuse to give back or dare to abstract or conceal a serf of the lord emperor or a district or land or anything that belongs to him; and that no one shall presume, through perjury or other wile, to conceal or abstract his fugitive fiscaline serfs who unjustly and fraudulently say that they are free.

That no one shall presume to rob or do any injury fraudulently to the churches of God or widows or orphans or pilgrims; for the lord emperor himself, after God and His saints, has constituted himself their protector and defender.

That no one shall dare to lay waste a benefice of the lord emperor, or to make it his own property.

That no one shall presume to neglect a summons to war from the lord emperor; and that no one of the counts shall be so presumptuous as to dare to dismiss thence any one of those who owe military service, either on account of relationship or flattery or gifts from any one.

That no one shall presume to impede at all in any way a ban or command of the lord emperor, or to dally with his work or to impede or to lessen or in any way to act contrary to his will or commands. And that no one shall dare to neglect to pay his dues or tax.

That no one, for any reason, shall make a practice in court of defending another unjustly, either from any desire of gain when the cause is weak, or by impeding a just judgment by his skill in reasoning, or by a desire of oppressing when the cause is weak. But each one shall answer for his own cause or tax or debt unless any one is infirm or ignorant of pleading; for these the *missi* or the chiefs who are in the court or the judge who knows the case in question shall plead before the court; or if it is necessary, such a person may be allowed as is acceptable to all and knows the case well; but this shall be done wholly according to the convenience of the chiefs or *missi* who are present. But in every case it shall be done in accordance with justice and the law; and that no one shall have the power to impede justice by a gift, reward, or any kind of evil flattery or from any hindrance of relationship. And that no one shall unjustly consent to another in anything, but that with all zeal and goodwill all shall be prepared to carry out justice.

For all the above mentioned ought to be observed by the imperial oath.

That bishops and priests shall live according to the canons and shall teach others to do the same.

That bishops, abbots, abbesses, who are in charge of others, with the greatest veneration shall strive to surpass their subjects in this diligence and shall not oppress their subjects with a harsh rule or tyranny, but with sincere love shall carefully guard the flock committed to them with mercy and charity or by the examples of good works. . . .

That bishops, abbots and abbesses, and counts shall be mutually in accord, following the law in order to render a just judgment with all charity and unity of peace, and that they shall live faithfully in accordance with the will of God, so that always everywhere through them and among them a just judgment shall be rendered. The poor, widows, orphans and pilgrims shall have consolation and defense from them; so that we, through their goodwill, may deserve the reward of eternal life rather than punishment. . . .

That counts and *centenarii*[1] shall compel all to do justice in every respect, and shall have such assistants in their ministries as they can securely confide in, who will observe law and justice faithfully, who will oppress the poor in no manner, who will not dare under any pretext, on account of flattery or reward, to conceal thieves, robbers, murderers, adulterers, magicians, wizards or witches, and all sacrilegious men, but instead will give them up that they may be punished and chastised in accordance with the law, so that, God granting it, all of these evils may be removed from the Christian people.

That judges shall judge justly in accordance with the written law, and not according to their own will.

And we command that no one in our whole kingdom shall dare to deny hospitality to rich or poor or pilgrims, that is, no one shall deny shelter and fire and water to pilgrims traversing our country in God's name, or to anyone travelling for the love of God or for the safety of his own soul. . . .

Concerning embassies coming from the lord emperor. That the counts and *centenarii* shall provide most carefully, as they desire the grace of the lord emperor, for the *missi* who are sent out, so that they may go through their departments without any delay; and he commands to all everywhere that they ought to see to it that no delay is encountered anywhere, but they shall cause them to go on their way in all haste and shall provide for them in such a manner as our *missi* may direct. . . .

And against those who announce the justice of the lord emperor, let no one presume to plot any injury or damage, or to stir up any enmity. But if any one shall have presumed, let him pay the imperial ban or, if he deserves a heavier punishment, it is commanded that he shall be brought to the emperor's presence. . . .

That all shall be fully and well prepared, whenever our order or proclamation shall come. But if any one shall then say that he was unprepared and shall have neglected our command, he shall be brought to the palace; and not only he, but also all who dare to transgress our ban or command. . . .

And that all shall be entirely of one mind with our *missi* in performing justice in every respect. And that they shall not permit the use of perjury at all, for it is necessary that this most evil crime shall be removed from the Christian people. But if any one after this shall have been proved a perjurer, let him know that he shall lose his right hand; and they shall be deprived of their property until we shall render our decision. . . .

---

[1]A *centenarius* is the ruler of a subdivision of a province or county.

Lastly, therefore, we desire all our decrees to be known in our whole kingdom through our *missi* now sent out, either among the men of the church, bishops, abbots, priests, deacons, canons, all monks or nuns, so that each one in his ministry or profession may keep our ban or decree, or where it may be fitting to thank the citizens for their good will, or to furnish aid, or where there may be need still of correcting anything. Likewise also to the laymen and in all places everywhere, whether they concern the guardianship of the holy churches or of widows and orphans and the weaker; or the robbing of them; or the arrangements for the assembling of the army; or any other matters; how they are to be obedient to our precept and will, or how they observe our ban, or how each one strives in all things to keep himself in the holy service of God; so that all these good things may be well done to the praise of omnipotent God, and we may return thanks where it is fitting. But where we believe there is anything unpunished, we shall so strive to correct it with all our zeal and will that with God's aid we may bring it to correction, both for our own eternal glory and that of all our faithful. Likewise we desire all the above to be fruitfully known by our counts or *centenarii*, our ministerials.

DISCUSSION QUESTIONS

1. What does this document reveal about Charlemagne's vision of himself and his empire? In what ways were his Christian beliefs central to both?

2. Why might Charlemagne have considered it necessary for all freemen to swear an oath of fidelity to him as emperor? How was the notion of fidelity crucial to the success of his government?

3. What do the articles suggest about the means by which Charlemagne sought to unify his empire?

2.
Resistance from Constantinople
Liutprand of Cremona, *Report to Otto I* (968)

The Carolingian successors of King Charlemagne (r. 768–814) could not sustain his unifying vision. Wracked by family squabbles, the empire was divided into three kingdoms in 843. The imperial title lived on, however, in the Ottonian dynasty that succeeded the Carolingians in Germany in the tenth century. Fashioning himself in Charlemagne's image, Otto I (r. 936–973) was the most powerful of these rulers. Crowned emperor in 962, Otto treated his Byzantine counterpart as an equal. To enhance his status, Otto dispatched his ambassador Liutprand (c. 920–972), a northern Italian bishop, to Constantinople in 968 to arrange the marriage of Otto's son to a Byzantine princess. With this goal in mind, Liutprand met with the Byzantine emperor Nicephorus Phocas (r. 963–969). As he describes in a report sent to Otto,

From *The Works of Liutprand of Cremona*, trans. F. A. Wright (New York: E. P. Dutton, 1930), 235–43.

excerpted here, his efforts were in vain, and the failed mission elucidates the widen-
ing gap between the emerging territorial kingdoms in the West and Byzantium.

> That the Ottos, the invincible august emperors of the Romans and the
> most noble Adelaide the august empress, may always flourish, prosper
> and triumph, is the earnest wish, desire and prayer of Liutprand bishop of
> the holy church of Cremona.

On the fourth of June we arrived at Constantinople, and after a miserable reception, meant as an insult to yourselves, we were given the most miserable and disgusting quarters. The palace where we were confined was certainly large and open,
but it neither kept out the cold nor afforded shelter from the heat. Armed soldiers
were set to guard us and prevent my people from going out, and any others from
coming in. This dwelling, only accessible to us who were shut inside it, was so far
distant from the emperor's residence that we were quite out of breath when we
walked there — we did not ride. To add to our troubles, the Greek wine we found
undrinkable because of the mixture in it of pitch, resin, and plaster. The house
itself had no water and we could not even buy any to quench our thirst. All this was
a serious "Oh dear me!" but there was another "Oh dear me" even worse, and that
was our warden, the man who provided us with our daily wants. If you were to
seek another like him, you certainly would not find him on earth; you might perhaps in hell. Like a raging torrent he poured upon us every calamity, every extor-
tion, every expense, every grief, and every misery that he could invent. . . .

On the fourth of June, as I said above, we arrived at Constantinople and
waited with our horses in heavy rain outside the Carian gate until five o'clock in
the afternoon. At five o'clock Nicephorus ordered us to be admitted on foot, for he
did not think us worthy to use the horses with which your clemency had provided
us, and we were escorted to the aforesaid hateful, waterless, draughty stone house.
On the sixth of June, which was the Saturday before Pentecost, I was brought before
the emperor's brother Leo, marshal of the court and chancellor; and there we tired
ourselves with a fierce argument over your imperial title. He called you not
emperor, which is Basileus in his tongue, but insultingly Rex, which is king in ours.
I told him that the thing meant was the same though the word was different, and
he then said that I had come not to make peace but to stir up strife. Finally he got
up in a rage, and really wishing to insult us received your letter not in his own hand
but through an interpreter. . . .

On the seventh of June, the sacred day of Pentecost, I was brought before
Nicephorus himself in the palace called Stephana, that is, the Crown Palace. He is
a monstrosity of a man, a dwarf, fat-headed and with tiny mole's eyes; disfigured
by a short, broad, thick beard half going gray; disgraced by a neck scarcely an inch
long; piglike by reason of the big close bristles on his head; in color an Ethiopian
and, as the poet [Juvenal] says, "you would not like to meet him in the dark"; a
big belly, a lean posterior, very long in the hip considering his short stature, small
legs, fair sized heels and feet; dressed in a robe made of fine linen, but old, foul
smelling, and discolored by age; shod with Sicyonian slippers; bold of tongue, a fox

by nature, in perjury and falsehood a Ulysses. My lords and august emperors, you always seemed comely to me; but how much more comely now! Always magnificent; how much more magnificent now! Always mighty; how much more mighty now! Always clement; how much more clement now! Always full of virtues; how much fuller now! At his left, not on a line with him, but much lower down, sat the two child emperors, once his masters, now his subjects. He began his speech as follows: —

It was our duty and our desire to give you a courteous and magnificent reception. That, however, has been rendered impossible by the impiety of your master, who in the guise of an hostile invader has laid claim to Rome; has robbed Berengar and Adalbert of their kingdom contrary to law and right; has slain some of the Romans by the sword, some by hanging, while others he has either blinded or sent into exile; and furthermore has tried to subdue to himself by massacre and conflagration cities belonging to our empire. His wicked attempts have proved unsuccessful, and so he has sent you, the instigator and furtherer of this villainy, under pretence of peace to act *comme un espion*, that is, as a spy upon us.

To him I made this reply: "My master did not invade the city of Rome by force nor as a tyrant; he freed her from a tyrant's yoke, or rather from the yoke of many tyrants. Was she not ruled by effeminate debauchers, and what is even worse and more shameful, by harlots? Your power, methinks, was fast asleep then; and the power of your predecessors, who in name alone are called emperors of the Romans, while the reality is far different. If they were powerful, if they were emperors of the Romans, why did they allow Rome to be in the hands of harlots?" . . .

"Come, let us clear away all trickeries and speak the plain truth. My master has sent me to you to see if you will give the daughter of the emperor Romanos and the empress Theophano to his son, my master the august emperor Otto. If you give me your oath that the marriage shall take place, I am to affirm to you under oath that my master in grateful return will observe to do this and this for you. Moreover he has already given you, his brother ruler, the best pledge of friendship by handing over Apulia, which was subject to his rule. . . .

"It is past seven o'clock," said Nicephorus "and there is a church procession which I must attend. Let us keep to the business before us. We will give you a reply at some convenient season."

I think that I shall have as much pleasure in describing this procession as my masters will have in reading of it. . . .

As Nicephorus, like some crawling monster, walked along, the singers began to cry out in adulation: "Behold the morning star approaches: the day star rises: in his eyes the sun's rays are reflected: Nicephorus our prince, the pale death of the Saracens." And then they cried again: "Long life, long life to our prince Nicephorus. Adore him, ye nations, worship him, bow the neck to his greatness." How much more truly might they have sung: — "Come, you miserable burnt-out coal; old woman in your walk, wood-devil in your look; clodhopper, haunter of byres, goat-footed, horned, double-limbed; bristly, wild, rough, barbarian, harsh, hairy, a rebel, a Cappadocian!" So, puffed up by these lying ditties, he entered St. Sophia, his masters the emperors following at a distance and doing him homage on the ground with the kiss of peace. His armor bearer, with an arrow for pen, recorded in the church the era in progress since the beginning of his reign. So those who did not see the ceremony know what era it is.

On this same day he ordered me to be his guest. But as he did not think me worthy to be placed above any of his nobles, I sat fifteenth from him and without a table cloth. Not only did no one of my suite sit at table with me; they did not even set eyes upon the house where I was entertained. At the dinner, which was fairly foul and disgusting, washed down with oil after the fashion of drunkards and moistened also with an exceedingly bad fish liquor, the emperor asked me many questions concerning your power, your dominions, and your army. My answers were sober and truthful; but he shouted out: — "You lie. Your master's soldiers cannot ride and they do not know how to fight on foot. The size of their shields, the weight of their cuirasses, the length of their swords, and the heaviness of their helmets, does not allow them to fight either way." Then with a smile he added: "Their gluttony also prevents them. Their God is their belly, their courage but wind, their bravery drunkenness. Fasting for them means dissolution, sobriety, panic. Nor has your master any force of ships on the sea. I alone have really stout sailors, and I will attack him with my fleets, destroy his maritime cities and reduce to ashes those which have a river near them. Tell me, how with his small forces will he be able to resist me even on land?" . . .

I wanted to answer and make such a speech in our defense as his boasting deserved; but he would not let me and added this final insult: "You are not Romans but Lombards." He even then was anxious to say more and waved his hand to secure my silence, but I was worked up and cried: "History tells us that Romulus, from whom the Romans get their name, was a fratricide born in adultery. He made a place of refuge for himself and received into it insolvent debtors, runaway slaves, murderers, and men who deserved death for their crimes. This was the sort of crowd whom he enrolled as citizens and gave them the name of Romans. From this nobility are descended those men whom you style 'rulers of the world.' But we Lombards, Saxons, Franks, Lotharingians, Bavarians, Swabians, and Burgundians, so despise these fellows that when we are angry with an enemy we can find nothing more insulting to say than — 'You Roman!' For us in the word Roman is comprehended every form of lowness, timidity, avarice, luxury, falsehood, and vice. You say that we are unwarlike and know nothing of horsemanship. Well, if the sins of the Christians merit that you keep this stiff neck, the next war will prove what manner of men you are, and how warlike we."

DISCUSSION QUESTIONS

1. How would you characterize Liutprand as an observer of the Byzantine court?

2. At the time of Liutprand's visit, Byzantium was enjoying renewed power and influence. How might this have shaped the Byzantine court's attitudes toward Liutprand and his master, Otto I?

3. Why did the Byzantine emperor's brother refer to Otto I as "Rex"? Why did Liutprand find this so insulting? What does this suggest about the ways in which the West and Byzantium had grown different both politically and culturally?

3.
The Macedonian Renaissance
Harbaville Triptych (c. 950)

His contempt aside, at the time of Liutprand of Cremona's visit, the Byzantine Empire was thriving. Ongoing military success had expanded its borders while infusing the imperial court with new wealth and power. Among the most striking features of the empire's vitality was a surge in artistic activity aimed at reviving the glory of Byzantium's past. With the iconoclastic period firmly behind them, the emperor and the local elite sponsored artists to craft Christian icons for both private and public worship. They, like ordinary Byzantines, believed icons were more than images; rather they were physical manifestations of the holy people they depicted and as such, possessed sacred power. The Harbaville Triptych is typical of Byzantine art in this period. Carved in ivory and intended for personal devotion, the triptych comprises a center panel and two wings that open and close. This design allowed for easy transport. When open, as it would have been when in use, the triptych measures nine and a half by eleven inches. The center panel is divided into two registers. At the top is a

The Bridgeman Art Library/Getty Images.

representation of Christ enthroned, with the Virgin Mary and Saint John the Baptist at his side as intercessors for humanity, a popular Byzantine image called the Deesis. *Below them stand five more saints, including St. Peter whose finger is pointed to draw the viewer's eye to Christ. Each inner wing panel includes two pairs of standing saints and one pair of saints in medallions. All four standing saints in the upper register are military saints, as their style of dress and attributes reveal. The saints in the lower register all bear a martyr's cross and wear a courtier's costume; this choice was customary for works connected to imperial circles. The names of the saints appear next to their heads.*

DISCUSSION QUESTIONS

1. Look closely at the human figures in the triptych. How would you describe them stylistically in terms of their shape and their clothes? Why do you think the sculptor paid such close attention to these details?

2. What effect do you think the overall composition and arrangement of the triptych may have had on viewers at the time? What do both suggest about the importance of icons in Byzantine society?

3. In what ways does the piece reflect the empire's newfound wealth and confidence in the tenth century?

4.
A New Islamic Dynasty
Ahmad al-Ya'qūbī, *Kitāb al-buldān* (Ninth Century)

At the same time Carolingian emperor Charlemagne (r. 768–814) was forging his empire, Islamic leaders were strengthening their own. In 750, a new dynasty, the Abbasids, seized control of the Islamic state, which they brought to new heights of power and influence. The foundation of a new capital city, Baghdad, in 762 by the Abbasids physically embodied the revolutionary nature of their rule. In the first fifty years of their reign, they transformed Baghdad into the hub of the Islamic state. An early historian of Islam and descendant of the Abbasid family, Ahmad al-Ya'qūbī (d. 897), experienced the dynamism of the city firsthand during his travels as a young man, and he later included his observations in a geographical work, Kitāb al-buldān, *which he wrote near the end of his life. Although composed after economic problems had begun to tarnish the Abbasids' luster,* Kitāb al-buldān *elucidates the cultural and economic forces binding the Islamic world together even at a time when the caliphate was fragmenting into separate political units.*

From Bernard Lewis, ed., *Islam from the Prophet Muhammad to the Capture of Constantinople,* vol. 2 (New York: Walker & Co., 1974), 69–73.

I begin with Iraq only because it is the center of this world, the navel of the earth, and I mention Baghdad first because it is the center of Iraq, the greatest city, which has no peer in the east or the west of the world in extent, size, prosperity, abundance of water, or health of climate, and because it is inhabited by all kinds of people, town-dwellers and country-dwellers. To it they come from all countries, far and near, and people from every side have preferred Baghdad to their own homelands. There is no country, the peoples of which have not their own quarter and their own trading and financial arrangements. In it there is gathered that which does not exist in any other city in the world. On its flanks flow two great rivers, the Tigris and the Euphrates, and thus goods and foodstuffs come to it by land and by water with the greatest ease, so that every kind of merchandise is completely available, from east and west, from Muslim and non-Muslim lands. Goods are brought from India, Sind, China, Tibet, the lands of the Turks, the Daylam, the Khazars, the Ethiopians, and others to such an extent that the products of the countries are more plentiful in Baghdad than in the countries from which they come. They can be procured so readily and so certainly that it is as if all the good things of the world are sent there, all the treasures of the earth assembled there, and all the blessings of creation perfected there.

Furthermore, Baghdad is the city of the Hashimites, the home of their reign, the seat of their sovereignty, where no one appeared before them and no kings but they have dwelt. Also, my own forbears have lived there, and one of them was governor of the city.

Its name is famous, and its fame widespread. Iraq is indeed the center of the world, for in accordance with the consensus of the astronomers recorded in the writings of ancient scholars, it is in the fourth climate, which is the middle climate where the temperature is regular at all times and seasons. It is very hot in the summer, very cold in the winter, and temperate in autumn and in spring. The passage from autumn to winter and from spring to summer is gradual and imperceptible, and the succession of the seasons is regular. So, the weather is temperate, the soil is rich, the water is sweet, the trees are thriving, the fruit luscious, the seeds are fertile, good things are abundant, and springs are easily found. Because of the temperate weather and rich soil and sweet water, the character of the inhabitants is good, their faces bright, and their minds untrammeled. The people excel in knowledge, understanding, letters, manners, insight, discernment, skill in commerce and crafts, cleverness in every argument, proficiency in every calling, and mastery of every craft. There is none more learned than their scholars, better informed than their traditionists, more cogent than their theologians, more perspicuous than their grammarians, more accurate than their readers, more skillful than their physicians, more melodious than their singers, more delicate than their craftsmen, more literate than their scribes, more lucid than their logicians, more devoted than their worshippers, more pious than their ascetics, more juridical than their judges, more eloquent than their preachers, more poetic than their poets, and more reckless than their rakes.

In ancient days, that is to say in the time of the Chosroes and the Persians, Baghdad was not a city, but only a village in the district of Bādārayā. The city in

Iraq which the Chosroes had chosen for their capital was al-Madā'in, seven para-sangs[1] from Baghdad. The audience chamber of Chosroes Anushirvan is still there. At that time there was nothing in Baghdad but a convent situated at a place called Qarn al-Ṣarāt, at the confluence of the Ṣarāt and the Tigris. This convent is called al-Dayr al-'Atīq [the ancient convent] and is still standing at the present time. It is the residence of the Catholicos, the head of the Nestorian Christians.

Nor does Baghdad figure in the wars of the Arabs at the time of the advent of Islam, since the Arabs founded Basra and Kūfa. Kūfa was founded in the year 17 [638] by Saʿd ibn Abī Waqqās al-Zuhrī, one of 'Umar ibn al-Khaṭṭāb's governors. Basra, too, was founded in the year 17 by 'Utba ibn Ghazwān al-Māzini of the tribe of Māzin of Qays, also a governor of 'Umar ibn al-Khaṭṭāb at that time. The Arabs settled down in these two places, but the important people, the notables, and the rich merchants moved to Baghdad.

The Umayyads lived in Syria and did not stay in Iraq. Mu'āwiya ibn Abī Sufyān, who had been governor of Syria in the name of 'Umar ibn al-Khaṭṭāb and then of 'Uthmān ibn 'Affān for twenty years, lived in Damascus with his family. When he seized power and sovereignty passed to him, he kept his residence and capital in Damascus, where he had his authority, his supporters, and his faction. The Umayyad kings after Mu'āwiya stayed in Damascus, since they were born there and knew no other place, and its people were their sole supporters.

Then the Caliphate came to the descendants of the paternal uncle of the Apostle of God, may God bless and save him and also his family, the line of 'Ab-bās ibn 'Abd al-Muṭṭālib. Thanks to clear discernment, sound intelligence, and perfect judgment, they saw the merits of Iraq, its magnificence, spaciousness, and central situation. They saw that it was not like Syria, with its pestilential air, narrow houses, rugged soil, constant diseases, and uncouth people; nor was it like Egypt, with changeable weather and many plagues, situated between a damp and fetid river, full of unhealthy mists that engender disease and spoil food, and the dry, bare mountains, so dry and salty and bad that no plant can grow nor any spring appear; nor like Ifriqiya, far from the peninsula of Islam and from the holy house of God, with uncouth people and many foes; nor like Armenia, remote, cold and icy, bar-ren, and surrounded by enemies; nor like the districts of the Jabal, harsh, rough, and snow-covered, the abode of the hard-hearted Kurds; nor like the land of Khurāsān, stretching to the east, surrounded on every side by rabid and war-like enemies; nor like the Ḥijāz where life is hard and means are few and the people's food comes from elsewhere, as Almighty God warned us in His book, through His friend Ibrāhīm, who said, "O Lord, I have given to my descendants as dwelling a valley without tillage" [Qur'an]; nor like Tibet, where, because of the foul air and food, the people are discolored, with stunted bodies and tufty hair.

When they understood that Iraq was the best of countries, the 'Abbasids decided to settle there. In the first instance the Commander of the Faithful, Abu'l-'Abbās, that is 'Abdallāh ibn Muhammad ibn 'Alī ibn 'Abdallāh ibn 'Abbās ibn 'Abd al-Muṭṭālib, stayed in Kūfa. Then he moved to Anbār and built a city on the banks

---

[1]**parasangs**: An ancient unit of distance totaling about four miles. [Ed.]

of the Euphrates which he called Hāshimiyya. Abu'l-'Abbās, may God be pleased with him, died before the building of this city was completed.

Then, when Abū Ja'far al-Manṣūr succeeded to the Caliphate, he founded a new city between Kūfa and Ḥīra, which he also called Hāshimiyya. He stayed there for a while, until the time when he decided to send his son, Muhammad al-Mahdī, to fight the Slavs in the year 140 [757–758]. He then came to Baghdad and stopped there, and asked, "What is the name of this place?" They answered, "Baghdad." "By God," said the Caliph, "this is indeed the city which my father Muhammad ibn 'Alī told me I must build, in which I must live, and in which my descendants after me will live. Kings were unaware of it before and since Islam, until God's plans for me and orders to me are accomplished. Thus, the traditions will be verified and the signs and proofs be manifest. Indeed, this island between the Tigris in the east and the Euphrates in the west is a marketplace for the world. All the ships that come up the Tigris from Wāsiṭ, Basra, Ubulla, Ahwāz, Fārs, 'Umān, Yamāma, Baḥrayn, and beyond will anchor here; wares brought on ships down the Tigris from Mosul, Diyār-Rabī'a, Ādharbayjān, and Armenia, and along the Euphrates from Diyār-Muḍar, Raqqa, Syria, the border marches, Egypt, and North Africa, will be brought and unloaded here. It will be the highway for the people of the Jabal, Iṣfahān, and the districts of Khurāsān. Praise be to God who preserved it for me and caused all those who came before me to neglect it. By God, I shall build it. Then I shall dwell in it as long as I live, and my descendants shall dwell in it after me. It will surely be the most flourishing city in the world."

DISCUSSION QUESTIONS

1. Considering Ahmad al-Ya'qūbī's family connections, to what extent can we accept his view of Baghdad, and why?

2. What does Ahmad al-Ya'qūbī reveal about the geographical breadth and ethnic diversity of the Islamic empire?

3. As described here, how did trade help unify the Islamic empire at a time when it was beginning to fragment politically?

5.
Advances in Medicine
Abū Bakr Muhammad ibn Zakarīyū Al-rāzī, *A Treatise on the Small-Pox and Measles* (c. 910)

Despite the rise of independent Islamic states in the ninth and tenth centuries, the Islamic world remained interconnected through language, commerce, and increasingly through learning. The Abbasid caliphs had set this process into motion by establishing research libraries and institutes for the study and translation of the classics of

From Abū Bakr Muhammad ibn Zakarīyū Al-rāzī, *A Treatise on the Small-Pox and Measles* (London: Sydenham Society, 1848), 24–25, 27–31.

Persia, India, and Greece. With the decline of the Abbasid dynasty, local rulers stepped in as patrons and supporters of science, math, medicine, and the arts. Muslim philosopher and physician Abū Bakr Muhammad ibn Zakarīyū Al-rāzī (c. 865–c. 925) was an influential product and propagator of the diffusion of Islamic learning and intellectual achievement. Born in the Iranian city of Rayy, Al-rāzī studied medicine in Baghdad and eventually became the director of a large hospital there. He wrote numerous philosophical and medical works, including A Treatise on the Small-Pox and Measles. *In the excerpt that follows, Al-rāzī sets forth his views on the cause of the disease, which he asserts neither ancient nor contemporary scholars had sufficiently addressed. He takes particular aim at Galen, a second-century Greek physician whose writings had been translated into Arabic. Although Al-rāzī's treatise was not the first work on the topic, it had a wide and enduring impact in the Muslim world and beyond. In the eighteenth century, it was translated twice into Latin at a time when Lady Mary Wortley Montagu brought public attention to the Turkish practice of inoculation against smallpox.*

In the name of God, the Compassionate, the Merciful.

. . . It happened on a certain night at a meeting in the house of a nobleman, of great goodness and excellence, and very anxious for the explanation and facilitating of useful sciences for the good of mankind, that, mention having been made of the Small-Pox, I then spoke what came into my mind on that subject. Whereupon our host (may God favor men by prolonging the remainder of his life,) wished me to compose a suitable, solid, and complete discourse on this disease, because there has not appeared up to this present time either among the ancients or the moderns an accurate and satisfactory account of it. And therefore I composed this discourse, hoping to receive my reward from the Almighty and Glorious God, and awaiting His good pleasure.

Of the Causes of the Small-Pox; How It Comes to Pass That Hardly Any One Escapes the Disease; and the Sum of What Galen Says Concerning It

As to any physician who says that the excellent Galen has made no mention of the Small-Pox, and was entirely ignorant of this disease, surely he must be one of those who have either never read his works at all, or who have passed over them very cursorily.

If, however, any one says that Galen has not mentioned any peculiar and satisfactory mode of treatment for this disease, nor any complete cause, he is certainly correct. . . . As for my own part, I have most carefully inquired of those who use both the Syriac and Greek languages, and have asked them about this matter; but there was not one of them who could add anything. . . . This I was much surprised at, and also how it was that Galen passed over this disease which occurs so frequently and requires such careful treatment, when he is so eager in finding out the causes and treatment of other maladies.

As to the moderns, although they have certainly made some mention of the treatment of the Small-Pox, (but without much accuracy and distinctness,) yet there is not one of them who has mentioned the cause of the existence of the disease, and how it comes to pass that hardly any one escapes it, or who has disposed the modes of treatment in their right places. And for this reason we hope that the reward of that man who encouraged us to compose this treatise, and also our own, will be doubled, since we have mentioned whatever is necessary for the treatment of this disease, and have arranged and carefully disposed every thing in its right place, by God's permission.

We will now begin therefore by mentioning the efficient cause of this distemper, and why hardly any one escapes it; and then we will treat of the other things that relate to it, section by section: and we will (with God's assistance,) speak on every one of these points with what we consider to be sufficient copiousness.

I say then that every man, from the time of his birth till he arrives at old age, is continually tending to dryness; and for this reason the blood of children and infants is much moister than the blood of young men, and still more so than that of old men. And besides this it is much hotter; as Galen testifies in his Commentary on the "Aphorisms," in which he says that "the heat of children is greater in quantity than the heat of young men, and the heat of young men is more intense in quality." And this also is evident from the force with which the natural processes, such as digestion and growth of body, are carried on in children. For this reason the blood of infants and children may be compared to must, in which the coction leading to perfect ripeness has not yet begun, nor the movement towards fermentation taken place; the blood of young men may be compared to must, which has already fermented and made a hissing noise, and has thrown out abundant vapors and its superfluous parts, like wine which is now still and quiet and arrived at its full strength; and as to the blood of old men, it may be compared to wine which has now lost its strength and is beginning to grow vapid and sour.

Now the Small-Pox arises when the blood putrefies and ferments, so that the superfluous vapors are thrown out of it, and it is changed from the blood of infants, which is like must, into the blood of young men, which is like wine perfectly ripened: and the Small-Pox itself may be compared to the fermentation and the hissing noise which take place in must at that time. And this is the reason why children, especially males, rarely escape being seized with this disease, because it is impossible to prevent the blood's changing from this state into its second state, just as it is impossible to prevent must (whose nature it is to make a hissing noise and to ferment,) from changing into the state which happens to it after its making a hissing noise and its fermentation. And the temperament of an infant or child is seldom such that it is possible for its blood to be changed from the first state into the second by little and little, and orderly, and slowly, so that this fermentation and hissing noise should not show itself in the blood: for a temperament, to change thus gradually, should be cold and dry; whereas that of children is just the contrary, as is also their diet, seeing that the food of infants consists of milk; and as for children, although their food does not consist of milk, yet it is nearer to it than is that of other ages; there is also a greater mixture in their food, and more movement after it; for which reason it is seldom that a child escapes this disease. Then afterwards alterations take place in their condition according to their temperaments, regimen, and natural disposition, the air that surrounds them, and the state of the vascular system both as to quantity and quality, for in some individuals the blood flows quickly, in others slowly, in some it is abundant, in others deficient, in some it is very bad in quality, in others less deteriorated.

As to young men, whereas their blood is already passed into the second state, its maturation is established, and the superfluous particles of moisture which necessarily cause putrefaction are now exhaled; hence it follows that this disease only happens to a few individuals among them, that is, to those whose vascular system abounds with too much moisture, or is corrupt in quality with a violent inflammation; or who in their childhood have had the Chicken-Pox, whereby the transition of the blood from the first into the second state has not been perfected. It takes place also in those who have a slight heat, or whose moisture is not copious; and to those who had the Chicken-Pox in their childhood, and are of a dry, lean habit of body, with slight and gentle heat; and who when they became young men, used a diet to strengthen and fatten their body, or a diet which corrupted their blood.

And as for old men, the Small-Pox seldom happens to them, except in pestilential, putrid, and malignant constitutions of the air, in which this disease is chiefly prevalent. For a putrid air, which has an undue proportion of heat and moisture, and also an inflamed air, promotes the eruption of this disease, by converting the spirit in the two ventricles of the heart to its own temperament, and then by means of the heart converting the whole of the blood in the arteries into a state of corruption like itself.[1]

DISCUSSION QUESTIONS

1. According to Al-rāzī, why did he write this treatise? What does his explanation suggest about Islamic attitudes toward science and its role in society?

2. As described by Al-rāzī, what is the cause of smallpox? What does his explanation reveal about his understanding of the human body?

3. Why do you think Al-rāzī invokes God in his treatise? Do you think it is less "scientific" as a result?

6.
The Faithful Vassal
Fulbert of Chartres, *Letter to William of Aquitaine* (1020)

Fragmented and under attack by outsiders, post-Carolingian Europe looked very different from the empire Charlemagne had envisioned. Counts and other local elites

---

From *Translations and Reprints from the Original Sources of European History*, vol. 4, no. 3 (Philadelphia: University of Pennsylvania Press, 1898), 23–24.

[1] This sentence affords a clear proof, that the ancients, while they considered the arteries to contain air, were also (at least after the time of Galen,) fully aware that blood was likewise to be found in them.

relied less on the king for new lands and offices and more on their own resources and networks. The glue binding these networks together was the notion of "fealty" by which local lords secured the personal loyalty and dependency of others, their "faithful men" (vassals). Duke William of Aquitaine, a very powerful lord in France who ruled from c. 995 to 1030, often found himself in conflict with his vassals. To clarify his and their obligations, he asked Fulbert, bishop of Chartres, to advise him on the matter. Fulbert's letter, written in 1020 and reproduced in full here, shows that many of the obligations were, like the Ten Commandments, negative ones.

To William most glorious duke of the Aquitanians, bishop Fulbert the favor of his prayers.

Asked to write something concerning the form of fealty, I have noted briefly for you on the authority of the books the things which follow. He who swears fealty to his lord ought always to have these six things in memory; what is harmless, safe, honorable, useful, easy, practicable. Harmless, that is to say that he should not be injurious to his lord in his body; safe, that he should not be injurious to him in his secrets or in the defenses through which he is able to be secure; honorable, that he should not be injurious to him in his justice or in other matters that pertain to his honor; useful, that he should not be injurious to him in his possessions; easy or practicable, that that good which his lord is able to do easily, he make not difficult, nor that which is practicable he make impossible to him.

However, that the faithful vassal should avoid these injuries is proper, but not for this does he deserve his holding; for it is not sufficient to abstain from evil, unless what is good is done also. It remains, therefore, that in the same six things mentioned above he should faithfully counsel and aid his lord, if he wishes to be looked upon as worthy of his benefice and to be safe concerning the fealty which he has sworn.

The lord also ought to act toward his faithful vassal reciprocally in all these things. And if he does not do this he will be justly considered guilty of bad faith, just as the former, if he should be detected in the avoidance of or the doing of or the consenting to them, would be perfidious and perjured.

I would have written to you at greater length, if I had not been occupied with many other things, including the rebuilding of our city and church which was lately entirely consumed in a great fire; from which loss though we could not for a while be diverted, yet by the hope of the comfort of God and of you we breathe again.

DISCUSSION QUESTIONS

1. According to Fulbert, what are the mutual duties of vassals and lords?
2. What do these duties reveal about the basis of local rule in post-Carolingian society?
3. What does the fact that William of Aquitaine asked a bishop for advice suggest about the relationship between secular and religious authorities at the time?

COMPARATIVE QUESTIONS

1. In what ways do Liutprand and Fulbert point to both the successes and failures of Charlemagne's political vision as revealed in the capitulary of the *missi*?

2. Based on Liutprand's account and the Harbaville Triptych, what factors shaped the Byzantine elites' self-understanding? What was Liutprand's attitude toward this understanding?

3. In what ways are Al-rāzī's intellectual achievements reflected in Ahmad al-Ya'qūbī's portrait of Baghdad?

4. How do Liutprand and Ahmad al-Ya'qūbī seek to enhance the image of their respective rulers? What does this suggest about the role of praise in both Eastern and Western cultures during the tenth century?

5. When viewed together, what do these documents reveal about the development of Byzantium, Islam, and western Europe as distinctive societies with their own identities in the ninth, tenth, and eleventh centuries?

CHAPTER 10

Commercial Quickening and Religious Reform

1050–1150

W estern Europe was alive with change in the late eleventh and early twelfth centuries. Trade and agricultural production were on the rise, promoting the development of a new, cash-based economy. A greater prevalence of wealth prompted a range of responses at all levels of medieval society. The first document set elucidates the innovative business arrangements that fueled the commercial revolution. With the economy booming, many ecclesiastical leaders feared that the church was becoming entangled in economic preoccupations. The second document suggests how this fear helped spark a religious reform movement that elevated the papacy to new heights of authority. The third document reveals this power in action when Pope Urban II called for the First Crusade in 1095. Heeding his call, tens of thousands of people from all walks of life left their homes to fight for God in the Holy Land. The fourth document allows us to see the crusade from a Muslim perspective as the crusaders made their way to Jerusalem. While the papacy expanded its reach through the First Crusade, the final document unveils how secular authorities strove to solidify their own power, buttressed by growing, fiscally minded bureaucracies and new ideologies of kingship.

1.
Medieval Business

Commenda *Contracts* (Eleventh–Twelfth Centuries)

Agricultural and commercial growth in the eleventh and twelfth centuries transformed Europe's landscape as new cities developed and old ones grew, all interconnected by local and long-distance trade networks. The creation of novel business agreements

From *Medieval Trade in the Mediterranean World*: Number LII of the *Records of Civilization, Sources and Studies*, ed. Austin P. Evans, trans. Robert S. Lopez and Irving W. Raymond (New York: Columbia University, 1961), 176–79.

through partnerships and contracts fueled the economic boom. One in particular was essential to the expansion of trade, the commenda *contract, sometimes translated as "business venture." The* commenda *had historical precedents but beginning in the tenth century it assumed unique characteristics in the Western Mediterranean, as illustrated in the examples below. Although known by different names in different places,* commenda *contracts all served the same purpose as legal tools for pooling capital and bringing together investors and managers for sea trade. Italy was a hub for these contracts as coastal cities like Genoa and Venice sought to establish and expand their maritime markets. The types of goods being traded varied widely; they included cotton, silk, sugar, gold, and spices. Sometimes both the investors and the traveling party provided capital for the venture (examples 1 and 3); other times, one party was the sole lender (example 4). When the traveling party returned, the terms of the contract were settled (example 2). In each instance, all parties involved shared the profits and the risks associated with the undertaking.*

The Venetian Commenda or Collegantia

1

Venice, August, 1073

In the name of the Lord God and of our Savior, Jesus Christ. In the year of the Incarnation of the same Redeemer of 1073, in the month of August, eleventh indiction, at Rialto,[1] I, Giovanni Lissado of Luprio together with my heirs, have received in *collegantia*[2] from you, Sevasto Orefice, son of Ser Trudimondo, and from your heirs, this [amount]: £200 [Venetian]. And I myself have invested £100 in it. And with this capital (*habere*) we have [acquired] two shares (*sortes*) in the ship of which Gosmiro da Molino is captain. And I am under obligation to bring all of this with me in *taxegio*[3] to Thebes in the ship in which the aforesaid Gosmiro da Molino sails as captain. Indeed, by this agreement and understanding of ours I promise to put to work this entire [capital] and to strive the best way I can. Then, if the capital is saved, we are to divide whatever profit the Lord may grant us from it by exact halves, without fraud and evil device. And whatever I can gain with those goods from any source, I am under obligation to invest all [of it] in the *collegantia*. And if all these goods are lost because of the sea or of [hostile] people, and this is proved — may this be averted — neither party ought to ask any of them from the other; if, however, some of them remain, in proportion as we invested so shall we share. Let this *collegantia* exist between us so long as our wills are fully agreed.

---

[1]Rialto ("high creek") is the original name of some of the islands which are now called Venice. Venice at first was the name of the entire region of which Rialto became the capital in the early ninth century.

[2]*collegantia*: The contracts are called *collegantia* according to the Venetian use. [Ed.]

[3]*Taxegium* is a word of Byzantine origin and means "commercial voyage" or "commercial journey."

But if I do not observe everything just as is stated above, I, together with my heirs, then promise to give and to return to you and your heirs everything in the double, both capital and profit (*caput et prode*), out of my land and my house or out of anything that I am known to have in this world.

Signature of the aforesaid Giovanni who requested this [instrument] to be made.

I, Pietro, witness, signed.

I, Lorenzo, witness, signed.

I, Gosmiro, witness, signed.

The full names of the witnesses are these: Pietro Gossoni; Lorenzo Scudaio; Gosmiro da Molino.

I, Domenico, cleric and notary, completed and certified [this instrument].

2

Venice, May, 1072[4]

In the name of the Lord God Almighty. In the year of the Incarnation of our Lord Jesus Christ 1072, in the month of May, tenth indiction, at Rialto. I, Domenico Zopulo, son of Vitale Zopulo junior, together with my heirs, do make to you, Giovanni Barozzi, son of Giovanni Barozzi, and to your heirs, full and irrevocable release[5] in regard to an instrument of record which you made to me, whereby I myself invested £50 in deniers[6] of good alloy and you by the same [instrument] invested £25, and [whereby] you went with all these goods in *taxegio* to Thebes in the ship of which Leone Orefice was captain. But now, since you have returned from said *taxegio*, you have rendered me a full, accurate, and true account of it, in regard to both the principal and the profit; under oath you have handed over everything to me and you have settled [accounts]. From now on you shall always remain released in regard to the principal and the profit or to the [penalty of the] double and to all that is stated in the said record, so that on no day and at no time [henceforth] are we to make any further demand or to exert [any more] pressure by any device, whether small or great. I, moreover, have returned to you the record itself. If a copy of it appears in my possession or in that of any man, it shall remain null and void, wholly without validity and force, because there is nothing left in it whereby we should make any further demand upon you. But if we at any time attempt to demand anything in regard to the clauses stated above, I, together with my heirs, promise to pay to you and to your heirs £5 in gold [as penalty], and this release shall [nevertheless] remain in force.

I, Domenico, signed by my hand.

I, Giovanni, witness, signed.

I, Domenico, witness, signed.

---

[4]. . . The parties and the witnesses belonged to the highest merchant nobility in Venice.

[5]*Securitatem*, literally, "security."

[6]**denier**: Coin used as a money of account; one pound was valued at the equivalent of 240 deniers. [Ed.]

I, Leone, witness, signed.

The full names of the witnesses are these: Giovanni, son of Pietro Michiel and Domenico, his brother; Leone, son of Domenico Michiel.

I, Giovanni, subdeacon and notary, completed and certified [this instrument].

The Genoese Commenda and Societas

3

[Genoa,] September 29, 1163

Witnesses: Simone Bucuccio, Ogerio Peloso, Ribaldo di Sauro, and Genoardo Tasca. Stabile and Ansaldo Garraton have formed a *societas*[7] in which, as they mutually declared, Stabile contributed £88 [Genoese] and Ansaldo £44. Ansaldo carries this *societas*, in order to put it to work, to Tunis or to wherever goes the ship in which he shall go—namely, [the ship] of Baldizzone Grasso and Girardo. On his return [he will place the proceeds] in the power of Stabile or of his messenger for [the purpose of] division. After deducting the capital, they shall divide the profits in half. Done in the chapter house, September 29, 1163, eleventh indiction.

In addition, Stabile gave his permission to send that money to Genoa by whatever ship seems most convenient to him [to Ansaldo].

4

[Genoa,] October 7, 1163

Witnesses: Bernizone Serra, Raimondo, Crispino and Pietro Vinattiere. I, Ingo Bedello, declare publicly that I am carrying £41 s.6 [Genoese] of goods belonging to Guglielmotto Ciriolo [invested] in silk and paper to Tunis, and from there to Genoa [where I shall place the proceeds] in the power of Guglielmotto or of his messenger. And he is not under obligation to contribute toward expenses in regard to them except in furnishing the [original] money. [Ingo] on his return [will place the proceeds] in the power of Guglielmotto or of his messenger and, after deducting the capital, he is to have one fourth of the profit. And Guglielmotto himself reserved as his right that there will be no expense for him in it. Done in the chapter house, October 7, 1163, eleventh indiction.

DISCUSSION QUESTIONS

1. The rise of a profit-based economy is one of the most distinctive features of this time period. How did the business arrangements described in these documents seek to maximize the profit of all parties involved?

2. What do these documents suggest about the extent of trade networks at the time and the types of goods being traded?

3. Do you see any similarities between these documents and modern business practices?

---

[7]*societas*: A bilateral commenda was called *societas* in Genoa, while *commenda* applied exclusively to the unilateral contract. [Ed.]

2.
Sources of the Investiture Conflict
Emperor Henry IV and Pope Gregory VII,
Letter and Excommunication (1076)

The commercial revolution helped spark not only economic changes but also religious ones. Pope Gregory VII (r. 1073–1085) became the driving force behind a movement for church reform, which strove to liberate the church from secular influence and wealth. His zeal brought him head-to-head with Emperor Henry IV (r. 1056–1106) who, claiming to be crowned by God, asserted the traditional right to oversee the church in his realm. These two documents illuminate each side of the debate. The first is a letter that Henry sent to the pope in January 1076 after Gregory had denounced him for not obeying papal mandates prohibiting, among other things, laymen from "investing" (that is, appointing) church leaders. In response, the pope excommunicated and deposed Henry. The lines of the conflict were thus drawn, pitting imperial and papal claims of authority against each other. Although the battle ended in 1122 with a compromise, the papacy emerged as a more powerful force than ever before.

Henry IV: Letter to Gregory VII

Henry, King not by usurpation, but by the pious ordination of God, to Hildebrand, now not Pope, but false monk:

You have deserved such a salutation as this because of the confusion you have wrought; for you left untouched no order of the Church which you could make a sharer of confusion instead of honor, of malediction instead of benediction.

For to discuss a few outstanding points among many: Not only have you dared to touch the rectors of the holy Church — the archbishops, the bishops, and the priests, anointed of the Lord as they are — but you have trodden them under foot like slaves who know not what their lord may do. In crushing them you have gained for yourself acclaim from the mouth of the rabble. You have judged that all these know nothing, while you alone know everything. In any case, you have sedulously used this knowledge not for edification, but for destruction, so greatly that we may believe Saint Gregory, whose name you have arrogated to yourself, rightly made this prophesy of you when he said: "From the abundance of his subjects, the mind of the prelate is often exalted, and he thinks that he has more knowledge than anyone else, since he sees that he has more power than anyone else."

And we, indeed, bore with all these abuses, since we were eager to preserve the honor of the Apostolic See. But you construed our humility as fear, and so you were emboldened to rise up even against the royal power itself, granted to us by

From *The Correspondence of Pope Gregory VII*, trans. Ephraim Emerton (New York: Columbia University Press, 1932), 90–91; and *Imperial Lives and Letters of the Eleventh Century*, trans. Theodor E. Mommsen and Karl F. Morrison (New York: Columbia University Press, 1962), 150–51.

God. You dared to threaten to take the kingship away from us — as though we had received the kingship from you, as though kingship and empire were in your hand and not in the hand of God.

Our Lord, Jesus Christ, has called us to kingship, but has not called you to the priesthood. For you have risen by these steps: namely, by cunning, which the monastic profession abhors, to money; by money to favor; by favor to the sword. By the sword you have come to the throne of peace, and from the throne of peace you have destroyed the peace. You have armed subjects against their prelates; you who have not been called by God have taught that our bishops who have been called by God are to be spurned; you have usurped for laymen the bishops' ministry over priests, with the result that these laymen depose and condemn the very men whom the laymen themselves received as teachers from the hand of God, through the imposition of the hands of bishops.

You have also touched me, one who, though unworthy, has been anointed to kingship among the anointed. This wrong you have done to me, although as the tradition of the holy Fathers has taught, I am to be judged by God alone and am not to be deposed for any crime unless — may it never happen — I should deviate from the Faith. For the prudence of the holy bishops entrusted the judgment and the deposition even of Julian the Apostate not to themselves, but to God alone. The true pope Saint Peter also exclaims, "Fear God, honor the king." You, however, since you do not fear God, dishonor me, ordained of Him.

Wherefore, when Saint Paul gave no quarter to an angel from heaven if the angel should preach heterodoxy, he did not except you who are now teaching heterodoxy throughout the earth. For he says, "If anyone, either I or an angel from heaven, preach any other gospel unto you than that which we have preached unto you, let him be accursed." Descend, therefore, condemned by this anathema and by the common judgment of all our bishops and of ourself. Relinquish the Apostolic See which you have arrogated. Let another mount the throne of Saint Peter, another who will not cloak violence with religion but who will teach the pure doctrine of Saint Peter.

I, Henry, King by the grace of God, together with all our bishops, say to you: Descend! Descend!

Gregory VII: Excommunication of Henry IV

O blessed Peter, prince of the Apostles, mercifully incline thine ear, we [sic] pray, and hear me, thy servant, whom thou hast cherished from infancy and hast delivered until now from the hand of the wicked who have hated and still hate me for my loyalty to thee. Thou art my witness, as are also my Lady, the Mother of God, and the blessed Paul, thy brother among all the saints, that thy Holy Roman Church forced me against my will to be its ruler. I had no thought of ascending thy throne as a robber, nay, rather would I have chosen to end my life as a pilgrim than to seize upon thy place for earthly glory and by devices of this world. Therefore, by thy favor, not by any works of mine, I believe that it is and has been thy will, that the Christian people especially committed to thee should render obedience to me, thy especially constituted representative. To me is given by thy grace the power of binding and loosing in Heaven and upon earth.

Wherefore, relying upon this commission, and for the honor and defense of thy Church, in the name of Almighty God, Father, Son and Holy Spirit, through thy power and authority, I deprive King Henry, son of the emperor Henry, who has rebelled against thy Church with unheard of audacity, of the government over the whole kingdom of Germany and Italy, and I release all Christian men from the allegiance which they have sworn or may swear to him, and I forbid anyone to serve him as king. For it is fitting that he who seeks to diminish the glory of thy Church should lose the glory which he seems to have.

And, since he has refused to obey as a Christian should or to return to the God whom he has abandoned by taking part with excommunicated persons, has spurned my warnings which I gave him for his soul's welfare, as thou knowest, and has separated himself from thy Church and tried to rend it asunder, I bind him in the bonds of anathema in thy stead and I bind him thus as commissioned by thee, that the nations may know and be convinced that thou art Peter and that upon thy rock the son of the living God has built his Church and the gates of hell shall not prevail against it.

DISCUSSION QUESTIONS

1. What does Henry IV mean by denouncing the pope as a "false monk"?
2. What do Henry's denunciations reveal about his conception of the source and the scope of his power as emperor?
3. How did Henry's self-image conflict with Gregory's understanding of his own authority as reflected in his excommunication and deposition of the emperor?

3.
Calling the First Crusade

Fulcher of Chartres, *Pope Urban II's Speech at Clermont* (1095)

The papacy emerged from the Gregorian reforms with enhanced power and prestige as the head of Western Christendom. Pope Urban II (r. 1088–1099) embraced his position of leadership and directed it toward a new cause: freeing Jerusalem and the Holy Land from the Seljuk Turks. They had seized control of the city as part of a broader expansionist campaign in Asia Minor. In need of military reinforcements to counter this threat, the Byzantine emperor called on the pope for help. Urban II's response is captured in the document that follows. It is a version of a speech he

From Oliver J. Thatcher and Edgar Holmes McNeal, *A Source Book for Medieval History* (New York: Charles Scribner's Sons, 1905), 516–17.

delivered to a large crowd in Clermont, France, in 1095 urging them to put down their weapons against one another and use them instead against the "infidel" in the Holy Land. Cleric Fulcher of Chartres (c. 1059–c. 1127) was present at the speech and was one of the tens of thousands who took up the pope's call to fight for God. He served as chaplain for one of the crusade leaders and recorded his experiences, including what he heard that day in Clermont, in a three-volume Chronicle. *His firsthand knowledge of events combined with the richness of his account make his* Chronicle *among the most reliable of all sources on the First Crusade.*

Although, O sons of God, you have promised more firmly than ever to keep the peace among yourselves and to preserve the rights of the church, there remains still an important work for you to do. Freshly quickened by the divine correction, you must apply the strength of your righteousness to another matter which concerns you as well as God. For your brethren who live in the east are in urgent need of your help, and you must hasten to give them the aid which has often been promised them. For, as the most of you have heard, the Turks and Arabs have attacked them and have conquered the territory of Romania [the Greek empire] as far west as the shore of the Mediterranean and the Hellespont, which is called the Arm of St. George. They have occupied more and more of the lands of those Christians, and have overcome them in seven battles. They have killed and captured many, and have destroyed the churches and devastated the empire. If you permit them to continue thus for awhile with impunity, the faithful of God will be much more widely attacked by them. On this account I, or rather the Lord, beseech you as Christ's heralds to publish this everywhere and to persuade all people of whatever rank, foot-soldiers and knights, poor and rich, to carry aid promptly to those Christians and to destroy that vile race from the lands of our friends. I say this to those who are present, it is meant also for those who are absent. Moreover, Christ commands it.

All who die by the way, whether by land or by sea, or in battle against the pagans, shall have immediate remission of sins. This I grant them through the power of God with which I am invested. O what a disgrace if such a despised and base race, which worships demons, should conquer a people which has the faith of omnipotent God and is made glorious with the name of Christ! With what reproaches will the Lord overwhelm us if you do not aid those who, with us, profess the Christian religion! Let those who have been accustomed unjustly to wage private warfare against the faithful now go against the infidels and end with victory this war which should have been begun long ago. Let those who, for a long time, have been robbers, now become knights. Let those who have been fighting against their brothers and relatives now fight in a proper way against the barbarians. Let those who have been serving as mercenaries for small pay now obtain the eternal reward. Let those who have been wearing themselves out in both body and soul now work for a double honor. Behold! on this side will be the sorrowful and poor, on that, the rich; on this side, the enemies of the Lord, on that, his friends. Let those who go not put off the journey, but rent their lands and collect money for their expenses; and as soon as winter is over and spring comes, let them eagerly set out on the way with God as their guide.

DISCUSSION QUESTIONS

1. Why does Urban II urge his audience to fight against the Turks? What language does he use to describe the crusaders and their journey? What language does he use to describe the Turks?

2. Why do you think this language motivated people in the audience like Fulcher of Chartres to join the crusade? What did the crusade have to offer them?

3. How does Urban II cast himself in this speech? How may it have strengthened the papacy's position in the church hierarchy?

4.
Arab Response to the First Crusade
Ibn al-Athīr, *A Muslim Perspective* (1097–1099)

In preaching the First Crusade, Pope Urban II called on the entire "race of Franks" to expel the enemies of God ("Turks" and "Arabs") from the Holy Land. As official accounts of the crusade make clear, Urban's words shaped the attitudes and actions of the crusaders as they made their way through Constantinople, south to the Seljuk capital of Nicaea, and then onward to Jerusalem, which they conquered in early June 1099. They saw themselves as God's army, which had the right and obligation to destroy "infidels." The document that follows reveals an entirely different perspective, that of Muslim leaders and soldiers fighting the crusaders along the way. It is drawn from a sweeping chronicle of Islamic history by Arab historian Ibn al-Athīr (1160–1233), who used a range of sources to describe the crusaders' activities and the Muslim response to them. For him, the crusaders were not men of God, but rather ruthless invaders who wreaked havoc on local peoples and holy sites.

How the Franks Took the City of Antioch

The power of the Franks and their increased importance were first manifested by their invasion of the lands of Islam and their conquest of part of them in the year 478 [1085–6], for [that was when] they took the city of Toledo and other cities of Spain, as we have already mentioned.

Then in the year 484 [1091–2] they attacked and conquered the island of Sicily, as we have also mentioned. They descended on the coasts of Ifrīqiya[1] and seized some part, which was then taken back from them. Later they took other parts, as you shall see.

When it was the year 490 [1096–7] they invaded Syria. The reason for their invasion was that their ruler, Baldwin, a relative of Roger the Frank who had conquered Sicily, gathered a great host of Franks and sent to Roger saying, "I have

From Ibn al-Athīr, *The Chronicle of Ibn al-Athīr for the Crusading Period* from *al-Kamil fi'l-Ta'rikh*, part 1, trans. D. S. Richards (Burlington, VT: Ashgate, 2006), 13–17, 21–22.

[1]The loose term for the eastern part of the Maghrib.

gathered a great host and I am coming to you. I shall proceed to Ifrīqiya to take it and I shall be a neighbor of yours." Roger assembled his men and consulted them about this. They said, "By the truth of the Gospel, this is excellent for us and them. The lands will become Christian lands." Roger raised his leg and gave a loud fart. "By the truth of my religion," he said, "there is more use in that than in what you have to say!" "How so?" they asked. "If they come to me," he replied, "I shall require vast expenditure and ships to convey them to Ifrīqiya and troops of mine also. If they take the territory it will be theirs and resources from Sicily will go to them. I shall be deprived of the money that comes in every year from agricultural revenues. If they do not succeed, they will return to my lands and I shall suffer from them. Tamīm will say, 'You have betrayed me and broken the agreement I have [with you].' Our mutual contacts and visits will be interrupted. The land of Ifrīqiya will be waiting for us. Whenever we find the strength we will take it."

He summoned Baldwin's envoy and said to him, "If you are determined to wage holy war on the Muslims, then the best way is to conquer Jerusalem. You will free it from their hands and have glory. Between me and the people of Ifrīqiya, however, are oaths and treaties." They therefore made their preparations and marched forth to Syria.

It has been said that the Alid rulers of Egypt[2] became fearful when they saw the strength and power of the Saljuq state, that it had gained control of Syrian lands as far as Gaza, leaving no buffer state between the Saljuqs and Egypt to protect them, and that Aqsīs[3] had entered Egypt and blockaded it. They therefore sent to the Franks to invite them to invade Syria, to conquer it and separate them and the [other] Muslims, but God knows best.

After they had decided to march to Syria, they went to Constantinople to cross the straits into Muslim lands, to travel on by land, for that would be easier for them. When they arrived, the Byzantine emperor refused them passage through his territory. He said, "I will not allow you to cross into the lands of Islam until you swear to me that you will surrender Antioch to me." His aim was to urge them to move into Islamic lands, assuming that Turks would not spare a single one of them, because he had seen how fierce they were and their control of the lands. They agreed to that and crossed the Bosphorus at Constantinople in the year 490 [1096–7].

They reached the lands of Qilij Arslān ibn Sulaymán ibn Qutlumish[4] namely Konya and other cities. Having arrived there, they were met by Qilij Arslān with his hosts, who resisted them. They put him to flight in Rajab 490 [July 1097] after a battle[5] and then traversed his lands into those of the son of the Armenian[6] which they marched through before emerging at Antioch and putting it under siege.

When the ruler Yaghī Siyān[7] heard of their coming, he feared the Christians in the city. He sent out the Muslim inhabitants by themselves and ordered them to

---

[2]I.e., the Fatimid caliphs.
[3]Alternative name for Atsiz ibn Uvak, a Turkoman chief who attacked Egypt in 1077.
[4]Saljuq sultan of Asia Minor (Rūm), died 1107.
[5]This is the battle of Dorylaeum.
[6]Perhaps Constantine I, son of Rupen I (1095–1102) is intended.
[7]Turkish emir, given Aleppo as fief by Sultan Malikshāh.

dig the moat. Then the next day he sent out the Christians also to dig the moat, unaccompanied by any Muslim. They labored on it until the evening but when they wished to enter the city he prevented them and said, "You can give me Antioch until I see how things will be with us and the Franks." They asked, "Who will look after our sons and our wives?" "I will look after them in your place," he replied. So they held back and took up residence in the Frankish camp. The Franks besieged the city for nine months. Yaghī Siyān displayed such courage, excellent counsel, resolution, and careful planning as had never been seen from anyone else. Most of the Franks perished. Had they remained in the numbers they set out with, they would have overwhelmed the lands of Islam. Yaghī Siyān protected the families of those Christians of Antioch, whom he had expelled, and restrained the hands that would do them harm.

After their siege of Antioch had lasted long, the Franks made contact with one of the men garrisoning the towers, who was an armorer, known as Rūzbah, and offered him money and grants of land. He was in charge of a tower next to the valley, which was built with a window overlooking the valley. After they had made an arrangement with this cursed armorer, they came to the window, which they opened and through which they entered. A large number climbed up on ropes. When they numbered more than five hundred, they blew the trumpet. That was at dawn. The defenders were already tired from many sleepless nights on guard. Yaghī Siyān awoke and asked what was happening. He was told, "That trumpet is from the citadel. No doubt it has already been taken." However, it was not from the citadel but merely from that tower. He was seized with fear, opened the city gate and left in headlong flight with thirty retainers. His deputy as governor of the city came and asked after him. He was told that he had fled, so he himself fled by another gate. That was a boon for the Franks. Had he held firm for a while, they would have perished. The Franks entered the city through the gate and sacked it, killing the Muslims that were there. This was in Jumada I [April-May 1098].[8] . . .

How the Muslims Marched against the Franks and What Befell Them

When Qiwām al-Dawla Karbughā[9] heard of the Franks' doings and their conquest of Antioch, he gathered his forces and marched to Syria. He camped at Jarj Dābiq,[10] where the troops of Syria, both Turks and Arabs, rallied to him, apart from those who were in Aleppo. There assembled with him Duqāq ibn Tutush,[11] Tughtakīn the Atabeg,[12] Janāh al-Dawla the lord of Homs,[13] Arslān Tāsh the lord of Sinjār,

---

[8] The city fell in fact in early June 1098.

[9] Governor of Mosul and other Mesopotamian towns, supporter of Barkyāruq and patron of Zankī.

[10] The "plain" near Dābiq in North Syria.

[11] Saljuq prince of Damascus.

[12] Zāhir al-Dīn Abū Mansūr Ṭughtakīn, freedman of Tutush and atabeg (i.e., regent/guardian) of Duqāq. Founder of the short-lived Būrid dynasty in Damascus.

[13] Atabeg of Ridwān ibn Tutush, ruled independently in Homs from 490/1097.

Suqmān ibn Artuq and other emirs, the likes of whom are not to be found. Hearing of this, the Franks' misfortunes increased and they were fearful because of their weakness and their shortage of provisions. The Muslims came and besieged them in Antioch, but Karbughā behaved badly towards the Muslims with him. He angered the emirs and lorded it over them, imagining that they would stay with him despite that. However, infuriated by this, they secretly planned to betray him, if there should be a battle, and they determined to give him up when the armies clashed.

The Franks, after they had taken Antioch, were left there for twelve days with nothing to eat. The powerful fed on their horses, while the wretched poor ate carrion and leaves. In view of this, they sent to Karbughā, asking him for terms to leave the city, but he did not grant what they sought. He said, "My sword alone will eject you."

The following princes were with them: Baldwin,[14] [Raymond of] St. Gilles,[15] Count Godfrey, the Count lord of Edessa,[16] and Bohemond the lord of Antioch, their leader. There was a monk there, of influence amongst them, who was a cunning man. He said to them, "The Messiah (blessings be upon Him) had a lance which was buried in the church at Antioch, which was a great building.[17] If you find it, you will prevail, but if you do not find it, then destruction is assured." He had previously buried a lance in a place there and removed the traces [of his digging]. He commanded them to fast and repent, which they did for three days. On the fourth day he took them all into the place, accompanied by the common people and workmen. They dug everywhere and found it as he had said. "Rejoice in your coming victory," he said to them.[18]

On the fifth day they went out of the gate in scattered groups of five or six or so. The Muslims said to Karbughā, "You ought to stand at the gate and kill all that come out, because now, when they are scattered, it is easy to deal with them." He replied, "No, do not do that. Leave them alone until they have all come out and then we can kill them." He did not allow his men to engage them. However, one group of Muslims did kill several that had come out but he came in person and ordered them to desist.

When the Franks had all come out and not one of them remained within, they drew up a great battle line. At that, the Muslims turned their backs in flight, firstly because of the contempt and the scorn with which Karbughā had treated them and secondly because he had prevented them from killing the Franks. Their flight was complete. Not one of them struck a blow with a sword, thrust with a spear or shot an arrow. The last to flee were Suqmān ibn Artuq and Janāḥ al-Dawla because they were stationed in ambush. Karbughā fled with them. When the Franks observed

---

[14]In Baldwin of Le Bourg, subsequently count of Edessa and then King Baldwin II.

[15]Count of Toulouse.

[16]Baldwin of Boulogne, count of Edessa and future Baldwin I, is meant, although he was not present at Antioch.

[17]This is the cathedral of St. Peter, called al-Qusyān.

[18]This lance, claimed to be the one used to pierce Jesus' side, was found in the Church of St. Peter by a Provencal, Peter Bartholomew.

this, they thought that it was a trick, since there had been no battle such as to cause a flight and they feared to pursue them. A company of warriors for the faith stood firm and fought zealously, seeking martyrdom. The Franks slew thousands of them and seized as booty the provisions, money, furnishings, horses and weapons that were in the camp. Their situation was restored and their strength returned. . . .

How the Franks (God Curse Them) Took Jerusalem

Jerusalem had been held by Tāj al-Dawla Tutush who assigned it to Emir Suqmān ibn Artuq the Turkoman. When the Franks defeated the Turks at Antioch and made slaughter amongst them, the power of the Turks weakened and they lost cohesion. When the Egyptians saw their weakness, they marched to Jerusalem, led by al-Afḍal ibn Badr al-Jamālī. There they besieged Suqmān and Īlghāzī, the sons of Artuq, and also their cousin Savanj and their nephew Yāqūtī. They set up forty and more trebuchets against the town and demolished parts of its wall. The inhabitants fought back and the fighting and the siege lasted somewhat over forty days, until the Egyptians took the city on terms in Sha'bān 489 [July 1096]. Al-Afḍal treated Suqmān, Īlghāzī and their followers well, gave them generous gifts and sent them on their way to Damascus. Subsequently they crossed the Euphrates. Suqmān took up residence in Edessa but Īlghāzī moved to Iraq.

The Egyptians appointed as deputy in Jerusalem a man called Iftikhār al-Dawla, who remained there until this present time, when the Franks attacked after they had besieged Acre but with no success. After their arrival they erected forty trebuchets or more and they constructed two towers, one on Mount Zion side but the Muslims burnt that one and killed all inside. After they had completely destroyed it by fire, their help was then called for, as the city defenses had been overwhelmed on the other side. The Franks did indeed take the city from the north in the forenoon of Friday, seven days remaining of Sha'bān [15 July 1099]. The inhabitants became prey for the sword. For a week the Franks continued to slaughter the Muslims. A group of Muslims took refuge in the Tower of David[19] and defended themselves there. They resisted for three days and then the Franks offered them safe-conduct, so they surrendered the place. The Franks kept faith with them and they departed at night for Ascalon, where they remained.

In the Aqsa Mosque the Franks killed more than 70,000, a large number of them being imams, ulema, righteous men, and ascetics, Muslims who had left their native lands and come to live a holy life in this august spot. The Franks took forty or more silver candlesticks from the Dome of the Rock, each of which weighed 3,600 dirhams, and also a silver candelabrum weighing forty Syrian rotls. They removed 150 small candlesticks of silver and twenty or so of gold. The booty they took was beyond counting.

DISCUSSION QUESTIONS

1. How does Ibn al-Athīr portray the crusaders and their leaders? What does he reveal about the organization and motives of the crusading armies in the process?

---

[19]I.e., the citadel, in Arabic called the Miḥrāb of David.

2. As described here, what factors contributed to the crusaders' military success against the Muslims?

3. According to Ibn al-Athīr, the Franks killed thousands of local residents when they took Jerusalem. How does Ibn al-Athīr describe the Franks' actions? How do you think his religious ideas may have shaped his account?

5.
The Power of William I
The Anglo-Saxon Chronicle (1085–1086)
and
Domesday Book (1086–1087)

While the papacy was expanding its authority in the eleventh century, regional rulers were doing much the same. William I, duke of Normandy and king of England (r. 1066–1087), provides a case in point, and his efforts on this front helped to make his twelfth-century successors the mightiest kings in Europe. Upon conquering his rival to the throne in the battle of Hastings in 1066, William consolidated his rule by preserving existing institutions and establishing new ones. Below is a contemporary description of King William from the Anglo-Saxon Chronicle, *a year-by-year account of English history from the birth of Christ to 1154. As it recounts, among William's many achievements was the commission of a comprehensive survey of England's land, livestock, taxes, and population, which was conducted in 1086–1087. Later condensed into two volumes, known as Domesday, the report paints a detailed picture of England's agricultural and urban landscape. An extract from the survey of the county of Norfolk follows. It bears witness not only to the minute level of record keeping the enterprise entailed but also to the king's immense resources and power.*

Anglo-Saxon Chronicle

In this year people said and declared for a fact, that Cnut, king of Denmark, son of King Swein, was setting out in this direction and meant to conquer this country with the help of Robert, count of Flanders, because Cnut was married to Robert's daughter. When William, king of England, who was then in Normandy — for he was in possession of both England and Normandy — found out about this, he went to England with a larger force of mounted men and infantry from France and Brittany than had ever come to this country, so that people wondered how this country could maintain all that army. And the king had all the army dispersed all over the country among his vassals, and they provisioned the army each in proportion

From *The Anglo-Saxon Chronicle*, trans. Dorothy Whitelock (New Brunswick, NJ: Rutgers University Press, 1961), 161–65; and *Translations and Reprints from the Original Sources of European History*, vol. 3 (Philadelphia: Department of History, University of Pennsylvania, 1912), 6–7.

to his land. And people had much oppression that year, and the king had the land near the sea laid waste, so that if his enemies landed, they should have nothing to seize on so quickly. But when the king found out for a fact that his enemies had been hindered and could not carry out their expedition — then he let some of the army go to their own country, and some he kept in this country over winter.

Then at Christmas, the king was at Gloucester with his council, and held his court there for five days, and then the archbishop and clerics had a synod for three days. There Maurice was elected bishop of London, and William for Norfolk, and Robert for Cheshire — they were all clerics of the king.

After this, the king had much thought and very deep discussion with his council about this country — how it was occupied or with what sort of people. Then he sent his men over all England into every shire and had them find out how many hundred hides there were in the shire, or what land and cattle the king himself had in the country, or what dues he ought to have in twelve months from the shire.[1] Also he had a record made of how much land his archbishops had, and his bishops and his abbots and his earls — and though I relate it at too great length — what or how much everybody had who was occupying land in England, in land or cattle, and how much money it was worth. So very narrowly did he have it investigated, that there was no single hide nor virgate of land, nor indeed (it is a shame to relate but it seemed no shame to him to do) one ox nor one cow nor one pig which was there left out, and not put down in his record; and all these records were brought to him afterwards. . . .

This King William of whom we speak was a very wise man,[2] and very powerful and more worshipful and stronger than any predecessor of his had been. He was gentle to the good men who loved God, and stern beyond all measure to those people who resisted his will. In the same place where God permitted him to conquer England, he set up a famous monastery and appointed monks for it,[3] and endowed it well. In his days the famous church at Canterbury was built,[4] and also many another over all England. Also, this country was very full of monks, and they lived their life under the rule of St. Benedict, and Christianity was such in his day that each man who wished followed out whatever concerned his order. Also, he was very dignified: three times every year he wore his crown, as often as he was in England. At Easter he wore it at Winchester, at Whitsuntide at Westminster, and at Christmas at Gloucester, and then there were with him all the powerful men over all England, archbishops and bishops, abbots and earls, thegns and knights. Also, he was a very stern and violent man, so that no one dared do anything contrary to his will. He had earls in his fetters, who acted against his will. He expelled bishops from their sees, and abbots from their abbacies, and put thegns in prison, and finally he did not spare his own brother, who was called Odo; he was a very powerful bishop in Normandy (his cathedral church was at Bayeux) and was the foremost man next the king, and had an earldom in England. And when the king was

---

[1]This initiative resulted in Domesday. A hide was a unit of land for taxation. [Ed.]
[2]The account that follows was clearly written by a man who had attended William's court.
[3]Battle Abbey.
[4]Lanfranc's rebuilding of Christ Church, Canterbury.

in Normandy, then he was master in this country; and he [the king] put *him* in prison. Amongst other things the good security he made in this country is not to be forgotten — so that any honest man could travel over his kingdom without injury with his bosom full of gold; and no one dared strike[5] another, however much wrong he had done him. And if any man had intercourse with a woman against her will, he was forthwith castrated.

He ruled over England, and by his cunning it was so investigated that there was not one hide of land in England that he did not know who owned it, and what it was worth, and then set it down in his record.[6] Wales was in his power, and he built castles there, and he entirely controlled that race. In the same way, he also subdued Scotland to himself, because of his great strength. The land of Normandy was his by natural inheritance, and he ruled over the county called Maine; and if he could have lived two years more, he would have conquered Ireland by his prudence and without any weapons. Certainly in his time people had much oppression and very many injuries:

He had castles built
And poor men hard oppressed.
The king was so very stark
And deprived his underlings of many a mark
Of gold and more hundreds of pounds of silver,
That he took by weight and with great injustice
From his people with little need for such a deed.
Into avarice did he fall
And loved greediness above all.
He made great protection for the game
And imposed laws for the same,
That who so slew hart or hind
Should be made blind.

He preserved the harts and boars
And loved the stags as much
As if he were their father.
Moreover, for the hares did he decree that they should go free.
Powerful men complained of it and poor men lamented it,
But so fierce was he that he cared not for the rancour of them all,
But they had to follow out the king's will entirely
If they wished to live or hold their land,
Property or estate, or his favour great.
Alas! woe, that any man so proud should go,
And exalt himself and reckon himself above all men!
May Almighty God show mercy to his soul
And grant unto him forgiveness for his sins.

---

[5]Or "kill."
[6]Domesday.

These things we have written about him, both good and bad, that good men may imitate their good points, and entirely avoid the bad, and travel on the road that leads us to the kingdom of heaven.

Extract from Domesday Survey of the County of Norfolk

The land of Robert Malet.

Fredrebruge Hundred and half. Glorestorp. Godwin, a freeman, held it. Two carucates[7] of land in the time of king Edward. Then and afterwards 8 villains[8]; now 3. Then and afterwards 3 bordars[9]; now 5. At all times 3 serfs, and 30 acres of meadow. At all times 2 carucates in demesne.[10] Then half a carucate of the men, and now. Woods for 8 swine, and 2 mills. Here are located 13 socmen,[11] of 40 acres of land. When it was received there were 2 horses, now 1. At all times 8 swine, then 20 sheep, and it is worth 60 shillings.

There is situated there, in addition, one berewick,[12] as the manor of Heuseda. In the time of king Edward, 1 carucate of land; then and afterwards 7 villains, now 5. At all times 12 bordars, and 3 serfs, and 40 acres of meadow; 1 mill. Woods for 16 swine and 1 salt pond and a half. Then 1 horse and now and 14 swine, 30 sheep, and 50 goats. In this berewick are located 3 socmen, of 10 acres of land, and it is worth 30 shillings. The two manors have 2 leagues in length and 4 firlongs in breadth. Whosoever is tenant there, returns 12 pence of the twenty shillings of geld.[13]

Scerpham Hundred Culverstestun Edric held it in the time of king Edward. Two carucates of land. At all times there were 4 villains, and 1 bordar, and 4 serfs; 5 acres of meadow and two carucates in the demesne. Then and afterwards 1 carucate, now one-half. At all times 1 mill and one fish-pond. Here is located 1 socmen of the king, of 40 acres of land; which his predecessors held only as commended and he claims his land from the gift of the king. Then and afterwards there was one carucate, now 2 oxen, and 2 acres of meadow. At all times two horses, and 4 geese; then 300 sheep, now 300 less 12; then 16 swine now 3. Then and afterwards it was worth 60 shillings, now 80; and there could be one plow. Walter of Caen holds it from Robert.

Heinstede Hundred. In Sasilingaham Edric, the predecessor of Robert Malet, held 2 sokes[14] and a half, of 66 acres of land, now Walter holds them. Then 9 bordars, now 13. At all times 3 carucates and a half among all, and 3 acres of meadow, and the eighth part of a mill; and under these 1 soke of 6 acres of land. At all times half a carucate. Then it was worth 30 shillings, now it returns 50 shillings.

---

[7]**carucates:** Ploughland; in this part of England, a carucate was used as a unit of tax assessment in lieu of the hide. [Ed.]

[8]**villains:** Peasants living in a village. [Ed.]

[9]**bordars:** Peasants occupying a lower rung on the economic ladder than villains. [Ed.]

[10]**demesne:** Land in lordship, meaning it was in the lord's personal possession or exploited exclusively for his benefit. [Ed.]

[11]**socmen:** Freemen (often peasants) who owed service to a lord. [Ed.]

[12]**berewick:** An outlying estate or one with a special function. [Ed.]

[13]**geld:** A land tax. [Ed.]

[14]**soke:** A lord's right of jurisdiction over specific places and people. [Ed.]

In Scotessa Ulcetel was tenant, a free man commended to Edric, in the time of king Edward of 30 acres of land. At that time 1 bordar, afterward and now 2. Then half a carucate, none afterward nor now. It was at all times worth 5 shillings and 4 pence; the same.

Discussion Questions

1. How does the *Anglo-Saxon Chronicle* describe William's method of rule in general? In what ways does the author present Domesday as a reflection of this rule?

2. Do you think that the Domesday extract supports the chronicle's account?

3. Do you think that the author of the chronicle was an objective observer? Why or why not? How does his account differ as a source from Domesday?

Comparative Questions

1. What do the Domesday survey and *commenda* contracts suggest about the basis of the medieval economy in the eleventh and twelfth centuries? What had changed from earlier periods? What remained the same?

2. How do you think Pope Gregory VII would have reacted to William I's relationship with the English church, as described in the *Anglo-Saxon Chronicle*, and why?

3. In what ways do both the investiture conflict between Henry IV and Pope Gregory VII and the First Crusade reflect the new power of the medieval papacy?

4. Look closely at the language Urban II and Ibn al-Athīr use to describe crusaders and Muslims. What similarities and differences do you see? What does this suggest about how the two sides viewed each other?

The Flowering
of the Middle Ages
1150–1215

R owdy students, brave knights, pious women, and powerful kings were just
a few of the people who infused medieval government, culture, and religion
with new vitality and confidence in the twelfth and early thirteenth centuries.
Some of the documents in this chapter illuminate how the vigor of the period
found expression in new approaches to learning (Documents 1 and 2), literary
styles (Document 3), and religious movements (Document 4). Despite the diversity of these sources, they reflect a heightened concern for regulating an individual's conduct as part of a larger group. The drive to codify and control behavior and
beliefs served a variety of purposes — from enhancing political authority and
social prestige to gaining salvation. As the lines delineating who fit into certain
groups became sharper, so too did those delineating who was to be excluded. Prejudice combined with religious zeal fueled violence and intolerance against an
ever-widening array of enemies, including the Byzantine Greeks (Document 5).

1.
New Learning

Peter Abelard, *The Story of My Misfortunes* (c. 1132)

*As cities grew in size throughout twelfth-century Europe, so too did the number of
people flocking to their gates, notably students hungry for knowledge. Schools associated with monasteries and cathedrals had been in place for centuries but another
model of learning gained prominence: the independent master with his own cohort of
students. The career of Peter Abelard (1079–1142) embodied the intellectual vitality
this second model had to offer. In his student days, he had wandered from school to*

From *The Letters of Abelard and Heloise*, trans. Betty Radice, rev. ed. M. T. Clanchy (London: Penguin Group, 2003), 19–24, 254–55.

school, increasingly dissatisfied with their scholarship. Although Abelard was trained in a traditional liberal arts curriculum, he was especially interested in logic as an analytical tool. Ultimately, he gained a name for himself as a master in his own right because of his innovative style of thinking and teaching. As he describes in the excerpt below from his autobiography, The Story of My Misfortunes, *his methods attracted both friends and foes. The passage opens with a description of his success as a teacher and how it set the stage for a confrontation with church officials in 1121. By this point in his life, he had entered a monastery but remained deeply engaged in academic pursuits.*

When it became apparent that God had granted me the gift for interpreting the Scriptures as well as secular literature, the numbers in my school began to increase for both subjects, while elsewhere they diminished rapidly. This roused the envy and hatred of the other heads of schools against me; they set out to disparage me in whatever way they could, and two of them[1] especially were always attacking me behind my back for occupying myself with secular literature[2] in a manner totally unsuitable to my monastic calling, and for presuming to set up as a teacher of sacred learning when I had had no teacher myself. Their aim was for every form of teaching in a school to be forbidden me, and for this end they were always trying to win over bishops, archbishops, abbots, in fact anyone of account in the Church whom they could approach.

Now it happened that I first applied myself to lecturing on the basis of our faith by analogy with human reason, and composed a theological treatise on divine unity and trinity[3] for the use of my students who were asking for human and logical reasons on this subject, and demanded something intelligible rather than mere words. In fact they said that words were useless if the intelligence could not follow them, that nothing could be believed unless it was first understood, and that it was absurd for anyone to preach to others what neither he nor those he taught could grasp with the understanding: the Lord himself had criticized such "blind guides of blind men."[4] After the treatise had been seen and read by many people it began to please everyone, as it seemed to answer all questions alike on this subject. It was generally agreed that the questions were peculiarly difficult and the importance of the problem was matched by the subtlety of my solution.

---

[1]Presumably Alberic of Rheims and Lotulf of Lombardy. They ran a school together in Rheims and were two of Abelard's main opponents at the Council of Soissons, described below. [Ed.]

[2]**occupying myself with secular literature**: This refers to the controversy in Abelard's time about whether monks should be contemplative or active. Monks should withdraw from the world; it was the business of the secular clergy and canons to deal with the laity. Hugh of St. Victor argued that Abelard should be devoted to prayer and not to teaching, now that he had become a monk.

[3]**a theological treatise on divine unity and trinity**: The title that Abelard gave to this book was *Theologia* (*Theology*), meaning in Greek "discussion" (*logos*) about the nature of "God" (*theos*). He did not know Greek, but giving the book a Greek title made it look impressive. The book discusses the doctrine of the Trinity and whether non-Christians share this belief.

[4]**"blind guides of blind men"**: Matthew 15:14.

My rivals were therefore much annoyed and convened a Council against me, prompted by my two old opponents, Alberic and Lotulf who, now that our former masters, William and Anselm, were dead, were trying to reign alone in their place and succeed them as their heirs. Both of them were heads of the school in Rheims, and there, by repeated insinuations, they were able to influence their archbishop, Ralph, to take action against me and, along with Conan, bishop of Palestrina, who held the office of papal legate in France at the time, to convene an assembly, which they called a Council, in the city of Soissons, where I was to be invited to come bringing my treatise on the Trinity. This was done, but before I could make my appearance, my two rivals spread such evil rumours about me amongst the clerks and people that I and the few pupils who had accompanied me narrowly escaped being stoned by the people on the first day we arrived, for having preached and written (so they had been told) that there were three Gods.

I called on the legate as soon as I entered the town, handed him a copy of the treatise for him to read and form an opinion, and declared myself ready to receive correction and make amends if I had written anything contrary to the Catholic faith. But he told me at once to take the book to the archbishop and my opponents, so that my accusers could judge me themselves and the words "Our enemies are judges"[5] be fulfilled in me. However, though they read and reread the book again and again they could find nothing they dared charge me with at an open hearing, so they adjourned the condemnation they were panting for until the final meeting of the Council. For my part, every day before the Council sat, I spoke in public on the Catholic faith in accordance with what I had written, and all who heard me were full of praise both for my exposition and for my interpretation. When the people and clerks saw this they began to say "'Here he is, speaking openly,'[6] and no one utters a word against him. The Council which we were told was expressly convened against him is quickly coming to an end. Can the judges have found that the error is theirs, not his?" This went on every day and added fuel to my enemies' fury.

And so one day Alberic sought me out with some of his followers, intent on attacking me. After a few polite words he remarked that something he had noticed in the book had puzzled him very much; namely, that although God begat God, and there is only one God, I denied that God had begotten Himself. I said at once that if they wished I would offer an explanation on this point. "We take no account of rational explanation," he answered, "nor of your interpretation in such matters; we recognize only the words of authority." "Turn the page," I said, "and you will find the authority." There was a copy of the book at hand, which he had brought with him, so I looked up the passage which I knew but which he had failed to see — or else he looked only for what would damage me. By God's will I found what I wanted at once: a sentence headed "Augustine, *On the Trinity*, Book One." "Whoever supposes that God has the power to beget Himself is in error, and the more so because it is not only God who lacks this power, but also any spiritual or corporeal creature. There is nothing whatsoever which can beget itself."

---

[5]**"Our enemies are judges"**: Deuteronomy 32:31.
[6]**"Here he is, speaking openly"**: John 7:26.

When his followers standing by heard this they blushed in embarrassment, but he tried to cover up his mistake as best he could by saying that this should be understood in the right way. To that I replied that it was nothing new, but was irrelevant at the moment as he was looking only for words, not interpretation. But if he was willing to hear an interpretation and a reasoned argument I was ready to prove to him that by his own words he had fallen into the heresy of supposing the Father to be His own Son. On hearing this he lost his temper and turned to threats, crying that neither my explanations nor my authorities would help me in this case. He then went off.

On the last day of the Council, before the session was resumed, the legate and the archbishop began to discuss at length with my opponents and other persons what decision to take about me and my book, as this was the chief reason for their being convened. They could find nothing to bring against me either in my words or in the treatise which was before them, and everyone stood silent for a while or began to retract his accusation, until Geoffrey, bishop of Chartres, who was out-standing among the other bishops for his reputation for holiness and the impor-tance of his see, spoke as follows:

> All of you, Sirs, who are here today know that this man's teaching, what-ever it is, and his intellectual ability have won him many followers and supporters wherever he has studied. He has greatly lessened the reputa-tion both of his own teachers and of ours, and his vine has spread its branches from sea to sea. If you injure him through prejudice, though I do not think you will, you must know that even if your judgement is deserved you will offend many people, and large numbers will rally to his defence; especially as in this treatise before us we can see nothing which deserves any public condemnation. . . .

At once my rivals broke in with an outcry: "Fine advice that is, to bid us com-pete with the ready tongue of a man whose arguments and sophistries could tri-umph over the whole world!" (But it was surely far harder to compete with Christ, and yet Nicodemus[7] asked for him to be given a hearing, as sanctioned by the law.) However, when the bishop could not persuade them to agree to his proposal, he tried to curb their hostility by other means, saying that the few people present were insufficient for discussing a matter of such importance, and this case needed longer consideration. His further advice was that my abbot, who was present, should take me back to my monastery, the Abbey of St. Denis, and there a larger number of more learned men should be assembled to go into the case thoroughly and decide what was to be done. The legate agreed with this last suggestion, and so did everyone else. Soon after, the legate rose to celebrate Mass before he opened the Council. Through Bishop Geoffrey he sent me the permission agreed on: I was to return to my monastery and await a decision.

---

[7]**Nicodemus:** The Pharisee who counselled that Jesus should be given a fair hearing (John 7:51). He was a secret supporter of Jesus (John 3:1–10) and assisted with his burial (John 19:39).

Then my rivals, thinking that they had achieved nothing if this matter were taken outside their diocese, where they would have no power to use force — it was plain that they had little confidence in the justice of their cause — convinced the archbishop that it would be an insult to his dignity if the case were transferred and heard elsewhere, and a serious danger if I were allowed to escape as a result. They hurried to the legate, made him reverse his decision and persuaded him against his better judgement to condemn the book without any inquiry, burn it immediately in the sight of all and condemn me to perpetual confinement in a different monastery. They said that the fact that I had dared to read the treatise in public and must have allowed many people to make copies without its being approved by the authority of the Pope the Church should be quite enough to condemn it, and that the Christian faith would greatly benefit if an example were made of me and similar presumption in many others were forestalled. As the legate was less of a scholar than he should have been, he relied largely on the advice of the archbishop, who in turn relied on theirs. When the bishop of Chartres saw what would happen he told me at once about their intrigues and strongly urged me not to take it too hard, as by now it was apparent to all that they were acting too harshly. He said I could be confident that such violence so clearly prompted by jealousy would discredit them and benefit me, and told me not to worry about being confined in a monastery as he knew that the papal legate was only acting under pressure, and would set me quite free within a few days of his leaving Soissons. So he gave me what comfort he could, both of us shedding tears.

I was then summoned and came at once before the Council. Without any questioning or discussion they compelled me to throw my book into the fire with my own hands, and so it was burnt.

DISCUSSION QUESTIONS

1. How would you describe Abelard's style of teaching? In his view, what should be the basis of all knowledge?

2. Why did some of Abelard's fellow scholars urge church officials to bring charges against him? What was the basis of their complaint? Why did they find him so threatening?

3. How did Abelard respond to the charges? What does his response reveal about the new ways of learning gaining ground in this period?

2.

Scholarly Pursuits and Youthful Frolics

Medieval University Life (Twelfth–Early Thirteenth Centuries)

The development of permanent centers of learning in the twelfth and thirteenth centuries in cities across Europe attests to the vitality of the age. As the following documents suggest, royal patronage and the formation of a sense of common identity among students were key to the rise of medieval universities as self-governing institutions. The first two documents consist of special privileges granted by King Frederick I (r. 1152–1190) of Germany in 1158 to all students within his domains, and by King Philip II of France (r. 1180–1223) in 1200 to students in Paris. In this way, students were enveloped within both rulers' growing bureaucracies as each strove to increase his power. The voices of students themselves are highlighted in the second pair of documents — two anonymous poems written by students in the twelfth century describing the anxieties and pleasures of their way of life.

From King Frederick I

After a careful consideration of this subject by the bishops, abbots, dukes, counts, judges, and other nobles of our sacred palace, we, from our piety, have granted this privilege to all scholars who travel for the sake of study, and especially, to the professors of divine and sacred laws, namely, that they may go in safety to the places in which the studies are carried on, both they themselves and their messengers, and may dwell there in security. For we think it fitting that, during good behavior, those should enjoy our praise and protection, by whose learning the world is enlightened to the obedience of God and of us, his ministers and the life of the subjects is moulded; and by a certain special love we defend them from all injuries.

For who does not pity those who exile themselves through love for learning, who wear themselves out in poverty in place of riches, who expose their lives to all perils and often suffer bodily injury from the vilest men — this must be endured with vexation. Therefore, we declare by this general and ever to be valid law, that in the future no one shall be so rash as to venture to inflict any injury on scholars, or to occasion any loss to them on account of a debt owed by an inhabitant of their province — a thing which we have learned is sometimes done by an evil custom. And let it be known to the violators of this constitution, and also to those who shall at the time be the rulers of the places, that a four-fold restitution of property shall be exacted from all and that, the mark of infamy being affixed to them by the law itself, they shall lose their office forever. . . .

We also order this law to be inserted among the imperial constitutions under the title, *ne filius pro patre, etc.*

Given at Roncaglia, in the year of our Lord 1158, in the month of November. . . .

From King Philip II

In the Name of the sacred and indivisible Trinity, amen. Philip, by the grace of God, King of the French.

Concerning the safety of the students at Paris in the future, by the advice of our subjects we have ordained as follows: we will cause all the citizens of Paris to

From Dana Carleton Munro, ed., *Translations and Reprints from the Original Sources of European History*, vol. 2, no. 3 (Philadelphia: University of Pennsylvania Press, 1898), 2–7; and *Wine, Women, and Song: Medieval Latin Students' Songs*, trans. John Addington Symonds (London: Chatto & Windus, 1907), 58–64.

swear that if any one sees an injury done to any student by any layman, he will testify truthfully to this, nor will any one withdraw in order not to see [the act]. And if it shall happen that any one strikes a student, except in self-defense, especially if he strikes the student with a weapon, a club or a stone, all laymen who see [the act] shall in good faith seize the malefactor or malefactors and deliver them to our judge; nor shall they withdraw in order not to see the act, or seize the malefactor, or testify to the truth. Also, whether the malefactor is seized in open crime or not, we will make a legal and full examination through clerks or laymen or certain lawful persons; and our count and our judges shall do the same. And if by a full examination we or our judges are able to learn that he who is accused, is guilty of the crime, then we or our judges shall immediately inflict a penalty, according to the quality and nature of the crime; notwithstanding the fact that the criminal may deny the deed and say that he is ready to defend himself in single combat, or to purge himself by the ordeal by water.

Also, neither our provost nor our judges shall lay hands on a student for any offense whatever; nor shall they place him in our prison, unless such a crime has been committed by the student, that he ought to be arrested. And in that case, our judge shall arrest him on the spot, without striking him at all, unless he resists, and shall hand him over to the ecclesiastical judge, who ought to guard him in order to satisfy us and the one suffering the injury. And if a serious crime has been committed, our judge shall go or shall send to see what is done with the student. . . .

In order, moreover, that these [decrees] may be kept more carefully and may be established forever by a fixed law, we have decided that our present provost and the people of Paris shall affirm by an oath, in the presence of the scholars, that they will carry out in good faith all the above-mentioned. And always in the future, whosoever receives from us the office of provost in Paris, among the other initiatory acts of his office, namely, on the first or second Sunday, in one of the churches of Paris, — after he has been summoned for the purpose, — shall affirm by an oath, publicly in the presence of the scholars, that he will keep in good faith all the above-mentioned. And that these decrees may be valid forever, we have ordered this document to be confirmed by the authority of our seal and by the characters of the royal name, signed below.

A Wandering Student's Petition

I, a wandering scholar lad,
    Born for toil and sadness,
Oftentimes am driven by
    Poverty to madness.

Literature and knowledge I
    Fain would still be earning,
Were it not that want of pelf[1]
    Makes me cease from learning.

---

[1]**pelf**: Money. [Ed.]

These torn clothes that cover me
  Are too thin and rotten;
Oft I have to suffer cold,
  By the warmth forgotten.

Scarce I can attend at church,
  Sing God's praises duly;
Mass and vespers both I miss,
  Though I love them truly.

Oh, thou pride of N —,
  By thy worth I pray thee
Give the suppliant help in need,
  Heaven will sure repay thee.

Take a mind unto thee now
  Like unto St. Martin;
Clothe the pilgrim's nakedness,
  Wish him well at parting.

So may God translate your soul
  Into peace eternal,
And the bliss of saints be yours
  In His realm supernal.

A Song of the Open Road

We in our wandering,
Blithesome and squandering,
      Tara, tantara, teino![2]

Eat to satiety,
Drink with propriety;
      Tara, tantara, teino!

Laugh till our sides we split,
Rags on our hides we fit;
      Tara, tantara, teino!

Jesting eternally,
Quaffing infernally:
      Tara, tantara, teino!

---

[2]This refrain appears to be intended to imitate a bugle call.

Craft's in the bone of us,
Fear 'tis unknown of us:
      Tara, tantara, teino!

When we're in neediness,
Thieve we with greediness:
      Tara, tantara, teino!

Brother catholical,
Man apostolical,
      Tara, tantara, teino!

Say what you will have done,
What you ask 'twill be done!
      Tara, tantara, teino!

Folk, fear the toss of the
Horns of philosophy!
      Tara, tantara, teino!

Here comes a quadruple
Spoiler and prodigal!
      Tara, tantara, teino!

License and vanity
Pamper insanity:
      Tara, tantara, teino!

As the Pope bade us do,
Brother to brother's true:
      Tara, tantara, teino!

Brother, best friend, adieu!
Now, I must part from you!
      Tara, tantara, teino!

When will our meeting be?
Glad shall our greeting be!
      Tara, tantara, teino!

Vows valedictory
Now have the victory;
      Tara, tantara, teino!

Clasped on each other's breast,
Brother to brother pressed,
      Tara, tantara, teino!

DISCUSSION QUESTIONS

1. Why might both Frederick I and Philip II have been concerned for students' welfare? What benefits do you think they gained from guaranteeing students certain privileges?

2. What do the kings' privileges reveal about the process of state building at the time? What role did official records, such as these, play in the process?

3. What picture of student life do the authors paint in the two poems? What similarities exist based on your own experiences as a student?

4. How do the student poems support the argument made by many historians that in the twelfth century, people became more aware of themselves as members of larger groups with similar concerns and objectives?

3.
Courtly Love

Chrétien de Troyes, *Lancelot: The Knight of the Cart* (c. 1170s)

Students were not the only group to gain a sense of group solidarity in the twelfth century. Nobles forged a common class identity during this period in part through new forms of vernacular literature that flourished in aristocratic circles. Long poems examining the relationships between knights and their lady loves were especially popular. The following excerpt is from one such poem, Lancelot: The Knight of the Cart, *written in Old French by Chrétien de Troyes (c. 1150–1190) in the 1170s. Attached to the court of the count and countess of Champagne in the city of Troyes, located southeast of Paris, Chrétien used his poems to entertain his audiences while instructing them in the ways of courtliness and proper knightly behavior. Set against the backdrop of King Arthur's court, the poem recounts the adventures of Arthur's best knight, Lancelot, in his quest to rescue Arthur's queen, Guinevere. She had been kidnapped by the villain, Méléagant, and was being held hostage in his castle. Lancelot's loyalty to his king was not the only emotion driving his quest; he was also passionately in love with Guinevere. In the scene that follows, he has just arrived at Méléagant's castle after having overcome numerous obstacles; these included crossing the Sword Bridge, which was composed of a razor sharp blade from end to end. Méléagant is enraged by Lancelot's success and, as described below, meets his adversary in combat while scores of people look on, including Guinevere and Méléagant's father, King Bademagu.*

And then the combatants, freed
For their fight, ordered the crowd

From Chrétien de Troyes, *Lancelot: The Knight of the Cart*, trans. Burton Raffel (New Haven, CT: Yale University Press, 1997), 113–21.

To withdraw, set their shields
In place, their arms through the straps,
And, aiming their spears, dashed

At each other, striking so fiercely
That the points went two arms deep,
And the shields split and shattered
To bits. Their horses, too,
Came smashing breastplate into
Breastplate, with incredible force,
And the crashing shock of shields
And helmets, horses and men,
Sounded for all the world
Like a towering clap of thunder,
And every strap and belt
And spur and rein and girth
Broke, and even the heavy
Saddles snapped at the bow,
And neither knight was shamed
Or surprised to be tossed to the ground,
As everything underneath him
Gave way. They leaped to their feet
And continued the combat like a pair
Of wild boars, not bothering with insults
Or boasts, but striking each other
With heavy blows of their steel
Swords, like men who violently
Hate one another. Their slashing
Strokes often cut
Through helmets and mail shirts, making
Blood spurt from the metal.
They fought savagely, giving
And taking mighty blows,
Cruel and heavy. Each
Assaulted the other on equal
Terms, neither able
To gain the slightest advantage.
But it could not last: he
Who had crossed the Sword Bridge was surely
Weakened by all his wounds,
As everyone watching knew,
And those who favored that knight
Were terribly worried, seeing
His strokes weaken, sensing
Him getting the worst, afraid
That Méléagant would seize

The upper hand and victory
Would be his. A buzzing murmur
Ran through the crowd. But up
In the tower, at a window, a wise
Girl was watching, and she thought
To herself the knight most certainly
Wasn't fighting so terrible
A battle for her, nor
For anyone standing in the crowd
Of ordinary people,
But strictly and solely for the queen
And no one else — and if
He knew she was at a window,
Watching from on high, it might give him
Strength and courage. And had she
Known his name, she'd have gladly
Told him (calling down
From the tower) that his love was there,
And he could glance up, and see her.
So she hurried to the queen and said,
"My lady, in the name of God,
For your sake and ours, please,
Tell me that knight's name,
If you know it, so I can offer him
Help." "Young lady," said the queen,
"Your request, it seems to me,
Contains nothing in any way
Hateful or wicked, but only
Concern for his good. As long
As I've known him, this knight's name
Has been Lancelot of the Lake."
"Oh God!" said the girl. "How my happy
Heart is leaping with joy!"
Then she jumped to the window and shouted,
As loud as she could, in a voice
That everyone heard: "Lancelot!
Turn your head up and look —
See who's here, watching!"
    As soon as he heard his name,
Lancelot turned and looked
Behind him, and saw, seated
High at an open window,
What more than anything else
In the world he wanted to see.
And then, from the moment he saw her,

He neither moved his head
Nor looked in any other
Direction, fighting with his back
To his enemy, and Méléagant
Immediately began to press him
As hard as he could, delighted
To think that, now, the knight
Could no longer face him and defend
Himself. And his countrymen, too,
Were delighted, while the men of Logres
Were so sick at heart they could not
Stand, many falling
To their knees, but many fainting
Away, stretched on the ground.
Sorrow and excitement were everywhere.
But the girl, high at her window,
Shouted down once more:
"Ah, Lancelot! Can you really
Be as stupid as you look?
You seemed to be all
That a knight should be, till now:
You had me convinced that God
Had never made a knight
Who could challenge you for courage
And strength and virtue. And now
We see you fighting backwards,
Looking away from your enemy!
Do your fighting with your face
Turned to this tower, so you'll see her
Better! Let her shine on you!"
Outraged at the insult, and deeply
Shamed, Lancelot bitterly
Cursed himself for letting
The combat go against him,
Here in the sight of them all.
With a leap, he drove behind
Méléagant, forcing
His enemy to stand with his back
To the tower. Méléagant
Struggled to regain his ground,
But Lancelot charged him, striking
So many powerful strokes,
Swinging with all his strength,
That he forced a further retreat,
Two or three unwilling,

Unwelcome steps. Between
The strength Love had lent him,
Offered in willing assistance,
And the hate swelling in his heart
As the battle wore on, all
His powers and quickness had returned.
Love and his mortal hate —
Fiercer than any ever
Known — combined to make him
So fearsome that Méléagant
Was suddenly afraid,
For never in all his life
Had an enemy seemed so strong,
Or pressed and hurt him so badly
As this knight was doing. He tried
As hard as he could to keep him
At a distance, feinting, ducking,
Bobbing, badly hurt
Each time he was hit. Lancelot
Wasted no breath on threats,
Kept driving him toward the tower
And the queen, over and over
Coming as close as he could,
Forcing Méléagant back,
Each time, barely a foot
Away from stepping out
Of her sight. So Lancelot led him
Up and down, this way
And that, always making him
Stop in front of his lady,
The queen, who'd set his heart
On fire, just knowing she was
Watching — a fiercely roaring,
Burning-hot flame impelling him
Straight at Méléagant
And pushing his helpless enemy
Forward and back like a cripple,
Tugging him along like a blind man
Or a beggar at the end of a rope.
The king saw his son
Utterly overwhelmed
And was filled with pity and compassion:
He had to help, if he could.
But the queen, he knew, was the only
Possible source of assistance,

So he turned to her and spoke:
"Lady, for as long as you've been
In my land you've had my love
And honor; I've served you well,
And always gladly, in every
Way I could. Let me
Ask you, now, to repay me.
And the gift I ask you to give me
Could only be granted out
Of the purest love. I can see
Quite well — there's not the slightest
Doubt — that my son has lost
This battle. And I speak to you, now,
Not on this score, but because
It's clear that Lancelot
Could easily kill him, if he chose to.
I hope you want that no more
Than I do — not that my son
Has treated you well — he hasn't —
But simply because I beg you
For your mercy. Let him live.
Let the final blow be withheld.
And thus you can tell me, if you choose,
How you value the honor
I've shown you." "Dear sir, if that's
What you want, I want it, too.
I certainly hate and loathe
Your son, for the best of reasons,
But you indeed have served me
So well that it pleases me
To please you by stopping the battle."
They had not whispered private
Words; both Lancelot
And Méléagant heard them.
Lovers are obedient men,
Cheerfully willing to do
Whatever the beloved, who holds
Their entire heart, desires.
Lancelot had no choice,
For if ever anyone loved
More truly than Pyramus
It was him. Hearing her response,
As soon as the final word
Fell from her mouth, declaring,
"Dear sir, if you want the battle

Stopped, I want that, too,"
Nothing in the world could have made him
Fight, or even move,
No matter if it cost his life.

DISCUSSION QUESTIONS

1. Based on this scene, how would you describe Lancelot? What effect does Guinevere have on the outcome of his fight with Méléagant, and why is this important
to understanding Lancelot's character?

2. In what ways do Lancelot's actions and attitudes embody the twelfth-century
ideal of a chivalric hero?

3. Why do you think this ideal may have appealed to Chrétien's aristocratic audience? Do you think they saw themselves as living up to this ideal?

4.
Franciscan Piety

St. Francis and St. Clare of Assisi, *Selected Writings*
(Thirteenth Century)

*The church was very much entwined in the world of wealth, power, and splendor
celebrated in the vernacular literature of the twelfth and early thirteenth centuries.
A variety of new religious movements emerged in reaction against the church's perceived worldliness and neglect of its pastoral mission. St. Francis of Assisi (c. 1182–
1226) founded what became the most popular and largest of these movements in
Europe, the Franciscans. These excerpts from his* Rule, *written in 1223, illuminate
the fundamental principles guiding the order. The Franciscans' message of poverty,
humility, and penance prompted people from all walks of life to follow their path,
including St. Clare of Assisi (1194–1253). Upon hearing St. Francis preach in 1212,
she established a community of pious women modeled after his ideals, which became
the Order of the Sisters of St. Francis. Although the sisters were eventually cloistered,
the following passages from Clare's* Testament *reveal not only how their ideals
remained true to those of St. Francis, but also how medieval women played an important role in cultivating new forms of piety.*

From Francis's *Rule*

This is the rule and way of living of the minorite brothers: namely to observe the
holy Gospel of our Lord Jesus Christ, living in obedience, without personal possessions, and in chastity. Brother Francis promises obedience and reverence to our

---

From Ernest Henderson, ed., *Select Historical Documents of the Middle Ages* (London:
G. Bell & Sons, 1921), 344–49; and *Francis and Clare: The Complete Works*, trans. Regis J.
Armstrong and Ignatius C. Brady (New York: Paulist Press, 1982), 226–32.

lord pope Honorius, and to his successors who canonically enter upon their office, and to the Roman Church. And the other brothers shall be bound to obey brother Francis and his successors.

If any persons shall wish to adopt this form of living, and shall come to our brothers, they shall send them to their provincial ministers; to whom alone, and to no others, permission is given to receive brothers. But the ministers shall diligently examine them in the matter of the catholic faith and the ecclesiastical sacraments. And if they believe all these, and are willing to faithfully confess them and observe them steadfastly to the end; and if they have no wives, or if they have them and the wives have already entered a monastery, or if they shall have given them permission to do so . . . the ministers shall say unto them the word of the holy Gospel, to the effect that they shall go and sell all that they have and strive to give it to the poor. But if they shall not be able to do this, their good will is enough. And the brothers and their ministers shall be on their guard and not concern themselves for their temporal goods; so that they may freely do with those goods exactly as God inspires them. . . . Afterwards there shall be granted to them the garments of probation: namely two gowns without cowls and a belt, and hose and a cape down to the belt; unless to these same ministers something else may at some time seem to be preferable in the sight of God. But, when the year of probation is over, they shall be received into obedience; promising always to observe that manner of living, and this Rule. . . .

I firmly command all the brothers by no means to receive coin or money, of themselves or through an intervening person. But for the needs of the sick and for clothing the other brothers, the ministers alone and the guardians shall provide through spiritual friends, as it may seem to them that necessity demands, according to time, place and cold temperature. This one thing being always regarded, that, as has been said, they receive neither coin nor money.

Those brothers to whom God has given the ability to labor, shall labor faithfully and devoutly; in such way that idleness, the enemy of the soul, being excluded, they may not extinguish the spirit of holy prayer and devotion; to which other temporal things should be subservient. As a reward, moreover, for their labor, they may receive for themselves and their brothers the necessaries of life, but not coin or money; and this humbly, as becomes the servants of God and the followers of most holy poverty.

The brothers shall appropriate nothing to themselves, neither a house, nor a place, nor anything; but as pilgrims and strangers in this world, in poverty and humility serving God, they shall confidently go seeking for alms. Nor need they be ashamed, for the Lord made Himself poor for us in this world. This is that height of most lofty poverty, which has constituted you my most beloved brothers heirs and kings of the kingdom of Heaven, has made you poor in possessions, has exalted you in virtues. . . .

All the brothers shall be bound always to have one of the brothers of that order as general minister and servant of the whole fraternity, and shall be firmly bound to obey him. . . .

The brothers may not preach in the bishopric of any bishop if they have been forbidden to by him. And no one of the brothers shall dare to preach at all to the people, unless he have been examined and approved by the general minister of this fraternity, and the office of preacher have been conceded to him. I also exhort those same brothers that, in the preaching which they do, their expressions shall be chaste and chosen, to the utility and edification of the people; announcing to them vices and virtues, punishment and glory, with briefness of discourse; for the words were brief which the Lord spoke upon earth.

The brothers who are the ministers and servants of the other brothers shall visit and admonish their brothers and humbly and lovingly correct them; not teaching them anything which is against their soul and against our Rule. But the brothers who are subjected to them shall remember that, before God, they have discarded their own wills. Wherefore I firmly command them that they obey their ministers in all things which they have promised God to observe, and which are not contrary to their souls and to our Rule. . . .

I firmly command all the brothers not to have suspicious intercourse or to take counsel with women. And, with the exception of those to whom special permission has been given by the Apostolic Chair, let them not enter nunneries. Neither may they become fellow god-parents with men or women, lest from this cause a scandal may arise among the brothers or concerning brothers.

Whoever of the brothers by divine inspiration may wish to go among the Saracens and other infidels, shall seek permission to do so from their provincial ministers. But to none shall the ministers give permission to go, save to those whom they shall see to be fit for the mission.

Furthermore, through their obedience I enjoin on the ministers that they demand from the lord pope one of the cardinals of the holy Roman Church, who shall be the governor, corrector and protector of that fraternity, so that, always subjected and lying at the feet of that same holy Church, steadfast in the catholic faith, we may observe poverty and humility, and the holy Gospel of our Lord Jesus Christ; as we have firmly promised.

From Clare's *Testament*

In the name of the Lord!

Among all the other gifts which we have received and continue to receive daily from our benefactor, *the Father of mercies* (2 Cor. 1:3), and for which we must express the deepest thanks to our glorious God, our vocation is a great gift. Since it is the more perfect and greater, we should be so much more thankful to Him for it. For this reason the Apostle writes: "Acknowledge your calling" (1 Cor. 1:26).

The Son of God became for us *the Way* which our Blessed Father Francis, His true lover and imitator, has shown and taught us by word and example.

Therefore, beloved Sisters, we must consider the immense gifts which God has bestowed on us, especially those which He has seen fit to work in us through His beloved servant, our blessed Father Francis, not only after our conversion but also while we were still [living among] the vanities of the world.

For, almost immediately after his conversion, while he had neither brothers nor companions, when he was building the Church of San Damiano in which he was totally filled with divine consolation, he was led to abandon the world completely. This holy man, in the great joy and enlightenment of the Holy Spirit, made a prophecy about us which the Lord fulfilled later. Climbing the wall of that church he shouted in French to some poor people who were standing nearby: "Come and help me build the Monastery of San Damiano, because ladies will dwell here who will glorify our heavenly Father throughout His holy Church by their celebrated and holy manner of life."

In this, then, we can consider the abundant kindness of God toward us. Because of His mercy and love, He saw fit to speak these words about our vocation and selection through His saint. And our most blessed Father prophesied not only for us, but also for those who were to come to this [same] holy vocation to which the Lord has called us.

With what solicitude and fervor of mind and body, therefore, must we keep the commandments of our God and Father, so that, with the help of the Lord, we may return to Him an increase of His *talents*. For the Lord Himself not only has set us as an example and mirror for others, but also for our [own] sisters whom the Lord has called to our way of life, so that they in turn will be a mirror and example to those living in the world. . . .

After the most high heavenly Father saw fit in His mercy and grace to enlighten my heart to do penance according to the example and teaching of our most blessed Father Francis, shortly after his own conversion, I, together with the few sisters whom the Lord had given me soon after my conversion, voluntarily promised him obedience, since the Lord had given us the Light of His grace through his holy life and teaching.

But when the Blessed Francis saw that, although we were physically weak and frail, we did not shirk deprivation, poverty, hard work, distress, or the shame or contempt of the world — rather, as he and his brothers often saw for themselves, we considered [all such trials] as great delights after the example of the saints and their brothers — he rejoiced greatly in the Lord. And moved by compassion for us, he promised to have always, both through himself and through his Order, the same loving care and special solicitude for us as for his own brothers.

And thus, by the will of God and our most blessed Father Francis, we went to dwell at the Church of San Damiano. There, in a short time, the Lord increased our number by His mercy and grace so that what He had predicted through His saint might be fulfilled. We had stayed in another place [before this], but only for a little while.

Later on he wrote a form of life for us, [indicating] especially that we should persevere always in holy poverty. And while he was living, he was not content to encourage us by many words and examples to love and observe holy poverty; [in addition] he also gave us many writings so that, after his death, we should in no way turn away from it. [In a similar way] the Son of God never wished to abandon this holy poverty while He lived in the world, and our most blessed Father Francis, following His footprints, never departed, either in example or teaching, from this holy poverty which he had chosen for himself and for his brothers.

Therefore, I, Clare, the handmaid of Christ and of the Poor Sisters of the Monastery of San Damiano — although unworthy — and the little plant of the holy Father, consider together with my sisters our most high profession and the command of so great a father. [We also take note] in some [sisters] of the frailty which we feared in ourselves after the death of our holy Father Francis, [He] who was our pillar of strength and, after God, our one consolation and support. [Thus] time and again, we bound ourselves to our Lady, most holy Poverty, so that, after my death, the Sisters present and to come would never abandon her.

And, as I have always been most zealous and solicitous to observe and to have the other sisters observe the holy poverty which we have promised the Lord and our holy Father Francis, so, too, the others who will succeed me in office should be bound always to observe it and have it observed by the other sisters. . . .

In the Lord Jesus Christ, I admonish and exhort all my Sisters, both those present and those to come, to strive always to imitate the way of holy simplicity, humility, and poverty and [to preserve] the integrity of [our] holy manner of life, as we were taught by our blessed Father Francis from the beginning of our conversion to Christ. Thus may they always remain *in the fragrance* of a good name, both among those who are afar off and those who are near. [This will take place] not by our own merits but solely by the mercy and grace of our Benefactor, the *Father of mercies*. . . .

I also beg that sister who will have the office [of caring for] the Sisters to strive to exceed others more by her virtues and holy life than by her office so that, encouraged by her example, the Sisters may obey her not so much out of duty but rather out of love. Let her also be prudent and attentive to her Sisters just as a good mother is to her daughters; and especially, let her take care to provide for them according to the needs of each one from the things which the Lord shall give. Let her also be so kind and so available that all [of them] may reveal their needs with trust and have recourse to her at any hour with confidence as they see fit, both for her sake and that of her Sisters.

But the sisters who are subjects should keep in mind that for the Lord's sake they have given up their own wills. Therefore I ask that they obey their mother as they have promised the Lord of their own free will so that, seeing the charity, humility, and unity they have toward one another, their mother might bear all the burdens of her office more lightly. Thus what is painful and bitter might be turned into sweetness for her because of their holy way of life. . . .

So that it may be observed better, I leave this writing for you, my dearest and most beloved Sisters, those present and those to come, as a sign of the blessing of the Lord and of our most blessed Father Francis and of my blessing — I who am your mother and servant.

DISCUSSION QUESTIONS

1. Based on his *Rule*, how would you characterize St. Francis's spirituality and sense of mission? Why might he have appealed to so many people at the time?

2. How does St. Clare echo Francis's ideals in her *Testament*?

3. What goals did Francis and Clare share in composing the *Rule* and *Testament*, respectively?

4. What do both documents reveal about contemporary attitudes toward women?

5.
The Sack of Constantinople
Annals of Niketas Choniatēs (1204)

As Europe became more confident and aggressive in the twelfth century, cracks began to appear in the edifice of the Byzantine state. The army and navy had lost much of their strength and, to make matters worse, in 1201 rival claimants to the imperial throne were embroiled in a dispute. This crisis coincided with the Roman Catholic pope's call for a new crusade to the Holy Land and served as a pretext for a detour by the crusaders to the Byzantine capital of Constantinople (present-day Istanbul). Fueled by religious zeal and prejudice, in April 1204 the crusaders swiftly and savagely sacked the city. Greek historian and imperial official Niketas Choniatēs (c. 1155–1215) witnessed the rampage firsthand, which he describes in the excerpt from his Annals *that follows. Other sources confirm many of the details of Niketas Choniatēs' account, although he clearly viewed the crusaders through a distinctive lens. Steeped in classical Greek, Christian, and Byzantine traditions, he was highly critical not only of the crusaders' violent acts but also of what he perceived as the barbarity underlying them. His criticism had little effect. Although the empire regained control of Constantinople in 1261, it was never again a dominant political force in the West.*

As dawn broke on . . . [9 April 1204], the warships and dromons approached the walls, and certain courageous warriors climbed the scaling ladders and discharged all manner of missiles against the towers' defenders. All through the day, a battle fraught with groanings was waged. The Romans had the upper hand: both the ships carrying the scaling ladders and the dromons transporting the horses were repulsed from the walls they had attacked without success, and many were killed by the stones thrown from the City's engines.

The enemy ceased all hostilities through the next day and the day after, . . . on the third day, . . . they again sailed towards the City and put in along the shore. By midday our forces prevailed, even though the fighting was more intense and furious than on the preceding Friday. Since it was necessary for the queen of cities to put on the slave's yoke, God allowed our jaws to be constrained with bit and curb because all of us, both priest and people, had turned away from him like a stiff-necked and unbridled horse. Two men on one of the scaling ladders nearest the Petria Gate, which was raised with great difficulty opposite the emperor, trusting themselves to fortune, were the first from among their comrades to leap down onto the tower facing them. When they drove off in alarm the Roman auxiliaries on watch, they waved their hands from above as a sign of joy and courage to embolden their countrymen. While they were jumping onto the tower, a knight by the name of Peter[1] entered through the gate situated there. He was deemed most

---

From Niketas Choniatēs, *O City of Byzantium, Annals of Niketas Choniatēs*, trans. Harry J. Magoulias (Detroit: Wayne State University Press, 1984), 312–17.

[1]This was Peter of Amiens, who led a party of ten knights and sixty sergeants. [Ed.]

capable of driving in rout all the battalions, for he was nearly nine fathoms tall and wore on his head a helmet fashioned in the shape of a towered city. The noblemen about the emperor and the rest of the troops were unable to gaze upon the front of the helm of a single knight so terrible in form and spectacular in size and took to their customary flight as the efficacious medicine of salvation. Thus, by uniting and fusing into one craven soul, the cowardly thousands, who had the advantage of a high hill, were chased by one man from the fortifications they were meant to defend. When they reached the Golden Gate of the Land walls, they pulled down the new-built wall there, ran forth, and dispersed, deservedly taking the road to perdition and utter destruction. The enemy, now that there was no one to raise a hand against them, ran everywhere and drew the sword against every age and sex. Each did not join with the next man to form a coherent battle array, but all poured out and scattered, since everyone was terrified of them.

That evening the enemy set fire to the eastern sections of the City . . . from there the flames spread to those areas that slope down to the sea and terminate in the vicinity of the Droungarios Gate. After despoiling the emperor's pavilion and taking the palace in Blachernai by assault without difficulty, they set up their general headquarters at the Pantepoptēs monastery. The emperor went hither and yon through the City's narrow streets, attempting to rally and mobilize the populace who wandered aimlessly about. Neither were they convinced by his exhortations nor did they yield to his blandishments, but the fiercely shaken aegis filled all with despair.

To continue with the remaining portions of my narrative, the day waned and night came on, and each and every citizen busied himself with removing and burying his possessions. Some chose to leave the City, and whoever was able hastened to save himself.

The enemy, who had expected otherwise, found no one openly venturing into battle or taking up arms to resist; they saw that the way was open before them and everything there for the taking. The narrow streets were clear and the crossroads unobstructed, safe from attack, and advantageous to the enemy. The populace, moved by the hope of propitiating them, had turned out to greet them with crosses and venerable icons of Christ as was customary during festivals of solemn processions. But their disposition was not at all affected by what they saw, nor did their lips break into the slightest smile, nor did the unexpected spectacle transform their grim and frenzied glance and fury into a semblance of cheerfulness. Instead, they plundered with impunity and stripped their victims shamelessly, beginning with their carts. Not only did they rob them of their substance but also the articles consecrated to God; the rest fortified themselves all around with defensive weapons as their horses were roused at the sound of the war trumpet.

What then should I recount first and what last of those things dared at that time by these murderous men? O, the shameful dashing to earth of the venerable icons and the flinging of the relics of the saints, who had suffered for Christ's sake, into defiled places! How horrible it was to see the Divine Body and Blood of Christ poured out and thrown to the ground! These forerunners of Antichrist, chief agents and harbingers of his anticipated ungodly deeds, seized as plunder the precious chalices and patens; some they smashed, taking possession of the ornaments embellishing them, and they set the remaining vessels on their tables to serve as bread dishes and wine goblets. Just as happened long ago, Christ was now disrobed and mocked, his garments were parted, and lots were cast for them by this race; and although his side was not pierced by the lance, yet once more streams of Divine Blood poured to the earth.

The report of the impious acts perpetrated in the Great Church[2] are unwelcome to the ears. The table of sacrifice, fashioned from every kind of precious material and fused by fire into one whole — blended together into a perfection of one multicolored thing of beauty, truly extraordinary and admired by all nations — was broken into pieces and divided among the despoilers, as was the lot of all the sacred church treasures, countless in number and unsurpassed in beauty. They found it fitting to bring out as so much booty the all-hallowed vessels and furnishings which had been wrought with incomparable elegance and craftsmanship from rare materials. In addition, in order to remove the pure silver which overlay the railing of the bema, the wondrous pulpit and the gates, as well as that which covered a great many other adornments, all of which were plated with gold, they led to the very sanctuary of the temple itself mules and asses with packsaddles; some of these, unable to keep their feet on the smoothly polished marble floors, slipped and were pierced by knives so that the excrement from the bowels and the spilled blood defiled the sacred floor. . . .

It was not that these crimes were committed in this fashion while others were not, or that some acts were more heinous than others, but that the most wicked and impious deeds were perpetrated by all with one accord. Did these madmen, raging thus against the sacred, spare pious matrons and girls of marriageable age or those maidens who, having chosen a life of chastity, were consecrated to God? Above all, it was a difficult and arduous task to mollify the barbarians with entreaties and to dispose them kindly towards us, as they were highly irascible and bilious and unwilling to listen to anything. Everything incited their anger, and they were thought fools and became a laughingstock. He who spoke freely and openly was rebuked, and often the dagger would be drawn against him who expressed a small difference of opinion or who hesitated to carry out their wishes.

. . . There were lamentations and cries of woe and weeping in the narrow ways, wailing at the crossroads, moaning in the temples, outcries of men, screams of women, the taking of captives, and the dragging about, tearing in pieces, and raping of bodies heretofore sound and whole. They who were bashful of their sex were led about naked, they who were venerable in their old age uttered plaintive cries, and the wealthy were despoiled of their riches. Thus it was in the squares, thus it was on the corners, thus it was in the temples, thus it was in the hiding places; for there was no place that could escape detection or that could offer asylum to those who came streaming in.

O City, City, eye of all cities, universal boast, supramundane wonder, wet nurse of churches, leader of the faith, guide of Orthodoxy, beloved topic of orations, the abode of every good thing! O City, that has drunk at the hand of the Lord the cup of his fury!

---

[2]**Great Church**: Hagia Sophia. [Ed.]

DISCUSSION QUESTIONS

1. What language does Choniatēs use to describe the crusaders and their actions? What does this suggest about Greek attitudes toward western Europeans and their culture?

2. How does Choniatēs portray the emperor and residents of the city? How did they react to the crusaders' actions?

3. What does Choniatēs reveal about the layout of Constantinople? Why do you think he included such details in his account?

4. Why does Choniatēs focus in particular on the crusaders' destruction of religious property? Why would this have been especially disturbing to him and other Byzantine Greeks?

COMPARATIVE QUESTIONS

1. What do Abelard's story and the privileges granted to students by Frederick I and Philip II suggest about the culture of learning at the time? Why was it so appealing to students? Why do you think political authorities were willing to grant them special privileges?

2. In what ways did the increase in wealth in twelfth-century Europe shape the ideals of Chrétien de Troyes and St. Francis?

3. How would you describe the roles of students as defined in Document 2 and of St. Francis and his followers in Document 4? What features do they share? How do they differ? Do you see any potential points of conflict?

4. Compare the behavior of the fictional hero Lancelot to that of the real-life crusaders described in the *Annals of Niketas Choniatēs*. What similarities and/or differences do you see? What do both sources suggest about Western aristocratic values and measures of self-worth at the time?

The Medieval Synthesis — and Its Cracks

1215–1340

H armony, order, and unity were the ideals sought by people from all walks of life in the medieval West between 1215 and 1340. Guided by the papacy, the church drove these efforts as it worked to codify religious doctrine and reform the laity. The first document illuminates scholasticism, an important force underlying these efforts that strove to summarize and reconcile all knowledge. Responding in kind, many laypeople, especially women, sought greater involvement in their religion and a deeper relationship with Christ. The second document captures the voice of one of these women, Hadewijch of Brabant (?–1248). The third document reveals the dark side of this trend as anti-Jewish feelings grew across Europe. The search for meaning in a world looking for unity also found literary and political expression. As reflected in the fourth document, vernacular literature blossomed beneath the pen of Italian poet Dante Alighieri (1265–1321), who harmonized heaven and earth through the language of poetry. At the same time, the fifth document set demonstrates how some monarchs instituted their own politics of control to broaden both the scope and basis of their power. Their success on this front brought them into conflict with other established authorities, notably the pope, who saw his influence severely weakened as a result.

1.
Reconciling Faith and Reason
Thomas Aquinas, *Summa Theologiae* (1273)

Dominican theologian and university professor Thomas Aquinas (c. 1225–1274) embodied the general search for harmony and order characteristic of the period

From *The Library of Original Sources: Ideas That Have Influenced Civilization, in the Original Documents, Translated*, vol. IV, ed. Oliver J. Thatcher (Metuchen, NJ: Mini-Print Corporation, 1971), 359–63.

1215–1340. Guided by the works of Aristotle, Aquinas embraced the power of human reason to examine important issues, both natural and divine. The title of his most famous work, Summa Theologiae, *reflects the confidence that he and other scholastics had in their ability to summarize knowledge for the benefit of teachers and students alike. Aquinas's systematic approach to this monumental task is embedded within the organization of the* Summa *itself. The material is divided into major topics, which in turn are divided into subtopics. He breaks down the content further still with "articles" where he poses a series of questions related to the corresponding subtopic. He then lays out the evidence for yes and no responses, ultimately guiding his reader to what he considers to be the correct conclusion. In doing so, Aquinas sought to convey not only theological fundamentals but also a way of thinking about complex issues in a logical and orderly way. The excerpt below is from the* Summa's *examination of the question of how we know that God exists, which for Aquinas was the essential starting point for understanding and explaining God's teachings.*

On the Existence of God

Article II. Whether the existence of God is demonstratable.

Let us proceed to the second point. It is objected (1) that the existence of God is not demonstratable: that God's existence is an article of faith, and that articles of faith are not demonstratable, because the office of demonstration is to prove, but faith pertains (only) to things that are not to be proven, as is evident from the Epistle to the Hebrews, XI. Hence that God's existence is not demonstratable.

Again, (2) that the subject matter of demonstration is that something exists, but in the case of God we cannot know what exists, but only what does not, as Damascenus[1] says (Of the Orthodox Faith, I.,4.) Hence that we cannot demonstrate God's existence.

Again, (3) that if God's existence is to be proved it must be from what He causes, and that what He effects is not sufficient for His supposed nature, since He is infinite, but the effects finite, and the finite is not proportional to the infinite. Since, therefore, a cause cannot be proved through an effect not proportional to itself, it is said that God's existence cannot be proved.

But against this argument the apostle says (Rom. I., 20), "The unseen things of God are visible through His manifest works." But this would not be so unless it were possible to demonstrate God's existence through His works. What ought to be understood concerning anything, is first of all, whether it exists.

Conclusion. It is possible to demonstrate God's existence, although not a priori (by pure reason), yet a posteriori from some work of His more surely known to us.[2]

In answer I must say that the proof is double. One is through the nature of a cause and is called *propter quid*: this is through the nature of preceding events

---

[1]John of Damascus (ca. 676–749), a Christian theologian. [Ed.]
[2]Here Aquinas is distinguishing between knowledge obtained through logic and reason (a priori) as opposed to from facts and observation (a posteriori). [Ed.]

simply. The other is through the nature of the effect, and is called *quia*, and is through the nature of preceding things as respects us.

Since the effect is better known to us than the cause, we proceed from the effect to the knowledge of the cause. From any effect whatsoever it can be proved that a corresponding cause exists, if only the effects of it are sufficiently known to us, for since effects depend on causes, the effect being given, it is necessary that a preceding cause exists. Whence, that God exists, although this is not itself known to us, is provable through effects that are known to us.

To the first objection above, I reply, therefore, that God's existence, and those other things of this nature that can be known through natural reason concerning God, as is said in Rom. I., are not articles of faith, but preambles to these articles. So faith presupposes natural knowledge, so grace nature, and perfection a perfectible thing. Nothing prevents a thing that is in itself demonstratable and knowable, from being accepted as an article of faith by someone that does not accept the proof of it.

To the second objection, I reply that, since the cause is proven from the effect, one must use the effect in the place of a definition of the cause in demonstrating that the cause exists; and that this applies especially in the case of God, because for proving that anything exists, it is necessary to accept in this method what the name signifies, not however that anything exists, because the question *what it is* is secondary to the question *whether it exists at all*. The characteristics of God are drawn from His works as shall be shown hereafter. Whence by providing that God exists through His works as shall be shown hereafter. Whence by proving that God exists through His works, we are able by this very method to see what the name God signifies.

To the third objection, I reply that, although a perfect knowledge of the cause cannot be had from inadequate effects, yet that from any effect manifest to us it can be shown that a cause does exist, as has been said. And thus from the works of God His existence can be proved, although we cannot in this way know Him perfectly in accordance with His own essence.

Article III. Whether God exists.

Let us proceed to the third article. It is objected (1) that God does not exist, because if one of two contradictory things is infinite, the other will be totally destroyed; that it is implied in the name God that there is a certain infinite goodness: if then God existed, no evil would be found. But evil is found in the world; therefore it is objected that God does not exist.

Again, that what can be accomplished through a less number of principles will not be accomplished through more. It is objected that all things that appear on the earth can be accounted for through other principles, without supposing that God exists, since what is natural can be traced to a natural principle, and what proceeds from a proposition can be traced to the human reason or will. Therefore that there is no necessity to suppose that God exists.

But as against this note what is said of the person of God (Exod. III., 14) *I am that I am.*

Conclusion. There must be found in the nature of things one first immovable Being, a primary cause, necessarily existing, not created; existing the most widely, good, even the best possible; the first ruler through the intellect, and the ultimate end of all things, which is God.

I answer that it can be proved in five ways that God exists. The first and plainest is the method that proceeds from the point of view of motion. It is certain and in accord with experience, that things on earth undergo change. Now everything that is moved is moved by something; nothing, indeed, is changed, except it is changed to something which it is in potentiality. Moreover, anything moves in accordance with something actually existing; change itself, is nothing else than to bring forth something from potentiality into actuality. Now nothing can be brought from potentiality to actual existence except through something actually existing: thus heat in action, as fire, makes fire-wood, which is hot in potentiality, to be hot actually, and through this process, changes itself. The same thing cannot at the same time be actually and potentially the same thing, but only in regard to different things. What is actually hot cannot be at the same time potentially hot, but it is possible for it at the same time to be potentially cold. It is impossible, then, that anything should be both mover and the thing moved, in regard to the same thing and in the same way, or that it should move itself. Everything, therefore, is moved by something else. If, then, that by which it is moved, is also moved, this must be moved by something still different, and this, again, by something else. But this process cannot go on to infinity (1) because there would not be any first mover, nor, because of this fact, anything else in motion, as the succeeding things would not move except because of what is moved by the first mover, just as a stick is not moved except through what is moved from the hand. Therefore it is necessary to go back to some first mover, which is itself moved by nothing, and this all men know as God.

The second proof is from the nature of the efficient cause. We find in our experience that there is a chain of causes: nor is it found possible for anything to be the efficient cause of itself, since it would have to exist before itself, which is impossible. Nor in the case of efficient causes causes can the chain go back indefinitely, because in all chains of efficient causes, the first is the cause of the middle, and these of the last, whether they be one or many. If the cause is removed, the effect is removed. Hence if there is not a first cause, there will not be a last, nor a middle. But if the chain were to go back infinitely, there would be no first cause, and thus no ultimate effect, nor middle causes, which is admittedly false. Hence we must presuppose some first efficient cause, which all call God.

The third proof is taken from the natures of the merely possible and necessary. We find that certain things either may or may not exist, since they are found to come into being and be destroyed, and in consequence potentially, either existent or non-existent. But it is impossible for all things that are of this character to exist eternally, because what *may* not exist, at length *will* not. If, then, all things were merely possible (mere accidents), eventually nothing among things would exist. If this is true, even now there would be nothing, because what does not exist, does not take its beginning except through something that does exist. If then nothing existed, it would be impossible for anything to begin, and there would now be nothing existing, which is admittedly false. Hence not all things are mere accidents, but there must be one necessarily existing being. Now every necessary thing either has a cause of its necessary existence, or has not. In the case of necessary things that have a cause for their necessary existence, the chain of causes cannot go back infinitely, just as not in the case of efficient causes, as proved. Hence there must be presupposed something necessarily existing through its own nature, not having a cause elsewhere but being itself the cause of the necessary existence of other things, — which all call God.

The fourth proof arises from the degrees that are found in things. For there is found a greater and a less degree of goodness, truth, nobility, and the like. But more or less are terms spoken of various things as they approach in diverse ways toward something that is the greatest, just as in the case of hotter (more hot) which approaches nearer the greatest heat. There exists therefore something that is the truest, and best, and most noble, and in consequence, the greatest being. For what are the greatest truths are the greatest beings, as is said in the Metaphysics Bk. II. 2. What moreover is the greatest in its way, in another way is the cause of all things of its own kind (or genus); thus fire, which is the greatest heat, is the cause of all heat, as is said in the same book (cf. Plato and Aristotle). Therefore there exists something that is the cause of the existence of all things and of the goodness and of every perfection whatsoever — and this we call God.

The fifth proof arises from the ordering of things for we see that some things which lack reason such as natural bodies are operated in accordance with a plan. It appears from this that they are operated always or the more frequently in this same way the closer they follow what is the Highest; whence it is clear that they do not arrive at the result by chance but because of a purpose. The things, moreover, that do not have intelligence do not tend toward a result unless directed by some one knowing and intelligent; just as an arrow is sent by an archer. Therefore there is something intelligent by which all natural things are arranged in accordance with a plan, — and this we call God.

In response to the first objection, then, I reply what Augustine says; that since God is entirely good, He would permit evil to exist in His works only if He were so good and omnipotent that He might bring forth good even from the evil. It therefore pertains to the infinite goodness of God that he permits evil to exist and from this brings forth good.

My reply to the second objection is that since nature is ordered in accordance with some defined purpose by the direction of some superior agent, those things that spring from nature must be dependent upon God, just as upon a first cause. Likewise what springs from a proposition must be traceable to some higher cause which is not the human reason or will, because this is changeable and defective and everything changeable and liable to non-existence is dependent upon some unchangeable first principle that is necessarily self-existent as has been shown.

DISCUSSION QUESTIONS

1. What objections does Aquinas think some people may have to the idea of God's existence?

2. What does he offer as proof against such objections? Summarize one of them in your own words.

3. In its most basic form, scholasticism was a method of logical inquiry and exposition. In what ways do both the content of this excerpt and its organization, notably Aquinas's use of objections and proofs, reflect these characteristics?

2.
A Female Mystic
Hadewijch of Brabant, *Letters and Poems* (1220–1240)

The body of religious work written or dictated by women during the thirteenth century is considerable and attests to heightened piety of laypeople across Europe. Often the line between the genres of writing was blurred as ordinary women explored different means of religious expression. Hadewijch of Brabant was one of many such women writers, and our knowledge of her comes primarily from her writings in her native Dutch, which include thirty-one letters, fourteen visions, forty-five stanzaic poems, and several other poems. Although criticized by members of her own, probably Beguine, community, Hadewijch nonetheless typifies many women writers of this period. She uses mystical and seemingly erotic language to describe a relationship with Christ. Love is a central concept throughout her work, which she consistently genders as female. For her, the word refers to her experience of the divine, far removed from the systematic doctrine of scholastic summas. Although some Beguines bordered on the edge of unorthodoxy and were at times accused of heresy, most works by female mystics fit harmoniously with the writings of such church leaders as St. Bernard of Clairvaux (1090–1153) and Richard (1123–1173) and Hugh of St. Victor (1096–1141).

Letter 11

Ah, dear child, may God give you what my heart desires for you, and may you love Him as He deserves. Still, I could never endure, dear child, that someone before me loved God as dearly as I. I believe that many loved Him as fondly and dearly, yet I could hardly bear that someone would know Him with such passion.

From the age of ten I have been overwhelmed with such passionate love that I would have died during the first two years of this experience if God had not granted me a power unknown to common people and made me recover with His own being. For He soon granted me reason, sometimes enlightened with many wonderful revelations, and I received many wonderful gifts from Him, when He let me feel His presence and showed Himself to me. I was aware of many signs that were between Him and me, as with friends who are used to concealing little and revealing much when their feelings for each other have grown most intimate, when they taste, eat, and drink and consume each other wholly. Through these many signs God, my lover, showed to me early in life, He made me gain much con-

---

From "The Brabant Mystic: Hadewijch," in *Medieval Women Writers*, ed. Katherina M. Wilson (Athens: University of Georgia Press, 1984), 193–95, 198–201.

fidence in Him, and I often thought that no one loved Him as dearly as I. But meanwhile reason made me see that my love for Him was not the dearest, though the strong bonds of our loving had prevented me from sensing or even believing this. Such then is my present state. I do no longer believe that my love for Him is the dearest, nor do I believe that there is one alive who loves God as dearly as I. Sometimes I am so enlightened with love that I realize my failure to give my beloved what He deserves; sometimes when I am blinded with love's sweetness, when I am tasting and feeling her, I realize she is enough for me; and sometimes when I am feeling so fulfilled in her presence, I secretly admit to her that she is enough for me.

Stanzaic Poem 8

Born is the new season as the old one that lasted so long is drawing to a close.
Those prepared to do love's service will receive her rewards: new comfort and
    new strength.
If they love her with the vigor of love, they will soon be one with love in love.

To be one with love is an awesome calling and those who long for it should spare
    no effort.
Beyond all reason they will give their all and go through all.
For love dwells so deep in the womb of the Father that her power will unfold only
    to those who serve her with utter devotion.

First the lover must learn charity and keep God's law.
Then he shall be blessed a hundredfold, and he shall do great things without great
    effort, and bear all pain without suffering.
And so his life will surpass human reason indeed.

Those who long to be one with love achieve great things, and shirk no effort.
They shall be strong and capable of any task that will win them the love of love,
    to help the sick or the healthy, the blind, the crippled or the wounded.
For this is what the lover owes to love.

He shall help the strangers and give to the poor and soothe the suffering when-
    ever he can.
He shall pay loyal service to God's friends, to saints and men, with a strength that
    is not human, by night and by day.
And when his strength seems to falter he will still place his trust in love.

Those who trust in love with all their being shall be given all they need.
For she brings comfort to the sad and guidance to those who cannot read.
Love will be pleased with the lover if he accepts no other comfort and trusts in
    her alone.

Those who desire to live in love alone with all their might and heart shall so
    dispose all things that they shall soon possess her all.

Stanzaic Poem 12

Like the noble season born to bring us flowers in the fields, so the noble ones are
    called to bear the yoke, the bonds of love.
Faith grows forever in their deeds, and noble flowers blossom and their fruits.
The world is fathomed with faith, and the lover dwells in highest love, one with
    her in everlasting friendship.

"My yoke is sweet, my burden light," love's lover speaks with words conceived in
    love.
And outside love their truth cannot be known: to those who do not dwell in love
    the burden is not light but heavy, and they suffer fears unknown to love.
For the servants' law is fear but love is the law of sons.

What is this burden light in love, this yoke so sweet?
It is that noble thrust inside, that touch of love in the beloved which makes him
    one with her, one will, one being, one beyond revoke.
And ever deeper digs desire and all that is dug up is drunk by love, for love's
    demands on love surpass the mind of man.

These things are beyond the mind of man: how the lover whom love has over-
    whelmed with love beholds the beloved so full of love.
For he rests not an hour, before he sails with love through all that is, and looks
    upon her splendor with devotion.
For in love's face he reads the designs she has for him, and in truth in love's face
    he sees clear and undeceived so many pains so sweet.

This he clearly sees: the lover must love in truth alone.
And when in truth he sees how little he does for love, his higher nature burns
    with rage and pain.
But from love's face, the lover learns to live a life devoted to the love of love.

This is a design that makes pain sweet, and the lover gives his all to love's
    fulfillment.

Things of great wonder come to those who give their all to love.
They will be glued to love with love, and with love they will fathom love.
All their secret veins will run into that stream where love gives love away, where
    love's friends are made drunk with love and filled with wonder at her passion.
And all this remains concealed to strangers, but to the wise it stands revealed.

God grant that all who crave love be well prepared for love, that they may live of
    her wealth alone, and draw her into their love.
No cruel stranger will ever cause them grief; their life is free and undisturbed,
    and well may they say, "I am all of love and love is all of me."
For what will harm them when they claim the sun, the moon, and all the stars?

DISCUSSION QUESTIONS

1. How does Hadewijch use gender imagery and language to express her feelings?

2. How would you describe Hadewijch's relationship with God and God's relationship with her?

3. What might have concerned some members of Hadewijch's community and some church authorities about her writings, as well as those of other female mystics? How did Hadewijch's approach challenge some accepted ways of thinking?

4. How does Hadewijch reflect the religious and cultural change of her times?

3.
Defining Outsiders

Thomas of Monmouth, *The Life and Martyrdom of St. William of Norwich* (c. 1173)

The church's efforts to reorder the world in the image of heaven helped to deepen popular piety but they also fostered intolerance. Jews in particular increasingly became objects of aggression in the thirteenth century, not only because of their religion but also because of their professional activities as moneylenders. The propagation of the belief that Jews secretly sacrificed Christian children — a belief that appeared in a fully developed form for the first time in The Life and Martyrdom of St. William of Norwich, *excerpted here — attests to the rise of anti-Jewish sentiment. This account was written by Thomas of Monmouth, a monk living in the English city of Norwich at the time when the events he describes allegedly took place. The evidence suggests that the body of a boy named William, who had met a violent death, was found in 1144. Thomas of Monmouth's story tells us more about the development of systematic anti-Jewish mentality than it does about historical facts, however. Although Jews had no rituals involving blood sacrifice, similar charges were made against them across Europe, often leading to their persecution.*

How He Was Wont to Resort to the Jews, and Having Been Chid by His Own People for So Doing, How He Withdrew Himself from Them

When therefore he was flourishing in this blessed boyhood of his and had attained to his eighth year [c. 1140], he was entrusted to the skinners[1] to be taught their craft. Gifted with a teachable disposition and bringing industry to bear upon it, in

---

From Thomas of Monmouth, *The Life and Miracles of St. William of Norwich*, trans. Augustus Jessopp and Montague Rhodes (Cambridge: Cambridge University Press, 1896), 14–17, 19–23. (Although *The Life and Martyrdom of St. William of Norwich* is the correct translation of the original Latin title, in English it is more generally known as *The Life and Miracles*.)

[1]**skinners**: Furriers. [Ed.]

a short time he far surpassed lads of his own age in the craft aforesaid, and he equaled some who had been his teachers. So leaving the country, by the drawing of a divine attraction he betook himself to the city and lodged with a very famous master of that craft, and some time passed away. He was seldom in the country, but was occupied in the city and sedulously gave himself to the practice of his craft, and thus reached his twelfth year.

Now, while he was staying in Norwich, the Jews who were settled there and required their cloaks or their robes or other garments (whether pledged to them, or their own property) to be repaired, preferred him before all other skinners. For they esteemed him to be especially fit for their work, either because they had learnt that he was guileless and skillful, or because attracted to him by their avarice they thought they could bargain with him for a lower price. Or, as I rather believe, because by the ordering of divine providence he had been predestined to martyrdom from the beginning of time, and gradually step by step was drawn on, and chosen to be made a mock of and to be put to death by the Jews, in scorn of the Lord's passion, as one of little foresight, and so the more fit for them. For I have learnt from certain Jews, who were afterwards converted to the Christian faith, how that at that time they had planned to do this very thing with some Christian, and in order to carry out their malignant purpose, at the beginning of Lent they had made choice of the boy William, being twelve years of age and a boy of unusual innocence. So it came to pass that when the holy boy, ignorant of the treachery that had been planned, had frequent dealings with the Jews, he was taken to task by Godwin the priest, who had the boy's aunt as his wife, and by a certain Wulward with whom he lodged, and he was prohibited from going in and out among them anymore. But the Jews, annoyed at the thwarting of their designs, tried with all their might to patch up a new scheme of wickedness, and all the more vehemently as the day for carrying out the crime they had determined upon drew near, and the victim which they had thought they had already secured had slipped out of their wicked hands. Accordingly, collecting all the cunning of their crafty plots, they found — I am not sure whether he was a Christian or a Jew — a man who was a most treacherous fellow and just the fitting person for carrying out their execrable crime, and with all haste — for their Passover was coming on in three days — they sent him to find out and bring back with him the victim which, as I said before, had slipped out of their hands.

How He Was Seduced by the Jews' Messenger

At the dawn of day, on the Monday after Palm Sunday, that detestable messenger of the Jews set out to execute the business that was committed to him, and at last the boy William, after being searched for with very great care, was found. When he was found, he got round him with cunning wordy tricks, and so deceived him with his lying promises. . . .

How on His Going to the Jews He Was Taken, Mocked, and Slain

Then the boy, like an innocent lamb, was led to the slaughter. He was treated kindly by the Jews at first, and, ignorant of what was being prepared for him, he was kept till the morrow. But on the next day, which in that year was the Passover for them,[2] after the singing of the hymns appointed for the day in the synagogue, the chiefs of the Jews . . . suddenly seized hold of the boy William as he was having his dinner and in no fear of any treachery, and ill-treated him in various horrible ways. For while some of them held him behind, others opened his mouth and introduced an instrument of torture which is called a teazle,[3] and, fixing it by straps through both jaws to the back of his neck, they fastened it with a knot as tightly as it could be drawn. After that, taking a short piece of rope of about the thickness of one's little finger and tying three knots in it at certain distances marked out, they bound round that innocent head with it from the forehead to the back, forcing the middle knot into his forehead and the two others into his temples, the two ends of the rope being most tightly stretched at the back of his head and fastened in a very tight knot. The ends of the rope were then passed round his neck and carried round his throat under his chin, and there they finished off this dreadful engine of torture in a fifth knot.

But not even yet could the cruelty of the torturers be satisfied without adding even more severe pains. Having shaved his head, they stabbed it with countless thorn-points, and made the blood come horribly from the wounds they made. And cruel were they and so eager to inflict pain that it was difficult to say whether they were more cruel or more ingenious in their tortures. For their skill in torturing kept up the strength of their cruelty and ministered arms thereto. And thus, while these enemies of the Christian name were rioting in the spirit of malignity around the boy, some of those present adjudged him to be fixed to a cross in mockery of the Lord's passion, as though they would say, "Even as we condemned the Christ to a shameful death, so let us also condemn the Christian, so that, uniting the Lord and his servant in a like punishment, we may retort upon themselves the pain of that reproach which they impute to us."

Conspiring, therefore, to accomplish the crime of this great and detestable malice, they next laid their blood-stained hands upon the innocent victim, and having lifted him from the ground and fastened him upon the cross, they vied with one another in their efforts to make an end of him. And we, after enquiring into the matter very diligently, did both find the house, and discovered some most certain marks in it of what had been done there. For report goes that there was there instead of a cross a post set up between two other posts, and a beam stretched across the midmost post and attached to the other on either side. And as we afterwards discovered, from the marks of the wounds and of the bands, the right hand and foot had been tightly bound and fastened with cords, but the left hand and foot were pierced with two nails: so in fact the deed was done by design that, in case at any time he should be found, when the fastenings of the nails were discovered it might not be supposed that he had been killed by Jews rather than by Christians. But while in doing these things they were adding pang to pang and wound to wound, and yet were not able to satisfy their heartless cruelty and their inborn hatred of the Christian name, lo! after all these many and great tortures, they

---

[2]In 1144, Easter fell on March 26 and Passover began on March 25.
[3]**teazle**: Wooden gag. [Ed.]

inflicted a frightful wound in his left side, reaching even to his inmost heart, and as though to make an end of all they extinguished his mortal life so far as it was in their power. And since many streams of blood were running down from all parts of his body, then, to stop the blood and to wash and close the wounds, they poured boiling water over him.

Thus then the glorious boy and martyr of Christ, William, dying the death of time in reproach of the Lord's death, but crowned with the blood of a glorious martyrdom, entered into the kingdom of glory on high to live for ever. Whose soul rejoiceth blissfully in heaven among the bright hosts of the saints, and whose body by the omnipotence of the divine mercy worketh miracles upon earth.

DISCUSSION QUESTIONS

1. What might Thomas of Monmouth have hoped to achieve in composing this text?

2. According to the text, the way the Jews murdered William was designed to mock the crucifixion of Christ. Why would this have been especially threatening to Christians at the time?

3. By the end of the twelfth century, William's cult was firmly established, and his tomb was the purported site of many miracles and visions. Why did people accept the story of his martyrdom and his status as a true saint?

4.
Imagining Hell

Dante Alighieri, *Divine Comedy* (1313–1321)

Like Hadewijch of Brabant, Dante Alighieri (1265–1321) combined poetry and the vernacular to explore the mysteries of faith and love. Born in Florence at a time rife with political struggles, Dante served in the city government and as a papal envoy, and eventually suffered exile from his beloved city. But Dante is most celebrated as one of the world's greatest poets. Through his artistry, Dante is widely credited with making Tuscan the language of Italy and spreading its use. His most famous poem, the Divine Comedy, *describes his imaginary trip from hell to purgatory to paradise. Written between 1313 and 1321, the poem functions at both literal and allegorical levels as Dante embarks on a journey to understand the meaning of life. The excerpt that follows is from the first part of the poem,* Inferno, *in which the pagan poet Virgil guides Dante through the circles of hell. Along the way, they meet a colorful cast of legendary and historical characters whose sins help Dante better understand his own sins, a crucial first step toward his ultimate salvation.*

From *The Inferno of Dante*, trans. Robert Pinsky (New York: Farrar, Straus and Giroux, 1994), 47–53.

Canto V

So I descended from first to second circle —
    Which girdles a smaller space and greater pain,
    Which spurs more lamentation. Minos[1] the dreadful
Snarls at the gate. He examines each one's sin,
    Judging and disposing as he curls his tail:
    That is, when an ill-begotten soul comes down,
It comes before him, and confesses all;
    Minos, great connoisseur of sin, discerns
    For every spirit its proper place in Hell,
And wraps himself in his tail with as many turns
    As levels down that shade will have to dwell.
    A crowd is always waiting: here each one learns
His judgment and is assigned a place in Hell.
    They tell; they hear — and down they all are cast.
    "You, who have come to sorrow's hospice, think well,"
Said Minos, who at the sight of me had paused
    To interrupt his solemn task mid-deed:
    "Beware how you come in and whom you trust,
Don't be deceived because the gate is wide."
    My leader answered, "Must you too scold this way?
    His destined path is not for you to impede:
Thus is it willed where every thing may be
    Because it has been willed. So ask no more."
    And now I can hear the notes of agony
In sad crescendo beginning to reach my ear;
    Now I am where the noise of lamentation
    Comes at me in blasts of sorrow. I am where
All light is mute, with a bellowing like the ocean
    Turbulent in a storm of warring winds,
    The hurricane of Hell in perpetual motion
Sweeping the ravaged spirits as it rends,
    Twists, and torments them. Driven as if to land,
    They reach the ruin: groaning, tears, laments,
And cursing of the power of Heaven. I learned
    They suffer here who sinned in carnal things —
    Their reason mastered by desire, suborned.
As winter starlings riding on their wings
    Form crowded flocks, so spirits dip and veer
    Foundering in the wind's rough buffetings,

---

[1]Minos is a mythological king and judge. Virgil casts him in the *Aeneid* as a judge of the underworld, and it is Dante who transforms him into a demonic creature.

Upward or downward, driven here and there
    With never ease from pain nor hope of rest.
    As chanting cranes will form a line in air,
So I saw souls come uttering cries — wind-tossed,
    And lofted by the storm. "Master," I cried,
    "Who are these people, by black air oppressed?"
"First among these you wish to know," he said,
    "Was empress of many tongues — she so embraced
    Lechery that she decreed it justified
Legally, to evade the scandal of her lust:
    She is that Semiramis[2] of whom we read,
    Successor and wife of Ninus, she possessed
The lands the Sultan rules. Next, she [Dido][3] who died
    By her own hand for love, and broke her vow
    To Sychaeus's ashes. After her comes lewd
And wanton Cleopatra. See Helen,[4] too,
    Who caused a cycle of many evil years;
    And great Achilles,[5] the hero whom love slew
In his last battle. Paris and Tristan[6] are here —"
    He pointed out by name a thousand souls
    Whom love had parted from our life, or more.
When I had heard my teacher tell the rolls
    Of knights and ladies of antiquity,
    Pity overwhelmed me. Half-lost in its coils,
"Poet," I told him, "I would willingly
    Speak with those two[7] who move along together,
    And seem so light upon the wind." And he:
"When they drift closer — then entreat them hither,
    In the name of love that leads them: they will respond."
    Soon their course shifted, and the merciless weather

---

[2]The ancient Assyrian queen Semiramis became legendary for sexual excess; one legend says that she legalized incest, to justify her own behavior.

[3]Dido is the Carthaginian queen who kills herself for love of Aeneas in Virgil's epic.

[4]Cleopatra, queen of Egypt, was the lover of both Julius Caesar and Mark Antony. Helen caused the rift that led to the Trojan War when she eloped with Paris.

[5]The idea that Achilles died for the love of the Trojan Polyxena was popular in the Middle Ages, but does not come from Homer.

[6]Tristan is a hero from medieval French romances, the lover of Iseult, the wife of his uncle, King Mark of Cornwall.

[7]Those two are Paolo and Francesca, historical contemporaries of Dante. Francesca was the wife of Gianciotto Malatesta of Rimini, but she fell in love with his brother, Paolo. Gianciotto murdered the lovers when they were discovered. The murder caused enormous scandal, and although Dante does not use Paolo's name at all, or Francesca's until line 103, there can be no doubt as to the identity of these lovers. The encounter that follows, in which Francesca tells Dante their sad tale, is one of the most celebrated passages in the *Commedia*.

Battered them toward us. I called against the wind,
    "O wearied souls! If Another [God][8] does not forbid,
    Come speak with us." As doves whom desire has summoned,
With raised wings steady against the current, glide
    Guided by will to the sweetness of their nest,
    So leaving the flock where Dido was, the two sped
Through the malignant air till they had crossed
    To where we stood — so strong was the compulsion
    Of my loving call. They spoke across the blast:
"O living soul, who with courtesy and compassion
    Voyage through black air visiting us who stained
    The world with blood: if heaven's King bore affection
For such as we are, suffering in this wind,
    Then we would pray to Him to grant you peace
    For pitying us in this, our evil end.
Now we will speak and hear as you may please
    To speak and hear, while the wind, for our discourse,
    Is still. My birthplace is a city[9] that lies
Where the Po finds peace with all its followers.
    Love, which in gentle hearts is quickly born,
    Seized him for my fair body — which, in a fierce
Manner that still torments my soul, was torn
    Untimely away from me. Love, which absolves
    None who are loved from loving, made my heart burn
With joy so strong that as you see it cleaves
    Still to him, here. Love gave us both one death.
    Caina awaits the one who took our lives."
These words were borne across from them to us.
    When I had heard those afflicted souls, I lowered
    My head, and held it so till I heard the voice
Of the poet ask, "What are you thinking?" I answered,
    "Alas — that sweet conceptions and passion so deep
    Should bring them here!" Then, looking up toward
The lovers: "Francesca, your suffering makes me weep
    For sorrow and pity — but tell me, in the hours
    Of sweetest sighing, how and in what shape
Or manner did Love first show you those desires
    So hemmed by doubt?" And she to me: "No sadness
    Is greater than in misery to rehearse
Memories of joy, as your teacher well can witness.
    But if you have so great a craving to measure
    Our love's first root, I'll tell it, with the fitness

---

[8]The direct mention of God is avoided in Hell.
[9]The city is Ravenna, on Italy's Adriatic (eastern) coast, Francesca's home.

Of one who weeps and tells. One day, for pleasure,
    We read of Lancelot,[10] by love constrained:
    Alone, suspecting nothing, at our leisure.
Sometimes at what we read our glances joined,
    Looking from the book each to the other's eyes,
    And then the color in our faces drained.
But one particular moment alone it was
    Defeated us: *the longed-for smile*, it said,
    Was kissed by that most noble lover: at this,
This one, who now will never leave my side,
    Kissed my mouth, trembling. A Galeotto,[11] that book!
    And so was he who wrote it; that day we read
No further." All the while the one shade spoke,
    The other at her side was weeping; my pity
    Overwhelmed me and I felt myself go slack:
Swooning as in death, I fell like a dying body.

DISCUSSION QUESTIONS

1. What transgressions have the people in Dante's second circle of hell committed?

2. What attitude does Dante express toward those who are in hell?

3. Dante is often portrayed as a "medieval" rather than a "Renaissance" poet. Why? What connections do you see in his poetry with the intellectual culture and Christian worldview of the time?

5.
The New Power of Medieval States

Pope Boniface VIII, *Unam Sanctam* (1302)
and
King Philip IV of France, *General Assembly of Paris* (1303)

In the thirteenth century, secular rulers throughout Europe sought to broaden their authority over people living within their lands, including the clergy. The pope vigorously resisted such efforts; as head of the universal church, the pope believed that he had exclusive jurisdiction over clerical matters. The documents below elucidate both sides of the argument against the backdrop of a bitter contest for power between Bon-

---

From *Documents of the Christian Church*, ed. Henry Bettenson (London: Oxford University Press, 1967), 115–16; and *Medieval Europe*, ed. Julius Kirshner and Karl F. Morrison (Chicago: University of Chicago Press, 1986), 390–91.

[10]Lancelot is a worthy knight in the Arthurian romances (see chapter 11, document 3). He betrays King Arthur, becoming the lover of Arthur's wife, Guinevere.

[11]Galeotto, or, in French, Gallehault, acted as messenger between Lancelot and Guinevere. The French version of his name has become a synonym for "pander" or "go-between."

iface VIII (r. 1294–1303) and King Philip IV of France (r. 1285–1314). The first is the papal bull Unam Sanctam *issued by Boniface to counter what he regarded as Philip's flagrant violations of clerical privilege. King Philip responded in kind by calling an assembly of his closest advisors to bring a host of charges against the pope, building on a strategy that he had already used in his conflict with Boniface. A year earlier, Philip had convened representatives of the clergy, nobles, and townspeople to garner support for his antipapal policies. His strategy succeeded in weakening the pope's claim to universal authority while laying the groundwork for the development of representative institutions in France.*

Unam Sanctam

We are obliged by the faith to believe and hold — and we do firmly believe and sincerely confess — that there is one Holy Catholic and Apostolic Church, and that outside this Church there is neither salvation nor remission of sins. . . . In which Church there is "one Lord, one faith, one baptism."[1] At the time of the flood there was one ark of Noah, symbolizing the one Church; this was completed in one cubit[2] and had one, namely Noah, as helmsman and captain; outside which all things on earth, we read, were destroyed. . . . Of this one and only Church there is one body and one head — not two heads, like a monster — namely Christ, and Christ's vicar is Peter, and Peter's successor, for the Lord said to Peter himself, "Feed My sheep."[3] "My sheep" He said in general, not these or those sheep; wherefore He is understood to have committed them all to him. . . .

And we learn from the words of the Gospel that in this Church and in her power are two swords, the spiritual and the temporal. For when the apostles said, "Behold, here" (that is, in the Church, since it was the apostles who spoke) "are two swords" — the Lord did not reply, "It is too much," but "It is enough."[4] Truly he who denies that the temporal sword is in the power of Peter, misunderstands the words of the Lord, "Put up thy sword into the sheath."[5] Both are in the power of the Church, the spiritual sword and the material. But the latter is to be used for the Church, the former by her; the former by the priest, the latter by kings and captains but at the will and by the permission of the priest. The one sword, then, should be under the other, and temporal authority subject to spiritual. For when the apostle says "there is no power but of God, and the powers that be are ordained of God"[6] they would not be so ordained were not one sword made subject to the other. . . .

Thus, concerning the Church and her power, is the prophecy of Jeremiah fulfilled, "See, I have this day set thee over the nations and over the kingdoms," etc.[7] If, therefore, the earthly power err, it shall be judged by the spiritual power; and if a

---

[1]Eph. iv. 5.
[2]Gen. vi. 16.
[3]John xxi. 17.
[4]Luke xxii. 38.
[5]John xviii. 11.
[6]Romans x. 1.
[7]Jer. i. 10.

lesser power err, it shall be judged by a greater. But if the supreme power err, it can only be judged by God, not by man; for the testimony of the apostle is "The spiritual man judgeth all things, yet he himself is judged of no man."[8] For this authority, although given to a man and exercised by a man, is not human, but rather divine, given at God's mouth to Peter and established on a rock for him and his successors in Him whom he confessed, the Lord saying to Peter himself, "Whatsoever thou shalt bind," etc.[9] Whoever therefore resists this power thus ordained of God, resists the ordinance of God. . . . Furthermore we declare, state, define and pronounce that it is altogether necessary to salvation for every human creature to be subject to the Roman pontiff.

General Assembly of Paris

We, Philip, by God's grace king of the French, have heard and understood the submissions and charges made by you, William of Plaisians, knight, and those previously made by our beloved and faithful Knight William of Nogaret, against Boniface, now presiding over the government of the Roman Church. We would gladly cover the shame of any father with our own mantle. Nevertheless, because of our fervor for the catholic faith, and the outstanding devotion we have for the sacrosanct Roman and universal Church, our mother and that of all the faithful, the spouse of Christ, following in the footsteps of our progenitors (who for the exaltation and the defense of ecclesiastical liberty and faith had no doubts at all about shedding their own blood), desiring to look after the interests of the faith and the state of the Church, in order to avoid the costs of a general scandal, we are unable under the pressure of conscience any longer to pass over said matters with closed eyes and pretended ignorance. Since Boniface's reputation has more and more often been vehemently and prominently burdened by frequently repeated complaints on these accounts, driven home by trustworthy men of great authority, since, when our faith is being destroyed, our own negligence, that of anybody else, and especially that of the kings and princes of the earth, who we know have received the power conferred upon us by the Lord in order to exalt and augment the faith, must be reproved, we assent to your requests in this respect, out of reverence for the divine name, reserving in all respects due honor and reverence to the sacrosanct Roman Church. We are prepared, and gladly offer ourselves, to the extent to which it falls within our purview, to lend our support, and to do so effectively, to the convocation and congregation of the said council,[10] so that in the said matters the truth may shine forth and all error recede, so that the state of the universal Church and of all Christendom, the faith, and the interests of the Holy Land may be taken thought for, and so that impending scandals and dangers may be countered. And we urgently request you archbishops, bishops, and other prelates here present, as sons of the Church and pillars of faith, called by the Lord to exer-

---

[8]1 Cor. ii. 15.

[9]Matt. xvi. 19.

[10]As part of the king's counterattack against Boniface, his minister had called for a general council to judge and depose the pope. [Ed.]

cise your part of the solicitude for the exaltation, augmentation, and conservation of the faith, and we beseech you by the bowels of Jesus Christ's mercy to devote every effort, as is fitting, to the convocation and congregation of the council, at which we are planning to be present in person, and to work in fitting ways and means effectively towards it.

There is need to ensure, however, that the said Boniface, who has already several times angrily and unlawfully threatened to proceed against us, will not, in trying to prevent his works of darkness, if there are any, from coming to light, directly or indirectly impede the convocation and congregation of the council, or, if he should fail in this endeavor, that he will not proceed against us, our state, churches, prelates, barons, and other faithful, vassals, and subjects, our lands or theirs, our kingdom and the kingdom's state, in any respect, abusing the spiritual sword, by excommunication, interdict, suspension, or in any other way, with the effect that our position in the same council would no longer be quite sound. We therefore call for review and appeal in writing, for ourselves and our adherents, and those wishing to adhere to us, to said general council, which we urgently petition be convoked, and to the true and legitimate supreme pontiff-to-be, and to others to whom one should be required to appeal, without withdrawing the appeal registered by said William of Nogaret, to which we adhered then and still adhere, urgently requesting testimonial letters of dismissal from you prelates and notaries, and expressly protesting our right to alter these calls for review and appeals where, when, and before whom we may consider it expedient.

DISCUSSION QUESTIONS

1. What does Boniface mean when he refers to temporal and spiritual swords? How does he define each and their relationship to each other?

2. How does Boniface use the swords as the basis for his claims for authority over Philip IV?

3. Describe Philip's response to these claims. How does he justify his actions against the pope? What does his argument suggest about his understanding of the basis of his rule?

COMPARATIVE QUESTIONS

1. What common assumptions about Europeans' religious and political identities do these documents share? In what ways does the conflict between Pope Boniface and King Philip IV of France reflect a shift in these assumptions?

2. How would you compare Hadewijch's search for religious understanding to that of Aquinas?

3. Compare and contrast the ways that Hadewijch and Dante approach the search for the soul's meaning. What similarities and differences do you see in their styles and use of language?

4. Hadewijch embodied the rise of intense lay piety in the twelfth and thirteenth centuries. How does this development relate to the intolerance for Jews revealed in *The Life and Martyrdom of St. William of Norwich*?

CHAPTER 13

Crisis and Renaissance

1340–1492

C urrents of both crisis and renewal swept through medieval society in the years 1340–1492. On the one hand, throughout the fourteenth century, Europeans faced myriad challenges, from pestilence to war to rebellions. On the other hand, the city-states of the northern Italian peninsula helped to spark a period of great creativity that historians often refer to as the Renaissance, which reached its peak in the 1400s. The documents in this chapter capture these twin themes, beginning with contemporary accounts of the catastrophic effects of the Black Death and the search for scapegoats, though many people viewed the plague as divine punishment. The Hundred Years' War (1337–1453) added to people's troubles as the kings of France and England battled for land and prestige. Both sides raised taxes to finance the war, leading to a wave of rebellions, including the English Peasants' Revolt of 1381, described in Document 2. The very church that at its height had claimed to be the spiritual and temporal head of Christendom could not help because it was a house divided and threatened by abuses and calls for reform, as the selections by Geoffrey Chaucer (c. 1342–1400; Document 3) and letters of Jan Hus (1427–1415; Document 4) reveal. At the same time, however, men of the upper classes in Italy defined themselves self-consciously as living in new times. For such men and a few women, this was a time of rebirth, distinct from what they viewed as a millennium of barbarism. Imitating the values and styles of antiquity, the Renaissance was defined by the *studia humanitatis* (roughly, the liberal arts), from which the term *humanism* was derived. The fifth document illustrates the application and possibilities of humanism, whereas the sixth document demonstrates that the realities of Italian life often did not match Renaissance ideals.

1.
Demographic Catastrophe

The Black Death (Fourteenth Century)

Few events in history have had such a shattering impact on every aspect of society as the plague, which reached Europe in 1347. The Black Death decimated a society already weakened by a demographic crisis, famines, and climatic disasters. It is esti-

mated that one-third of Europe's population died in the first wave of plague, which was followed by repeated outbreaks. Some cities may have lost over half their people in 1347–1348 alone. Though the devastation was social, psychological, economic, political, and even artistic, many historians believe that in the long term the plague led to significant changes and even improvements in Western life. The following documents describe the arrival of the plague in various places and responses to it, including searches for its cause and people on whom to fix blame. The plague ultimately precipitated much of the crisis that characterized the fourteenth century.

From Ordinances against the Spread of Plague, Pistoia

2 May, 1348

1. So that the sickness which is now threatening the region around Pistoia shall be prevented from taking hold of the citizens of Pistoia, no citizen or resident of Pistoia, wherever they are from or of what condition, status or standing they may be, shall dare or presume to go to Pisa or Lucca; and no one shall come to Pistoia from those places; penalty 500 pence. And no one from Pistoia shall receive or give hospitality to people who have come from those places; same penalty. And the guards who keep the gates of the city of Pistoia shall not permit anyone travelling to the city from Pisa or Lucca to enter; penalty 10 pence from each of the guards responsible for the gate through which such an entry has been made. But citizens of Pistoia now living within the city may go to Pisa and Lucca, and return again, if they first obtain permission from the common council — who will vote on the merits of the case presented to them. The licence is to be drawn up by the notary of the *anziani* and gonfalonier of the city.[1] And this ordinance is to be upheld and observed from the day of its ratification until 1 October, or longer if the council sees fit.

2. No one, whether from Pistoia or elsewhere, shall dare or presume to bring or fetch to Pistoia, whether in person or by an agent, any old linen or woollen cloths, for male or female clothing or for bedspreads; penalty 200 pence, and the cloth to be burnt in the public piazza of Pistoia by the official who discovered it.[2]

From Rosemary Horrox, ed. and trans., *The Black Death* (Manchester: Manchester University Press, 1994), 16–21, 23, 194–97, 207, 208, 219–22.

[1]The official rulers of Italian cities were the commune (a word which does not have its modern egalitarian connotations). They appointed a *podestà*, often a nobleman from outside the region, as their salaried chief executive. By the fourteenth century this arrangement was mirrored in many cities by the more broadly based *popolo*, represented by a governing council of *anziani* (elders). The *capitano del popolo* corresponded, in background and role, to the *podestà* of the commune.

[2]Later outbreaks of plague in Italian cities were often associated with the movement of cloth, and this requirement suggests that the connection may already have been noted. Contemporaries — who were not aware of the role played by fleas in the transmission of the disease — explained the connection as due to the trapping of corrupt air within the folds of fabric.

However it shall be lawful for citizens of Pistoia travelling within Pistoia and its territories to take linen and woollen cloths with them for their own use or wear, provided that they are in a pack or fardle weighing 30 lb or less. And this ordinance to be upheld and observed from the day of its ratification until 1 January. And if such cloth has already been brought into Pistoia, the bringer must take it away within three days of the ordinance's ratification; same penalty.

3. The bodies of the dead shall not be removed from the place of death until they have been enclosed in a wooden box, and the lid of planks nailed down[3] so that no stench can escape, and covered with no more than one pall, coverlet or cloth; penalty 50 pence to be paid by the heirs of the deceased or, if there are no heirs, by the nearest kinsmen in the male line. The goods of the deceased are to stand as surety for the payment of the penalty. Also the bodies are to be carried to burial in the same box; same penalty. So that the civic officials can keep a check on this, the rectors of the chapels in Pistoia must notify the *podestà* and *capitano* when a corpse is brought into their chapel, giving the dead man's name and the contrada in which he was living when he died; same penalty. As soon as he has been notified, the *podestà* or *capitano* must send an official to the place, to find out whether this chapter of the ordinances is being observed, along with the other regulations governing funerals, and to punish those found guilty. And if the *podestà* or *capitano* is remiss in carrying out these orders he must be punished by those who appointed him; same penalty. But these regulations should not apply to the poor and destitute of the city, who are dealt with under another civic ordinance.

4. To avoid the foul stench which comes from dead bodies each grave shall be dug two and a half armslength deep, as this is reckoned in Pistoia;[4] penalty 10 pence from anyone digging or ordering the digging of a grave which infringes the statute.

5. No one, of whatever condition, status or standing, shall dare or presume to bring a corpse into the city, whether coffined or not; penalty 25 pence. And the guards at the gates shall not allow such bodies to be brought into the city; same penalty, to be paid by every guard responsible for the gate through which the body was brought.

6. Any person attending a funeral shall not accompany the corpse or its kinsmen further than the door of the church where the burial is to take place, or go back to the house where the deceased lived, or to any other house on that occasion; penalty 10 pence. Nor is he to go [to] the week's mind of the deceased; same penalty.[5]

7. When someone dies, no one shall dare or presume to give or send any gift to the house of the deceased, or to any other place on that occasion, either before or after the funeral, or to visit the house, or eat there on that occasion; penalty 25 pence. This shall not apply to the sons and daughters of the deceased, his blood

---

[3]The bodies of ordinary people were generally buried in shrouds, although they might be carried to church in a coffin. This ordinance probably implies that they were to be buried in a coffin.

[4]A *bracchio* in Pistoia measured between two and two and a half feet.

[5]This last sentence refers to a ban on attendance at the commemorative mass one week after a death.

brothers and sisters and their children, or to his grandchildren. The *podestà* and *capitano*, when notified by the rector as in chapter 3, must send an official to enquire whether anything has been done to the contrary and to punish those responsible.

From Gabriele de' Mussis (d. 1356), a Lawyer in Piacenza

In 1346, in the countries of the East, countless numbers of Tartars and Saracens were struck down by a mysterious illness which brought sudden death. . . . An eastern settlement under the rule of the Tartars called Tana, which lay to the north of Constantinople and was much frequented by Italian merchants, was totally abandoned after an incident there which led to its being besieged and attacked by hordes of Tartars who gathered in a short space of time. The Christian merchants, who had been driven out by force, were so terrified of the power of the Tartars that, to save themselves and their belongings, they fled in an armed ship to Caffa, a settlement in the same part of the world which had been founded long ago by the Genoese.

Oh God! See how the heathen Tartar races, pouring together from all sides, suddenly invested the city of Caffa and besieged the trapped Christians there for almost three years. There, hemmed in by an immense army, they could hardly draw breath, although food could be shipped in, which offered them some hope. But behold, the whole army was affected by a disease which overran the Tartars and killed thousands upon thousands every day. It was as though arrows were raining down from heaven to strike and crush the Tartars' arrogance. All medical advice and attention was useless; the Tartars died as soon as the signs of disease appeared on their bodies: swellings in the armpit or groin caused by coagulating humors, followed by a putrid fever.

The dying Tartars, stunned and stupefied by the immensity of the disaster brought about by the disease, and realizing that they had no hope of escape, lost interest in the siege. But they ordered corpses to be placed in catapults and lobbed into the city in the hope that the intolerable stench would kill everyone inside. What seemed like mountains of dead were thrown into the city, and the Christians could not hide or flee or escape from them, although they dumped as many of the bodies as they could in the sea. And soon the rotting corpses tainted the air and poisoned the water supply, and the stench was so overwhelming that hardly one in several thousand was in a position to flee the remains of the Tartar army. Moreover, one infected man could carry the poison to others, and infect people and places with the disease by look alone. No one knew, or could discover, a means of defense.

Thus almost everyone who had been in the East, or in the regions to the south and north, fell victim to sudden death after contracting this pestilential disease, as if struck by a lethal arrow which raised a tumor on their bodies. The scale of the mortality and the form which it took persuaded those who lived, weeping and lamenting, through the bitter events of 1346 to 1348 — the Chinese, Indians, Persians, Medes, Kurds, Armenians, Cilicians, Georgians, Mesopotamians, Nubians, Ethiopians, Turks, Egyptians, Arabs, Saracens and Greeks (for almost all the East has been affected) that the last judgment had come. . . .

As it happened, among those who escaped from Caffa by boat were a few sailors who had been infected with the poisonous disease. Some boats were bound for Genoa, others went to Venice and to other Christian areas. When the sailors reached these places and mixed with the people there, it was as if they had brought evil spirits with them: every city, every settlement, every place was poisoned by the contagious pestilence. . . .

Scarcely one in seven of the Genoese survived. In Venice, where an inquiry was held into the mortality, it was found that more than 70 percent of the people had died, and that within a short period 20 out of 24 excellent physicians had died. The rest of Italy, Sicily and Apulia and the neighboring regions maintain that they have been virtually emptied of inhabitants. The people of Florence, Pisa and Lucca, finding themselves bereft of their fellow residents, emphasize their losses. The Roman Curia at Avignon, the provinces on both sides of the Rhône, Spain, France, and the Empire cry up their griefs and disasters — all of which makes it extraordinarily difficult for me to give an accurate picture.

By contrast, what befell the Saracens can be established from trustworthy accounts. In the city of Babylon alone (the heart of the Sultan's power), 480,000 of his subjects are said to have been carried off by the disease in less than three months in 1348 — and this is known from the Sultan's register which records the names of the dead, because he receives a gold bezant for each person buried. . . .

I am overwhelmed, I can't go on. Everywhere one turns there is death and bitterness to be described. The hand of the Almighty strikes repeatedly, to greater and greater effect. The terrible judgment gains power as time goes by.

From Herman Gigas, a Franciscan Friar in Germany, Whose Account Goes until 1349

In 1347 there was such a great pestilence and mortality throughout almost the whole world that in the opinion of well-informed men scarcely a tenth of mankind survived. The victims did not linger long, but died on the second or third day. . . . Some say that it was brought about by the corruption of the air; others that the Jews planned to wipe out all the Christians with poison and had poisoned wells and springs everywhere. And many Jews confessed as much under torture: that they had bred spiders and toads in pots and pans, and had obtained poison from overseas; and that not every Jew knew about this, only the more powerful ones, so that it would not be betrayed. . . . [M]en say that bags full of poison were found in many wells and springs.

From Heinrich Truchess, a Former Papal Chaplain and Canon of Constance

The persecution of the Jews began in November 1348, and the first outbreak in Germany was at Sölden, where all the Jews were burnt on the strength of a rumor that they had poisoned wells and rivers, as was afterwards confirmed by their own confessions and also by the confessions of Christians whom they had corrupted. . . . Within the revolution of one year, that is from All Saints [1 November]

1348 until Michaelmas [29 September] 1349 all the Jews between Cologne and Austria were burnt and killed for this crime, young men and maidens and the old along with the rest. And blessed be God who confounded the ungodly who were plotting the extinction of his church.

Papal Bull *Sicut Judeis* of Clement VI Issued in July 1348

Recently, however, it has been brought to our attention by public fame — or more accurately, infamy — that numerous Christians are blaming the plague with which God, provoked by their sins, has afflicted the Christian people, on poisonings carried out by the Jews at the instigation of the devil, and that out of their own hotheadedness they have impiously slain many Jews, making no exception for age or sex; and that the Jews have been falsely accused of such outrageous behavior. . . . [I]t cannot be true that the Jews, by such a heinous crime, are the cause or occasion of the plague, because throughout many parts of the world the same plague, by the hidden judgment of God, has afflicted and afflicts the Jews themselves and many other races who have never lived alongside them.

We order you by apostolic writing that each of you upon whom this charge has been laid, should straitly command those subject to you, both clerical and lay . . . not to dare (on their own authority or out of hot-headedness) to capture, strike, wound or kill any Jews or expel them from their service on these grounds; and you should demand obedience under pain of excommunication.

DISCUSSION QUESTIONS

1. What explanations do these documents offer for the onset of plague? What do they suggest about the extent of Europeans' understanding of the disease and how it spread?

2. What strategies did the city of Pistoia adopt to prevent the spread of infection? How did those strategies differ from the ones described by Herman Gigas and Heinrich Truchess?

3. What do the accounts by Mussis and the bull of Pope Clement VI have in common? How did different groups of people react to the plague?

2.
Crisis and Change

Thomas Walsingham, *Peasant Rebels in London* (1381)

Thomas Walsingham (d. 1422) was the Benedictine author of six chronicles, including a portion of the famous "St. Alban's Chronicle." Although little is known of his life, his description of the Peasants' Revolt is a riveting and, by the standards of the time, reliable account of events early in the reign of King Richard II (r. 1377–1399).

From Thomas Walsingham, "Historia Anglicana I," in R. B. Dobson, *The Peasants' Revolt of 1381*, 2d ed. (London: Macmillan, 1983), 169–76, 178–81.

The revolt, one of the largest of its kind, was a response to noble demands on a popu-lation experiencing declining incomes as a result of the Black Death, the costs of war with France, and the realm's poor administration. The poll tax imposed on adult males in 1380 sparked a rebellion, led by Wat Tyler (d. 1381) and preacher John Ball, of townsmen and peasants in southeastern England. The larger causes can be found in the final breakdown of serfdom — a breakdown vigorously opposed by a nobility in decline and supported by a peasantry with new opportunities brought about by the scarcity of laborers.

On the next day [Corpus Christi] the rebels went in and out of London and talked with the simple commons of the city about the acquiring of liberty and the seizure of the traitors, especially the duke of Lancaster whom they hated most of all; and in a short time easily persuaded all the poorer citizens to support them in their con-spiracy. And when, later that day, the sun had climbed higher and grown warm and the rebels had tasted various wines and expensive drinks at will and so had become less drunk than mad (for the great men and common people of London had left all their cellars open to the rebels), they began to debate at length about the traitors with the more simple men of the city. Among other things they assembled and set out for the Savoy, the residence of the duke of Lancaster, unrivaled in splendor and nobility within England, which they then set to the flames. . . . This news so delighted the common people of London that, thinking it particularly shameful for others to harm and injure the duke before themselves, they imme-diately ran there like madmen, set fire to the place on all sides and so destroyed it. In order that the whole community of the realm should know that they were not motivated by avarice, they made a proclamation that no one should retain for his own use any object found there under penalty of execution. Instead they broke the gold and silver vessels, of which there were many at the Savoy, into pieces with their axes and threw them into the Thames or the sewers. They tore the golden cloths and silk hangings to pieces and crushed them underfoot; they ground up rings and other jewels inlaid with precious stones in small mortars, so that they could never be used again. . . .

After these malicious deeds, the rebels destroyed the place called the "Temple Bar" (in which the more noble apprentices of the law lived) because of their anger . . . and there many muniments which the lawyers were keeping in custody were con-sumed by fire. Even more insanely they set fire to the noble house of the Hospital of St. John at Clerkenwell so that it burnt continuously for the next seven days. . . .

For who would ever have believed that such rustics, and most inferior ones at that, would dare (not in crowds but individually) to enter the chamber of the king and of his mother with their filthy sticks; and undeterred by any of the soldiers, to stroke and lay their uncouth and sordid hands on the beards of several most noble knights. Moreover, they conversed familiarly with the soldiers asking them to be faithful to the ribalds and friendly in the future. . . . [They] gained access singly and in groups to the rooms in the Tower, they arrogantly lay and sat on the king's bed while joking; and several asked the king's mother to kiss them. . . . The rebels, who had formerly belonged to the most lowly condition of serf, went in and out like lords; and swineherds set themselves above soldiers. . . .

When the archbishop finally heard the rebels coming, he said to his men with great fortitude: "Let us go with confidence, for it is better to die when it can no longer help to live. At no previous time of my life could I have died in such security of conscience." A little later the executioners entered crying, "Where is that traitor to the kingdom? Where the despoiler of the common people?" . . . [They] dragged the archbishop along the passages by his arms and hood to their fellows once outside the gates on Tower Hill. . . . Words could not be heard among their horrible shrieks but rather their throats sounded with the bleating of sheep, or, to be more accurate, with the devilish voices of peacocks. . . .

Scarcely could the archbishop finish [his] speech before the rebels broke out with the horrible shout that they feared neither an interdict nor the Pope; all that remained for him, as a man false to the community and treasonable to the realm was to submit his neck to the executioners' swords. The archbishop now realized that his death was imminent and inevitable. . . . He was first struck severely but not fatally in the neck. He put his hand to the wound and said: "Ah! Ah! this is the hand of God." As he did not move his hand from the place of sorrow the second blow cut off the top of his fingers as well as severing part of the arteries. But the archbishop still did not die, and only on the eighth blow, wretchedly wounded in the neck and on the head, did he complete what we believe is worthy to be called his martyrdom. . . .

Nor did they show any reverence to any holy places but killed those whom they hated even if they were within churches and in sanctuary. I have heard from a trustworthy witness that thirty Flemings were violently dragged out of the church of the Austin Friars in London and executed in the open street. . . .

On the next day, Saturday 15 June (the feasts of Saints Vitus and Modestus), behold, the men of Kent showed themselves no less persistent in their wicked actions than on the previous day: they continued to kill men and to burn and destroy houses. The king sent messengers to the Kentishmen telling them that their fellows had left to live in peace henceforward and promising that he would give them too a similar form of peace if they would accept it. The rebels' greatest leader was called "Walter Helier" or "Tylere" (for such names had been given to him because of his trade), a cunning man endowed with much sense if he had decided to apply his intelligence to good purposes. . . .

On this the king, although a boy and of tender age, took courage and ordered the mayor of London to arrest Tyler. The mayor, a man of incomparable spirit and bravery, arrested Tyler without question and struck him a blow on the head which hurt him badly. Tyler was soon surrounded by the other servants of the king and pierced by sword thrusts in several parts of his body. His death, as he fell from his horse to the ground, was the first incident to restore to the English knighthood their almost extinct hope that they could resist the commons. . . .

But the king, with marvelous presence of mind and courage for so young a man, spurred his horse towards the commons and rode around them, saying, "What is this, my men? What are you doing? Surely you do not wish to fire on your own king? Do not attack me and do not regret the death of that traitor and ruffian. For I will be your king, your captain, and your leader. Follow me into the field where you can have all the things you would like to ask for." . . .

The commons were allowed to spend the night under the open sky. However the king ordered that the written and sealed charter which they had requested should be handed to them in order to avoid more trouble at that time. He knew that Essex was not yet pacified nor Kent settled; and the commons and rustics of both counties were ready to rebel if he failed to satisfy them quickly. . . .

Once they had this charter, the commons returned to their homes. But still the earlier evils by no means ceased.

DISCUSSION QUESTIONS

1. How does Thomas Walsingham's class and position affect his recording of events? How does he describe the different classes of society?

2. What does the account suggest about economic and political conditions in late-fourteenth-century England?

3. How did the rebels choose their targets, both human and material? What were they seeking? Against what were they protesting?

4. What was the rebels' attitude toward religious authority? What might explain their actions in this regard?

3.
Satirizing the Church

Geoffrey Chaucer, *The Pardoner's Prologue* (1387–1400)

Geoffrey Chaucer (c. 1342–1400) wore many hats in his native England: soldier, diplomat, customs official, and politician. Yet it was his talent as a poet deeply in tune with pressing social and religious issues that gained him fame. In the late fourteenth century, he composed one of the great works of world literature, The Canterbury Tales, in Middle English. Here he claims to narrate the story of thirty pilgrims who embark on a journey to Thomas Becket's shrine at Canterbury. Each pilgrim is supposed to tell two stories to pass the time. The men and women, collectively representing most social classes and professions of the day, tell tales that are bawdy parodies of society, religion, and gender roles. Yet, at the same time, the stories also provide shrewd insights into human behavior and social evils. The following tale, told by the Pardoner, a medieval indulgence preacher, represents the worst of religion at a time of crisis in the church. Known as the Great Schism (1378–1417), two men claimed their right to the papacy, sparking increasingly vocal calls for reform. The Pardoner personified what many Christians regarded as the clergy's failings. Instead of using his preaching skills to teach the Christian life, the Pardoner is a con artist and hypocrite who willingly deceives to enrich himself and to eat well — two of Catholic Christianity's deadly sins: avarice and gluttony.

From Geoffrey Chaucer, *The Canterbury Tales*, trans. into modern English J. U. Nicolson (New York: Covici Friede Publishers, 1870), 293–96.

"Masters," quoth he, "in churches, when I preach,
I am at pains that all shall hear my speech,
And ring it out as roundly as a bell,
For I know all by heart the thing I tell.
My theme is always one, and ever was:
'Radix malorum est cupiditas.'[1]
    "First I announce the place whence I have come,
And then I show my pardons, all and some.
Our liege-lord's seal on my patent perfect,
I show that first, my safety to protect,
And then no man's so bold, no priest nor clerk,
As to disturb me in Christ's holy work;
And after that my tales I marshal all.
Indulgences of pope and cardinal,
Of patriarch and bishop, these I do
Show, and in Latin speak some words, a few,
To spice therewith a bit my sermoning
And stir men to devotion, marveling.
Then show I forth my hollow crystal-stones,
Which are crammed full of rags, aye, and of bones;
Relics are these, as they think, every one.
Then I've in latten box a shoulder bone
Which came out of a holy Hebrew's sheep.
'Good men,' say I, 'my words in memory keep;
If this bone shall be washed in any well,
Then if a cow, calf, sheep, or ox should swell
That's eaten snake, or been by serpent stung,
Take water of that well and wash its tongue,
And 'twill be well anon; and furthermore,
Of pox and scab and every other sore
Shall every sheep be healed that of this well
Drinks but one draught; take heed of what I tell.
And if the man that owns the beasts, I trow,
Shall every week, and that before cock-crow,
And before breakfast, drink thereof a draught,
As that Jew taught of yore in his priestcraft,
His beasts and all his store shall multiply.
And, good sirs, it's a cure for jealousy;
For though a man be fallen in jealous rage,
Let one make of this water his pottage
And nevermore shall he his wife mistrust,
Though he may know the truth of all her lust,

---

[1]"Greed is the root of all evil."

Even though she'd taken two priests, aye, or three.
    "'Here is a mitten, too, that you may see.
Who puts his hand therein, I say again,
He shall have increased harvest of his grain,
After he's sown, be it of wheat or oats,
Just so he offers pence or offers groats.
    "'Good men and women, one thing I warn you,
If any man be here in church right now
That's done a sin so horrible that he
Dare not, for shame, of that sin shriven be,
Or any woman, be she young or old,
That's made her husband into a cuckold,
Such folk shall have no power and no grace
To offer to my relics in this place.
But whoso finds himself without such blame,
He will come up and offer, in God's name,
And I'll absolve him by authority
That has, by bull, been granted unto me.'
    "By this fraud have I won me, year by year,
A hundred marks, since I've been pardoner.
I stand up like a scholar in pulpit,
And when the ignorant people all do sit,
I preach, as you have heard me say before,
And tell a hundred false japes, less or more.
I am at pains, then, to stretch forth my neck,
And east and west upon the folk I beck,
As does a dove that's sitting on a barn.
With hands and swift tongue, then, do I so yarn
That it's a joy to see my busyness.
Of avarice and of all such wickedness
Is all my preaching, thus to make them free
With offered pence, the which pence come to me.
For my intent is only pence to win,
And not at all for punishment of sin.
When they are dead, for all I think thereon
Their souls may well black-berrying have gone!
For, certainly, there's many a sermon grows
Ofttimes from evil purpose, as one knows;
Some for folks' pleasure and for flattery,
To be advanced by all hypocrisy,
And some for vainglory, and some for hate.
For, when I dare not otherwise debate,
Then do I sharpen well my tongue and sting
The man in sermons, and upon him fling
My lying defamations, if but he
Has wronged my brethren or — much worse — wronged me.

For though I mention not his proper name,
Men know whom I refer to, all the same,
By signs I make and other circumstances.
Thus I pay those who do us displeasances.
Thus spit I out my venom under hue
Of holiness, to seem both good and true.

"But briefly my intention I'll express;
I preach no sermon, save for covetousness.
For that my theme is yet, and ever was,
'*Radix malorum est cupiditas.*'
Thus can I preach against that self-same vice
Which I indulge, and that is avarice.
But though myself be guilty of that sin,
Yet can I cause these other folk to win
From avarice and really to repent.
But that is not my principal intent.
I preach no sermon, save for covetousness;
This should suffice of that, though, as I guess.

"Then do I cite examples, many a one,
Out of old stories and of time long gone,
For vulgar people all love stories old;
Such things they can re-tell well and can hold.
What? Think you that because I'm good at preaching
And win me gold and silver by my teaching
I'll live of my free will in poverty?
No, no, that's never been my policy!
For I will preach and beg in sundry lands;
I will not work and labor with my hands,
Nor baskets weave and try to live thereby,
Because I will not beg in vain, say I.
I will none of the apostles counterfeit;
I will have money, wool, and cheese, and wheat,
Though it be given by the poorest page,
Or by the poorest widow in village,
And though her children perish of famine.
Nay! I will drink good liquor of the vine
And have a pretty wench in every town.
But hearken, masters, to conclusion shown:
Your wish is that I tell you all a tale.
Now that I've drunk a draught of musty ale,
By God, I hope that I can tell something
That shall, in reason, be to your liking.
For though I am myself a vicious man,
Yet I would tell a moral tale, and can,
The which I'm wont to preach more gold to win.
Now hold your peace! my tale I will begin."

DISCUSSION QUESTIONS

1. What methods does the Pardoner use to convince people to buy his indulgences? Why might these methods have been effective?

2. From the Pardoner's tale, what do you learn about saints' relics?

3. Although the tale is satiric, it is filled with examples of abuses in the church of Chaucer's day. What examples are described?

4.
Preaching Reform

Jan Hus, *Letters* (1408–1415)

Like Chaucer, Jan Hus (1372–1415) lived in the midst of the anxiety and strife caused by the Great Schism. He, too, was a vocal critic of the church, but from a very different platform. A professor at the University of Prague in Bohemia and an ordained priest, in 1402 Hus was appointed rector of the Bethlehem Chapel. The chapel had been founded in 1391 to fill a gap in the city's divine services by providing preaching in the Czech language. Hus wholeheartedly embraced his position and used it to call for reform. Influenced by the writings of English scholar, John Wycliffe (c. 1330– 1384), Hus targeted a range of issues for criticism, including immorality within the priesthood, resistance to preaching and reading the Bible in the vernacular, and opposition to all Christians receiving both the bread and wine during communion. While he garnered considerable support among nobles and commoners alike, his views outraged many high church officials, including the archbishop of Prague, ultimately leading to his excommunication and exile in 1412. When invited to the Council of Constance in 1414 to defend his views, he gladly accepted. He was immediately imprisoned upon his arrival, however, which set the stage for his trial and execution in 1415. Aside from his sermons and other works, Hus was a prolific letter writer up to the very moment of his death. The letters below illuminate Hus at each stage in his career: as preacher and pastor in Prague, in exile, and in prison in Constance.

To Archbishop Zbyněk

Prague

After 6 July 1408

I commend my humble self in the faith and truth of our Lord Jesus Christ.[1]

Most reverend Father!

From *The Letters of John Hus*, trans. Matthew Spinka (New York: Roman and Littlefield, 1972), 22–23, 79–84, 165–67.

[1] . . . The youthful Archbishop Zbyněk, who assumed the office in August 1403, had been favourably inclined toward the reforms, particularly toward Hus. However, during the five years he occupied the see of Prague, the anti-reformist party sought to gain him to their side, and by 1408 they partly succeeded. . . .

Very often I repeat to myself that not long ago after your enthronement Your Paternity had set up the rule that whenever I should observe some defect in the administration, that I should instantly report such defect in person, or in Your absence by writing. This rule now compels me to express myself: how is it that fornicating and otherwise criminal priests walk about freely and without rigorous correction like unbroken bulls and lusty stallions,[2] with outstretched necks, while humble priests, who uproot the thorns of sin, who fulfil the duties of your administration with proper devotion, are not avaricious, but offer themselves freely for God's sake to the labour of proclaiming the gospel — these are jailed as heretics and suffer exile for the very proclamation of the gospel? O Father, what sort of devotion is it to prohibit the proclamation of the gospel — the duty which Christ commanded His disciples in the first place, saying: "Preach the gospel to every creature"?[3] What kind of discretion is it to hinder the diligent and faithful worker from work? In truth I suppose that it is not Your Paternity, but other people's heinousness which disseminates such things. What poor priests will dare to fight against criminal conduct? Who will dare to make known vices?

"The harvest is truly plentiful, but the labourers are few," that is, the real ones. Therefore, Father, "pray the Lord of the harvest that He send faithful labourers into His harvest."[4] It rests with Your Paternity to reap the whole harvest of the kingdom of Bohemia, to gather it into the Lord's barn, and in the day of your death to give account from each sheaf. How will Your Paternity be able to gather into the Lord's barn so many sheaves, if you deprive the labourers of the scythe of the preacher's word to please the idlers, who themselves do not reap and obstruct others in doing so, as soon as they touch with the word of the Lord upon their vices? . . .

Therefore, most reverend Father, open the inner, or the inward eye! Love the good, take note of the bad! Do not succumb to the flattery of the lovers of ostentation and avarice, but delight in the humble and the lovers of poverty! Drive the laggards to work, do not obstruct those who faithfully labour in the Lord's harvest. For the Word is not bound, whereby the salvation of souls is accomplished.

I would write more, but the duty of preaching the gospel does not permit. . . .

To the Praguers

In exile
c. November 1412

Master John Hus, in hope a priest and servant of the Lord Jesus Christ, to all who love God truly, confess His law, and await the appearing of the Saviour, with Whom they desire to dwell forever — "grace and peace from God the Father and from the Lord Jesus Christ, Who offered Himself in death for our sins, that He might rescue us from this miserable world and from eternal damnation, in accordance with the will of God the Father, to Whom be glory for ever. Amen."[5]

---

[2]Jer. 5:8.
[3]Mark 16:15.
[4]Matt. 9:37–8.
[5]Paraphrase of Gal. 1:3–5.

Dearly beloved, having heard of your desire for and progress in the law of God, I thank God in joy, and pray that He may grant you perfect understanding, that knowing the wiles of the Antichrist and of his messengers, you would not allow yourselves to be led astray from God's truth. I trust in His holy grace, that He will fulfil in you the good He began,[6] and will not permit you to fall away from His truth, which many have forsaken in fear, being in greater terror of miserable man than of the Almighty God who has the power to kill and to give life, to condemn and to save,[7] to preserve His faithful servants in temptation and to grant him — in lieu of the minute suffering — eternal life of immense joy. . . .

Therefore stand fast in the truth which you have learned: everything you do, do as God's sons. Trust that as Christ has conquered, you also will conquer. Remember Him who endured persecution from sinners, that you would not grow weary in your good desire. All of you, "laying aside every weight and every sin, let us run with perseverance the race that is set before us, looking to Jesus, the creator and perfector of our faith, who for the joy that was set before Him endured the cross, despising the shame, and is already seated at the right hand of God."[8] . . .

Our gracious king, master, and father, beloved brother, the mighty creator and our merciful Redeemer indeed said: "If the world hates you, know that it has hated me first. If you were of the world, the world would love its own; but because you are not of the world, but that I chose you out of the world, therefore the world hates you. Remember the word that I said to you: A servant is not greater than his master. If they persecuted me, they will persecute you; if they kept my word, they will keep yours also. But all this they will do to you for my name's sake, for they do not know Him who sent me."[9] . . .

Thus spoke the Saviour, warning His future disciples, teaching and comforting them, warning them to conduct themselves carefully, recognize the ravening wolves by their deeds, who wish to devour the whole world by their covetousness. He taught them to know the false prophets by the fact that they do not agree with the true prophets in word or deed; and to regard as false Christs those who assert that they are Christ's principal disciples, while in reality they are His chief foes. They would gladly stifle His word — if they could — for it is contrary to their pride, avarice, simony, fornication, and other deeds.

At first they attacked all the chapels to prevent the Word of God from being preached there;[10] but Christ did not allow it. Now I hear that they decided to pull down Bethlehem,[11] and prohibited preaching in the churches where their iniquity is denounced. But I trust God that they will not succeed in this. At first they spread their nets of citations and excommunications for Hus,[12] and have already caught

---

[6]Phil. 1:6.
[7]James 4:12.
[8]Heb. 12:1–2.
[9]John 15:18–21.
[10]This refers to the prohibition of Pope Alexander V of 20 December 1409, whereby preaching in all but the parochial, cathedral, and monastic churches was forbidden. . . .
[11]The papal command to do so was received in Prague before the end of September 1412.
[12]It could also be understood as "goose," since that is what his name means.

many. But because goose is a lazy bird, domestic, not flying high, their net has begun to tear; likewise many other birds who fly high to God by their [writings] and their lives will tear their nets. They issued citations, threatened with excommunications as with a wooden snare and in the end shot an arrow from the Antichrist's quiver when they stopped the divine service and praise. The more they wish to conceal their wickedness, the more they reveal it; and the more they desire to be free, the more work they have; and the more they endeavour to establish their traditions like nets, the more they tear them; and by seeking to have the worldly peace, they have lost it along with the spiritual. Wishing to harm others, they harm themselves even more. . . .

I write you this message, dearest brothers and beloved sisters, that you may stand firm in the truth you have learned, would not fear the citations, nor attend less than before the hearing of the Word of God on account of their cruel threats. . . .

Finally, I beseech you, dearly beloved, pray for those who proclaim God's truth with His grace; also pray for me, that I may write and preach more against the malice of the Antichrist, and that when need is the greatest, God may place me in the battle-array to defend His truth.

For know for certain that I do not flinch from yielding my miserable life for God's truth in danger or death. For I know that nothing is lacking to you in God's word; but that day by day the truth of the gospel is being spread ever wider. Nevertheless, I desire to live for those who suffer violence and need the preaching of the Word of God, in order that thus the malice of Antichrist may be revealed, so that the godly can escape it. On that account I preach elsewhere and minister as priest to others, in the knowledge that the will of God is thus fulfilled in me. . . .

To His Friends in Bohemia

Constance, Franciscan monastery
10 June 1415

Master John Hus,[13] in hope a servant of God, to all the faithful Czechs who love the Lord God and will love Him, sends his wish that the Lord may grant them to dwell and die in His grace and to live forever in the joy of heaven. Amen.

Faithful and dear to God lords and ladies,[14] both rich and poor!

I beseech and admonish you that you obey the Lord God, extol His word, and gladly hear and follow it. I pray that you hold that truth of God which I have drawn from the law of God, and have preached and written from the teachings of the saints. I also beseech you that if anyone has heard at my preaching or in private anything contrary to the truth of God, or if I have written it anywhere — which, I trust God, there is none of it — that he does not hold it. I also beseech you that if anyone saw in me any levity of morals in speaking or actions, that he does not hold them, but that he pray God for me that He may be pleased to forgive me. I beseech

---

[13]. . . The letter was written in expectation that the next day Hus would be sentenced to death.

[14]The address may be understood as including nobles; otherwise, it should be "masters and mistresses."

the priests, particularly those who labour in the Word of God, that they love good morals and extol and honour them. I beseech them to beware of deceitful men, and particularly of unworthy priests. . . .

I beseech the lords that they deal mercifully with their poor and rule them justly. I beseech the burghers that they carry on their commerce justly. I beseech the craftsmen that they do their work faithfully and have their living from it. I beseech the servants that they serve their masters and mistresses faithfully. I beseech the masters that they, living worthily, teach their pupils faithfully; first of all to love God, and to study for the sake of His praise and the benefit of the community, as well as for the sake of their salvation — but not for the sake of avarice or of worldly prosperity. I beseech the students and other pupils that they obey and follow their masters in the good, and that they study diligently for the sake of God's praise and their own and other people's salvation.

I beseech all together that they give thanks and be grateful for the diligence of the [following] lords: Lord Wenceslas of Dubá otherwise of Leštno, Lord John of Chlum, Lord Henry of Plumlov, Lord William Zajíc, Lord Myška,[15] and the other lords from Bohemia and Moravia, as well as the faithful lords of the Polish kingdom; for they, as God's brave defenders and supporters of the truth, have many times risen up against the whole Council and have brought proofs and arguments in order to secure my liberation. Especially believe what Lord Wenceslas of Dubá and Lord John of Chlum say, for they were present at the Council when for several days I defended myself. They know which Czechs brought many unworthy accusations against me, and how the whole Council shouted at me, and how I answered to what they demanded of me. . . .

I wrote this letter to you in prison, in chains, expecting tomorrow the sentence of death, in full hope in God that I swerve not from His truth nor recant the errors that the false witnesses have witnessed against me. How the Lord God has dealt graciously with me and has remained with me in strange temptations you shall learn when with God's help we shall meet in His joy. . . .

I also beseech, particularly you Praguers, to be kind toward Bethlehem as long as the Lord God will be pleased that the Word of God be preached there. For the devil has become enraged at that place and has incited pastors and canons against it, perceiving that his kingdom was being ruined there. I trust the Lord God that He will preserve that place according to His will and will increase its benefits through others more than He has done through my unworthy self.

Also I beseech you that you love one another, permit not the good to be oppressed by violence, and desire that everyone learns the truth.

DISCUSSION QUESTIONS

1. What aspects of the contemporary church did Hus criticize and why? What do his criticisms reveal about his vision for the church and its pastors? In what ways did he himself seek to live out this vision?

---

[15]Henry of Plumlov was the principal Moravian noble; Zajíc and Myška were members of Sigismund's entourage.

2. What specific actions did Hus's detractors take against him and his supporters? Why do you think the archbishop of Prague and other church officials may have found his views threatening?

3. What advice did Hus give to his supporters in Prague while he was imprisoned in Constance? What does this letter suggest about the basis of his support? Do you think this may help to explain why many people in Bohemia reacted angrily to his execution?

5.
Extolling Humanism

Giovanni Rucellai and Leonardo Bruni,
Florence in the Quattrocento (1427 and 1457)

The Petrarchan ideal of humanism, which had refocused attention on the classics with special attention to language and letters, was given new expression in the 1400s. While Francesco Petrarch (1304–1374) had found answers to many of his life questions through introspection, civic humanists felt that a true life could only be lived within the hustle and bustle of Italian city politics. A civic humanist was one who applied humanism's academic principles to the active, political life. The first document is by Giovanni Rucellai (1403–1481), a merchant connected through marriage and patronage to two great families of Florence, the Strozzis and Medicis, who made their fortunes in business and banking, respectively. The second document is a funeral oration for a leading citizen, given in the midst of the wars with Milan by Leonardo Bruni (1369–1444), a noted scholar of the Greek language who served as Florence's chancellor and official historian. Both men paint portraits of Florence and the ideal Renaissance man.

Rucellai's "A Merchant's Praise of Florence"

Most people believe that our age, from 1400 onward, is the most fortunate period in Florence's history. I shall now explain why this is so. It is commonly believed that since 1400 the Italians have been superior to all other nations in the art of war, whereas before 1400 the northern Europeans were thought to be peerless. Thanks to their intelligence, astuteness, cunning, and strategic ability, the Italians are now the best at seizing cities and winning battles. In this age, moreover, there are more outstanding scholars of Greek, Latin, and Hebrew in Florence than ever before. . . . Our men of letters have revived the elegance of the ancient style that has long been lost and forgotten. Those who have participated in the government of the city since 1400 have surpassed all their predecessors. Likewise, the dominion of Florence has considerably expanded. . . .

From Stefano Ugo Baldassarri and Arielle Saiber, eds., *Images of Quattrocento Florence: Selected Writings in Literature, History, and Art* (New Haven, CT: Yale University Press, 2000), 73–75; and Benjamin G. Kohl and Alison Andrews Smith, eds., *Major Problems in the History of the Italian Renaissance* (Lexington, MA: D. C. Heath, 1995), 279–82.

There have not been such accomplished masters in joinery and woodcarving since the days of antiquity: they are able to produce such skillfully designed works in perspective that a painter could not do any better. The same can be said of our masters in painting and drawing, whose ability, sense of proportion, and precision are so great that Giotto and Cimabue would not even be accepted as their pupils. Similarly, we cannot forget to mention our excellent tapestry makers and goldsmiths.

Never before have men and women dressed in such expensive and elegant clothing. Women wear brocade and embroidered gowns covered with jewels and saunter through the streets in their French-style hats that cost at least two hundred florins apiece. Neither the city nor the countryside has ever had such an abundance of household goods. . . .

This age has also had four notable citizens who deserve to be remembered. The first one is Palla di Nofri Strozzi, who possessed all seven of the things necessary for a man's happiness: a worthy homeland, noble and distinguished ancestors, a good knowledge of Greek and Latin, refinement, physical beauty, a good household, and honestly earned wealth. . . . Then we have Cosimo de' Medici, probably not only the richest Florentine, but the richest Italian of all time. . . . The third citizen I shall mention is Messer Leonardo di Francesco Bruni. Although he was born in Arezzo, he was an honorary citizen of Florence. He had a unique knowledge of and expertise in Greek, Hebrew, and Latin and was more famous than any rhetorician after Cicero. . . . Finally, Filippo, son of Ser Brunellesco, was a master architect and sculptor. He was an accomplished geometer and . . . is the one who rediscovered ancient Roman building techniques.

The earnings of the Florentine commune are now greater than ever. In this period, both in our city and in its countryside, people have witnessed tremendous wars and political upheaval, the like of which were never seen in the past. Churches and hospitals are richer than ever, better supplied with gold and silk paraments and precious silver. There are numerous friars and priests caring for these places, which the faithful visit constantly. Men and women attend Mass and other religious ceremonies with greater devotion than ever. . . .

The citizens have never had so much wealth, merchandise, and property, nor have the Monte's[1] interests ever been so conspicuous; consequently, the sums spent on weddings, tournaments, and various forms of entertainment are greater than ever before. Between 1418 and 1423 Florence's wealth was probably at its height. At the time, in the Mercato Nuovo and the streets nearby, there were seventy-two exchange banks.

Bruni's Funeral Oration for Nanni Strozzi, 1427

This is an exceptional funeral oration because it is appropriate neither to weep or lament. . . . His first claim to fame is conferred on him because of his country's merit. For the homeland is the first and chief basis of human happiness and more worthy of our veneration than even our own parents. If we begin therefore by praising the motherland, we will be starting in the right order.

---

[1]Monte della Doti (dowry fund) was a credit fund established by Florence in 1425 to help well-to-do families finance in advance their daughters' marriages. [Ed.]

He was born in the most spacious and greatest of cities, wide-ruling and endowed with the mightiest power, without question the foremost of all the Etruscan cities. Indeed, it is second to none of the cities of Italy either in origin, wealth, or size. . . . The Tuscans had been the chief people of Italy and supreme both in authority and wealth. Before the foundation of the Roman empire their power was so great that they had the seas on both sides of Italy under their control and governed the whole length of the country. . . . Finally, this one people diffused the worship of the immortal gods as well as learning and letters throughout Italy. . . .

What city, therefore, can be more excellent, more noble? What descended from more glorious antecedents? . . . [Our fathers] so established and governed it that they were in no way inferior to their own fathers in virtue. Sustained by the most sacred laws, the state was ruled by them with such wisdom that they served as an example of good moral behavior for other peoples and had no need to take others as their model. . . .

Worthy of praise as well are those who are its present-day citizens. They have augmented the power received from their predecessors even more by adding Pisa and a number of other great cities to their empire through their virtue and valor in arms. . . .

Our form of governing the state aims at achieving liberty and equality for each and every citizen. Because it is equal in all respects it is called a popular government. We tremble before no lord nor are we dominated by the power of a few. All enjoy the same liberty, governed only by law and free from fear of individuals. Everyone has the same hope of attaining honors and of improving his condition provided he is industrious, has talent and a good sober way of life. For our city requires virtue and honesty in its citizens. . . .

This is true liberty and equality in a city to fear the power of no one nor dread injury from them; to experience equality of law among the citizens and the same opportunity of ruling the state. These advantages cannot be had where one man rules or a few. . . .

This capacity for a free people to attain honors and this ability to pursue one's goals serve in a marvelous way to excite men's talents. For with the hope of honors extended, men raise themselves and surge upward; excluded they become lifeless. . . . Our citizens excel so greatly in talents and intelligence that few equal them and none surpass them. They have vivacity and industry and alacrity and agility in acting with a greatness of spirit equal to all challenges.

We thrive not only in governing the republic, in domestic arts, and in engaging in business everywhere, but we are also distinguished for military glory. . . .

What now shall I say about literature and scholarship in which all concede that Florence is the chief and most splendid leader? . . . But I am speaking about those more civilized and lofty studies which are considered more excellent and worthy of everlasting immortal glory. For who is able to name a poet in our generation or in the last one who is not Florentine? Who but our citizens recalled this skill at eloquence, already lost, to light, to practical use, and to life? Who but they understood Latin literature, already abject, prostrate and almost dead, and raised it up, restored and reclaimed it from destruction? . . . For the same reason, should not our city be proclaimed the parent of the Latin language . . . ? Now the knowledge of Greek literature, which had decayed in Italy for more than seven hundred years, has been revived and restored by our city. . . . Finally, these humanities most excellent and of highest value, especially relevant for human beings, necessary both for private and public life, adorned with a knowledge of letters worthy of free men, have originated in our city and are now thriving throughout Italy. The city enjoys such resources and wealth that I fear to arouse jealousy by referring to its inexhaustible supply of money. This is demonstrated by the long Milanese war waged at an almost incredible cost. . . . Now at the end of the war men are more prompt in paying their taxes than they were at the beginning of the war.

DISCUSSION QUESTIONS

1. Bruni's funeral oration for Nanni Strozzi seems to have little to do with the man himself. What is its true subject? What are its possible purposes?

2. What do both Bruni and Rucellai see as the desirable attributes of a citizen? Why do they portray the city of Florence as a model for other cities?

3. What role does wealth play in both Petrarchan and civic humanism?

4. In these documents, how do Greece and Rome serve as models for Florence?

6.
Women's Place in Renaissance Italy
Alessandra, *Letters from a Widow*
and
Matriarch of a Great Family (1450–1465)

Although there were differences by region, women in medieval and Renaissance Europe were usually under legal guardianship — typically that of a father or husband. Although women of the lower classes may have had more freedom in terms of work and marriage early in their lives, their upper-class counterparts gained their greatest prestige and power through widowhood. Alessandra (1407–1471) married Matteo Strozzi (c. 1397–1435), a wealthy merchant whose business had branches throughout Europe. But when Matteo died of the effects of the plague while exiled for being in opposition to Cosimo de' Medici (1389–1464), Alessandra's financial situation became more difficult because she had sons and daughters to marry and a great household to maintain. She engaged in lengthy correspondence with her sons about political, marital, and economic conditions that affected the family. The following excerpts from letters to her son Filippo show some of the realities of Italian life during the Renaissance — exile; political danger if one did not agree with the ruling faction; marriages that were contracted solely for reasons of politics, honor, and clientage; and slavery.

From Eric Cochrane and Julius Kirshner, eds., *University of Chicago Readings in Western Civilization, 5: The Renaissance* (Chicago: University of Chicago Press, 1986), 109, 113–17.

To Filippo, 1450

Really, as long as there are young girls in the house, you do nothing but work for them, so when she leaves I will have no one to attend to but you three. And when I get the house in a little better shape I would love it if you would think about coming home. You would have no cause to be ashamed with what there is now, and you could do honor to any friend who dropped in to see you at home. But two or three years from now it will all be much better. And I would love to get you a wife; you're of an age now to know how to manage the help and to give me some comfort and consolation. I have none. . . .

You know that some time ago I bought Cateruccia, our slave, and for several years now, though I haven't laid a hand on her, she has behaved so badly toward me and the children that you wouldn't believe it if you hadn't seen it. Our Lorenzo could tell you all about it. . . . I've always suffered it because I can't chastise her, and besides I thought you would come once a month so that we could come to a decision together or she could be brought to better obedience. For several months now she has been saying and is still saying that she doesn't want to stay here, and she is so moody that no one can do a thing with her. If it weren't for love of Lesandra, I would have told you to sell her, but because of her malicious tongue, I want to see Lesandra safely out of the house first. But I don't know if I can hold out that long: mark my words, I'm going to get her out of my sight because I don't want this constant battle. She pays no more attention to me than if I were the slave and she were the mistress, and she threatens us all so that Lesandra and I are both afraid of her.

To Filippo, 1459

It grieves me, my son, that I'm not near you to take some of these troublesome things off your hands. You should have told me the first day Matteo fell sick so I could have jumped on a horse and been there in just a few days. But I know that you didn't do it for fear I would get sick or would be put to trouble. . . . I have been told that in the honors you arranged for the burial of my son you did honor to yourself as well as to him. You did all the better to pay him such honor there, since here they don't usually do anything for those who are in your condition [that is, in exile]. Thus I am pleased that you did so. Here these two girls, who are unconsolable over the death of their brother, and I have gone into mourning, and because I had not yet gotten the woolen cloth to make a mantle for myself, I have gotten it now and I will pay for it.

To Filippo, 1465

I told you in my other [letter] what happened about 60[1] [the daughter of Francesco Tanagli], and there's nothing new there. And you have been advised that there is no talk of 59 [a woman who belonged to the Adimari family] until we have placed

---

[1]Because much of her family was already in exile or in political danger, Alessandra used numbers to refer to possible marriage alliances, eliminating the danger of seeming to be associated with certain factions, even during the negotiation phase.

the older girl. 13 [Marco Parenti] believes we should do nothing further until we can see our way clearly concerning these two and see what way they will go. Considering their age, this shouldn't take too long. It's true that my wish would be to see both of you with a companion, as I have told you many times before. That way when I die I would think you ready to take the step all mothers want — seeing their sons married — so your children could enjoy what you have acquired with enormous effort and stress over the long years. To that end, I have done my very best to keep up the little I have had, foregoing the things that I might have done for my soul's sake and for that of our ancestors. But for the hope I have that you will take a wife (in the aim of having children), I am happy to have done so. So what I would like would be what I told you. Since then I have heard what Lorenzo's wants are and how he was willing to take her to keep me happy, but that he would be just as glad to wait two years before binding himself to the lady. I have thought a good deal about the matter, and it seems to me that since nothing really advantageous to us is available, and since we have time to wait these two years, it would be a good idea to leave it at that unless something unexpected turns up. Otherwise, it doesn't seem to me something that requires immediate thought, particularly considering the stormy times we live in these days, when so many young men on this earth are happy to inhabit it without taking a wife. The world is in a sorry state, and never has so much expense been loaded on the backs of women as now. No dowry is so big that when the girl goes out she doesn't have the whole of it on her back, between silks and jewels. . . . If 60 works out well, we could sound out the possibility of the other girl for him. There's good forage there if they were to give her, and at any [other] time it would have been a commendable move. As things are going now, it seems to me better to wait and see a while for him. . . . This way something may come of it, and they will not offer a wife without money, as people are doing now, since it seems superfluous to those who are giving 50 to give her a dowry. 13 wrote you that 60's father touched on the matter with him in the way I wrote you about. He says that you should leave it to us to see to it and work it out. For my part, I've done my diligent best, and I can't think what more I could have done — for your consolation than my own. . . .

Niccolò has gone out of office, and although he did some good things, they weren't the ones I would have wanted. Little honor has been paid to him or to the other outgoing magistrates, either when they were in office, or now that they have stepped down. Our scrutineer was quite upset about it, as were we, but I feel that what was done will collapse, and it is thought they will start fresh. This Signoria has spent days in deliberation, and no one can find out anything about them. They have threatened to denounce whoever reveals anything as a rebel, so things are being done in total secrecy. I have heard that 58 [the Medici] is everything and 54 [the Pitti] doesn't stand a chance. For the moment, it looks to me as if they will get back to 56 [the Pucci] in the runoffs, if things continue to go as now. May God, who can do all, set this city right, for it is in a bad way. Niccolò went in proudly and then lost heart — as 14's [Soderini] brother said, "He went in a lion and he will go out a lamb," and that's just what happened to him. When he saw the votes were going against him, he began to humble himself. Now, since he left office, he goes about accompanied by five or six armed men for fear. . . . It would have been better for him if [he had never been elected], for he would never have made so many enemies. . . .

[T]hink about having Niccolò Strozzi touch on the matter with Giovanfrancesco for 45 [Lorenzo], if you think it appropriate. Although I doubt that she would deign [to marry] so low, still, it sometimes happens that you look in places that in other times you wouldn't have dreamed of, by the force of events — deaths or other misfortunes. So think about it.

DISCUSSION QUESTIONS

1. What is Alessandra's role as matriarch of her family?
2. What is her view of the politics of the city in her day?
3. What is Alessandra's relation to her slave? How does the existence of slavery affect your view of Florence's vaunted "liberty for all"?
4. How were marriages formed among the middle and upper classes? What was required before one could marry?

COMPARATIVE QUESTIONS

1. What connections can you draw between the plague and the peasant rebellions that swept over Europe during the decades after 1347?
2. What do Hus's and Chaucer's views of the church have in common? What does this suggest about the effects of the Great Schism and perceived abuses within the church on Europeans' spiritual life?
3. Compare the portraits of Florentine life and politics painted in Documents 5 and 6. What similarities and differences do you see? What does this suggest about the limitations of Renaissance ideals?
4. One of historian Jacob Burckhardt's chapters in *The Civilization of the Renaissance* is entitled "The Discovery of Man and the World." What is "new" about the Renaissance? What could be considered a continuation of medieval ideas?

Global Encounters and the Shock of the Reformation

1492–1560

I n the late fifteenth century, Europe stood on the threshold of profound transformations within its borders and beyond. Portuguese fleets had opened up new trade routes extending along the West African coast to Calicut, India, the hub of the spice trade. Their success whet Europeans' appetite for maritime exploration, with Spain ultimately taking the lead. The Spaniards' colonization of the Caribbean was in full gear by 1500, and from there they moved westward into Mexico. The first two documents illuminate aspects of the Spanish conquest of Mexico from both Spanish and native perspectives. As they suggest, European colonization permanently changed the lives of native peoples of the Americas, often with devastating results. The third document reveals that some Europeans openly criticized colonization while at the same time embracing the opportunities it provided to spread Catholic Christianity. Catholicism had long been a unifying force in the West. In the early sixteenth century, however, the religious landscape shifted dramatically. Problems within the Catholic church combined with the spirit and methods of the Renaissance to usher in the Protestant Reformation, a time of questioning, reform, and revolt. The fourth and fifth documents allow us to see the Reformation through the eyes of two of its leaders, Martin Luther and John Calvin. Together, their ideas helped to shatter the religious unity of Europe forever. As the final document attests, despite the many challenges it faced, Catholicism underwent its own process of change and renewal.

1.
Worlds Collide

Bernal Díaz del Castillo, *The True History of the Conquest of New Spain* (c. 1567)

By the mid-sixteenth century, Spain had built an empire in the Americas that extended from Mexico to Chile. The Spanish crown especially prized Mexico, then called "New Spain," because of the precious metals (gold and silver) found there. Numerous Spanish accounts of the conquest of Mexico have survived, perhaps none more vivid than that of Bernal Díaz del Castillo (1495–1583). Díaz had been in the thick of colonization from an early age, having joined a Spanish expedition to Panama in 1514 and two more to Mexico before meeting up with Hernán Cortés (1485–1547) in Cuba. In 1519, Cortés led a group of fellow adventurers, including Díaz, to the Mexican heartland, which they ultimately brought under Spanish control. By the mid-1550s, Díaz had begun to record his version of events, which he called The True History of the Conquest of New Spain, *to counter what he considered to be "false" histories by people who had not participated in the conquest. Díaz was also sensitive to critics of the colonists' treatment of native peoples. Completed around 1567, the book languished in obscurity until its publication in 1632. In the excerpt that follows, Díaz recounts a key moment in the conquest—the Spaniards' arrival in Tenochtitlán, the Aztec capital, on November 8, 1519. Here Cortés and his men were greeted by the Aztec leader, Moctezuma, with great hospitality. In its close attention to detail, Díaz's description reveals a blend of wonder and disdain underlying Spanish attitudes toward Aztec civilization.*

When Cortés was told that the Great Montezuma was approaching, and he saw him coming, he dismounted from his horse, and when he was near Montezuma, they simultaneously paid great reverence to one another. Montezuma bade him welcome and our Cortés replied through Doña Marina[1] wishing him very good health. And it seems to me that Cortés, through Doña Marina, offered him his right hand, and Montezuma did not wish to take it, but he did give his hand to Cortés and then Cortés brought out a necklace which he had ready at hand, made of glass stones, which I have already said are called Margaritas, which have within them many patterns of diverse colors, these were strung on a cord of gold and with musk so that it should have a sweet scent, and he placed it round the neck of the Great Montezuma and when he had so placed it he was going to embrace him, and those great Princes who accompanied Montezuma held back Cortés by the arm so that he should not embrace him, for they considered it an indignity.

Then Cortés through the mouth of Doña Marina told him that now his heart rejoiced at having seen such a great Prince, and that he took it as a great honor that he had come in person to meet him and had frequently shown him such favor.

Then Montezuma spoke other words of politeness to him, and told two of his nephews who supported his arms, the Lord of Texcoco and the Lord of Coyoacan, to go with us and show us to our quarters, and Montezuma with his other two relations,

From Bernal Díaz del Castillo, *The True History of the Conquest of New Spain*, vol. 2, trans. Alfred Percival Maudslay (London: The Hakluyt Society, 1910), 41–44, 55–59.

[1]A Nahua slave of a Maya cacique, she was given to Cortés by the Maya after their defeat at Potonchan. Speaking both Nahuatl and Yucatec Maya, she (and the ex-Maya captive Gerónimo de Aguilar) became crucial interpreters for Cortés as he entered the world of the Mexica. She was also the mother of Cortés's illegitimate son, Martín. See Stuart B. Schwartz, ed., *Victors and Vanquished: Spanish and Nahua Views of the Conquest of Mexico* (Boston: Bedford/St. Martin's, 2000), 251. [Schwartz's note.]

the Lord of Cuitlahuac and the Lord of Tacuba who accompanied him, returned to the city, and all those grand companies of Caciques[2] and chieftains who had come with him returned in his train. . . . Thus space was made for us to enter the streets of Mexico, without being so much crowded. But who could now count the multitude of men and women and boys who were in the streets and on the azoteas, and in canoes on the canals, who had come out to see us. It was indeed wonderful, and, now that I am writing about it, it all comes before my eyes as though it had happened but yesterday. Coming to think it over it seems to be a great mercy that our Lord Jesus Christ was pleased to give us grace and courage to dare to enter into such a city; and for the many times He has saved me from danger of death, as will be seen later on, I give Him sincere thanks, and in that He has preserved me to write about it, although I cannot do it as fully as is fitting or the subject needs. Let us make no words about it, for deeds are the best witnesses to what I say here and elsewhere.

Let us return to our entry to Mexico. They took us to lodge in some large houses, where there were apartments for all of us, for they had belonged to the father of the Great Montezuma, who was named Axayaca, and at that time Montezuma kept there the great oratories for his idols, and a secret chamber where he kept bars and jewels of gold, which was the treasure that he had inherited from his father Axayaca, and he never disturbed it. They took us to lodge in that house, because they called us Teules, and took us for such, so that we should be with the Idols or Teules which were kept there. However, for one reason or another, it was there they took us, where there were great halls and chambers canopied with the cloth of the country for our Captain, and for every one of us beds of matting with canopies above, and no better bed is given, however great the chief may be, for they are not used. And all these palaces were [coated] with shining cement and swept and garlanded.

As soon as we arrived and entered into the great court, the Great Montezuma took our Captain by the hand, for he was there awaiting him, and led him to the apartment and saloon where he was to lodge, which was very richly adorned according to their usage, and he had at hand a very rich necklace made of golden crabs, a marvelous piece of work, and Montezuma himself placed it round the neck of our Captain Cortés, and greatly astonished his [own] Captains by the great honor that he was bestowing on him. When the necklace had been fastened, Cortés thanked Montezuma through our interpreters, and Montezuma replied — "Malinche, you and your brethren are in your own house, rest awhile," and then he went to his palaces which were not far away, and we divided our lodgings by companies, and placed the artillery pointing in a convenient direction, and the order which we had to keep was clearly explained to us, and that we were to be much on the alert, both the cavalry and all of us soldiers. A sumptuous dinner was provided for us according to their use and custom, and we ate it at once. So this was our lucky and daring entry into the great city of Tenochtitlan, Mexico. . . .

---

[2]A Taino word meaning ruler, brought from the Indies to Mexico by the Spanish and used to refer to native rulers in Mexico and Latin America in general. See Schwartz, *Victors and Vanquished*, 254. [Schwartz's note.]

Thanks to our Lord Jesus Christ for it all. . . .

Let us leave this talk and go back to our story of what else happened to us, which I will go on to relate. . . .

The next day Cortés decided to go to Montezuma's palace, and he first sent to find out what he intended doing and to let him know that we were coming. . . .

When Montezuma knew of our coming he advanced to the middle of the hall to receive us, accompanied by many of his nephews, for no other chiefs were permitted to enter or hold communication with Montezuma where he then was, unless it were on important business. Cortés and he paid the greatest reverence to each other and then they took one another by the hand and Montezuma made him sit down on his couch on his right hand, and he also bade all of us to be seated on seats which he ordered to be brought.

Then Cortés began to make an explanation through our interpreters Doña Marina and Aguilar, and said that he and all of us were rested, and that in coming to see and converse with such a great Prince as he was, we had completed the journey and fulfilled the command which our great King and Prince had laid on us. But what he chiefly came to say on behalf of our Lord God had already been brought to his [Montezuma's] knowledge through his ambassadors, Tendile, Pitalpitoque and Quintalbor, at the time when he did us the favor to send the golden sun and moon to the sand dunes; for we told them then that we were Christians and worshipped one true and only God, named Jesus Christ, who suffered death and passion to save us, and we told them that a cross (when they asked us why we worshipped it) was a sign of the other Cross on which our Lord God was crucified for our salvation, and that the death and passion which He suffered was for the salvation of the whole human race, which was lost, and that this our God rose on the third day and is now in heaven, and it is He who made the heavens and the earth, the sea and the sands, and created all the things there are in the world, and He sends the rain and the dew, and nothing happens in the world without His holy will. That we believe in Him and worship Him, but that those whom they look upon as gods are not so, but are devils, which are evil things, and if their looks are bad their deeds are worse, and they could see that they were evil and of little worth, for where we had set up crosses such as those his ambassadors had seen, they dared not appear before them, through fear of them, and that as time went on they would notice this.

The favor he now begged of him was his attention to the words that he now wished to tell him; then he explained to him very clearly about the creation of the world, and how we are all brothers, sons of one father, and one mother who were called Adam and Eve, and how such a brother as our great Emperor, grieving for the perdition of so many souls, such as those which their idols were leading to Hell, where they burn in living flames, had sent us, so that after what he [Montezuma] had now heard he would put a stop to it and they would no longer adore these Idols or sacrifice Indian men and women to them, for we were all brethren, nor should they commit sodomy or thefts. He also told them that, in course of time, our Lord and King would send some men who among us lead very holy lives, much better than we do, who will explain to them all about it, for at present we merely came to give them due warning, and so he prayed him to do what he was asked and carry it into effect.

As Montezuma appeared to wish to reply, Cortés broke off his argument, and to all of us who were with him he said: "with this we have done our duty considering it is the first attempt."

Montezuma replied — "Señor Malinche, I have understood your words and arguments very well before now, from what you said to my servants at the sand dunes, this about three Gods and the Cross, and all those things that you have preached in the towns through which you have come. We have not made any answer to it because here throughout all time we have worshipped our own gods, and thought they were good, as no doubt yours are, so do not trouble to speak to us any more about them at present. Regarding the creation of the world, we have held the same belief for ages past, and for this reason we take it for certain that you are those whom our ancestors predicted would come from the direction of the sunrise." . . .

. . . Then Cortés and all of us answered that we thanked him sincerely for such signal good will, and Montezuma said, laughing, for he was very merry in his princely way of speaking: "Malinche, I know very well that these people of Tlaxcala with whom you are such good friends have told you that I am a sort of God or Teul, and that everything in my houses is made of gold and silver and precious stones, I know well enough that you are wise and did not believe it but took it as a joke. Behold now, Señor Malinche, my body is of flesh and bone like yours, my houses and palaces of stone and wood and lime; that I am a great king and inherit the riches of my ancestors is true, but not all the nonsense and lies that they have told you about me, although of course you treated it as a joke, as I did your thunder and lightning."

Cortés answered him, also laughing, and said that opponents and enemies always say evil things, without truth in them, of those whom they hate, and that he well knew that he could not hope to find another Prince more magnificent in these countries, and, that not without reason had he been so vaunted to our Emperor.

While this conversation was going on, Montezuma secretly sent a great Cacique, one of his nephews who was in his company, to order his stewards to bring certain pieces of gold, which it seems must have been put apart to give to Cortés, and ten loads of fine cloth, which he apportioned, the gold and mantles between Cortés and the four captains, and to each of us soldiers he gave two golden necklaces, each necklace being worth ten pesos, and two loads of mantles. The gold that he then gave us was worth in all more than a thousand pesos and he gave it all cheerfully and with the air of a great and valiant prince.

Discussion Questions

1. How does Díaz describe Tenochtitlán and the Aztec leader Moctezuma? What impressed him in particular? What does he seem to criticize, and why?

2. How does Díaz portray Cortés and his interactions with Moctezuma? What was the role of Doña Marina in their exchanges?

3. In what ways is Díaz's account colored by his own preconceptions and beliefs as a European in a foreign land?

4. Based on this account, what motivated Díaz and other conquistadors? What did the New World have to offer them?

2.
Illustrating a Native Perspective
Lienzo de Tlaxcala (c. 1560)

Like Bernal Díaz del Castillo, the peoples of central Mexico had a stake in recording the momentous events unfolding around them, for they had long believed that remembering the past was essential to their cultural survival. Traditionally, local peoples used pictoriographic representations to record legends, myths, and historical events. After the Spaniards' arrival, indigenous artists borrowed from this tradition to produce their own accounts of the conquest, including the image below. It is one of a series contained in the Lienzo de Tlaxcala, *painted on cloth in the mid-sixteenth*

xff F1219.L58 LAM .06, Courtesy of The Bancroft Library, University of California, Berkeley.

century. Apparently, the Lienzo was created for the Spanish viceroy to commemorate the alliance of the Tlaxcalans with the Spaniards. The Tlaxcalans were enemies of the Aztecs and after initial resistance to the Spanish invasion decided to join their forces. This particular image depicts two related events. The first is the meeting between the Aztec leader Moctezuma and Hernán Cortés in Tenochtitlán in August 1519. Cortés is accompanied by Doña Marina, his translator and cultural mediator; Moctezuma appears with warriors at his side. Rather than showing Moctezuma in his traditional garb, the artist dressed him in the manner of the Tlaxcalans. Both sit in European-style chairs, a nod to European artistic influence, and a Tlaxcalan headdress is suspended in the air between them. Game and fowl offered to the Spaniards are portrayed at the bottom. Within a week of this meeting, Cortés imprisoned Moctezuma in his own palaces with the Tlaxcalans' help. Moctezuma the prisoner appears in the upper right of the image as an old, weak ruler whose sun has set.

DISCUSSION QUESTIONS

1. In what ways do the artist's depictions of Cortés and Moctezuma differ? In what ways are they the same?

2. Why do you think the artist chose to depict Moctezuma in Tlaxcalan dress? How was this choice related to the artist's audience and the message he sought to convey?

3. What are the possible strengths and weaknesses of using pictures to record and convey information?

3.
Defending Native Humanity
Bartolomé de Las Casas, *In Defense of the Indians* (c. 1548–1550)

Indigenous peoples in the Americas suffered heavily under Spanish colonization. Millions died as the result of war and disease, and many who remained were used as forced labor. The Amerindians' fate did not go unnoticed in Europe, where the ethical and legal basis of their harsh treatment became the subject of significant debate. Charles V, king of Spain and the Holy Roman Emperor, added fuel to the fire. In 1550, he ordered a panel of lawyers and theologians at the University of Valladolid to evaluate the positions of two prominent opposing voices on the issue, Juan Ginés de Sepúlveda (1490–1573) and Bartolomé de Las Casas (1474–1566). Drawing heavily on Aristotle's notion that hierarchy was natural, Sepúlveda argued that the Spanish had the right to enslave Amerindians because they were an inferior and less civilized people. Las Casas, whose response is excerpted below, rejected Sepúlveda's position,

From *In Defense of the Indians*, trans. Stafford Poole (DeKalb: Northern Illinois University Press, 1974), 41–46.

based in part on his own experience living in Spanish America. Here he witnessed firsthand the devastating human impact of colonization and was ultimately swayed by the local Dominicans' campaign against the mistreatment of Indians. He joined the order and thereafter was a vocal advocate for Amerindians until his death in 1566. Although the Valladolid panel did not declare a winner, in the end, Las Casas's views did not hold the day in the New World.

As a result of the points we have proved and made clear, the distinction the Philosopher [Aristotle] makes between the two above-mentioned kinds of barbarian is evident. For those he deals with in the first book of the *Politics*, and whom we have just discussed, are barbarians without qualification, in the proper and strict sense of the word, that is, dull witted and lacking in the reasoning powers necessary for self-government. They are without laws, without king, etc. For this reason they are by nature unfitted for rule.

However, he admits, and proves, that the barbarians he deals with in the third book of the same work have a lawful, just, and natural government. Even though they lack the art and use of writing, they are not wanting in the capacity and skill to rule and govern themselves, both publicly and privately. Thus they have kingdoms, communities, and cities that they govern wisely according to their laws and customs. Thus their government is legitimate and natural, even though it has some resemblance to tyranny. From these statements we have no choice but to conclude that the rulers of such nations enjoy the use of reason and that their people and the inhabitants of their provinces do not lack peace and justice. Otherwise they could not be established or preserved as political entities for long. This is made clear by the Philosopher and Augustine. Therefore not all barbarians are irrational or natural slaves or unfit for government. Some barbarians, then, in accord with justice and nature, have kingdoms, royal dignities, jurisdiction, and good laws, and there is among them lawful government.

Now if we shall have shown that among our Indians of the western and southern shores (granting that we call them barbarians and that they are barbarians) there are important kingdoms, large numbers of people who live settled lives in a society, great cities, kings, judges and laws, persons who engage in commerce, buying, selling, lending, and the other contracts of the law of nations, will it not stand proved that the Reverend Doctor Sepúlveda has spoken wrongly and viciously against peoples like these, either out of malice or ignorance of Aristotle's teaching, and, therefore, has falsely and perhaps irreparably slandered them before the entire world? From the fact that the Indians are barbarians it does not necessarily follow that they are incapable of government and have to be ruled by others, except to be taught about the Catholic faith and to be admitted to the holy sacraments. They are not ignorant, inhuman, or bestial. Rather, long before they had heard the word Spaniard they had properly organized states, wisely ordered by excellent laws, religion, and custom. They cultivated friendship and, bound together in common fellowship, lived in populous cities in which they wisely administered the affairs of both peace and war justly and equitably, truly governed by laws that at very many points surpass ours, and could have won the admiration of the sages of Athens. . . .

Now if they are to be subjugated by war because they are ignorant of polished literature, let Sepúlveda hear Trogus Pompey:

> Nor could the Spaniards submit to the yoke of a conquered province until Caesar Augustus, after he had conquered the world, turned his victorious armies against them and organized that barbaric and wild people as a province, once he had led them by law to a more civilized way of life.

Now see how he called the Spanish people barbaric and wild. I would like to hear Sepúlveda, in his cleverness, answer this question: Does he think that the war of the Romans against the Spanish was justified in order to free them from barbarism? And this question also: Did the Spanish wage an unjust war when they vigorously defended themselves against them?

Next, I call the Spaniards who plunder that unhappy people torturers. Do you think that the Romans, once they had subjugated the wild and barbaric peoples of Spain, could with secure right divide all of you among themselves, handing over so many head of both males and females as allotments to individuals? And do you then conclude that the Romans could have stripped your rulers of their authority and consigned all of you, after you had been deprived of your liberty, to wretched labors, especially in searching for gold and silver lodes and mining and refining the metals? And if the Romans finally did that, . . . [would you not judge] that you also have the right to defend your freedom, indeed your very life, by war? Sepúlveda, would you have permitted Saint James to evangelize your own people of Córdoba in that way? For God's sake and man's faith in him, is this the way to impose the yoke of Christ on Christian men? Is this the way to remove wild barbarism from the minds of barbarians? Is it not, rather, to act like thieves, cut-throats, and cruel plunderers and to drive the gentlest of people headlong into despair? The Indian race is not that barbaric, nor are they dull witted or stupid, but they are easy to teach and very talented in learning all the liberal arts, and very ready to accept, honor, and observe the Christian religion and correct their sins (as experience has taught) once priests have introduced them to the sacred mysteries and taught them the word of God. They have been endowed with excellent conduct, and before the coming of the Spaniards, as we have said, they had political states that were well founded on beneficial laws.

Now if Sepúlveda had wanted, as a serious man should, to know the full truth before he sat down to write with his mind corrupted by the lies of tyrants, he should have consulted the honest religious who have lived among those peoples for many years and know their endowments of character and industry, as well as the progress they have made in religion and morality. . . .

From this it is clear that the basis for Sepúlveda's teaching that these people are uncivilized and ignorant is worse than false. Yet even if we were to grant that this race has no keenness of mind or artistic ability, certainly they are not, in consequence, obliged to submit themselves to those who are more intelligent and to adopt their ways, so that, if they refuse, they may be subdued by having war waged against them and be enslaved, as happens today. For men are obliged by the natural law to do many things they cannot be forced to do against their will. We are bound by the natural law to embrace virtue and imitate the uprightness of good men. No one, however, is punished for being bad unless he is guilty of rebellion. Where the Catholic faith has been preached in a Christian manner and as it ought to be, all men are bound by the natural law to accept it, yet no one is forced to accept the faith of Christ. No one is punished because he is sunk in vice, unless he is rebellious or harms the property and persons of others. No one is forced to embrace virtue and show himself as a good man. . . .

. . . Therefore, not even a truly wise man may force an ignorant barbarian to submit to him, especially by yielding his liberty, without doing him an injustice. This the poor Indians suffer, with extreme injustice, against all the laws of God and of men and against the law of nature itself.

DISCUSSION QUESTIONS

1. Why does Las Casas reject Sepúlveda's argument? What is the basis of his reasoning?

2. How does Las Casas depict Amerindian civilization? What attributes does he highlight and why?

3. Why does Las Casas cite the example of Rome's conquest of Spain under Caesar Augustus to support his point?

4. Despite Las Casas's vigorous defense of the Indians, what prejudices and assumptions of his own did he bring to bear in this work?

4.
Scripture and Salvation

Martin Luther, *Freedom of a Christian* (1520)

German monk Martin Luther's attempt to reform the Catholic church from within developed into a new branch of Christianity known as Protestantism. After his excommunication by Pope Leo X in 1520, Luther published several treatises that attacked church authority, clerical celibacy, and the sacraments while elucidating his evangelical theology. He set forth the guiding principles of his beliefs with particular clarity in Freedom of a Christian. *Although originally written in Latin and addressed to the pope, the tract was soon translated into German and widely circulated among Luther's ever-growing number of followers. In the excerpt that follows, Luther defined what became a central tenet of the reform movement: faith in Christ and his promise of salvation is all that a Christian needs to be saved from sin.*

Many people have considered Christian faith an easy thing, and not a few have given it a place among the virtues. They do this because they have not experienced it and have never tasted the great strength there is in faith. It is impossible to write

From Martin Luther, *Christian Liberty*, ed. Harold J. Grimm (Philadelphia, PA: Fortress Press, 1957), 6–10.

well about it or to understand what has been written about it unless one has at one time or another experienced the courage which faith gives a man when trials oppress him. But he who has had even a faint taste of it can never write, speak, meditate, or hear enough concerning it. It is a living "spring of water welling up to eternal life," as Christ calls it in John 4 [:14].

As for me, although I have no wealth of faith to boast of and know how scant my supply is, I nevertheless hope that I have attained to a little faith, even though I have been assailed by great and various temptations; and I hope that I can discuss it, if not more elegantly, certainly more to the point, than those literalists and sub-tile disputants have previously done, who have not even understood what they have written. . . .

First, let us consider the inner man to see how a righteous, free, and pious Christian, that is, a spiritual, new, and inner man, becomes what he is. It is evident that no external thing has any influence in producing Christian righteousness or freedom. . . . It does not help the soul if the body is adorned with the sacred robes of priests or dwells in sacred places or is occupied with sacred duties or prays, fasts, abstains from certain kinds of food, or does any work that can be done by the body and in the body. . . .

One thing, and only one thing, is necessary for Christian life, righteousness, and freedom. That one thing is the most holy Word of God, the gospel of Christ, as Christ says, John 11 [:25], "I am the resurrection and the life; he who believes in me, though he die, yet shall he live"; and John 8 [:36], "So if the Son makes you free, you will be free indeed"; and Matt. 4 [:4], "Man shall not live by bread alone, but by every word that proceeds from the mouth of God." Let us then consider it certain and firmly established that the soul can do without anything except the Word of God and that where the Word of God is missing there is no help at all for the soul. If it has the Word of God it is rich and lacks nothing since it is the Word of life, truth, light, peace, righteousness, salvation, joy, liberty, wisdom, power, grace, glory, and of every incalculable blessing. . . .

You may ask, "What then is the Word of God, and how shall it be used, since there are so many words of God?" I answer: The Apostle explains this in Romans 1. The Word is the gospel of God concerning his Son, who was made flesh, suffered, rose from the dead, and was glorified through the Spirit who sanctifies. To preach Christ means to feed the soul, make it righteous, set it free, and save it, provided it believes the preaching. Faith alone is the saving and efficacious use of the Word of God. . . . Therefore it is clear that, as the soul needs only the Word of God for its life and righteousness, so it is justified by faith alone and not any works. . . .

When you have learned this you will know that you need Christ, who suffered and rose again for you so that, if you believe in him, you may through this faith become a new man in so far as your sins are forgiven and you are justified by the merits of another, namely, of Christ alone. . . .

DISCUSSION QUESTIONS

1. According to Luther, what is faith and where does it come from?

2. How can an individual Christian become a "new man" through such faith?

3. By defining faith alone as essential to salvation, in what ways does Luther undermine basic Catholic teachings?

4. What authority does Luther draw on to defend his point of view? What does this reveal about the basis of his theology?

5.
Reforming Christianity
John Calvin, *Articles Concerning Predestination* (c. 1560)
and
The Necessity of Reforming the Church (1543)

Studying in Paris at the same time as Ignatius of Loyola (1491–1556) in 1533–1534, Frenchman John Calvin (1509–1564) became a convert to the reform movement. Fleeing the dangers of Paris, Calvin settled in Geneva and produced the first edition of his famous treatise, Institutes of the Christian Religion, *in 1536. With Guillaume Farel (1489–1565), he began to implement a program of religious and moral reform. Calvin and Farel soon clashed with the city's leaders, who were unwilling to go along with the radical disciplinary measures they proposed, as the measures would have made the city a virtual theocracy — a state governed by officials in the name of God. Although banished from the city in 1537, Calvin and Farel were invited back in 1540. Calvin then began to build a godly city, making Geneva a haven for reformers and a training ground for preachers. The first excerpt that follows, "Articles Concerning Predestination," was written late in Calvin's life and is one of the simplest explanations of his doctrine. The second excerpt, from "The Necessity of Reforming the Church," addresses the problem of idolatry, especially the cult of the saints.*

Articles Concerning Predestination

Before the first man was created, God in his eternal counsel had determined what he willed to be done with the whole human race.

In the hidden counsel of God it was determined that Adam should fall from the unimpaired condition of his nature, and by his defection should involve all his posterity in sentence of eternal death.

Upon the same decree depends the distinction between elect and reprobate:[1] as he adopted some for himself for salvation, he destined others for eternal ruin.

While the reprobate are the vessels of the just wrath of God, and the elect vessels of his compassion, the ground of the distinction is to be sought in the pure will of God alone, which is the supreme rule of justice.

From *Calvin: Theological Treatises*, vol. 22, trans. Rev. J. K. S. Reid (Philadelphia, PA: The Westminster Press, 1954), 179, 188–91.

[1]Reprobates refer to those who were damned. [Ed.]

While the elect receive the grace of adoption by faith, their election does not depend on faith but is prior in time and order.

As the beginning of faith and perseverance in it arises from the gratuitous election of God, none are truly illuminated with faith, and none granted the spirit of regeneration, except those whom God elects. But it is necessary that the reprobate remain in their blindness or be deprived of such portion of faith as is in them.

While we are elected in Christ, nevertheless that God reckons us among his own is prior in order to his making us members of Christ.

While the will of God is the supreme and primary cause of all things, and God holds the devil and the godless subject to his will, nevertheless God cannot be called the cause of sin, nor the author of evil, nor subject of any guilt. . . .

The Necessity of Reforming the Church

. . . Both sides confess that in the sight of God idolatry is an execrable crime. But when we attack the worship of images, our adversaries immediately take the opposite side, and lend support to the crime which they had with us verbally condemned. . . . For they strenuously defend the veneration of images, though they condemn idolatry. But these ingenious men deny that the honor which they pay to images is worship, as if, when compared with ancient idolatry, it were possible to see any difference. Idolaters pretended that they worshipped the celestial gods, though under corporeal figures which represented them. What else do our adversaries pretend? But is God satisfied with such excuses? Did the prophets on this account cease to rebuke the madness of the Egyptians, when, out of the secret mysteries of their theology, they drew subtle distinctions under which to screen themselves? What too do we suppose the brazen serpent which the Jews worshipped to have been, but something which they honored as a representation of God? . . .

I have not yet adverted to the grosser superstitions, though these cannot be confined to the ignorant, since they are approved by public consent. They adorn their idols now with flowers and chaplets, now with robes, vests, girdles, purses, and frivolities of every kind. They light tapers and burn incense before them, and carry them on their shoulders in solemn state. They assemble from long distances to one statue, though they have similar things at home. Likewise, though in one shrine there may be several images, of the Virgin Mary, or someone else, they pass these by, and one is frequented as if it were more divine. When they pray to the image of Christopher or Barbara, they mutter the Lord's Prayer and the angel's salutation. The fairer or dingier the images are, the greater is their excellence supposed to be. They find new commendation in fabulous miracles. Some they pretend to have spoken, others to have extinguished a fire in the church by trampling on it, others to have moved of their own accord to a new abode, others to have dropped from heaven. While the whole world teems with these and similar delusions, and the fact is perfectly notorious, we who have brought back the worship of the one God to the rule of his Word, who are blameless in this matter, and have purged our churches, not only of idolatry but of superstition also, are accused of violating the worship of God, because we have discarded the worship of images. . . .

. . . As to the matter of relics, it is almost incredible how impudently the world has been cheated. I can mention three relics of our Savior's circumcision; likewise fourteen nails which are exhibited for the three by which the soldiers cast lots; two inscriptions that were placed over the cross; three blades of the spear by which our Savior's side was pierced, and about five sets of linen clothes which wrapped his body in the tomb. Besides they show all the articles used at the institution of the Lord's Supper, and endless absurdities of this kind. There is no saint of any celebrity of whom two or three bodies are not in existence. I can name the place where a piece of pumice-stone was long held in high veneration as the skull of Peter. Decency will not permit me to mention fouler exhibitions. It is therefore undeservedly that we are blamed for having studied to purify the Church of God from such impurities.

In regard to the worship of God, our adversaries next accuse us, because, in omitting trivialities not only foolish but also tending to hypocrisy, we worship God more simply. . . .

DISCUSSION QUESTIONS

1. Describe the doctrine of predestination according to Calvin. How were the elect and reprobate "chosen"?

2. What potential problems might arise from a person's belief that he or she was predestined to election or damnation?

3. To whom does Calvin compare Catholics in their "worship" of saints and relics, and why?

4. What specific evidence does Calvin provide to undermine the cult of the saints?

6.
Responding to Reformation

St. Ignatius of Loyola, *A New Kind of Catholicism*
(1546, 1549, 1553)

The interests of Ignatius of Loyola (1491–1556), born of a Spanish noble family, cen-tered more on chivalry than religion before his serious injury at the Battle of Pam-plona in 1520. While recovering, he experienced a conversion when he began reading the only books available to him, The Golden Legend *(about saints' lives) and the* Life of Christ. *After begging and spending time at the monastery of Montserrat, he began work on* The Spiritual Exercises, *a manual of discernment for the pilgrim journeying to God. After studying at the University of Paris, Ignatius, Francis Xavier (1506–1552), and other friends made vows of chastity and poverty, determining to travel to*

From Joseph A. Munitiz and Philip Endean, eds. and trans., *Saint Ignatius of Loyola, Personal Writings: Reminiscences, Spiritual Diary, Select Letters, Including the Text of The Spiritual Exercises* (New York: Penguin Books, 1996), 165, 166, 230, 233–34, 257, 259, 262–63.

Jerusalem. When this became impossible, they went to Italy. The Society of Jesus (the Jesuits), founded by Ignatius and his early companions, was officially recognized by Pope Paul III in 1540 as a new order directly under the papacy. Its spirituality would be expressed most prominently in teaching and missionary work. The following letters of Ignatius reveal a new form of Catholic spiritual expression that was active and apostolic in its orientation. It was less a "response" to Protestantism than a model for Catholic life and work. Along with the works of other early Jesuits, it embodied a new spirit that so many had sought but not found in the late medieval church.

Conduct at Trent: On Helping Others, 1546

Our main aim [to God's greater glory] during this undertaking at Trent is to put into practice (as a group that lives together in one appropriate place) preaching, confessions and readings, teaching children, giving good example, visiting the poor in the hospitals, exhorting those around us, each of us according to the different talents he may happen to have, urging on as many as possible to greater piety and prayer. . . .

In their preaching they should not refer to points of conflict between Protestants and Catholics, but simply exhort all to upright conduct and to ecclesiastical practice, urging everyone to full self-knowledge and to greater knowledge and love of their Creator and Lord, with frequent allusions to the Council. At the end of each session, they should (as has been mentioned) lead prayers for the Council.

They should do the same with readings as with sermons, trying their best to influence people with greater love of their Creator and Lord as they explain the meaning of what is read; similarly, they should lead their hearers to pray for the Council. . . .

They should spend some time, as convenient, in the elementary teaching of youngsters, depending on the means and disposition of all involved, and with more or less explanation according to the capacity of the pupils. . . . Let them visit the almshouses once or twice a day, at times that are convenient for the patients' health, hearing confessions and consoling the poor, if possible taking them something, and urging them to the sort of prayers mentioned above for confession. If there are three of ours in Trent, each should visit the poor at least once every four days.

When they are urging people in their dealings with them to go to confession and communion, to say mass frequently, to undertake the Spiritual Exercises and other good works, they should also be urging them to pray for the Council.

It was said that there are advantages in being slow to speak and measured in one's statements when doctrinal definitions are involved. The opposite is true when one is urging people to look to their spiritual progress. Then one should be eloquent and ready to talk, full of sympathy and affection.

Spreading God's Word in a German University, 1549

The aim that they should have above all before their eyes is that intended by the Supreme Pontiff who has sent them: to help the University of Ingolstadt, and as far as is possible the whole of Germany, in all that concerns purity of faith, obedience to the Church, and firmness and soundness of doctrine and upright living. . . .

They must be very competent in them, and teach solid doctrine without many technical terms (which are unpopular), especially if these are hard to understand. The lectures should be learned yet clear, sustained in argument yet not long-winded, and delivered with attention to style. . . . Besides these academic lectures, it seems opportune on feast days to hold sermons on Bible readings, more calculated to move hearts and form consciences than to produce learned minds. . . . They should make efforts to attract their students into a friendship of spiritual quality, and if possible towards confession and making the Spiritual Exercises, even in the full form, if they seem suitable to join the Society. . . .

On occasion they should give time to works of mercy of a more visible character, such as in hospitals and prisons and helping other kinds of poor; such works arouse a "sweet fragrance" in the Lord. Opportunity may also arise to act as peacemakers in quarrels and to teach basic Christian doctrine to the uneducated. Taking account of local conditions and the persons concerned, prudence will dictate whether they should act themselves or through others.

They should make efforts to make friends with the leaders of their opponents, as also with those who are most influential among the heretics or those who are suspected of it yet seem not absolutely immovable. They must try to bring them back from their error by sensitive skill and signs of love. . . . All must try to have at their finger-tips the main points concerning dogmas of faith that are subjects of controversy with heretics, especially at the time and place when they are present, and with those persons with whom they are dealing. Thus they will be able, whenever opportunity arises, to put forward and defend the Catholic truth, to refute errors and to strengthen the doubtful and wavering, whether by lectures and sermons or in the confessional and in conversations. . . .

It will be helpful to lead people, as far as possible, to open themselves to God's grace, exhorting them to a desire for salvation, to prayer, to alms, and to everything that conduces to receiving grace or increasing it. . . .

Let [the duke] understand also what glory it will mean for him if he is the first to introduce into Germany seminaries in the form of such colleges, to foster sound doctrine and religion.

The Final Word on Obedience, 1553, to the Brothers in Portugal

To form an idea of the exceptional intrinsic value of this obedience in the eyes of God Our Lord, one should weigh both the worth of the noble sacrifice offered, involving the highest human power, and the completeness of the self-offering undertaken, as one strips oneself of self, becoming a "living victim" pleasing to the Divine Majesty. Another indication is the intensity of the difficulty experienced as one conquers self for love of God, opposing the natural human inclination felt by us all to follow our own opinions. . . .

Let us be unpretentious and let us be gentle! God Our Lord will grant the grace to enable you, gently and lovingly, to maintain constantly the offering you have made to Him. . . .

All that has been said does not exclude your bringing before your superiors a contrary opinion that may have occurred to you, once you have prayed about the matter and you feel that it would be proper and in accord with your respect for God to do so. . . . Such is the model on which divine Providence "gently disposes all things," so that the lower via the middle, and the middle via the higher, are led to their final ends. . . . The same can be seen upon the earth with respect to all secular constitutions that are duly established, and with respect to the ecclesiastical hierarchy, which is subordinated to you in virtue of holy obedience to select among the many routes open to you that which will bring you back to Portugal as soon and as safely as possible. So I order you in the name of Christ Our Lord to do this, even if it will be so as to return soon to India. . . . Firstly, you are well aware how important for the upkeep and advancement of Christianity in those lands, as also in Guinea and Brazil, is the good order that the King of Portugal can grant from his kingdom. When a prince of such Christian desires and holy intentions as is the King of Portugal receives information from someone of your experience about the state of affairs in those parts, you can imagine what influence this will have on him to do much more in the service of God Our Lord and for the good of those countries that you will describe to him. . . .

You are also aware how important it is for the good of the Indies that the persons sent there should be suitable for the aim that one is pursuing in those and in other lands. . . . Quite apart from all these reasons, which apply to furthering the good of India, it seems to me that you would fire the King's enthusiasm for the Ethiopian project, which has been planned for so many years without anything effective having been seen. Similarly, with regard to the Congo and Brazil, you could give no small help from Portugal, which you cannot do from India as there are not the same commercial relations. If people in India consider that your presence is important given your post, you can continue to act as superior no less from Portugal than from Japan or China, and probably much better. Just as you have gone away on other occasions for longer periods, do the same now.

Discussion Questions

1. What does the Catholic life mean to Ignatius?

2. What advice does Ignatius offer about dealing with the problem of heresy?

3. What role will Jesuits play throughout Europe and the rest of the world according to Ignatius's instructions?

4. How does Ignatius think political leaders can be enlisted to support the aims of the reform movement?

Comparative Questions

1. How do Bernal Díaz del Castillo, the *Lienzo de Tlaxcala*, and Bartolomé de Las Casas portray native peoples? Can you trust these portraits? What do they reveal about the ways in which Europeans and native peoples viewed themselves?

2. According to Las Casas, Amerindians were not "barbarians" because they had many marks of "civilization," including cities and self-sustaining governments. What evidence can you find in Díaz to support this view?

3. What similarities and/or differences do you see among Luther, Calvin, and Ignatius's models of Christian life?

4. How do you think Las Casas might have responded to Ignatius's advice to Jesuit missionaries in Portugal? What does this suggest about the role of Catholic Christianity in European colonization?

CHAPTER 15

Wars of Religion and Clash of Worldviews

1560–1648

For kings, nobles, and ordinary folk alike, the late sixteenth through mid-seventeenth centuries were a time of turmoil and change, as the following documents illustrate. Religious wars galvanized much of Europe during this period, fueled by both ecclesiastical and lay leaders' attempts to maintain the commonly held idea that political and social stability depended on religious conformity. With the escalation of violence, however, some people came to question, and in some cases openly criticize, conventional views about the basic order of governance. They argued successfully that peace would come only if state interests took precedence over religious ones. Europeans' views of the earth and the heavens also expanded because of the rise of new scientific methods. At the same time, the lure of traditional beliefs remained strong within communities struggling to make sense of the upheavals occurring around them.

1.
Legislating Tolerance
Henry IV, *Edict of Nantes* (1598)

The promulgation of the Edict of Nantes in 1598 by King Henry IV (r. 1589–1610) marked the end of the French Wars of Religion by recognizing French Protestants as a legally protected religious minority. Drawing largely on earlier edicts of pacification, the Edict of Nantes was composed of ninety-two general articles, fifty-six secret articles, and two royal warrants. The two series of articles represented the edict proper and were registered by the highest courts of law in the realm (parlements). The

Modernized English text adapted from Edmund Everard, *The Great Pressures and Grievances of the Protestants in France* (London, 1681), 1–5, 10, 14, 16.

following excerpts from the general articles reveal the triumph of political concerns over religious conformity on the one hand, and the limitations of religious tolerance in early modern France on the other.

Henry, by the grace of God, King of France, and Navarre, to all present, and to come, greeting. Among the infinite mercies that it has pleased God to bestow upon us, that most signal and remarkable is, his having given us power and strength not to yield to the dreadful troubles, confusions, and disorders, which were found at our coming to this kingdom, divided into so many parties and factions, that the most legitimate was almost the least, enabling us with constancy in such manner to oppose the storm, as in the end to surmount it, now reaching a part of safety and repose for this state . . . For the general difference among our good subjects, and the particular evils of the soundest parts of the state, we judged might be easily cured, after the principal cause (the continuation of civil war) was taken away. In which having, by the blessing of God, well and happily succeeded, all hostility and wars through the kingdom being now ceased, we hope that we will succeed equally well in other matters remaining to be settled, and that by this means we shall arrive at the establishment of a good peace, with tranquility and rest. . . . Among our said affairs . . . one of the principal has been the complaints we have received from many of our Catholic provinces and cities, that the exercise of the Catholic religion was not universally re-established, as is provided by edicts or statutes heretofore made for the pacification of the troubles arising from religion; as well as the supplications and remonstrances which have been made to us by our subjects of the Reformed religion, regarding both the non-fulfillment of what has been granted by the said former laws, and that which they desired to be added for the exercise of their religion, the liberty of their consciences and the security of their persons and fortunes; presuming to have just reasons for desiring some enlargement of articles, as not being without great apprehensions, because their ruin has been the principal pretext and original foundation of the late wars, troubles, and commotions. Now not to burden us with too much business at once, as also that the fury of war was not compatible with the establishment of laws, however good they might be, we have hitherto deferred from time to time giving remedy herein. But now that it has pleased God to give us a beginning of enjoying some rest, we think we cannot employ ourself better than to apply to that which may tend to the glory and service of His holy name, and to provide that He may be adored and prayed unto by all our subjects: and if it has not yet pleased Him to permit it to be in one and the same form of religion, that it may at the least be with one and the same intention, and with such rules that may prevent among them all troubles and tumults. . . . For this cause, we have upon the whole judged it necessary to give to all our said subjects one general law, clear, pure, and absolute, by which they shall be regulated in all differences which have heretofore risen among them, or may hereafter rise, wherewith the one and other may be contented, being framed according as the time requires: and having had no other regard in this deliberation than solely the zeal we have to the service of God, praying that He would from this time forward render to all our subjects a durable and established peace. . . . We have by this edict or statute perpetual and irrevocable said, declared, and ordained, saying, declaring, and ordaining;

That the memory of all things passed on the one part and the other, since the beginning of the month of March 1585 until our coming to the crown, and also during the other preceding troubles, and the occasion of the same, shall remain extinguished and suppressed, as things that had never been. . . .

We prohibit to all our subjects of whatever state and condition they be, to renew the memory thereof, to attack, resent, injure, or provoke one another by reproaches for what is past, under any pretext or cause whatsoever, by disputing, contesting, quarrelling, reviling, or offending by factious words; but to contain themselves, and live peaceably together as brethren, friends, and fellow-citizens, upon penalty for acting to the contrary, to be punished for breakers of peace, and disturbers of the public quiet.

We ordain, that the Catholic religion shall be restored and re-established in all places, and quarters of this kingdom and country under our obedience, and where the exercise of the same has been interrupted, to be there again, peaceably and freely exercised without any trouble or impediment. . . .

And not to leave any occasion of trouble and difference among our subjects, we have permitted and do permit to those of the Reformed religion, to live and dwell in all the cities and places of this our kingdom and countries under our obedience, without being inquired after, vexed, molested, or compelled to do any thing in religion, contrary to their conscience. . . .

We permit also to those of the said religion to hold, and continue the exercise of the same in all the cities and places under our obedience, where it was by them established and made public at several different times, in the year 1586, and in 1597.

In like manner the said exercise may be established, and re-established in all the cities and places where it has been established or ought to be by the Statute of Pacification, made in the year 1577 . . .

We prohibit most expressly to all those of the said religion, to hold any exercise of it . . . except in places permitted and granted in the present edict. As also not to exercise the said religion in our court, nor in our territories and countries beyond the mountains, nor in our city of Paris, nor within five leagues of the said city. . . .

We prohibit all preachers, readers, and others who speak in public, to use any words, discourse, or propositions tending to excite the people to sedition; and we enjoin them to contain and comport themselves modestly, and to say nothing which shall not be for the instruction and edification of the listeners, and maintaining the peace and tranquility established by us in our said kingdom. . . .

They [French Protestants] shall also be obliged to keep and observe the festivals of the Catholic Church, and shall not on the same days work, sell, or keep open shop, nor likewise the artisans shall not work out of their shops, in their chambers or houses privately on the said festivals, and other days forbidden, of any trade, the noise whereof may be heard outside by those that pass by, or by the neighbors. . . .

We ordain, that there shall not be made any difference or distinction upon the account of the said religion, in receiving scholars to be instructed in the universities, colleges, or schools, nor of the sick or poor into hospitals, sick houses or public almshouses. . . .

We will and ordain, that all those of the Reformed religion, and others who have followed their party, of whatever state, quality or condition they be, shall be obliged and constrained by all due and reasonable ways, and under the penalties contained in the said edict or statute relating thereunto, to pay tithes to the curates, and other ecclesiastics, and to all others to whom they shall appertain. . . .

To the end to re-unite so much the better the minds and good will of our subjects, as is our intention, and to take away all complaints for the future; we declare all those who make or shall make profession of the said Reformed religion, to be capable of holding and exercising all estates, dignities, offices, and public charges whatsoever. . . .

We declare all sentences, judgments, procedures, seizures, sales, and decrees made and given against those of the Reformed religion, as well living as dead, from the death of the deceased King Henry the Second our most honored Lord and father in law, upon the occasion of the said religion, tumults and troubles since happening, as also the execution of the same judgments and decrees, from henceforward canceled, revoked, and annulled. . . .

Those also of the said religion shall depart and desist henceforward from all practices, negotiations, and intelligences, as well within or without our kingdom; and the said assemblies and councils established within the provinces, shall readily separate, and also all the leagues and associations made or to be made under any pretext, to the prejudice of our present edict, shall be cancelled and annulled, . . . prohibiting most expressly to all our subjects to make henceforth any assessments or levies of money, fortifications, enrollments of men, congregations and assemblies of other than such as are permitted by our present edict, and without arms. . . .

We give in command to the people of our said courts of parlement, chambers of our courts, and courts of our aids, bailiffs, chief-justices, provosts and other of our justices and officers to whom it appertains, and to their lieutenants, that they cause to be read, published, and registered this present edict and ordinance in their courts and jurisdictions, and the same keep punctually, and the contents of the same to cause to be enjoined and used fully and peaceably to all those to whom it shall belong, ceasing and making to cease all troubles and obstructions to the contrary, for such is our pleasure: and in witness hereof we have signed these presents with our own hand; and to the end to make it a thing firm and stable for ever, we have caused to put and endorse our seal to the same. Given at *Nantes* in the month of April in the year of Grace 1598, and of our reign the ninth.

Signed

HENRY

DISCUSSION QUESTIONS

1. What are the edict's principal objectives?

2. In what ways does the edict balance the demands of both French Catholics and Protestants?

3. What limits does the edict place on Protestants' religious rights?

4. Did Henry IV regard this edict as a permanent solution to the religious divisions in the realm? Why or why not?

2.
Barbarians All

Michel de Montaigne, *Of Cannibals* (1580s)

The Edict of Nantes was a victory not only for Henry IV but also for the politiques, *moderate French Catholics and Calvinists who advocated putting the viability of the state ahead of religious uniformity. Their support of religious toleration emerged in direct response to the violence and futility of civil war. French nobleman Michel de Montaigne (1533–1592) was among the most influential voices of moderation and open-mindedness in war-torn France. Alongside his public life as a lawyer and government official, Montaigne was a prolific writer who invented a new genre in European literature, the essay, as a concise form of expression. An excerpt from one of his best-known essays, "Of Cannibals," follows. Here Montaigne casts his gaze in two directions: at newly colonized peoples in the Americas and at his fellow citizens consumed by religious hatred. In the process, he questions the basis of Europeans' supposed moral and cultural superiority over the "barbarians" of the New World.*

I had with me for a long time a man that had lived ten or twelve years in that other world which has been discovered in our century, in the place where Villegaignon landed, which he called Antarctic France.[1] This discovery of so vast a country seems worthy of consideration. I do not know if I can be sure that in the future there may not be another such discovery made, so many greater men than we having been deceived in this. I am afraid our eyes are bigger than our bellies and that we have more curiosity than capacity. We grasp at all, but catch nothing but wind. . . .

This man that I had was a plain ignorant fellow, which is a condition fit to bear true witness; for your sharp sort of men are much more curious in their observations and notice a great deal more, but they gloss them; and to give the greater weight to their interpretation and make it convincing, they cannot forbear to alter the story a little. They never represent things to you simply as they are, they slant them and mask them according to the aspect they saw in them; and to give authority to their judgment and to attract you to it, they are willing to contribute something there to the matter, lengthening it and amplifying it. We should have a man either of irreproachable veracity, or so simple that he has not wherewithal to contrive and to give a color of truth to false tales, and who has not espoused any cause. Mine was such a one; and, besides that, he has diverse times brought me several seamen and merchants whom he had known on that voyage. I do, therefore, content myself with his information without inquiring what the cosmographers say about it. . . .

Now to return to my subject, I find that there is nothing barbarous and savage in this nation according to what I have been told, except that everyone gives the

---

From Michel de Montaigne, *Montaigne: Selected Essays*, ed. Blanchard Bates, trans. C. Cotton and W. C. Hazlit (New York: Modern Library, 1949), 74, 77–79, 82–84.

[1]Brazil, where he arrived in 1557.

title of barbarism to everything that is not according to his usage; as, indeed, we have no other criterion of truth and reason than the example and pattern of the opinions and customs of the country wherein we live. There is always the perfect religion, there the perfect government, there the perfect and accomplished usage in all things. They are savages in the same way that we say fruits are wild, which nature produces of herself and by her ordinary course; whereas, in truth, we ought rather to call those wild whose natures we have changed by our artifice and diverted from the common order. In the former, the genuine, most useful, and natural virtues and properties are vigorous and active, which we have degenerated in the latter, and we have only adapted them to the pleasure of our corrupted palate. And yet, for all this, the flavor and delicacy found in various uncultivated fruits of those countries are excellent to our taste, worthy rivals of ours. . . .

These nations then seem to me to be barbarous so far as having received very little fashioning from the human mind and as being still very close to their original simplicity. The laws of Nature govern them still, very little vitiated by ours. . . .

. . . [T]here is no manner of traffic, no knowledge of letters, no science of numbers, no name of magistrate or of political superiority; no use of servitude, riches, or poverty; no contracts, no successions, no dividing of properties, no employments, except those of leisure; no respect of kindred, except for the common bond; no clothing, no agriculture, no metal, no use of wheat or wine. The very words that signify lying, treachery, dissimulation, avarice, envy, detraction, and pardon were never heard of. . . .

They have wars with the nations that live farther inland beyond their mountains, to which they go quite naked and without other arms than their bows and wooden swords pointed at one end like the points of our spears. The obstinacy of their battles is wonderful; they never end without slaughter and bloodshed; for as to running away and fear, they know not what it is. Everyone for a trophy brings home the head of an enemy he has killed and fixes it over the door of his house. After having a long time treated their prisoners well and with all the luxuries they can think of, he to whom the prisoner belongs forms a great assembly of his acquaintances. He ties a rope to one of the arms of the prisoner, by the end of which he holds him some paces away for fear of being struck, and gives to the friend he loves best the other arm to hold in the same manner; and they two, in the presence of all the assembly, dispatch him with their swords. After that they roast him and eat him among them and send some pieces to their absent friends. They do not do this, as some think, for nourishment, . . . but as a representation of an extreme revenge. And its proof is that having observed that the Portuguese, who were in league with their enemies, inflicted another sort of death on them when they captured them, which was to bury them up to the waist, shoot the rest of the body full of arrows, and then hang them; they thought that these people from the other world (as men who had sown the knowledge of a great many vices among their neighbors and were much greater masters in all kind of wickedness than they) did not exercise this sort of revenge without reason, and that it must needs be more painful than theirs, and they began to leave their old way and to follow this. I am not sorry that we should take notice of the barbarous horror of such acts, but I am sorry that, seeing so clearly into their faults, we should be so blind to our own. I conceive there is more barbarity in eating a man alive than in eating him dead, in tearing by tortures and the rack a body that is still full of feeling, in roasting him by degrees, causing him to be bitten and torn by dogs and swine (as we have not only read, but lately seen, not among inveterate enemies, but among neighbors and fellow-citizens, and what is worse, under color of piety and religion), than in roasting and eating him after he is dead. . . .

We may, then, well call these people barbarians in respect to the rules of reason, but not in respect to ourselves, who, in all sorts of barbarity, exceed them. Their warfare is in every way noble and generous and has as much excuse and beauty as this human malady is capable of; it has with them no other foundation than the sole jealousy of valor. Their disputes are not for the conquests of new lands, for they still enjoy that natural abundance that supplies them without labor and trouble with all things necessary in such abundance that they have no need to enlarge their borders. And they are still in that happy stage of desiring only as much as their natural necessities demand; all beyond that is superfluous to them.

DISCUSSION QUESTIONS

1. How does Montaigne describe the Amerindians?

2. How does Amerindian culture compare to that of Europeans? Who is more barbaric and why? Why does Montaigne make such a comparison?

3. What does this essay suggest about the ways in which the colonization of the New World affected European identity and self-understanding?

3.
Defending Religious Liberty

Apology of the Bohemian Estates (May 25, 1618)

Even as Henry IV worked to bring peace between French Catholics and Calvinists, an even bloodier chapter in European religious wars lay ahead. By the early 1600s, Calvinists had grown in numbers and political clout in the Holy Roman Empire; but unlike their French counterparts, they did not enjoy full legal recognition. The kingdom of Bohemia was a hotbed of Calvinist discontent within the empire. Bolstered by a long tradition of defending their religious liberty, in 1609 the nobles, knights, and city-dwellers who met in the local Bohemian legislature (estates) had gained a series of concessions, much to the outrage of the king-elect, Ferdinand II. Working in tandem with regents ruling in the name of the current king and Holy Roman Emperor, Matthias, Ferdinand moved to suppress both Protestantism and local estates under imperial rule. The Protestant leaders reacted angrily, hurling two representatives of the king and their secretary out a window during a meeting to protest Ferdinand's demands. This event, the so-called defenestration of Prague, marked the first salvo in

From *The Thirty Years War: A Documentary History*, ed. and trans. Tryntje Helfferich (Indianapolis: Hackett Publishing Company, Inc., 2009), 20–23, 29–30.

the Thirty Years' War. The document below is an extract from the Protestant rebels' Apology *defending their actions in Prague. To garner support for their cause, they had the* Apology *published across Europe. Thus from its very onset, the war would be waged in battle and in the court of public opinion.*

Apology, or Letter of Excuse, Concerning the Inevitable Causes That Forced All Three Estates of the Commendable Kingdom of Bohemia Who Receive the Body and Blood of the Lord Christ in Both Kinds[1] to Act in Their Own Defense

We, the representatives of the lords, knights, and cities of Prague, Kuttenberg, and other places: all three estates of this kingdom of Bohemia who receive the body and blood of our Lord Jesus Christ in both kinds, who confess to the Bohemian Confession,[2] and who are now assembled at the castle of Prague, unanimously make it known, both in the name of those present and also on behalf of all those absent, that:

In previous years, all three estates and inhabitants of the kingdom have faced, suffered, and endured many and various kinds of terrible hardships and tribulations in both political and ecclesiastical affairs. These were instigated and provoked by evil and turbulent people, both clergy and laymen, but especially by members of the Jesuit sect, whose impetuses, writings, and endeavors have always been aimed primarily toward fraudulently subjugating not only His Majesty,[3] but also all Protestant residents and estates of this entire kingdom under the lordship of the Roman See,[4] a foreign authority. Hereafter, however, in the years 1609 and [16]10 a perfect peace was erected. The Letter of Majesty[5] of His Imperial Majesty of blessed memory, Emperor Rudolph [II],[6] as well as an accommodation[7] made

---

[1]Inspired by the message of Jan Hus (see chapter 13, document 4), Christians in Bohemia had gained the right to receive Communion in both kinds in the mid-fifteenth century. They later became the core of the Protestant movement in the region. [Ed.]

[2]The Bohemian Confession was a statement of faith made at the 1575 Diet of Prague. It was generally based on the Lutheran Augsburg Confession (1530), but was vague enough eventually to represent a basic point of agreement for all non-Catholics in Bohemia, including the Brethren, Lutherans, and Calvinists.

[3]The king of Bohemia, King Matthias, was both Holy Roman Emperor and king of Bohemia. [Ed.]

[4]The papacy.

[5]The Letter of Majesty was signed by Emperor Rudolph II on July 9, 1609. It affirmed the Bohemian Confession, guaranteed religious freedom in the kingdom, established a unified Protestant consistory for church government, gave control of the University of Prague to the Protestants, allowed the estates to appoint twenty-four religious Defenders, and allowed the estates to keep their existing churches and build new ones on crown lands.

[6]Emperor Rudolph II (1552–1612) was king of Bohemia from 1575 to 1611. . . .

[7]The accommodation, also referred to elsewhere as the union, was an agreement made between the Protestant and Catholic estates over certain points of contention not covered by the Letter of Majesty.

by both sides (Catholics and Protestants) and a general diet,[8] all forcefully confirmed and approved that no side would molest the other; but rather, according to the accommodation that they had made and erected between them, both Catholics and Protestants might and ought freely and peacefully to serve the Lord God everywhere, in any place, and without any interruption by either ecclesiastic or temporal authority. And all of this and more was contained and indicated by the said Letter of Majesty, the accommodation, and the general diet.

At the assumption of his reign in this kingdom and following the customs of this land, His Imperial Majesty, now our most gracious king and lord, also admirably and powerfully approved and confirmed this — not only generally, but also specifically.

Yet nevertheless, the above-mentioned enemies of the king, land, and general peace spared no effort to find a way to negate the concord (which had been both desired and confirmed) and to carry out their evil, extremely dangerous, and pernicious intentions toward this kingdom and our successors. Thus even at the time when the above-mentioned peace and accommodation were being made and ratified, they advanced other persons who were, like them, Catholics; and they refused to subscribe to the Letter of Majesty and the erected accommodation, or to the amnesty.[9] . . . Instead they strove to abolish completely all of this, truly proving their malicious disposition and intentions toward quite a few members of the estates. . . .

[The authors accuse these men, whom they call traitors, of attempting to block the proper line of royal succession in order to undermine Bohemian Protestantism.]

Then, using the Jesuits and other tools of theirs, [these enemies] once again began to issue a variety of abuse, slander, and denunciations against Protestants, giving people to understand, both in public writings and by word of mouth, that we were heretics, with whom (according to their teaching) one was not bound to keep any faith, either promised or proscribed, no matter its importance. They also dishonored us with all kinds of ignominious names and demonstrated great contempt for our teachings and the Protestant religion, and in their libelous publications also proclaimed that Protestants and all of those who were not Roman Catholic had rejected a life of honor: thereby animating the secular authorities to use fire and sword to eradicate Protestantism. And so that they could all the more easily deceive the people and provoke and bring about mistrust among the Protestant members of the estates, the enemies of this territory and of the common peace also tried to sow division among the Defenders[10] (who, with the gracious approval and ratification of His Majesty, had for very good reasons been decreed by us to be protectors of our religion — something that the oft-mentioned Letter of Majesty

---

[8] A general diet was a meeting of the full Bohemian parliament. In addition to serving as the principal political and legislative body, the Bohemian diet also claimed the right to elect the king.

[9] The amnesty was proclaimed by Rudolph II in order to protect both Catholics and non-Catholics from punishment for their actions prior to the issuance of the Letter of Majesty.

[10] The Defenders were a group of twenty-four men appointed by the estates, whose job it was to protect the religious liberties and rights of non-Catholics in the kingdom.

had granted and approved), and thereby to abolish completely the Protestant consistory.[11] . . .

Furthermore, it is more than sufficiently known and evident that, desiring to place honorable people under suspicion and cause them trouble, they [our enemies] brought everything to bear against them — even if it ran contrary to all right, equitableness, and every good order — and used both unusual and usual means to take numerous people's belongings and subject them to great hardships. Especially when it came to Evangelicals, they withheld, at the very least, their rights and justice, and tried to make black seem white, white black, loyal and obedient subjects of His Imperial Majesty disloyal, and, on the contrary, the disloyal loyal. Meanwhile they honored and elevated frivolous and evil people while helping to belittle and bring into contempt those who were well behaved. At the same time, they badly plagued, on account of religion, not only their own subjects but also those of the entire land, including without distinction both those under His Imperial Majesty's control and those who belonged to the ecclesiastical properties; and they used unheard-of atrocities to force people to convert to the Catholic religion against their will and against the clear language of the Letter of Majesty. Indeed, the royal judges' threats against the royal free cities brought several of these cities to the point at which they were forced to agree no longer to stand with the estates [of Bohemia], nor to be counted among their number. [The enemies] planned to do even more evil things, and when we asked them if their advice [to the emperor] had not caused the above-mentioned letter and our denunciation, they neither could, nor did, deny it.

For these above-enumerated reasons, we proceeded against two of their members — namely, Wilhelm Slawata von Chlum und Kosumberg and Jaroslav Borsita von Martinitz, otherwise known as Smeczensky[12] — as destroyers of the law and the common peace, and also because they did not keep in mind the offices and positions in which they found themselves, but instead evilly misused them toward the belittlement of the authority of His Imperial Majesty, our king and lord, as well as toward the abolishment of the common peace in this kingdom of Bohemia. And after determining from their past publications that they were indeed such as they appeared to be, in accordance with the old custom we threw both of them, along with a secretary (their sycophant who had, among other things, caused great disruptions in the towns of Prague), out the window.[13] And we shall proceed further against them (for they are still living) and their goods, as well as against all those whom they represent and defend, those who wish to persecute us or anyone else by whatever ways or means, and equally all who are destroyers of the Letter of Majesty and union, or who would perpetrate similar crimes. . . .

To which end, we, at this, our assembly at the castle of Prague, have established a kingdomwide system of defense for the good of His Imperial Majesty and this kingdom (our dear fatherland), and for the protection of our wives and children from all kinds of danger. And through this action we do not intend to do

---

[11]The consistory was the instrument of church government. . . .

[12]Two of the regents assembled to hear the estates' grievances. [Ed.]

[13]This act, the Defenestration of Prague, occurred on May 23, 1618.

anything against His Imperial Majesty, our most gracious king and lord, nor desire to cause any inopportuneness for peaceable people or our dear Catholic friends (as long as they themselves desire to live in peace). For it is commonly recognized and known that by this action no further layperson or clergyman shall be harmed, nor any tumult result, but rather good peace shall be maintained everywhere — both in the cities of Prague and in the entire kingdom — except only for the above-listed unavoidable reasons, and then only when we neither should nor can do otherwise or any less.

DISCUSSION QUESTIONS

1. Whom do the estates target as their enemies and why? How do they use the *Apology* as a means of justifying their actions against imperial authority?

2. Why do you think the estates chose not to target the king and Holy Roman Emperor, Matthias, for criticism? In what ways do you think this may have reflected their strategy to win support for their cause?

3. What does this document suggest about the religious causes of the Thirty Years' War? How did politics come into play?

4.
The Scientific Challenge

Galileo, *Letter to the Grand Duchess Christina* (1615)

Italian-born and educated, Galileo Galilei (1564–1642) was among the most illustrious proponents of the new science in the seventeenth century. Early in his studies, he embraced the theory held by Nicolaus Copernicus (1473–1543) that the sun, not the Earth, was at the center of the universe. Having improved on the newly invented telescope in 1609, Galileo was able to substantiate the heliocentric view through his observations of the moon and planets. Because Galileo's work challenged both traditional scientific and religious views, it sparked considerable controversy. In the letter excerpted here, written in 1615 to Grand Duchess Christina of Tuscany, an important Catholic patron of learning, Galileo defends the validity of his findings while striving to separate matters of religious faith from the study of natural phenomena.

Galileo Galilei to The Most Serene Grand Duchess Mother

Some years ago, as Your Serene Highness well knows, I discovered in the heavens many things that had not been seen before our own age. The novelty of these things, as well as some consequences which followed from them in contradiction to the physical notions commonly held among academic philosophers, stirred up against me no small number of professors — as if I had placed these things in the sky with my own hands in order to upset nature and overturn the sciences. . . .

From *Discoveries and Opinions of Galileo*, trans. Stillman Drake (New York: Doubleday, 1957), 175–86.

Well, the passage of time has revealed to everyone the truths that I previously set forth. . . . But some, besides allegiance to their original error, possess I know not what fanciful interest in remaining hostile not so much toward the things in question as toward their discoverer. No longer being able to deny them, these men now take refuge in obstinate silence, but being more than ever exasperated by that which has pacified and quieted other men, they divert their thoughts to other fancies and seek new ways to damage me. . . .

Persisting in their original resolve to destroy me and everything mine by any means they can think of, these men are aware of my views in astronomy and philosophy. They know that as to the arrangement of the parts of the universe, I hold the sun to be situated motionless in the center of the revolution of the celestial orbs while the earth rotates on its axis and revolves about the sun. . . .

Now as to the false aspersions which they so unjustly seek to cast upon me, I have thought it necessary to justify myself in the eyes of all men, whose judgment in matters of religion and of reputation I must hold in great esteem. I shall therefore discourse of the particulars which these men produce to make this opinion detested and to have it condemned not merely as false but as heretical. To this end they make a shield of their hypocritical zeal for religion. They go about invoking the Bible, which they would have minister to their deceitful purposes. Contrary to the sense of the Bible and the intention of the holy Fathers, if I am not mistaken, they would extend such authorities until even in purely physical matters — where faith is not involved — they would have us altogether abandon reason and the evidence of our senses in favor of some biblical passage, though under the surface meaning of its words this passage may contain a different sense. . . .

The reason produced for condemning the opinion that the earth moves and the sun stands still is that in many places in the Bible one may read that the sun moves and the earth stands still. Since the Bible cannot err, it follows as a necessary consequence that anyone takes an erroneous and heretical position who maintains that the sun is inherently motionless and the earth movable.

With regard to this argument, I think in the first place that it is very pious to say and prudent to affirm that the holy Bible can never speak untruth — whenever its true meaning is understood. But I believe nobody will deny that it is often very abstruse, and may say things which are quite different from what its bare words signify. Hence in expounding the Bible if one were always to confine oneself to the unadorned grammatical meaning, one might fall into error. Not only contradictions and propositions far from true might thus be made to appear in the Bible, but even grave heresies and follies. Thus it would be necessary to assign to God feet, hands, and eyes, as well as corporeal and human affections, such as anger, repentance, hatred, and sometimes even the forgetting of things past and ignorance of those to come. These propositions uttered by the Holy Ghost were set down in that manner by the sacred scribes in order to accommodate them to the capacities of the common people, who are rude and unlearned. For the sake of those who deserve to be separated from the herd, it is necessary that wise expositors should produce the true senses of such passages, together with the special reasons for which they were set down in these words. This doctrine is so widespread and so definite with all theologians that it would be superfluous to adduce evidence for it.

Hence I think that I may reasonably conclude that whenever the Bible has occasion to speak of any physical conclusion (especially those which are very abstruse and hard to understand), the rule has been observed of avoiding confusion in the minds of the common people which would render them contumacious toward the higher mysteries. Now the Bible, merely to condescend to popular capacity, has not hesitated to obscure some very important pronouncements, attributing to God himself some qualities extremely remote from (and even contrary to) His essence. Who, then, would positively declare that this principle has been set aside, and the Bible has confined itself rigorously to the bare and restricted sense of its words, when speaking but casually of the earth, of water, of the sun, or of any other created thing? Especially in view of the fact that these things in no way concern the primary purpose of the sacred writings, which is the service of God and the salvation of souls — matters infinitely beyond the comprehension of the common people.

This being granted, I think that in discussions of physical problems we ought to begin not from the authority of scriptural passages, but from sense-experiences and necessary demonstrations; for the holy Bible and the phenomena of nature proceed alike from the divine Word, the former as the dictate of the Holy Ghost and the latter as the observant executrix of God's commands. It is necessary for the Bible, in order to be accommodated to the understanding of every man, to speak many things which appear to differ from the absolute truth so far as the bare meaning of the words is concerned. But Nature, on the other hand, is inexorable and immutable; she never transgresses the laws imposed upon her, or cares a whit whether her abstruse reasons and methods of operations are understandable to men. For that reason it appears that nothing physical which sense-experience sets before our eyes, or which necessary demonstrations prove to us, ought to be called in question (much less condemned) upon the testimony of biblical passages which may have some different meaning beneath their words. For the Bible is not chained in every expression to conditions as strict as those which govern all physical effects; nor is God any less excellently revealed in Nature's actions than in the sacred statements of the Bible. . . .

From this I do not mean to infer that we need not have an extraordinary esteem for the passages of holy Scripture. On the contrary, having arrived at any certainties in physics, we ought to utilize these as the most appropriate aids in the true exposition of the Bible and in the investigation of those meanings which are necessarily contained therein, for these must be concordant with demonstrated truths. I should judge that the authority of the Bible was designed to persuade men of those articles and propositions which, surpassing all human reasoning, could not be made credible by science, or by any other means than through the very mouth of the Holy Spirit.

Yet even in those propositions which are not matters of faith, this authority ought to be preferred over that of all human writings which are supported only by bare assertions or probable arguments, and not set forth in a demonstrative way. This I hold to be necessary and proper to the same extent that divine wisdom surpasses all human judgment and conjecture.

But I do not feel obliged to believe that that same God who has endowed us with senses, reason, and intellect has intended to forego their use and by some other means to give us knowledge which we can attain by them. He would not require us to deny sense and reason in physical matters which are set before our eyes and minds by direct experience or necessary demonstrations. This must be especially true in those sciences of which but the faintest trace (and that consisting of conclusions) is to be found in the Bible. Of astronomy, for instance, so little is found that none of the planets except Venus are so much as mentioned, and this only once or twice under the name of "Lucifer." If the sacred scribes had had any intention of teaching people certain arrangements and motions of the heavenly bodies, or had they wished us to derive such knowledge from the Bible, then in my opinion they would not have spoken of these matters so sparingly in comparison with the infinite number of admirable conclusions which are demonstrated in that science. . . .

From these things it follows as a necessary consequence that, since the Holy Ghost did not intend to teach us whether heaven moves or stands still, whether its shape is spherical or like a discus or extended in a plane, nor whether the earth is located at its center or off to one side, then so much the less was it intended to settle for us any other conclusion of the same kind. And the motion or rest of the earth and the sun is so closely linked with the things just named, that without a determination of the one, neither side can be taken in the other matters. Now if the Holy Spirit has purposely neglected to teach us propositions of this sort as irrelevant to the highest goal (that is, to our salvation), how can anyone affirm that it is obligatory to take sides on them, and that one belief is required by faith, while the other side is erroneous? Can an opinion be heretical and yet have no concern with the salvation of souls? Can the Holy Ghost be asserted not to have intended teaching us something that does concern our salvation? I would say here something that was heard from an ecclesiastic of the most eminent degree: "That the intention of the Holy Ghost is to teach us how one goes to heaven, not how heaven goes." . . .

From this it is seen that the interpretation which we impose upon passages of Scripture would be false whenever it disagreed with demonstrated truths. And therefore we should seek the incontrovertible sense of the Bible with the assistance of demonstrated truth, and not in any way try to force the hand of Nature or deny experiences and rigorous proofs in accordance with the mere sound of words that may appeal to our frailty. . . .

To that end they would forbid him the use of reason, divine gift of Providence, and would abuse the just authority of holy Scripture — which, in the general opinion of theologians, can never oppose manifest experiences and necessary demonstrations when rightly understood and applied. If I am correct, it will stand them in no stead to go running to the Bible to cover up their inability to understand (let alone resolve) their opponents' arguments.

DISCUSSION QUESTIONS

1. What do you think was Galileo's goal in writing this letter to the Grand Duchess?

2. What is the basis of the attacks against Galileo by his critics?

3. According to Galileo, what role should the Bible play in scientific inquiry?

4. How does this document lend support to historians who have credited Galileo for helping to popularize the principles and methods of the new science?

5.
The Persecution of Witches

The Trial of Suzanne Gaudry (1652)

Even as the new science gained support, most Europeans continued to believe in the supernatural, especially at this time of religious wars, economic decline, and social strife. This belief found violent expression in a wave of witchcraft persecutions across Europe between 1560 and 1640. The following selections from the trial records of Suzanne Gaudry attest to the predominant notion that witches were agents of the devil. Although conducted at a time when the number of witch hunts and persecutions were in decline, her trial attests to the persistence of a deeply felt fear among many people regarding the presence of diabolical forces in everyday life.

At Ronchain, 28 May, 1652. . . . Interrogation of Suzanne Gaudry, prisoner at the court of Rieux. Questioned about her age, her place of origin, her mother and father.

— Said that she is named Suzanne Gaudry, daughter of Jean Gaudry and Marguerite Gerné, both natives of Rieux, but that she is from Esgavans, near Odenarde, where her family had taken refuge because of the wars, that she was born the day that they made bonfires for the Peace between France and Spain, without being able otherwise to say her age.

Asked why she has been taken here.

— Answers that it is for the salvation of her soul.

— Says that she was frightened of being taken prisoner for the crime of witchcraft.

Asked for how long she has been in the service of the devil.

— Says that about twenty-five or twenty-six years ago she was his lover, that he called himself Petit-Grignon, that he would wear black breeches, that he gave her the name Magin, that she gave him a pin with which he gave her his mark on the left shoulder, that he had a little flat hat; said also that he had his way with her two or three times only.

Asked how many times she has been at the nocturnal dance.

— Answers that she has been there about a dozen times, having first of all renounced God, Lent, and baptism; that the site of the dance was at the little marsh of Rieux, understanding that there were diverse dances. The first time, she did not recognize anyone there, because she was half blind. The other times, she saw and

---

From Alan C. Kors and Edward Peters, eds., *Witchcraft in Europe, 1100–1700: A Documentary History* (Philadelphia: University of Pennsylvania Press, 1972), 266–75.

recognized there Noelle and Pasquette Gerné, Noelle the wife of Nochin Quin-chou and the other of Paul Doris, the widow Marie Nourette, not having recognized others because the young people went with the young people and the old people with the old. [. . .]

Interrogated on how and in what way they danced.
— Says that they dance in an ordinary way, that there was a guitarist and some whistlers who appeared to be men she did not know; which lasted about an hour, and then everyone collapsed from exhaustion.
    Inquired what happened after the dance.
— Says that they formed a circle, that there was a king with a long black beard dressed in black, with a red hat, who made everyone do his bidding, and that after the dance he made a . . . [the word is missing in the text], and then everyone disappeared. . . .

Questioned if she has abused the Holy Communion.
— Says no, never, and that she has always swallowed it. Then says that her lover asked her for it several times, but that she did not want to give it to him.
    After several admonitions were sent to her, she has signed this

Mark
X
Suzanne Gaudry

Second Interrogation, May 29, 1652, in the Presence of the Afore-Mentioned

This prisoner, being brought back into the chamber, was informed about the facts and the charges and asked if what she declared and confessed yesterday is true.
— Answers that if it is in order to put her in prison it is not true; then after having remained silent said that it is true.
    Asked what is her lover's name and what name has he given himself.
— Said that his name is Grinniou and that he calls himself Magnin.
    Asked where he found her the first time and what he did to her.
— Answers that it was in her lodgings, that he had a hide, little black breeches, and a little flat hat; that he asked her for a pin, which she gave to him, with which he made his mark on her left shoulder. Said also that at the time she took him oil in a bottle and that she had thoughts of love.
    Asked how long she has been in subjugation to the devil.
— Says that it has been about twenty-five or twenty-six years, that her lover also then made her renounce God, Lent, and baptism, that he has known her carnally three or four times, and that he has given her satisfaction. And on the subject of his having asked her if she wasn't afraid of having a baby, says that she did not have that thought.
    Asked how many times she found herself at the nocturnal dance and carol and who she recognized there.

— Answers that she was there eleven or twelve times, that she went there on foot with her lover, where the third time she saw and recognized Pasquette and Noelle Gerné, and Marie Homitte, to whom she never spoke, for the reason that they did not speak to each other. And that the sabbat took place at the little meadow. . . .

Asked what occurred at the dance and afterwards.
— Says that right after the dance they put themselves in order and approached the chief figure, who had a long black beard, dressed also in black, with a red hat, at which point they were given some powder, to do with it what they wanted; but that she did not want to take any.
    Charged with having taken some and with having used it evilly.
— Says, after having insisted that she did not want to take any, that she took some, and that her lover advised her to do evil with it; but that she did not want to do it.
    Asked if, not obeying his orders, she was beaten or threatened by him, and what did she do with this powder.
— Answers that never was she beaten; she invoked the name of the Virgin [and answered] that she threw away the powder that she had, not having wanted to do any evil with it.
    Pressed to say what she did with this powder. Did she not fear her lover too much to have thrown it away?
— Says, after having been pressed on this question, that she made the herbs in her garden die at the end of the summer, five to six years ago, by means of the powder, which she threw there because she did not know what to do with it. [. . .]

Charged once more with having performed some malefice with this powder, pressed to tell the truth.
— Answers that she never made any person or beast die; then later said that she made Philippe Cornié's red horse die, about two or three years ago, by means of the powder, which she placed where he had to pass, in the street close to her home.
    Asked why she did that and if she had had any difficulty with him.
— Says that she had had some difficulty with his wife, because her cow had eaten the leeks. [. . .]

After having been admonished to think of her conscience, was returned to prison after having signed this

Mark
X
Suzanne Gaudry

Deliberation of the Court of Mons — June 3, 1652

The under-signed advocates of the Court of Mons have seen these interrogations and answers. They say that the aforementioned Suzanne Gaudry confesses that she is a witch, that she has given herself to the devil, that she has renounced God, Lent, and baptism, that she has been marked on the shoulder, that she has cohabited with him and that she has been to the dances, confessing only to have cast a spell upon and caused to die a beast of Philippe Cornié; but there is no evidence for this, excepting a prior statement. For this reason, before going further, it will be necessary to become acquainted with, to examine and to probe the mark, and to hear Philippe Cornié on the death of the horse and on when and in what way he died. . . .

Deliberation of the Court of Mons — June 13, 1652

[The Court] has reviewed the current criminal trial of Suzanne Gaudry, and with it the trial of Antoinette Lescouffre, also a prisoner of the same office.

It appeared [to the Court] that the office should have the places probed where the prisoners say that they have received the mark of the devil, and after that, they must be interrogated and examined seriously on their confessions and denials, this having to be done, in order to regulate all this definitively. . . .

Deliberation of the Court of Mons — June 22, 1652

The trials of Antoinette Lescouffre and Suzanne Gaudry having been described to the undersigned, advocates of the Court of Mons, and [the Court] having been told orally that the peasants taking them to prison had persuaded them to confess in order to avoid imprisonment, and that they would be let go, by virtue of which it could appear that the confessions were not so spontaneous:

They are of the opinion that the office, in its duty, would do well, following the two preceding resolutions, to have the places of the marks that they have taught us about probed, and if it is found that these are ordinary marks of the devil, one can proceed to their examination; then next to the first confessions, and if they deny [these], one can proceed to the torture, given that they issue from bewitched relatives, that at all times they have been suspect, that they fled to avoid the crime [that is to say, prosecution for the crime of witchcraft], and that by their confessions they have confirmed [their guilt], notwithstanding that they have wanted to revoke [their confessions] and vacillate. . . .

Third Interrogation, June 27, in the Presence of the Afore-Mentioned

This prisoner being led into the chamber, she was examined to know if things were not as she had said and confessed at the beginning of her imprisonment.

— Answers no, and that what she has said was done so by force.

Asked if she did not say to Jean Gradé that she would tell his uncle, the mayor, that he had better be careful . . . and that he was a Frank.

— Said that that is not true.

Pressed to say the truth, that otherwise she would be subjected to torture, having pointed out to her that her aunt was burned for this same subject.

— Answers that she is not a witch.

Interrogated as to how long she has been in subjection to the devil, and pressed that she was to renounce the devil and the one who misled her.

— Says that she is not a witch, that she has nothing to do with the devil thus that she did not want to renounce the devil, saying that he has not misled her, and upon inquisition of having confessed to being present at the carol, she insisted that although she had said that, it is not true, and that she is not a witch.

Charged with having confessed to having made a horse die by means of a powder that the devil had given her.

— Answers that she said it, but because she found herself during the inquisition pressed to say that she must have done some evil deed; and after several admonitions to tell the truth:

She was placed in the hands of the officer of the *haultes oeuvres* [the officer in charge of torture], throwing herself on her knees, struggling to cry, uttering several exclamations, without being able, nevertheless, she shed a tear. Saying at every moment that she is not a witch.

The Torture

On this same day, being at the place of torture.

This prisoner, before being strapped down, was admonished to maintain herself in her first confessions and to renounce her lover.

— Said that she denies everything she has said, and that she has no lover. Feeling herself being strapped down, says that she is not a witch, while struggling to cry.

Asked why she fled outside the village of Rieux.

— Says that she cannot say it, that God and the Virgin Mary forbid her to; that she is not a witch. And upon being asked why she confessed to being one, said that she was forced to say it.

Told that she was not forced, that on the contrary she declared herself to be a witch without any threat.

— Says that she confessed it and that she is not a witch, and being a little stretched [on the rack] screams ceaselessly that she is not a witch, invoking the name of Jesus and of Our Lady of Grace, not wanting to say any other thing.

Asked if she did not confess that she had been a witch for twenty-six years.

— Says that she said it, that she retracts it, crying Jésus-Maria, that she is not a witch.

Asked if she did not make Philippe Cornié's horse die, as she confessed.

— Answers no, crying Jésus-Maria, that she is not a witch.

The mark having been probed by the officer, in the presence of Doctor Bouchain, it was adjudged by the aforesaid doctor and officer truly to be the mark of the devil.

Being more tightly stretched upon the torture-rack, urged to maintain her confessions.

— Said that it was true that she is a witch and that she would maintain what she had said.

Asked how long she has been in subjugation to the devil.

— Answers that it was twenty years ago that the devil appeared to her, being in her lodgings in the form of a man dressed in a little cow-hide and black breeches.

Interrogated as to what her lover was called.

— Says that she said Petit-Grignon, then, being taken down [from the rack] says upon interrogation that she is not a witch and that she can say nothing.

Asked if her lover has had carnal copulation with her, and how many times.

— To that she did not answer anything; then, making believe that she was ill, not another word could be drawn from her.

As soon as she began to confess, she asked who was alongside of her, touching her, yet none of those present could see anyone there. And it was noticed that as soon as that was said, she no longer wanted to confess anything.

Which is why she was returned to prison.

Verdict

July 9, 1652

In the light of the interrogations, answers and investigations made into the charge against Suzanne Gaudry, coupled with her confessions, from which it would appear that she has always been ill-reputed for being stained with the crime of witchcraft, and seeing that she took flight and sought refuge in this city of Valenciennes, out of fear of being apprehended by the law for this matter; seeing how her close family were also stained with the same crime, and the perpetrators executed; seeing by her own confessions that she is said to have made a pact with the devil, received the mark from him, which in the report of *sieur* Michel de Roux was judged by the medical doctor of Ronchain and the officer of *haultes oeuvres* of Cambrai, after having proved it, to be not a natural mark but a mark of the devil, to which they have sworn with an oath; and that following this, she had renounced God, Lent, and baptism and had let herself be known carnally by him, in which she received satisfaction. Also, seeing that she is said to have been a part of nocturnal carols and dances. Which are crimes of divine lèse-majesty:

For expiation of which the advice of the under-signed is that the office of Rieux can legitimately condemn the aforesaid Suzanne Gaudry to death, tying her to a gallows, and strangling her to death, then burning her body and burying it there in the environs of the woods.

At Valenciennes, the 9th of July, 1652. To each [member of the Court] 4 *livres*, 16 *sous*. . . . And for the trip of the aforementioned Roux, including an escort of one soldier, 30 *livres*.

DISCUSSION QUESTIONS

1. According to the trial record, why was Suzanne Gaudry targeted for persecution? What does this reveal about contemporary beliefs in witches and their powers?

2. How would you characterize the legal procedures used in this trial? How might the procedures help to explain the widespread consistency in the content of confessions throughout the period of witchcraft persecutions?

3. What does this document suggest about the religious anxieties of the times?

COMPARATIVE QUESTIONS

1. How do the Edict of Nantes, "Of Cannibals," and Galileo's letter support scholars who argue that amidst the conflicts of this period, many European leaders and thinkers increasingly gave precedence to secular concerns over religious ones?

2. Despite the gradual trend in Europe toward secularization during the seventeenth century, what do the *Apology*, Galileo's letter, and Suzanne Gaudry's trial records reveal about the continued importance of religion in shaping Europeans' self-understanding?

3. What do "Of Cannibals" and the witchcraft trial suggest about the role of violence in European society and culture?

4. In what ways is Galileo's emphasis on the value of observation and personal experience reflected in the Gaudry trial? What does this suggest about the impact of the new science on traditional beliefs?

CHAPTER 16

Absolutism, Constitutionalism, and the Search for Order

1640–1715

T he wars over religion not only left bitter memories in late seventeenth-century Europe but also ruined economies and weakened governments. In response, many people sought to impose order on the turbulent world in a variety of ways. All of the documents in this chapter reveal that politically, the quest for stability fueled the development of two rival systems of state building—absolutism and constitutionalism. Despite their differences, rulers within both systems centralized power and expanded bureaucracies, casting an increasingly wide net over their subjects' lives. The first document shows that the sinews of the state extended into the New World as European nations (in this case France) continued their quest for land, treasure, and cultural influence there. Not everyone submitted willingly to the expansion of state power, however. On the one hand, such resistance could have permanent repercussions, as it did during the English civil war and the ensuing debate over the nature of authority (Documents 2–4). On the other hand, challenges to increased state control elsewhere in Europe ultimately were no match for established governments, as the final document illustrates.

1.
Mercantilism in the Colonies
Jean-Baptiste Colbert, *Instructions* (1667, 1668)
and
A Royal Ordinance (1669)

As monarchs sought to consolidate and enhance their power in the seventeenth century, they looked to colonization in the New World as a vital component of their state-building strategies. These strategies included a series of economic policies known as mercantilism designed to maximize domestic and colonial commerce and industry for the state's benefit, all under the watchful eye of government bureaucrats. Jean-Baptiste Colbert (1619–1683), chief minister of finance and commerce during the reign of Louis XIV, was an especially active practitioner of mercantilism. For Colbert, the government's intervention in the economy went hand in hand with strengthening the king's rule at home and abroad. For this reason, he extended his mercantilist policies to France's colonies in the northern Americas and the Caribbean islands. The documents below allow us to see these policies in action as Colbert worked to exert stronger royal control over the organization and regulation of French colonial affairs.

Instructions from Colbert to M. de la Rabesnières de Treillebois, Ship's Captain, October 1, 1667

The King, having resolved to send a squadron of his ships to America in the Antilles Islands, commanded by Mr. de la Rabesnières de Treillebois, His Majesty wanted to inform [Treillebois] of the plans [the King] has proposed for this voyage, to guide his voyage so that it gains the advantages expected from his zeal, capacity, and experience in naval matters.

Thus, he will be informed that the plan of His Majesty is:

1. To assure the peace and tranquility of his subjects inhabiting these islands.

2. To assure the possession of the islands to the West India Company[1] that His Majesty has created, to fortify its commerce, in excluding foreigners, and to oblige the inhabitants to submit themselves willingly to the regulations and ordinances of the Company.

3. To show to the English on the island of Barbados that His Majesty wants to protect [the Antilles] more strongly than ever before, in order to invite them to live in peace and execute in good faith the treaties between His Majesty and the King of England. . . .

5. To exclude from the commerce of the [Antilles] all foreigners. . . . His Majesty desires that in the visits that [Treillebois] will make on all the islands, if he encounters some foreign vessels, he will require them to justify whether or not they have permission from the West India Company. If they do, he will make them execute [the terms of this permission] punctually. But if they do not, His Majesty desires that [Treillebois] prevents them from loading or unloading anything in the islands, that he gives them 24 hours to raise their sails and leave, and if this time passes, he seizes or sinks them, His Majesty previously having forbidden all foreigners from trafficking in the islands. His Majesty also wants him to visit all foreign ships and to reclaim the Frenchmen whom he finds in their crews.

From Pierre Clément, ed., *Lettres Instructions et Mémoires de Colbert.* vol. 3, pt. 2, *Instructions au Marquis de Seignlay: Colonies* (Paris, 1865), trans. David Kammerling Smith in *The West in the Wider World*, vol. 2, by Richard Lim and David K. Smith (New York: Bedford/St. Martin's, 2003), 398, 400–401, 402–5, 657.

[1]The West India Company was a privately owned company that was granted a royal charter and monopolistic privileges to trade in the West Indies.

Instructions from Colbert to M. de Bouteroue, Departing as Intendant[2] for Justice, Police, and Finances in Canada, April 5, 1668

Principal Issues to Which the Intendant Sent by the King to
Canada Should Apply Himself

Immediately after his arrival, he [Bouteroue] must make a general census of all the inhabitants of the country, noting their age, sex, and estate, marital status, and number of children.

Inform himself, every three months, of the number of deaths, births, and marriages.

Renew the census every year to know if the colony has grown.

The growth of the colony must be the guiding principle and goal of all the intendant's conduct, so that he is never satisfied on this point, and must apply himself incessantly to find all the expedients imaginable to preserve the inhabitants, to multiply them by marriages, and to attract new people. . . .

Excite, by all methods possible, the people to work to clear land for good agriculture, to establish manufacturing, and to develop some maritime trade. . . .

Investigate with great care the mines within the country, such as those of coal, iron, and lead, and establish work there. . . .

With regard to spiritual matters, the opinion of [those in the colony] is that the bishop of Pétrée[3] and the Jesuits establish their authority too strongly by the fear of excommunications and by the too strict of life that they want to maintain.

The intendant must observe all which occurs on this issue without taking part in blaming their [the Jesuits'] conduct, but only in regarding and esteeming them as men of an exemplary piety who have contributed a lot to the discovery and preservation of this country, intervening occasionally to bring them to soften this excessive strictness. It is very important that the bishop and the Jesuits never become aware that he would want to censure their conduct because he would render himself nearly useless to the service of the King. . . .

Up to now, it seems that the maxim of the Jesuits has been to not call the natural inhabitants of this country into common life with the French, either by giving them common lands and housing, by the education of their children, or by marriages. Their [the Jesuits'] reason was that they believe they will conserve the principles and holiness of our religion more purely in keeping the converted savages in their ordinary form of life rather than in bringing them among the French. As it is very easy to see how this maxim is far removed from all good management, as much for religion as for the State, it is necessary to act gently to make them change it and employ all temporal authority to attract the savages [to live] among the French, this which can be done by marriages and by the education of their children.

---

[2]An official appointed by the king to represent royal authority in a French province or colony. Intendants served a crucial role in extending royal authority throughout the realm.
[3]François Xavier de Laval-Montmorency (1621–1708), appointed bishop of Pétrée (or Petraea) and vicar-apostolic of Canada in 1658.

The commerce of wine and liquor with the savages . . . was a subject of per-petual conflict between the bishop of Pétrée and the Jesuits, on one hand, and the principal inhabitants and those who trade in this country, on the other. The Bishop and the Jesuits have claimed that these liquors intoxicate the savages, that the sav-ages are not able to take them in moderation, and that drunkenness makes them lazy in hunting and gives them all sorts of bad habits, as much for religion as for the State. The principal inhabitants and the traders, to the contrary, claim that the desire to have liquor, which is traded by everyone, obliges the savages to go hunt with more diligence. It is necessary to examine these two sentiments, and the intendant give his reasoned opinion to the King.

Royal Ordinance, April 5, 1669

The king . . . [having reviewed documents on] the number of Frenchmen that the King has sent [to Canada] the previous four or five years, the number of families established there, the lands that have been cleared and cultivated, and everything that concerns the situation in that land, and having recognized the considerable growth that this colony has received by the care taken with it, it is hoped that in continuing these same cares, [the colony] will be able to support itself in a few years. And desiring that the inhabitants of this land participate in the favors that His Majesty has made to his people in consideration of the multiplicity of infants and to induce them to marriage, His Majesty has ordered and orders that in the future all the inhabitants of [the colony] who have as many as 10 living children, born in legitimate marriages, and being neither priests, monks, nor nuns, will be paid a pension of 300 livres[4] annually, the money being remitted in the colony. And those who have a dozen children, 400 livres.

His Majesty desires further that it be paid by the orders of the intendant to all boys who marry at 20 years of age and younger and girls at 16 and younger,[5] 20 livres each on the day of their marriages, which will be called "the gift of the king." . . .

[Ordered that] there be made a general division of all the inhabitants by par-ishes and villages; that some honors be created for the principal inhabitants who take care of the affairs of each town . . . ; that those who have the greatest number of children always be given preference over others, unless some reason prevents it; that there be established some pecuniary penalty payable to the local hospitals against the fathers who do not marry off their children at the age of 20 for boys and 16 for girls.

Discussion Questions

1. How would you describe the policies Colbert sought to implement in French colonies? How do they reflect mercantilist principles?

---

[4]French money of account.
[5]In seventeenth-century France, the average age of first marriage for men and women was mid- to late twenties.

2. In what ways were Colbert's policies designed to extend the crown's authority? What evidence do these documents provide regarding the role of government bureaucracy in this process?

3. What were some of Colbert's tactics for enhancing France's demographic and cultural presence in the colonies? What do his tactics suggest about European attitudes toward indigenous peoples? In what ways did the Jesuits challenge these attitudes?

2.
Regime Change
The Trial of Charles I (January 1649)

The seventeenth century was particularly turbulent in England, where Protestants, Catholics, royalists and parliamentary supporters vied for power. The English king Charles I (r. 1625–1649) had long chaffed under Parliament's demands for participation in government. Adamant in his belief in his divine right to rule, Charles worked to strengthen his grip over Parliament, setting the stage for war. As the conflict spilled over onto the battlefield in 1642, each side accused the other of undermining the ancient legal rights of the people and the legal balance between the king and the two houses of Parliament enshrined in the English constitution. Parliamentary forces ultimately defeated the king's army and Charles surrendered in 1646. Three years later he was brought before a parliamentary high court for trial on the charge of treason. Lasting a week, the proceedings culminated in Charles's condemnation and a death sentence. He was beheaded on January 30, 1649, as a huge crowed looked on. When set against the backdrop of the civil war, the trial raised a host of enduring questions regarding the nature of political authority. Below are extracts from the first three days of the proceedings when the king and his opponents each laid the foundations of their case.

Having again placed himself in his Chair, with his face towards the Court, silence being again ordered, the Lord President stood up, and said,

LORD PRESIDENT: Charles Stuart, king of England, the Commons of England assembled in Parliament being deeply sensible of the calamities that have been brought upon this nation, which is fixed upon you as the principal author of it, have resolved to make inquisition for blood; and according to that debt and duty they owe to justice, to God, the kingdom, and themselves, and according to the fundamental power that rests in themselves, they have resolved to bring you to Trial and Judgment; and for that purpose have constituted this High Court of Justice, before which they are brought.

This said, Mr. Cook, Solicitor for the Commonwealth standing within a bar on the right hand of the Prisoner, offered to speak; but the king having a staff in his

---

From *State Trials: Political and Social*, vol. I, ed. H. L. Stephen (London: Duckworth and Co., 1899), 78–87, 89, 91–94.

hand, held it up, and laid it on the said Mr. Cook's shoulder two or three times, bidding him hold. Nevertheless, the Lord President ordering him to go on, he said,

MR. COOK: My lord, I am commanded to charge Charles Stuart King of England, in the name of the Commons of England, with Treason and High Misdemeanors; I desire the said Charge may be read.

The said Charge being delivered to the Clerk of the Court, the Lord President ordered it should be read; but the king bid him hold. Nevertheless, being commanded by the Lord President to read it, the Clerk begun, and the Prisoner sat down again in his chair, looking sometimes on the High Court, sometimes up to the Galleries; and having risen again, and turned about to behold the guards and spectators, sat down, looking very sternly, and with a countenance not at all moved, till these words, viz.: — "Charles Stuart to be a Tyrant and Traitor," etc. were read; at which he laughed, as he sat, in the face of the Court.

The Charge being read, the Lord President replied;

LORD PRESIDENT: Sir, You have now heard your Charge, containing such matter as appears in it; you find, that in the close of it, it is prayed to the Court, in the behalf of the commons of England, that you answer to your Charge. The Court expects your Answer.

KING: . . . Remember I am your king, your lawful king, and what sins you bring upon your heads, and the judgment of God upon this land; think well upon it, I say, think well upon it, before you go further from one sin to a greater; therefore let me know by what lawful authority I am seated here, and I shall not be unwilling to answer. In the mean time, I shall not betray my trust; I have a trust committed to me by God, by old and lawful descent; I will not betray it, to answer to a new unlawful authority; therefore resolve me that and you shall hear more of me.

LORD PRESIDENT: If you had been pleased to have observed what was hinted to you by the Court, at your first coming hither, you would have known by what authority; which authority requires you, in the name of the people of England, of which you are elected king, to answer them.

KING: No. Sir, I deny that.

LORD PRESIDENT: If you acknowledge not the authority of the Court, they must proceed.

KING: I do tell them so; England was never an elective kingdom, but an hereditary kingdom, for near these thousand years; therefore let me know by what authority I am called hither. I do stand more for the Liberty of my people, than any here that come to be my pretended Judges; and therefore let me know by what lawful authority I am seated here, and I will answer it; otherwise I will not answer it. . . .

LORD PRESIDENT: The Court expects you should give them a final Answer; their purpose is to adjourn to Monday next; if you do not satisfy yourself, though we do tell you our authority, we are satisfied with our authority, and it is upon God's authority and the kingdom's; and that peace you speak of will be kept in the doing of justice, and that is our present work. . . .

At the High Court of Justice sitting in Westminster Hall, Monday, January 22, 1649. . . .

LORD PRESIDENT: Sir, You may remember at the last Court you were told the occasion of your being brought hither, and you heard a Charge read against you, containing a Charge of High Treason and other high crimes against this realm of England: you heard likewise, that it was prayed in the behalf of the People, that you should give an Answer to that Charge, that thereupon such proceedings might be had, as should be agreeable to justice. You were then pleased to make some scruples concerning the authority of this Court, and knew not by what authority you were brought hither; you did divers times propound your questions, and were as often answered. That it was by authority of the Commons of England assembled in parliament, that did think fit to call you to account for those high and capital Misdemeanours wherewith you were then charged. Since that the Court hath taken into consideration what you then said; they are fully satisfied with their own authority, and they hold it fit you should stand satisfied with it too; and they do require it, that you do give a positive and particular Answer to this Charge that is exhibited against you; they do expect you should either confess or deny it; if you deny, it is offered in the behalf of the kingdom to be made good against you; their authority they do avow to the whole world, that the whole kingdom are to rest satisfied in, and you are to rest satisfied with it. And therefore you are to lose no more time, but to give a positive Answer thereunto.

KING: When I was here last, it is very true, I made that question; truly if it were only my own particular case, I would have satisfied myself with the protestation I made the last time I was here against the Legality of this Court, and that a king cannot be tried by any superior jurisdiction on earth; but it is not my case alone, it is the Freedom and the Liberty of the people of England; and do you pretend what you will, I stand more for their Liberties. For if power without law may make laws, may alter the fundamental laws of the kingdom, I do not know what subject he is in England, that can be sure of his life, or any thing that he calls his own: therefore when that I came here, I did expect particular reasons to know by what law, what authority you did proceed against me here. And therefore I am a little to seek what to say to you in this particular, because the affirmative is to be proved, the negative often is very hard to do: but since I cannot persuade you to do it, I shall tell you my reasons as short as I can — My Reasons why in conscience and the duty I owe to God first, and my people next, for the preservation of their lives, liberties, and estates I conceive I cannot answer this, till I be satisfied of the legality of it. All proceedings against any man whatsoever ——

LORD PRESIDENT: Sir, I must interrupt you, which I would not do, but that what you do is not agreeable to the proceedings of any court of justice: You are about to enter into argument, and dispute concerning the Authority of this Court, before whom you appear as a Prisoner, and are charged as an high Delinquent: if you take upon you to dispute the Authority of the Court, we may not do it, nor will any court give way unto it: you are to submit unto it, you are to give a punctual and direct Answer, whether you will answer your charge or no, and what your Answer is.

KING: Sir, By your favour, I do not know the forms of law: I do know law and reason, though I am no lawyer professed; but I know as much law as any gentleman in England; and therefore (under favour) I do plead for the Liberties of the People of England more than you do: and therefore if I should impose a belief upon any man, without reasons given for it, it were unreasonable: but I must tell you, that that reason that I have, as thus informed, I cannot yield unto it.

LORD PRESIDENT: Sir, I must interrupt you, you may not be permitted; you speak of law and reason; it is fit there should be law and reason, and there is both against you. Sir, the Vote of the Commons of England assembled in parliament, it is the reason of the kingdom, and they are these that have given to that law, according to which you should have ruled and reigned. Sir, you are not to dispute our Authority, you are told it again by the Court. Sir, it will be taken notice of, that you stand in contempt of the Court, and your contempt will be recorded accordingly. . . .

At the High Court of Justice sitting in Westminster Hall, Tuesday, January 23, 1649. . . .

LORD PRESIDENT: Sir, you have heard what is moved by the Counsel on the behalf of the kingdom against you. . . . You were told, over and over again, That the Court did affirm their own jurisdiction; that it was not for you, nor any other man, to dispute the jurisdiction of the supreme and highest Authority of England, from which there is no appeal, and touching which there must be no dispute; yet you did persist in such carriage, as you gave no manner of obedience, nor did you acknowledge any authority in them, nor the High Court that constituted this Court of Justice. Sir, I must let you know from the Court, that they are very sensible of these delays of yours, and that they ought not, being thus authorised by the supreme Court of England, to be thus trifled withal; and that they might in justice, if they pleased, and according to the rules of justice, take advantage of these delays and proceed to pronounce judgment against you; yet nevertheless they are pleased to give direction, and on their behalfs I do require you, that you make a positive Answer unto this Charge that is against you, Sir, in plain terms, for Justice knows no respect of persons; you are to give your positive and final Answer in plain English, whether you be Guilty or Not Guilty of these Treasons laid to your charge.

The King, after a little pause, said,

KING: When I was here yesterday, I did desire to speak for the Liberties of the people of England; I was interrupted; I desire to know yet whether I may speak freely or not.

LORD PRESIDENT: Sir, you have had the Resolution of the Court upon the like question the last day, and you were told that having such a Charge of so high a nature against you, and your work was, that you ought to acknowledge the jurisdiction of the Court, and to answer to your Charge. Sir, if you answer to your Charge, which the Court gives you leave now to do, though they might have taken the advantage of your contempt; yet if you be able to answer to your Charge, when you have once answered, you shall be heard at large, make the best defence you can. . . .

KING: For the Charge, I value it not a rush; it is the Liberty of the People of England that I stand for. For me to acknowledge a new Court that I never heard of before, I that am your King, that should be an example to all the people of England for to uphold justice, to maintain the old laws: indeed I do not know how to do it. You spoke very well the first day that I came here (on Saturday) of the obligations that I had laid upon me by God, to the maintenance of the Liberties of my people; the same obligation you spake of, I do acknowledge to God that I owe to him, and to my people, to defend as much as in me lies the ancient laws of the kingdom: therefore, until that I may know that this is not against the fundamental Laws of the kingdom, by your favour I can put in no particular Charge. If you will give me time, I will shew you my Reasons why I cannot do it, and this ——

Here, being interrupted, he said,

By your favor, you ought not to interrupt me: How I came here, I know not; there's no law for it to make your king your prisoner. . . .

Here the Lord President said, Sir, you must know the pleasure of the Court.

KING: By your favour, sir.

LORD PRESIDENT: Nay, sir, by your favour, you may not be permitted to fall into those discourses; you appear as a Delinquent, you have not acknowledged the authority of the Court, the Court craves it not of you; but once more they command you to give your positive Answer. — Clerk, do your duty.

KING: Duty, Sir!

The Clerk reads.

"Charles Stuart, king of England, you are accused in behalf of the commons of England of divers Crimes and Treasons, which Charge hath been read unto you: the Court now requires you to give your positive and final Answer, by way of confession or denial of the Charge."

KING: Sir, I say again to you, so that I might give satisfaction to the people of England of the clearness of my proceeding, not by way of Answer, not in this way, but to satisfy them that I have done nothing against that trust that has been committed to me, I would do it; but to acknowledge a new Court, against their Privileges, to alter the fundamental laws of the kingdom — sir, you must excuse me.

LORD PRESIDENT: Sir, this is the third time that you have publicly disowned this Court, and put an affront upon it. How far you have preserved the privileges of the people, your actions have spoke it; but truly, Sir, men's intentions ought to be known by their actions; you have written your meaning in bloody characters throughout the whole kingdom. But, Sir, you understand the pleasure of the Court. — Clerk, Record the Default. — And, Gentlemen, you that took charge of the Prisoner, take him back again.

DISCUSSION QUESTIONS

1. According to the prosecution, why did Parliament have both a duty and a right to bring charges against the king?

2. What does the high court's argument suggest about its understanding of the role of Parliament in governance and its relationship to the monarchy?

3. In his defense, why does the king refuse to acknowledge the court's authority to bring charges against him? In doing so, what did he reveal about his understanding of the basis of royal authority?

3.
Civil War and Social Contract

Thomas Hobbes, *Leviathan* (1651)

Thomas Hobbes (1588–1679), an English philosopher with close aristocratic and royalist ties, viewed England's troubles as an indictment of traditional political thinking. According to Hobbes, in their natural state humans were violent and prone to war. Absolute authority was the only way to counter this threat to social order. Whether this authority rested in a king or parliament was immaterial to Hobbes; what mattered was that it gained its power from a social contract, or "covenant," between ruler and ruled. Individuals agreed to relinquish their right to govern themselves to an absolute ruler in exchange for collective peace and defense. Hobbes published his views in 1651 in his book Leviathan, *most of which he wrote during the final stage of the English civil war while living in exile in France, where he was the tutor of the future king Charles II. The excerpt that follows speaks not only to Hobbes's understanding of human nature, absolute authority, and the social contract but also to the relationship among them.*

Of the Difference of Manners

By manners, I mean not here decency of behavior; as how one man should salute another, or how a man should wash his mouth, or pick his teeth before company, and such other points of the small morals; but those qualities of mankind that concern their living together in peace and unity. . . .

. . . [I]n the first place, I put for a general inclination of all mankind a perpetual and restless desire of power after power, that ceaseth only in death. And the cause of this is not always that a man hopes for a more intensive delight than he has already attained to, or that he cannot be content with a moderate power, but because he cannot assure the power and means to live well, which he hath present, without the acquisition of more. And from hence it is that kings, whose power is greatest, turn their endeavors to the assuring it at home by laws, or abroad by wars: and when that is done, there succeedeth a new desire; in some, of fame from new conquest; in others, of ease and sensual pleasure; in others, of admiration, or being flattered for excellence in some art or other ability of the mind. . . .

Of the Natural Condition of Mankind as Concerning Their Felicity and Misery

Nature hath made men so equal in the faculties of body and mind as that, though there be found one man sometimes manifestly stronger in body or of quicker mind than another, yet when all is reckoned together the difference between man and man is not so considerable as that one man can thereupon claim to himself any

From Thomas Hobbes, *Leviathan*, Renascence Editions, at www.luminarium.org/renascence-editions/hobbes/leviathan.html.

benefit to which another may not pretend as well as he. For as to the strength of body, the weakest has strength enough to kill the strongest, either by secret machination or by confederacy with others that are in the same danger with himself.

And as to the faculties of the mind, setting aside the arts grounded upon words, and especially that skill of proceeding upon general and infallible rules, called science, which very few have and but in few things, as being not a native faculty born with us, nor attained, as prudence, while we look after somewhat else, I find yet a greater equality amongst men than that of strength. For prudence is but experience, which equal time equally bestows on all men in those things they equally apply themselves unto. That which may perhaps make such equality incredible is but a vain conceit of one's own wisdom, which almost all men think they have in a greater degree than the vulgar; that is, than all men but themselves, and a few others, whom by fame, or for concurring with themselves, they approve. For such is the nature of men that howsoever they may acknowledge many others to be more witty, or more eloquent or more learned, yet they will hardly believe there be many so wise as themselves; for they see their own wit at hand, and other men's at a distance. But this proveth rather that men are in that point equal, than unequal. For there is not ordinarily a greater sign of the equal distribution of anything than that every man is contented with his share.

From this equality of ability ariseth equality of hope in the attaining of our ends. And therefore if any two men desire the same thing, which nevertheless they cannot both enjoy, they become enemies; and in the way to their end (which is principally their own conservation, and sometimes their delectation only) endeavor to destroy or subdue one another. And from hence it comes to pass that where an invader hath no more to fear than another man's single power, if one plant, sow, build, or possess a convenient seat, others may probably be expected to come prepared with forces united to dispossess and deprive him, not only of the fruit of his labor, but also of his life or liberty. And the invader again is in the like danger of another. . . .

. . . [M]en have no pleasure (but on the contrary a great deal of grief) in keeping company where there is no power able to overawe them all. For every man looketh that his companion should value him at the same rate he sets upon himself, and upon all signs of contempt or undervaluing naturally endeavors, as far as he dares (which amongst them that have no common power to keep them in quiet is far enough to make them destroy each other), to extort a greater value from his contemners, by damage; and from others, by the example. So that in the nature of man, we find three principal causes of quarrel. First, competition; secondly, diffidence; thirdly, glory. The first maketh men invade for gain; the second, for safety; and the third, for reputation. The first use violence, to make themselves masters of other men's persons, wives, children, and cattle; the second, to defend them; the third, for trifles, as a word, a smile, a different opinion, and any other sign of undervalue, either direct in their persons or by reflection in their kindred, their friends, their nation, their profession, or their name. Hereby it is manifest that during the time men live without a common power to keep them all in awe, they are in that condition which is called war; and such a war as is of every man against every man. For war consisteth not in battle only, or the act of fighting, but in a tract of time, wherein the will to contend by battle is sufficiently known: and therefore the notion of time is to be considered in the nature of war, as it is in the nature of weather. For as the nature of foul weather lieth not in a shower or two of rain, but in an inclination thereto of many days together: so the nature of war consisteth not in actual fighting, but in the known disposition thereto during all the time there is no assurance to the contrary. All other time is peace.

Whatsoever therefore is consequent to a time of war, where every man is enemy to every man, the same consequent to the time wherein men live without other security than what their own strength and their own invention shall furnish them withal. In such condition there is no place for industry, because the fruit thereof is uncertain: and consequently no culture of the earth; no navigation, nor use of the commodities that may be imported by sea; no commodious building; no instruments of moving and removing such things as require much force; no knowledge of the face of the earth; no account of time; no arts; no letters; no society; and which is worst of all, continual fear, and danger of violent death; and the life of man, solitary, poor, nasty, brutish, and short. . . .

Of the Causes, Generation, and Definition of a Commonwealth

The final cause, end, or design of men (who naturally love liberty, and dominion over others) in the introduction of that restraint upon themselves, in which we see them live in Commonwealths, is the foresight of their own preservation, and of a more contented life thereby; that is to say, of getting themselves out from that miserable condition of war which is necessarily consequent, as hath been shown, to the natural passions of men when there is no visible power to keep them in awe, and tie them by fear of punishment to the performance of their covenants. . . .

The only way to erect such a common power, as may be able to defend them from the invasion of foreigners, and the injuries of one another, and thereby to secure them in such sort as that by their own industry and by the fruits of the earth they may nourish themselves and live contentedly, is to confer all their power and strength upon one man, or upon one assembly of men, that may reduce all their wills, by plurality of voices, unto one will: which is as much as to say, to appoint one man, or assembly of men, to bear their person; and every one to own and acknowledge himself to be author of whatsoever he that so beareth their person shall act, or cause to be acted, in those things which concern the common peace and safety; and therein to submit their wills, every one to his will, and their judgments to his judgment. This is more than consent, or concord; it is a real unity of them all in one and the same person, made by covenant of every man with every man, in such manner as if every man should say to every man: I authorize and give up my right of governing myself to this man, or to this assembly of men, on this condition; that thou give up, thy right to him, and authorize all his actions in like manner. This done, the multitude so united in one person is called a COMMONWEALTH; in Latin, CIVITAS. This is the generation of that great LEVIATHAN, or rather, to speak more reverently, of that mortal god to which we owe, under the immortal God, our peace and defense. For by this authority, given him by every particular man in the Commonwealth, he hath the use of so much power and strength conferred on him that, by terror thereof, he is enabled to form the wills of them all, to peace at home, and mutual aid against their enemies abroad. And in him consisteth the essence of the Commonwealth; which, to define it, is: one person, of whose acts a great multitude, by mutual covenants one with another, have made themselves every one the author, to the end he may use the strength and means of them all as he shall think expedient for their peace and common defense. . . .

Of the Rights of Sovereigns by Institution

A Commonwealth is said to be instituted when a multitude of men do agree, and covenant, every one with every one, that to whatsoever man, or assembly of men, shall be given by the major part the right to present the person of them all, that is to say, to be their representative; every one, as well he that voted for it as he that voted against it, shall authorize all the actions and judgments of that man, or assembly of men, in the same manner as if they were his own, to the end to live peaceably amongst themselves, and be protected against other men.

From this institution of a Commonwealth are derived all the rights and faculties of him, or them, on whom the sovereign power is conferred by the consent of the people assembled.

First, because they covenant, it is to be understood they are not obliged by former covenant to anything repugnant hereunto. And consequently they that have already instituted a Commonwealth, being thereby bound by covenant to own the actions and judgments of one, cannot lawfully make a new covenant amongst themselves to be obedient to any other, in anything whatsoever, without his permission. And therefore, they that are subjects to a monarch cannot without his leave cast off monarchy and return to the confusion of a disunited multitude; nor transfer their person from him that beareth it to another man, other assembly of men: for they are bound, every man to every man, to own and be reputed author of all that already is their sovereign shall do and judge fit to be done; so that any one man dissenting, all the rest should break their covenant made to that man, which is injustice: and they have also every man given the sovereignty to him that beareth their person; and therefore if they depose him, they take from him that which is his own, and so again it is injustice. Besides, if he that attempteth to depose his sovereign be killed or punished by him for such attempt, he is author of his own punishment, as being, by the institution, author of all his sovereign shall do; and because it is injustice for a man to do anything for which he may be punished by his own authority, he is also upon that title unjust. And whereas some men have pretended for their disobedience to their sovereign a new covenant, made, not with men but with God, this also is unjust: for there is no covenant with God but by mediation of somebody that representeth God's person, which none doth but God's lieutenant who hath the sovereignty under God. But this pretence of covenant with God is so evident a lie, even in the pretenders' own consciences, that it is not only an act of an unjust, but also of a vile and unmanly disposition.

Secondly, because the right of bearing the person of them all is given to him they make sovereign, by covenant only of one to another, and not of him to any of them, there can happen no breach of covenant on the part of the sovereign; and consequently none of his subjects, by any pretence of forfeiture, can be freed from his subjection. That he which is made sovereign maketh no covenant with his subjects before hand is manifest; because either he must make it with the whole multitude, as one party to the covenant, or he must make a several covenant with every man. With the whole, as one party, it is impossible, because as they are not one person: and if he make so many several covenants as there be men, those covenants after he hath the sovereignty are void; because what act soever can be pretended by any one of them for breach thereof is the act both of himself, and of all the rest, because done in the person, and by the right of every one of them in particular. Besides, if any one or more of them pretend a breach of the covenant made by the sovereign at his institution, and others or one other of his subjects, or himself alone, pretend there was no such breach, there is in this case no judge to decide the controversy: it returns therefore to the sword again; and every man recovereth the right of protecting himself by his own strength, contrary to the design they had in the institution. It is therefore in vain to grant sovereignty by way of precedent covenant. The opinion that any monarch receiveth his power by covenant, that is to say, on condition, proceedeth from want of understanding this easy truth: that covenants being but words, and breath, have no force to oblige, contain, constrain, or protect any man, but what it has from the public sword; that is, from the untied hands of that man, or assembly of men, that hath the sovereignty, and whose actions are avouched by them all, and performed by the strength of them all, in him united. But when an assembly of men is made sovereign, then no man imagineth any such covenant to have passed in the institution: for no man is so dull as to say, for example, the people of Rome made a covenant with the Romans to hold the sovereignty on such or such conditions; which not performed, the Romans might lawfully depose the Roman people. That men see not the reason to be alike in a monarchy and in a popular government proceedeth from the ambition of some that are kinder to the government of an assembly, whereof they may hope to participate, than of monarchy, which they despair to enjoy.

Thirdly, because the major part hath by consenting voices declared a sovereign, he that dissented must now consent with the rest; that is, be contented to avow all the actions he shall do, or else justly be destroyed by the rest. For if he voluntarily entered into the congregation of them that were assembled, he sufficiently declared thereby his will, and therefore tacitly covenanted, to stand to what the major part should ordain: and therefore if he refuse to stand thereto, or make protestation against any of their decrees, he does contrary to his covenant, and therefore unjustly. And whether he be of the congregation or not, and whether his consent be asked or not, he must either submit to their decrees or be left in the condition of war he was in before; wherein he might without injustice be destroyed by any man whatsoever.

Fourthly, because every subject is by this institution author of all the actions and judgments of the sovereign instituted, it follows that whatsoever he doth, can be no injury to any of his subjects; nor ought he to be by any of them accused of injustice. For he that doth anything by authority from another doth therein no injury to him by whose authority he acteth: but by this institution of a Commonwealth every particular man is author of all the sovereign doth; and consequently he that complaineth of injury from his sovereign complaineth of that whereof he himself is author, and therefore ought not to accuse any man but himself; no, nor himself of injury, because to do injury to oneself is impossible. It is true that they that have sovereign power may commit iniquity, but not injustice or injury in the proper signification.

Fifthly, and consequently to that which was said last, no man that hath sovereign power can justly be put to death, or otherwise in any manner by his subjects punished. For seeing every subject is author of the actions of his sovereign, he punisheth another for the actions committed by himself.

DISCUSSION QUESTIONS

1. How does Hobbes describe human nature? How might the events of the English civil war have shaped his views?

2. What is Hobbes's definition of the "Leviathan"? How is his definition linked to his understanding of the basis and role of absolute authority?

3. What does Hobbes mean by the "covenant" between sovereign and subject? How did this differ from the traditional understanding of absolute authority based on divine right?

4. According to Hobbes, did subjects bound by this covenant have the right to challenge sovereign power? Why or why not?

4.
The Consent of the Governed

John Locke, *The Second Treatise of Government* (1690)

Hobbes's fellow Englishman John Locke (1632–1704) likewise viewed the tumults of his day with a critical eye. Although the English civil war ended with the restoration of Charles II to the throne, new troubles loomed. Charles openly sympathized with Catholics, as did his brother and heir, James II. Fearful of the ties between Catholicism and French absolutism, in 1678 Parliament denied the right of a Catholic to inherit the crown. Charles resisted this move, sparking a succession crisis. Locke fled to the Dutch Republic in 1683 with his patron, the Earl of Shaftesbury, who opposed a Catholic monarch. While abroad, Locke worked on his Two Treatises of Government, *which he published upon his return to England after the Glorious Revolution of 1688. A selection from the* Second Treatise *follows. As it reveals, although Locke shared Hobbes's interest in the origins of civil society, his anti-absolutist stance stood in sharp contrast to Hobbes's position. For Locke, ultimate authority rests in the will of the majority of propertied men who, in exchange for protection, endow the state with the authority to rule over them. Yet this power is not limitless. Just as the majority*

From John Locke, *Second Treatise on Government*, at www.ilt.columbia.edu/academic/digitexts/locke/second/locke2nd.txt.

grants the state its power, so too can it justifiably resist it if it fails to fulfill its part of the social contract.

Of the Beginning of Political Societies

Men being, as has been said, by nature, all free, equal, and independent, no one can be put out of this estate, and subjected to the political power of another, without his own consent. The only way whereby any one divests himself of his natural liberty, and puts on the bonds of civil society, is by agreeing with other men to join and unite into a community for their comfortable, safe, and peaceable living one amongst another, in a secure enjoyment of their properties, and a greater security against any, that are not of it. This any number of men may do, because it injures not the freedom of the rest; they are left as they were in the liberty of the state of nature. When any number of men have so consented to make one community or government, they are thereby presently incorporated, and make one body politic, wherein the majority have a right to act and conclude the rest. . . .

And thus every man, by consenting with others to make one body politic under one government, puts himself under an obligation, to every one of that society, to submit to the determination of the majority, and to be concluded by it; or else this original compact, whereby he with others incorporates into one society, would signify nothing, and be no compact, if he be left free, and under no other ties than he was in before in the state of nature. For what appearance would there be of any compact? what new engagement if he were no farther tied by any decrees of the society, than he himself thought fit, and did actually consent to? This would be still as great a liberty, as he himself had before his compact, or any one else in the state of nature hath, who may submit himself, and consent to any acts of it if he thinks fit. . . .

Whosoever therefore out of a state of nature unite into a community, must be understood to give up all the power, necessary to the ends for which they unite into society, to the majority of the community, unless they expressly agreed in any number greater than the majority. And this is done by barely agreeing to unite into one political society, which is all the compact that is, or needs be, between the individuals, that enter into, or make up a commonwealth. And thus that, which begins and actually constitutes any political society, is nothing but the consent of any number of freemen capable of a majority to unite and incorporate into such a society. And this is that, and that only, which did, or could give beginning to any lawful government in the world.

Of the Ends of Political Society and Government

If man in the state of nature be so free, as has been said; if he be absolute lord of his own person and possessions, equal to the greatest, and subject to nobody, why will he part with his freedom? why will he give up this empire, and subject himself to the dominion and control of any other power? To which it is obvious to answer, that though in the state of nature he hath such a right, yet the enjoyment of it is very uncertain, and constantly exposed to the invasion of others: for all being kings as much as he, every man his equal, and the greater part no strict observers of equity and justice, the enjoyment of the property he has in this state is very unsafe, very unsecure. This makes him willing to quit a condition, which, however free, is full of fears and continual dangers: and it is not without reason, that he seeks out, and is willing to join in society with others, who are already united, or have a mind to unite, for the mutual preservation of their lives, liberties and estates, which I call by the general name, property.

The great and chief end, therefore, of men's uniting into commonwealths, and putting themselves under government, is the preservation of their property. To which in the state of nature there are many things wanting.

First, there wants an established, settled, known law, received and allowed by common consent to be the standard of right and wrong, and the common measure to decide all controversies between them: for though the law of nature be plain and intelligible to all rational creatures; yet men being biased by their interest, as well as ignorant for want of study of it, are not apt to allow of it as a law binding to them in the application of it to their particular cases.

Secondly, In the state of nature there wants a known and indifferent judge, with authority to determine all differences according to the established law: for every one in that state being both judge and executioner of the law of nature, men being partial to themselves, passion and revenge is very apt to carry them too far, and with too much heat, in their own cases; as well as negligence, and unconcernedness, to make them too remiss in other men's.

Thirdly, In the state of nature there often wants power to back and support the sentence when right, and to give it due execution. They who by any injustice offended, will seldom fail, where they are able, by force to make good their injustice; such resistance many times makes the punishment dangerous, and frequently destructive, to those who attempt it.

Thus mankind, notwithstanding all the privileges of the state of nature, being but in an ill condition, while they remain in it, are quickly driven into society. Hence it comes to pass, that we seldom find any number of men live any time together in this state. The inconveniences that they are therein exposed to, by the irregular and uncertain exercise of the power every man has of punishing the transgressions of others, make them take sanctuary under the established laws of government, and therein seek the preservation of their property. It is this makes them so willingly give up every one his single power of punishing, to be exercised by such alone, as shall be appointed to it amongst them; and by such rules as the community, or those authorized by them to that purpose, shall agree on. And in this we have the original right and rise of both the legislative and executive power, as well as of the governments and societies themselves.

For in the state of nature, to omit the liberty he has of innocent delights, a man has two powers.

The first is to do whatsoever he thinks fit for the preservation of himself, and others within the permission of the law of nature: by which law, common to them all, he and all the rest of mankind are one community, make up one society, distinct from all other creatures. And were it not for the corruption and viciousness of degenerate men, there would be no need of any other; no necessity that men should separate from this great and natural community, and by positive agreements combine into smaller and divided associations.

The other power a man has in the state of nature, is the power to punish the crimes committed against that law. Both these he gives up, when he joins in a private, if I may so call it, or particular politic society, and incorporates into any commonwealth, separate from the rest of mankind.

The first power, viz. of doing whatsoever he thought for the preservation of himself, and the rest of mankind, he gives up to be regulated by laws made by the society, so far forth as the preservation of himself, and the rest of that society shall require; which laws of the society in many things confine the liberty he had by the law of nature.

Secondly, The power of punishing he wholly gives up, and engages his natural force, (which he might before employ in the execution of the law of nature, by his own single authority, as he thought fit) to assist the executive power of the society, as the law thereof shall require: for being now in a new state, wherein he is to enjoy many conveniences, from the labor, assistance, and society of others in the same community, as well as protection from its whole strength; he is to part also with as much of his natural liberty, in providing for himself, as the good, prosperity, and safety of the society shall require; which is not only necessary, but just, since the other members of the society do the like.

But though men, when they enter into society, give up the equality, liberty, and executive power they had in the state of nature, into the hands of the society, to be so far disposed of by the legislative, as the good of the society shall require; yet it being only with an intention in every one the better to preserve himself, his liberty, and property; (for no rational creature can be supposed to change his condition with an intention to be worse) the power of the society, or legislative constituted by them, can never be supposed to extend farther, than the common good; but is obliged to secure every one's property, by providing against those three defects above mentioned, that made the state of nature so unsafe and uneasy. And so whoever has the legislative or supreme power of any commonwealth, is bound to govern by established standing laws, promulgated and known to the people, and not by extemporary decrees; by indifferent and upright judges, who are to decide controversies by those laws; and to employ the force of the community at home, only in the execution of such laws, or abroad to prevent or redress foreign injuries, and secure the community from inroads and invasion. And all this to be directed to no other end, but the peace, safety, and public good of the people.

DISCUSSION QUESTIONS

1. According to Locke, what is man's natural state? What are its chief characteristics?

2. Why would men relinquish the natural state to form a government? What advantages does government offer?

3. How does Locke describe the relationship between a government and its subjects? What are its terms and conditions?

4. How does Locke's proposed system guard against absolute or arbitrary power?

5.
Opposing Serfdom

Ludwig Fabritius, *The Revolt of Stenka Razin* (1670)

Despite its geographic and cultural isolation from the rest of Europe, Russia watched its neighbors carefully and crafted its own brand of absolutism. In the process, Tsar Alexei (r. 1645–1676) legally combined millions of slaves and free peasants into a single serf class bound to the land and their aristocratic masters. Not everyone passively accepted this fate, however. In 1667, a Cossack named Stenka Razin (c. 1630–1671) led a revolt against serfdom that gained considerable support among people whose social and economic status was threatened by the tsar's policies, including soldiers from peasant stock. Razin's ultimate defeat at the hands of the tsar explains the close ties between the Russian government's enhanced power and the enforcement of serfdom. Ludwig Fabritius (1648–1729), a Dutch soldier who lived in Russia from 1660 to 1677 while employed as a military expert in the Russian army, wrote the following account of one stage of the revolt.

Then Stenka with his company started off upstream, rowing as far as Tsaritsyn, whence it took him only one day's journey to Panshin, a small town situated on the Don. Here he began straightaway quietly gathering the common people around him, giving them money, and promises of great riches if they would be loyal to him and help to exterminate the treacherous boyars.[1]

This lasted the whole winter, until by about spring he had assembled 4,000 to 5,000 men. With these he came to Tsaritsyn and demanded the immediate surrender of the fortress; the rabble soon achieved their purpose, and although the governor tried to take refuge in a tower, he soon had to give himself up as he was deserted by one and all. Stenka immediately had the wretched governor hanged; and all the goods they found belonging to the Tsar and his officers as well as to the merchants were confiscated and distributed among the rabble.

Stenka now began once more to make preparations. Since the plains are not cultivated, the people have to bring their corn from Nizhniy-Novgorod and Kazan down the Volga in big boats known as *nasady*, and everything destined for Astrakhan has first to pass Tsaritsyn. Stenka Razin duly noted this, and occupied the whole of the Volga, so that nothing could get through to Astrakhan. Here he captured a few hundred merchants with their valuable goods, taking possession of all kinds of fine linen, silks, striped silk material, sables, soft leather, ducats, talers, and many thousands of rubles in Russian money and merchandise of every description. . . .

In the meantime four regiments of *streltsy* [musketeers] were dispatched from Moscow to subdue these brigands. They arrived with their big boats and as they were not used to the water, were easily beaten. Here Stenka Razin gained possession

From Anthony Glenn Cross, ed., *Russia under Western Eyes, 1517–1825* (Boston: St. Martin's Press, 1971), 120–23.

[1]This term refers to a class of noblemen.

of a large amount of ammunition and artillery-pieces and everything else he required. While the above-mentioned [musketeers] were sent from Moscow, about 5,000 men were ordered up from Astrakhan by water and by land to capture Stenka Razin. As soon as he had finished with the former, he took up a good position, and, being in possession of reliable information regarding our forces, he left Tsaritsyn and came to meet us half way at Chernyy Yar, confronting us before we had suspected his presence or received any information about him. We stopped at Chernyy Yar for a few days and sent out scouts by water and by land, but were unable to obtain any definite information. On 10 July [sic: June] a council of war was held at which it was decided to advance and seek out Stenka. The next morning, at 8 o'clock, our look-outs on the water came hurriedly and raised the alarm as the Cossacks were following at their heels. We got out of our boats and took up battle positions. General Knyaz Semen Ivanovich Lvov went through the ranks and reminded all the men to do their duty and to remember the oath they had taken to His Majesty the Tsar, to fight like honest soldiers against these irresponsible rebels, whereupon they all unanimously shouted: "Yes, we will give our lives for His Majesty the Tsar, and will fight to the last drop of our blood."

In the meantime Stenka prepared for battle and deployed on a wide front; to all those who had no rifle he gave a long pole, burnt a little at one end, and with a rag or small hook attached. They presented a strange sight on the plain from afar, and the common soldiers imagined that, since there were so many flags and standards, there must be a host of people. They [the common soldiers] held a consultation and at once decided that this was the chance for which they had been waiting so long, and with all their flags and drums they ran over to the enemy. They began kissing and embracing one another and swore with life and limb to stand together and to exterminate the treacherous boyars, to throw off the yoke of slavery, and to become free men.

The general looked at the officers and the officers at the general, and no one knew what to do; one said this, and another that, until finally it was decided that they and the general should get into the boats and withdraw to Astrakhan. But the rascally [musketeers] of Chernyy Yar stood on the walls and towers, turning their weapons on us and opened fire; some of them ran out of the fortress and cut us off from the boats, so that we had no means of escape. In the meantime those curs of ours who had gone over to the Cossacks came up from behind. We numbered about eighty men, officers, noblemen, and clerks. Murder at once began. Then, however, Stenka Razin ordered that no more officers were to be killed, saying that there must be a few good men among them who should be pardoned, whilst those others who had not lived in amity with their men should be condemned to well-deserved punishment by the Ataman and his *Krug*. A *Krug* is a meeting convened by the order of the Ataman, at which the Cossacks stand in a circle with the standard in the center; the Ataman then takes his place beside his best officers, to whom he divulges his wishes, ordering them to make these known to the common brothers and to hear their opinion on the matter. . . .

A *Krug* was accordingly called and Stenka asked through his chiefs how the general and his officers had treated the soldiers under their command. Thereupon the unscrupulous curs, [musketeers] as well as soldiers, unanimously called out that there was not one of them who deserved to remain alive, and they all asked that their father Stepan Timofeyevich Razin should order them to be cut down. This was granted with the exception of General Knyaz Semen Ivanovich Lvov, whose life was specially spared by Stenka himself. The officers were now brought in order of rank out of the tower, into which they had been thrown bound hand and foot the previous day, their ropes were cut and they were led outside the gate. When all the bloodthirsty curs had lined up, each was eager to deal his former superior the first blow, one with the sword, another with the lance, another with the scimitar, and others again with martels, so that as soon as an officer was pushed into the ring, the curs immediately killed him with their many wounds; indeed, some were cut to pieces and straightaway thrown into the Volga. My stepfather, Paul Rudolf Beem, and Lt. Col. Wundrum and many other officers, senior and junior, were cut down before my eyes.

My own time had not yet come: this I could tell by the wonderful way in which God rescued me, for as I — half-dead — now awaited the final blow, my [former] orderly, a young soldier, came and took me by my bound arms and tried to take me down the hill. As I was already half-dead, I did not move and did not know what to do, but he came back and took me by the arms and led me, bound as I was, through the throng of curs, down the hill into the boat and immediately cut my arms free, saying that I should rest in peace here and that he would be responsible for me and do his best to save my life. . . . Then my guardian angel told me not to leave the boat, and left me. He returned in the evening and brought me a piece of bread which I enjoyed since I had had nothing to eat for two days.

The following day all our possessions were looted and gathered together under the main flag, so that both our bloodthirsty curs and the Cossacks got their share.

DISCUSSION QUESTIONS

1. What do you think motivated Razin and his followers to take action?

2. Why were Razin and his forces able to defeat the tsar's soldiers?

3. With whom do you think Fabritius's sympathies lay, and why?

COMPARATIVE QUESTIONS

1. What do these documents suggest about the basis of authority in constitutional and absolutist states? What features differentiated them as systems of government? What features did they share?

2. What similarities and differences do you see between Locke's and Hobbes's views of human nature and government?

3. In what ways were both Hobbes and Locke responding to the debate over political authority evident in Charles I's trial?

4. Based on Charles I's trial and the account of Stenka Razin's revolt, what set the English and Russian states apart politically, culturally, and socially? How may this help to explain why Charles I's autocratic rule failed in England while the tsar's flourished in Russia?

The Atlantic System and Its Consequences

1700–1750

T he growth of European domestic economies and overseas colonization during the eighteenth century infused Europe with money, new products, and a new sense of optimism about the future. Yet, as the first document illustrates, the good times came at a horrible price for millions of African slaves who formed the economic backbone of the Atlantic system by toiling on plantations in New World colonies. Meanwhile, Europeans back home enjoyed slave-produced goods. New forms of social interaction emerged hand in hand with new consumption patterns, most notably at coffeehouses. The second document gives us a flavor of early coffeehouse culture in London, where these establishments first appeared in Europe. Changes were also under way on the political front, with the stabilization of the European state system. Consequently, states such as Russia shone more brightly over the political landscape while others lost their luster. The third document set illuminates Tsar Peter I's diverse strategies for transforming Russia into a great power closely modeled on its western European counterparts. The fourth and fifth documents reveal that intellectual circles were also ablaze with change as scholars and writers cast political, social, and religious issues in a new critical and secular light.

1.
Captivity and Enslavement

Olaudah Equiano, *The Interesting Narrative of the Life of Olaudah Equiano Written by Himself* (1789)

The autobiography of Olaudah Equiano (c. 1745–1797) puts a human face on the eighteenth-century Atlantic slave trade and its human consequences. As he describes, he was born in what is now Nigeria and was captured by local raiders and sold into slavery in his early teens. He gained his freedom in 1766 and soon thereafter became a vocal supporter of the English abolitionist movement. He published his autobiography in 1789, a best seller in its day, with numerous editions published in Britain and America. In the following excerpt, Equiano recounts his journey on the slave ship that took him away from his homeland, his freedom, and his very identity. Millions of others shared this same fate. Scholars have recently challenged this account, pointing to new evidence that suggests Equiano was born a slave in South Carolina, so probably early parts of his autobiography drew on the oral history of other slaves rather than on Equiano's personal experience. Regardless of where the truth lies, his book is invaluable as one of the very few texts written in English during the eighteenth century by a person of African descent.

The first object which saluted my eyes when I arrived on the coast was the sea, and a slave ship which was then riding at anchor and waiting for its cargo. These filled me with astonishment, which was soon converted into terror when I was carried on board. I was immediately handled and tossed up to see if I were sound by some of the crew, and I was now persuaded that I had gotten into a world of bad spirits and that they were going to kill me. Their complexions too differing so much from ours, their long hair and the language they spoke (which was very different from any I had ever heard) united to confirm me in this belief. Indeed such were the horrors of my views and fears at the moment that, if ten thousand worlds had been my own, I would have freely parted with them all to have exchanged my condition with that of the meanest slave in my own country. When I looked round the ship too and saw a large furnace or copper boiling and a multitude of black people of every description chained together, every one of their countenances expressing dejection and sorrow, I no longer doubted of my fate; and quite overpowered with horror and anguish, I fell motionless on the deck and fainted. When I recovered a little I found some black people about me, who I believed were some of those who had brought me on board and had been receiving their pay; they talked to me in order to cheer me, but all in vain. I asked them if we were not to be eaten by those white men with horrible looks, red faces, and loose hair. They told me I was not, and one of the crew brought me a small portion of spirituous liquor in a wine glass, but being afraid of him I would not take it out of his hand. One of the blacks therefore took it from him and gave it to me, and I took a little down my palate, which instead of reviving me, as they thought it would, threw me into the greatest consternation at the strange feeling it produced, having never tasted such any liquor before. Soon after this the blacks who brought me on board went off, and left me abandoned to despair.

I now saw myself deprived of all chance of returning to my native country or even the least glimpse of hope of gaining the shore, which I now considered as friendly; and I even wished for my former slavery in preference to my present situation, which was filled with horrors of every kind, still heightened by my ignorance of what I was to undergo. I was not long suffered to indulge my grief; I was

From Paul Edwards, ed., *Equiano's Travels: His Autobiography*, abridged (London: Heinemann, 1967), 25–32.

soon put down under the decks, and there I received such a salutation in my nostrils as I had never experienced in my life: so that with the loathsomeness of the stench and crying together, I became so sick and low that I was not able to eat, nor had I the least desire to taste anything. I now wished for the last friend, death, to relieve me; but soon, to my grief, two of the white men offered me eatables, and on my refusing to eat, one of them held me fast by the hands and laid me across I think the windlass, and tied my feet while the other flogged me severely. I had never experienced anything of this kind before, and although, not being used to the water, I naturally feared that element the first time I saw it, yet nevertheless could I have got over the nettings I would have jumped over the side, but I could not; and besides, the crew used to watch us very closely who were not chained down to the decks, lest we should leap into the water: and I have seen some of these poor African prisoners most severely cut for attempting to do so, and hourly whipped for not eating. This indeed was often the case with myself. In a little time after, amongst the poor chained men I found some of my own nation, which in a small degree gave ease to my mind. I inquired of these what was to be done with us; they gave me to understand we were to be carried to these white people's country to work for them. I then was a little revived, and thought if it were no worse than working, my situation was not so desperate: but still I feared I should be put to death, the white people looked and acted, as I thought, in so savage a manner; for I had never seen among my people such instances of brutal cruelty, and this not only shewn towards us blacks but also to some of the whites themselves. One white man in particular I saw, when we were permitted to be on deck, flogged so unmercifully with a large rope near the foremast that he died in consequence of it; and they tossed him over the side as they would have done a brute. This made me fear these people the more, and I expected nothing less than to be treated in the same manner. . . . At last, when the ship we were in had got in all her cargo, they made ready with many fearful noises, and we were all put under deck so that we could not see how they managed the vessel. But this disappointment was the last of my sorrow. The stench of the hold while we were on the coast was so intolerably loathsome that it was dangerous to remain there for any time, and some of us had been permitted to stay on the deck for the fresh air; but now that the whole ship's cargo were confined together it became absolutely pestilential. The closeness of the place and the heat of the climate, added to the number in the ship, which was so crowded that each had scarcely room to turn himself, almost suffocated us. This produced copious perspirations, so that the air soon became unfit for respiration from a variety of loathsome smells, and brought on a sickness among the slaves, of which many died, thus falling victims to the improvident avarice, as I may call it, of their purchasers. This wretched situation was again aggravated by the galling of the chains, now become insupportable, and the filth of the necessary tubs, into which the children often fell and were almost suffocated. The shrieks of the women and the groans of the dying rendered the whole a scene of horror almost inconceivable. Happily perhaps for myself I was soon reduced so low here that it was thought necessary to keep me almost always on deck, and from my extreme youth I was not put in fetters. In this situation I expected every hour to share the fate of my companions, some of whom were almost daily brought upon deck at the point of death, which I began to hope would soon put an end to my miseries. . . . At last we came in sight of the island of Barbados, at which the whites on board gave a great shout and made many signs of joy to us. We did not know what to think of this, but as the vessel drew nearer we plainly saw the harbor and other ships of different kinds and sizes, and we soon anchored amongst them off Bridgetown. Many merchants and planters now came on board, though it was in the evening. They put us in separate parcels and examined us attentively. They also made us jump, and pointed to the land, signifying we were to go there. . . . We were not many days in the merchant's custody before we were sold after their usual manner, which is this: On a signal given, (as the beat of a drum) the buyers rush at once into the yard where the slaves are confined, and make choice of that parcel they like best. The noise and clamor with which this is attended and the eagerness visible in the countenances of the buyers serve not a little to increase the apprehensions of the terrified Africans, who may well be supposed to consider them as the ministers of that destruction to which they think themselves devoted. In this manner, without scruple, are relations and friends separated, most of them never to see each other again. I remember in the vessel in which I was brought over, in the men's apartment there were several brothers who, in the sale, were sold in different lots; and it was very moving on this occasion to see and hear their cries at parting. O, ye nominal Christians! might not an African ask you, Learned you this from your God who says unto you, Do unto all men as you would men should do unto you?

DISCUSSION QUESTIONS

1. What are Equiano's impressions of the white men on the ship and their treatment of the slaves? How does this treatment reflect the slave traders' primary concerns?

2. What message do you think Equiano sought to convey to his readers? Based on this message, to whom do you think his book especially appealed?

2.
A "Sober and Wholesome Drink"

A Brief Description of the Excellent Vertues of That Sober and Wholesome Drink, Called Coffee (1674)

The expansion of the slave trade in the late seventeenth and eighteenth centuries was directly linked to Europeans' appetite for the commodities slave labor produced, including coffee. European travelers and merchants had first noticed people drinking coffee in the Middle East in the late sixteenth century, and its consumption slowly spread from there into Europe. With the drink came the rise of a new type of gathering place, the coffeehouse. In 1652, a Greek merchant who had learned to make coffee

---

Transcription of original, as reproduced in Markman Ellis, ed., *Eighteenth-Century Coffee-House Culture*, vol. 1, *Restoration Satire* (London: Pickering & Chatto, 2006), 129.

while working in a Turkish trading port opened the first coffeehouse in western Europe in London. The number of coffeehouses in London, and eventually all over Europe, exploded when western European trading nations moved into the business of coffee production. Coffeehouses became places for men to meet for company and conversation, often with a political bent. The broadsheet transcribed here illuminates the origins of coffeehouse culture as merchants sought to entice customers to partake in the "sober and wholesome drink" and the sociability of the coffeehouse. Composed of two poems, the broadsheet was printed in 1674, most likely as an advertisement for coffee, coffeehouses, and the retail coffee business of Paul Greenwood situated in the heart of London's textile district. The first poem contrasts the detrimental effects of alcohol with the "sober and merry" effects of coffee. The second describes the rules of behavior coffeehouse patrons were expected to follow. Scholars have suggested that, despite its slightly satirical tone, the poem is an accurate portrayal of the regulations governing coffeehouses and may have been printed on large sheets of paper and posted on the walls of coffeehouses in London.

A Brief Description of the Excellent Vertues of that Sober and Wholesome Drink, called Coffee, and its incomparable effects in preventing or curing most diseases incident to humane bodies (London, printed for Paul Greenwood . . . who selleth the best Arabian Coffee-Powder and Chocolate, made in Cake or in Roll, after the Spanish Fashion, &c., 1674).[1]

When the sweet Poison of the Treacherous Grape,
Had Acted on the world a General Rape;
Drowning our very Reason and our Souls
In such deep Seas of large o'reflowing Bowls,
That New Philosophers Swore they could feel
The Earth to Stagger, as her Sons did Reel:
When Foggy Ale, leavying up mighty Trains
Of muddy Vapors, had besieg'd our Brains;
And Drink, Rebellion, and Religion too,
Made Men so Mad, they knew not what to do;
Then Heaven in Pity, to Effect our Cure,
And stop the Ragings of that Calenture,
First sent amongst us this All-*healing-Berry*,
At once to make us both *Sober* and *Merry*.
      Arabian coffee, a Rich Cordial

---

[1]**Chocolate, made in Cake or in Roll, after the Spanish Fashion:** chocolate is made from the fermented, roasted, and ground beans of the cocoa tree (*Theobroma cacao*). Imported from Spanish America, chocolate was sold as a bitter paste made up into small cylindrical cakes or rolls, which were used in the preparation of hot drinks with the addition of water, sugar, and sometimes eggs. Only in the nineteenth century was eating chocolate developed.

To Purse and Person Beneficial,
Which of so many Vertues doth partake
Its Country's called *Felix* for its sake.[2]
From the Rich Chambers of the Rising Sun,

. . .

COFFEE arrives, that Grave and wholesome Liquor,
That heals the Stomack, makes the Genius quicker,
Relieves the Memory, Revives the Sad,
And cheers the Spirits, without making Mad;

. . .

Its constant Use the sullenest Griefs will Rout,
Remove the Dropsie, gives ease to the Gout,[3]

. . .

A Friendly Entercourse[4] it doth Maintain
Between the Heart, the Liver, and the Brain,

. . .

Nor have the LADIES reason to Complain,
As fumbling Doe-littles[5] are apt to Faign;
COFFEE's no Foe to their obliging Trade,
By it Men rather are more active made;
'Tis stronger Drink, and base adulterate Wine;
Enfeebles Vigor, and makes Nature Pine;
Loaden with which, th' Impotent Sott is Led
Like a Sowe'd Hogshead to a Misses Bed;[6]
But this Rare Settle-Brain prevents those Harms,[7]
Conquers Old Sherry, and brisk Claret Charms.
Sack, I defie thee with an open Throat,
Whilst Truly COFFEE is my Antedote

. . .

---

[2]**Country's called** *Felix*: Arabia Felix (Arabia the happy), the name of one of three zones of the Arabian peninsula in classical geography, roughly corresponding to modern Yemen.
[3]**Dropsie . . . Gout**: dropsy, a morbid condition characterized by the accumulation of watery fluid in the serous cavities; gout, a disease characterized by the painful inflammation of the smaller joints (*Oxford English Dictionary*).
[4]**Entercourse**: intercourse, communication between something, here the heart, liver, and brain.
[5]**fumbling Doe-littles**: one who does little, a lazy person (*OED*).
[6]**th' Impotent . . . to a Misses Bed**: a complicated disparagement: a sot is one who dulls or stupefies himself with drink, here to the state of impotence, who must be induced to visit a young woman's bed, like a pickled or soused pig's head (an unwieldy and unrewarding dish).
[7]**Settle-Brain**: something that calms the brain (*OED*).

The RULES and ORDERS of the COFFEE-HOUSE.[8]
Enter Sirs Freely, But first if you please,
Peruse our Civil-Orders,[9] which are these.
First, Gentry, Tradesmen, all are welcome hither,
And may without Affront sit down Together:
Pre-eminence of Place, none here should Mind,[10]
But take the next fit Seat that he can find:
Nor need any, if Finer Persons come,
Rise up for to assigne to them his Room;
To limit Mens Expense, we think not fair,
But let him forfeit Twelve-pence that shall Swear:
He that shall any Quarrel begin,
Shall give each Man a Dish t'Atone the Sin;
And so shall He, whose Complements extend
So far to drink in COFFEE to his Friend;
Let Noise of loud Disputes be quite forborn,
No Maudlin Lovers[11] here in Corners Mourn,
But all be Brisk, and Talk, but not too much
On Sacred things, Let none presume to touch,
Nor Profane Scripture, or sawcily wrong
Affairs of State[12] with an Irreverent Tongue:
Let Mirth be Innocent, an each Man see,
That all his Jests without Reflection be;
To keep the House more Quiet, and from Blame,
We Banish hence Cards, Dice, and every Game:
Nor can allow of Wagers, that Exceed
Five shillings, which oft-times much Trouble Breed;
Let all that's lost, or forfeited be spent
In such Good Liquor as the House doth Vent,
And Customers endeavor to their Powers,
For to observe still seasonable Howers.

---

[8]**The RULES . . . COFFEE-HOUSE:** an ironic title for a satire on coffee-house sociability. "Rules and Orders" is a commonplace phrase in legal discourse, signifying the administrative regulations of certain judicial institutions, especially courts of law, or the body of rules followed by an assembly.

[9]**Civil-Orders:** the civil laws. A term in legal debate current in the period.

[10]**Pre-eminence of Place, none here should Mind:** seats around the table in the coffee-room were not organized hierarchically, referring to the custom in coffee-houses, that each man should take the next free seat around the table.

[11]**Maudlin Lovers:** men who discuss their illicit gallantries and amors in a mawkish or sentimental manner, one of the ordeals of the coffee-house.

[12]**Affairs of State:** transactions concerning the state or nation, politics. The coffee-houses had come to be emblematic locations for debate on public affairs by those outside the court and ministry, where it was still assumed that ordinary people did not need to know about the state and its affairs.

Lastly, let each Man what he calls for Pay,
And so you're welcome to come every Day.

DISCUSSION QUESTIONS

1. What does the imprint of the broadsheet suggest about changing consumption patterns at the time and their links to Europe's growing worldwide economic links?

2. According to the first poem, what were the medicinal effects of coffee? How might these effects have contributed to coffeehouses' growing popularity?

3. Based on the "Rules and Orders," what type of people frequented early coffeehouses? How would you describe their social interactions there?

4. Why do you think these rules legislated against swearing, disputes, and noise in coffeehouses?

3.
Westernizing Russian Culture

Peter I, *Decrees and Statutes* (1701–1723)

During the eighteenth century, European states turned much of their attention to the political and military scene burgeoning within Europe, vying to keep one step ahead of their rivals. Russian tsar Peter I (r. 1689–1725) was especially successful at this game, transforming Russia into a formidable European power with all the trappings of an absolutist state, including a strong army and centralized bureaucracy. After spending time abroad, notably in England and the Dutch Republic, Peter came to admire western European technology, commerce, and customs and worked relentlessly to refashion Russia accordingly. For him, Westernization was more than an act of admiration; it provided him with powerful tools for enhancing Russia's status on the European stage. Below are several decrees and a statute he issued seeking to reform various aspects of Russian life and society, all with the aim of bringing them more in line with western European models.

The Decree on "German" Dress, 1701

Western ["German"] dress shall be worn by all the boyars, okol'nichie,[1] members of our councils and of our court . . . gentry of Moscow, secretaries . . . provincial gentry, deti boiarskie,[2] gosti,[3] government officials, strel'tsy,[4] members of the guilds

---

From *A Source Book for Russian History from Early Times to 1917*, vol. 2, ed. George Vernadsky (New Haven, CT: Yale University Press, 1972), 347, 357–58; and *Peter the Great*, ed. L. Jay Oliva (Englewood Cliffs, NJ: Prentice-Hall, Inc., 1970), 44–45.

[1]**boyars, okol'nichie:** Nobles of the highest and second-highest rank, respectively. [Ed.]
[2]**boiarskie:** Sons of boyars. [Ed.]
[3]**gosti:** Merchants who often served the tsar in some capacity. [Ed.]
[4]**strel'tsy:** Members of the imperial guard stationed in Moscow. [Ed.]

purveying for our household, citizens of Moscow of all ranks, and residents of provincial cities . . . excepting the clergy (priests, deacons, and church attendants) and peasant tillers of the soil. The upper dress shall be of French or Saxon cut, and the lower dress and underwear — [including] waistcoat, trousers, boots, shoes, and hats — shall be of the German type. They shall also ride German saddles. [Likewise] the womenfolk of all ranks, including the priests', deacons', and church attendants' wives, the wives of the dragoons, the soldiers, and the strel'tsy, and their children, shall wear Western ["German"] dresses, hats, jackets, and underwear — undervests and petticoats — and shoes. From now on no one [of the above-mentioned] is to wear Russian dress or Circassian coats, sheepskin coats, or Russian peasant coats, trousers, boots, and shoes. It is also forbidden to ride Russian saddles, and the craftsmen shall not manufacture them or sell them at the marketplaces. [Note: For a breach of this decree a fine was to be collected at the town gates: forty copecks from a pedestrian and two rubles from a mounted person.]

The Decree on the Shaving of Beards and Moustaches, January 16, 1705

A decree to be published in Moscow and in all the provincial cities: Henceforth, in accordance with this, His Majesty's decree, all court attendants . . . provincial service men, government officials of all ranks, military men, all the gosti, members of the wholesale merchants' guild, and members of the guilds purveying for our household must shave their beards and moustaches. But, if it happens that some of them do not wish to shave their beards and moustaches, let a yearly tax be collected from such persons: from court attendants . . . provincial service men, military men, and government officials of all ranks — 60 rubles per person; from the gosti and members of the wholesale merchants' guild of the first class — 100 rubles per person; from members of the wholesale merchants' guild of the middle and the lower class [and] . . . from [other] merchants and townsfolk — 60 rubles per person; . . . from townsfolk [of the lower rank], boyars' servants, stagecoachmen, waggoners, church attendants (with the exception of priests and deacons), and from Moscow residents of all ranks — 30 rubles per person. Special badges shall be issued to them from the Prikaz of Land Affairs [of Public Order] . . . which they must wear. . . . As for the peasants, let a toll of two half-copecks per beard be collected at the town gates each time they enter or leave a town; and do not let the peasants pass the town gates, into or out of town, without paying this toll.

Decree on the Invitation to Foreigners, April 17, 1702

It is sufficiently known in all the lands which the Almighty has placed under our rule, that since our accession to the throne all our efforts and intentions have tended to govern this realm in such a way that all of our subjects should, through our care for the general good, become more and more prosperous. For this end we have always tried to maintain internal order, to defend the State against invasion, and in every possible way to improve and to extend trade. With this purpose we have been compelled to make some necessary and salutary changes in the administration, in order that our subjects might more easily gain a knowledge of matters of which they were before ignorant, and become more skilful in their commercial relations. We have therefore given orders, made dispositions, and founded institutions indispensable for increasing our trade with foreigners, and shall do the same in future. Nevertheless we fear that matters are not in such a good condition as we desire, and that our subjects cannot in perfect quietness enjoy the fruits of our labours, and we have therefore considered still other means to protect our frontier from the invasion of the enemy, and to preserve the rights and privileges of our State, and the general peace of all Christians, as is incumbent on a Christian monarch to do. To attain these worthy aims, we have endeavoured to improve our military forces, which are the protection of our State, so that our troops may consist of well-drilled men, maintained in perfect order and discipline. In order to obtain greater improvement in this respect, and to encourage foreigners, who are able to assist us in this way, as well as artists and artisans profitable to the State, to come in numbers to our country, we have issued this manifesto, and have ordered printed copies of it to be sent throughout Europe. And as in our residence of Moscow, the free exercise of religion of all other sects, although not agreeing with our church, is already allowed, so shall this be hereby confirmed anew in such wise that we, by the power granted to us by the Almighty, shall exercise no compulsion over the consciences of men, and shall gladly allow every Christian to care for his own salvation at his own risk.

The Statute of the College of Manufactures, December 3, 1723

His Imperial Majesty is diligently striving to establish and develop in the Russian Empire such manufacturing plants and factories as are found in other states, for the general welfare and prosperity of his subjects. He [therefore] most graciously charges the College of Manufactures to exert itself in devising the means to introduce, with the least expense, and to spread in the Russian Empire these and other ingenious arts, and especially those for which materials can be found within the empire; [the College of Manufactures] must also consider the privileges that should be granted to those who might wish to found manufacturing plants and factories.

His Imperial Majesty gives permission to everyone, without distinction of rank or condition, to open factories wherever he may find suitable. This provision must be made public everywhere. . . .

In granting a privilege to establish a factory, the college must take care not to debar others who might later wish to establish similar factories. For competition between manufacturers may not only help industrial growth but also ameliorate the quality of goods and keep prices at a reasonable level, thereby benefiting all His Majesty's subjects. At the same time, in cases where existing factories are sufficient for the general needs, the college must see to it that the creation of new ones does not lead to a deterioration of original manufactures, especially through the production of inferior goods, even though they may sell at a low price. . . .

Factory owners must be closely supervised, in order that they have at their plants good and experienced [foreign] master craftsmen, who are able to train Russians in such a way that these, in turn, may themselves become masters, so that their produce may bring glory to the Russian manufactures. . . .

The factories and plants that have been built or will be built at His Majesty's expense should be turned over to private individuals as soon as they are put into good condition; let the college exert itself to this end. . . .

By the former decrees of His Majesty commercial people were forbidden to buy villages [i.e., to own serfs], the reason being that they were not engaged in any other activity beneficial for the state save commerce; but since it is now clear to all that many of them have started to found manufacturing establishments and build plants, both in companies and individually, which tend to increase the welfare of the state — and many of them have already started production; therefore permission is granted both to the gentry and to men of commerce to acquire villages for these factories without hindrance, [but] with the permission of the College of Manufactures, on the condition, however, that such villages remain permanently attached to the said factories. . . .

In order to stimulate voluntary immigration of various craftsmen from other countries into the Russian Empire, and to encourage them to establish factories and manufacturing plants freely and at their own expense, the College of Manufactures must send appropriate announcements to the Russian envoys accredited at foreign courts. The envoys should then, in an appropriate way, bring these announcements to the attention of men of various professions, urge them to come to settle in Russia, and help them to move.

DISCUSSION QUESTIONS

1. Why do you think Peter I targeted the appearance of Russians as part of his Westernization policy? What benefits do you think he hoped to gain?

2. Why did Peter I want to encourage foreigners to move to Russia? What did he offer them as incentives?

3. What do the decree on foreigners and the statute of the College of Manufactures suggest about Peter I's understanding of the role of commerce in building the power of the Russian state? In what ways was this understanding in line with broader changes in the European economy at the time?

4.
Early Enlightenment

Voltaire, *Letters Concerning the English Nation* (1733)

As Europe's economy expanded and its state system stabilized, many people were infused with a sense of optimism in human nature and its potential for improvement.

From *The Enlightenment: A Comprehensive Anthology*, ed. Peter Gay (New York: Simon and Schuster, 1973), 162–66.

This sentiment found expression in an intellectual movement known as the Enlightenment, the term used to describe a group of writers and scholars who brought a new critical, scientific, and secular approach to the study of society and its problems. François-Marie Arouet (1694–1778), known by his pen name, Voltaire, was the most prominent early Enlightenment writer. After one of several clashes with church and state officials in his native France, Voltaire left the country, ultimately finding himself in 1726 in England, where he lived for several years. While there, Voltaire learned English and became an admiring observer of English political institutions and customs, using comparison with them to criticize religious intolerance and Catholic censorship in France. All the while, Voltaire wrote letters to his friends intended to amuse them with his observations while rallying them around the principles of the Enlightenment. In this selection from a letter on John Locke, Voltaire develops the argument that religion should be considered a matter of faith and conscience and be separated from arguments concerning philosophy.

Such a multitude of reasoners having written the romance of the soul, a sage at last arose who gave, with an air of the greatest modesty, the history of it. Mr. Locke has displayed the human soul in the same manner as an excellent anatomist explains the springs of the human body. He everywhere takes the light of physics for his Guide. He sometimes presumes to speak affirmatively, but then he presumes also to doubt. Instead of concluding at once what we know not, he examines gradually what we would know. He takes an infant at the instant of his Birth; he traces, step by step, the progress of his understanding; examines what things he has in common with beasts, and what he possesses above them. Above all he consults himself; the being conscious that he himself thinks.

I shall leave, says he, to those who know more of this matter than myself, the examining whether the soul exists before or after the organization of our bodies. But I confess that it is my lot to be animated with one of those heavy souls which do not think always; and I am even so unhappy as not to conceive that it is more necessary the soul should think perpetually than that bodies should be for ever in motion.

With regard to myself, I shall boast that I have the honour to be as stupid in this particular as Mr. Locke. No one shall ever make me believe that I think always; and I am as little inclined as he could be to fancy that some weeks after I was conceived I was a very learned soul, knowing at that time a thousand things which I forgot at my birth, and possessing when in the womb (though to no manner of purpose) knowledge which I lost the instant I had occasion for it, and which I have never since been able to recover perfectly.

Mr. Locke, after having destroyed innate ideas; after having fully renounced the vanity of believing that we think always; after having laid down, from the most solid principles, that ideas enter the mind through the senses; having examined our simple and complex ideas; having traced the human mind through its several operations; having showed that all the languages in the world are imperfect, and the great abuse that is made of words every moment; he at last comes to consider the extent or rather the narrow limits of human knowledge. It was in this chapter he presumed to advance, but very modestly, the following words: "We shall, perhaps, never be capable of knowing, whether a Being, purely material, thinks or not." This sage assertion was, by more divines than one, looked upon as a scandalous declaration that the soul is material and mortal. Some Englishmen, devout after their way, sounded an alarm. The superstitious are the same in society as cowards in an army; they themselves are seized with a panic fear, and communicate it to others. It was loudly exclaimed that Mr. Locke intended to destroy religion; nevertheless, religion had nothing to do in the affair, it being a question purely philosophical, altogether independent of faith and revelation. Mr. Locke's opponents needed but to examine, calmly and impartially, whether the declaring that matter can think implies a contradiction, and whether God is able to communicate thought to matter. But divines are too apt to begin their declarations with saying that God is offended when people differ from them in opinion. . . . If I might presume to give my opinion on so delicate a subject after Mr. Locke, I would say that men have long disputed on the nature and the immortality of the soul. With regard to its immortality, it is impossible to give a demonstration of it, since its nature is still the subject of controversy; which, however, must be thoroughly understood before a person can be able to determine whether it be immortal or not. Human reason is so little able, merely by its own strength, to demonstrate the immortality of the soul, that it was absolutely necessary religion should reveal it to us. It is of advantage to society in general that mankind should believe the soul to be immortal; faith commands us to do this; nothing more is required, and the matter is cleared up at once. But it is otherwise with respect to its nature; it is of little importance to religion, which only requires the soul to be virtuous, what substance it may be made of. It is a clock which is given us to regulate, but the artist has not told us of what materials the spring of this clock is composed.

I am a body and, I think, that's all I know of the matter. Shall I ascribe to an unknown cause what I can so easily impute to the only second cause I am acquainted with? Here all the School philosophers interrupt me with their arguments and declare that there is only extension and solidity in bodies, and that there they can have nothing but motion and figure. Now, motion, figure, extension and solidity cannot form a thought, and consequently the soul cannot be matter. All this, so often repeated, mighty series of reasoning, amounts to no more than this: I am absolutely ignorant what matter is; I guess but imperfectly some properties of it; now, I absolutely cannot tell whether these properties may be joined to thought. As I therefore know nothing, I maintain positively that matter cannot think. In this manner do the Schools reason.

Mr. Locke addressed these gentlemen in the candid, sincere manner following: At least confess yourselves to be as ignorant as I. Neither your imaginations nor mine are able to comprehend in what manner a body is susceptible of ideas; and do you conceive better in what manner a substance, of what kind soever, is susceptible of them? As you cannot comprehend either matter or spirit, why will you presume to assert anything?

The superstitious man comes afterwards, and declares that all those must be burnt for the good of their souls who so much as suspect that it is possible for the body to think without any foreign assistance. But what would these people say should they themselves be proved irreligious? And, indeed, what man can presume to assert, without being guilty at the same time of the greatest impiety, that it is impossible for the Creator to form matter with thought and sensation? Consider only, I beg you, what a dilemma you bring yourselves into, you who confine in this manner the power of the Creator. Beasts have the same organs, the same sensations, the same perceptions as we; they have memory, and combine certain ideas. In case it was not in the power of God to animate matter and inform it with sensation, the consequence would be either that beasts are mere machines or that they have a spiritual soul.

Methinks it is clearly evident that beasts cannot be mere machines, which I prove thus: God has given them the very same organs of sensation as to us: If therefore they have no sensation, God has created a useless thing; now, according to your own confession, God does nothing in vain; he therefore did not create so many organs of sensation merely for them to be uninformed with this faculty; consequently beasts are not mere machines. Beasts, according to your assertion, cannot be animated with a spiritual soul; you will therefore, in spite of yourself, be reduced to this only assertion, *viz.* that God has endued the organs of beasts, who are mere matter, with the faculties of sensation and perception, which you call instinct in them. But why may not God, if he pleases, communicate to our more delicate organs that faculty of feeling, perceiving and thinking which we call human reason? To whatever side you turn, you are forced to acknowledge your own ignorance and the boundless power of the Creator. Exclaim therefore no more against the sage, the modest philosophy of Mr. Locke, which, so far from interfering with religion, would be of use to demonstrate the truth of it, in case Religion wanted any such support. For what philosophy can be of a more religious nature than that which, affirming nothing but what it conceives clearly, and conscious of its own weakness, declares that we must always have recourse to God in our examining of the first principles.

Besides, we must not be apprehensive that any philosophical opinion will ever prejudice the religion of a country. Though our demonstrations clash directly with our mysteries, that's nothing to the purpose, for the latter are not less revered upon that account by our Christian philosophers, who know very well that the objects of reason and those of faith are of a very different nature. Philosophers will never form a religious sect, the reason of which is, their writings are not calculated for the vulgar, and they themselves are free from enthusiasm. If we divide mankind into twenty parts, it will be found that nineteen of these consist of persons employed in manual labour, who will never know that such a man as Mr. Locke existed. In the remaining twentieth part how few are readers? And among such as are so, twenty amuse themselves with romances to one who studies philosophy. The thinking part of mankind are confined to a very small number, and these will never disturb the peace and tranquillity of the world.

Neither Montaigne, Locke, Bayle, Spinoza, Hobbes, Lord Shaftesbury, Collins nor Toland lighted up the firebrand of discord in their countries; this has generally been the work of divines, who, being at first puffed up with the ambition of becoming chiefs of a sect, soon grew very desirous of being at the head of a party. But what do I say? All the works of the modern philosophers put together will never make so much noise as even the dispute which arose among the Franciscans merely about the fashion of their sleeves and of their cowls.

Discussion Questions

1. How does Voltaire describe Locke's approach to human understanding and knowledge?

2. Why do you think Voltaire admired this approach? In what ways did it reflect his own thinking as an Enlightenment writer?

3. Notice Voltaire's frequent use of contrast between faith and reason, religion and philosophy, faith and nature. Why are such contrasts important to Voltaire's argument? And why did some people object to making them in the first place?

5.
Questioning Women's Submission

Mary Astell, *Reflections upon Marriage* (1706)

Like Voltaire, English author Mary Astell (1666–1731) helped to shape the course of the Enlightenment by surveying society with a critical eye. First published anonymously in 1700, Reflections upon Marriage, *one of her best-known books, highlights Astell's keen interest in the institution of marriage, education, and relations between the sexes. Only the third edition (published in 1706) divulged her gender, but still not her name. As the following excerpt reveals, Astell held a dim view of women's inequality in general and of their submissive role in marriage in particular. She argues that one should abhor the use of arbitrary power within the state, and so, too, within the family. Among the book's principal goals was to present spinsterhood as a viable alternative to marriage. Perhaps not surprisingly, Astell herself never married.*

These Reflections being made in the Country, where the Book that occasioned them came but late to Hand, the *Reader* is desired to excuse their Unseasonableness as well as other Faults; and to believe that they have no other Design than to Correct some Abuses, which are not the less because Power and Prescription seem to Authorize them. If any are so needlessly curious as to enquire from what Hand they come, they may please to know, that it is not good Manners to ask, since the Title-Page does not tell them: We are all of us sufficiently Vain, and without doubt the Celebrated Name of *Author,* which most are so fond of, had not been avoided but for very good Reasons: To name but one; *Who will care to pull upon themselves an Hornet's nest?* 'Tis a very great Fault to regard rather who it is that Speaks, than what is Spoken; and either to submit to Authority, when we should only yield to Reason; or if Reason press too hard, to think to ward it off by Personal Objections and Reflections. Bold Truths may pass while the Speaker is Incognito, but are not endured when he is known; few Minds being strong enough to bear what Contradicts their Principles and Practices without Recriminating when they can. And

From Bridget Hill, ed., *The First English Feminist: Reflections upon Marriage and Other Writings by Mary Astell* (New York: St. Martin's Press, 1986), 69–76.

tho' to tell the Truth be the most Friendly Office, yet whosoever is so hardy as to venture at it, shall be counted an Enemy for so doing.

Thus far the old Advertisement, when the Reflections first appeared, A.D. 1700.

But the *Reflector*, who hopes *Reflector* is not bad English, now Governor is happily of the feminine Gender, had as good or better have said nothing; For People by being forbid, are only excited to a more curious Enquiry. A certain Ingenuous Gentleman (as she is informed) had the Good-Nature to own these Reflections, so far as to affirm that he had the Original M.S. in his Closet, a Proof she is not able to produce, and so to make himself responsible for all their Faults, for which she returns him all due Acknowledgment. However, the Generality being of Opinion, that a Man would have had more Prudence and Manners than to have Published such unseasonable Truths, or to have betrayed the *Arcana Imperii* of his Sex, she humbly confesses, that the Contrivance and Execution of this Design, which is unfortunately accused of being so destructive to the government, of the Men I mean, is entirely her own. She neither advised with Friends, nor turned over Ancient or Modern Authors, nor prudently submitted to the Correction of such as are, or such as *think* they are good Judges, but with an *English* Spirit and Genius, set out upon the Forlorn Hope, meaning no hurt to any body, nor designing any thing but the Publick Good, and to retrieve, if possible, the Native Liberty, the Rights and Privileges of the Subject.

Far be it from her to stir up Sedition of any sort, none can abhor it more; and she heartily wishes that our Masters would pay their Civil and Ecclesiastical Governors the same Submission, which they themselves extract from their Domestic Subjects. Nor can she imagine how she any way undermines the Masculine Empire, or blows the Trumpet of Rebellion to the Moiety of Mankind. Is it by exhorting Women, not to expect to have their own Will in any thing, but to be entirely Submissive, when once they have made choice of a Lord and Master, though he happen not to be so Wise, so Kind, or even so Just a Governor as was expected? She did not indeed advise them to think his Folly Wisdom, nor his Brutality that Love and Worship he promised in his Matrimonial Oath, for this required a Flight of Wit and Sense much above her poor Ability, and proper only to Masculine Understandings. However she did not in any manner prompt them to Resist, or to Abdicate the Perjured Spouse, though the Laws of GOD and the Land make special Provision for it, in a case wherein, as is to be feared, few Men can truly plead Not Guilty.

'Tis true, through Want of Learning, and of that Superior Genius which Men as Men lay claim to, she was ignorant of the *Natural Inferiority* of our Sex, which our Masters lay down as a Self-Evident and Fundamental Truth.[1] She saw nothing in the Reason of Things, to make this either a Principle or a Conclusion, but much

---

[1]Possibly a reference to William Nichols, D.D., *The Duty of Inferiours Towards Their Superiours in Five Practical Discourses* (1701), in which he argued that man possesses "a higher state of natural perfection and dignity, and thereupon puts in a just claim of superiority, which everything which is of more worth has a right to, over that which has less" (pp. 87–88).

to the contrary; it being Sedition at least, if not Treason to assert it in this Reign. For if by the Natural Superiority of their Sex, they mean that every Man is by Nature superior to every Woman, which is the obvious meaning, and that which must be stuck to if they would speak Sense, it would be a Sin in *any* Woman to have Dominion over *any* Man, and the greatest Queen ought not to command but to obey her Footman, because no Municipal Laws can supersede or change the Law of Nature; so that if the dominion of the Men be such, the *Salique Law*, as unjust as *English Men* have ever thought it, ought to take place over all the Earth, and the most glorious Reigns in the *English, Danish, Castilian*, and other Annals, were wicked Violations of the Law of Nature!

If they mean that *some* Men are superior to *some* Women, this is no great Discovery; had they turned the Tables they might have seen that *some* Women are Superior to *some* Men. Or had they been pleased to remember their Oaths of Allegiance and Supremacy, they might have known that *One* Woman is superior to *All* the Men in these Nations, or else they have sworn to very little purpose. And it must not be supposed, that their Reason and Religion would suffer them to take Oaths, contrary to the Law of Nature and Reason of things.

By all which it appears, that our Reflector's Ignorance is very pitiable, it may be her Misfortune but not her Crime, especially since she is willing to be better informed, and hopes she shall never be so obstinate as to shut her Eyes against the Light of Truth, which is not to be charged with Novelty, how late soever we may be blessed with the Discovery. Nor can Error, be it as Ancient as it may, ever plead Prescription against Truth. And since the only way to remove all Doubts, to answer all Objections, and to give the Mind entire Satisfaction, is not by *Affirming*, but by *Proving*, so that every one may see with their *own* Eyes, and Judge according to the best of their *own* Understandings, She hopes it is no Presumption to insist on this Natural Right of Judging for her self, and the rather, because by quitting it, we give up all the Means of Rational Conviction. Allow us then as many Glasses as you please to help our Sight, and as many good Arguments as you can afford to Convince our Understandings: But don't exact of us we beseech you, to affirm that we see such things as are only the Discovery of Men who have quicker Senses; or that we understand and Know what we have by Hearsay only, for to be so excessively Complaisant, is neither to see nor to understand.

That the Custom of the World has put Women, generally speaking, into a State of Subjection, is not denied; but the Right can no more be proved from the Fact, than the Predominancy of Vice can justify it. A certain great Man has endeavored to prove by Reasons not contemptible, that in the Original State of things the Woman was the Superior, and that her Subjection to the Man is an Effect of the Fall, and the Punishment of her Sin. And that Ingenious Theorist Mr. *Whiston*[2] asserts, That before the Fall there was a greater equality between the two Sexes.

---

[2]William Whiston (1667–1752), divine, mathematician, and Newtonian. Author of many works including *A New Theory of the Earth* (1696). He succeeded Newton as the Lucasian Professor and did much to popularize Newton's ideas. In 1710 he was deprived of his chair for casting doubt on the doctrine of the Trinity.

However this be 'tis certainly no Arrogance in a Woman to conclude, that she was made for the Service of GOD, and that this is her End. Because GOD made all Things for Himself, and a Rational Mind is too noble a Being to be Made for the Sake and Service of any Creature. The Service she at any time becomes obliged to pay to a Man, is only a Business by the Bye. Just as it may be any Man's Business and Duty to keep Hogs; he was not Made for this, but if he hires himself out to such an Employment, he ought conscientiously to perform it. Nor can anything be concluded to the contrary from St. *Paul's* Argument, *I Cor. II.* For he argues only for Decency and Order, according to the present Custom and State of things. Taking his Words strictly and literally, they prove too much, in that *Praying and Prophecying in the Church* are allowed the Women, provided they do it with their Head Covered, as well as the Men; and no inequality can be inferred from hence, their Reverence to the Sacred Oracles who engage them in such Disputes. And therefore the blame be theirs, who have unnecessarily introduced them in the present Subject, and who by saying that the *Reflections* were not agreeable to Scripture, oblige the Reflector to shew that those who affirm it must either mistake her Meaning, or the Sense of Holy Scripture, or both, if they think what they say, and do not find fault merely because they resolve to do so. For had she ever writ any thing contrary to those sacred Truths, she would be the first in pronouncing its Condemnation.

But what says the Holy Scripture? It speaks of Women as in a State of Subjection, and so it does of the *Jews* and *Christians* when under the Dominion of the *Chaldeans* and *Romans*, requiring of the one as well as of the other a quiet submission to them under whose Power they lived. But will any one say that these had a *Natural Superiority* and Right to Dominion? that they had a superior Understanding, or any Pre-eminence, except what their greater Strength acquired? Or that the other were subjected to their Adversaries for any other Reason but the Punishment of their sins, and in order to their Reformation? Or for the Exercise of their Vertue, and because the Order of the World and the Good of Society required it?

If Mankind had never sinned, Reason would always have been obeyed, there would have been no struggle for Dominion, and Brutal Power would not have prevailed. But in the lapsed State of Mankind, and now that Men will not be guided by their Reason but by their Appetites, and do not what they *ought* but what they *can*, the Reason, or that which stands for it, the Will and Pleasure of the Governor is to be the Reason of those who will not be guided by their own, and must take place for Order's sake, although it should not be conformable to right Reason. Nor can there be any Society great or little, from Empires down to private Families, with a last Resort, to determine the Affairs of that Society by an irresistible Sentence. Now unless this Supremacy be fixed somewhere, there will be a perpetual Contention about it, such is the love of Dominion, and let the Reason of things be what it may, those who have least Force, or Cunning to supply it, will have the Disadvantage. So that since Women are acknowledged to have least Bodily strength, their being commanded to obey is in pure kindness to them and for their Quiet and Security, as well as for the Exercise of their Vertue. But does it follow that Domestic Governors have more Sense than their Subjects, any more than that other Governors have? We do not find that any Man thinks the worse of his own Understanding because another has superior Power; or concludes himself less capable of a

Post of Honor and Authority, because he is not Preferred to it. How much time would lie on Men's hands, how empty would the Places of Concourse be, and how silent most Companies, did Men forbear to Censure their Governors, that is in effect to think themselves Wiser. Indeed Government would be much more desirable than it is, did it invest the Possessor with a superior Understanding as well as Power. And if mere Power gives a Right to Rule, there can be no such thing as Usurpation; but a Highway-Man so long as he has strength to force, has also a Right to require our Obedience.

Again, if Absolute Sovereignty be not necessary in a State, how comes it to be so in a family? or if in a Family why not in a State; since no Reason can be alledged for the one that will not hold more strongly for the other? If the Authority of the Husband so far as it extends, is sacred and inalienable, why not of the Prince? The Domestic Sovereign is without Dispute Elected, and the Stipulations and Contract are mutual, is it not then partial in Men to the last degree, to contend for, and practice that Arbitrary Dominion in their Families, which they abhor and exclaim against in the State? For if Arbitrary Power is evil in itself, and an improper Method of Governing Rational and Free Agents, it ought not to be Practiced any where; Nor is it less, but rather more mischievous in Families than in Kingdoms, by how much 100000 Tyrants are worse than one. What though a Husband can't deprive a Wife of Life without being responsible to the Law, he may however do what is much more grievous to a generous Mind, render Life miserable, for which she has no Redress, scarce Pity which is afforded to every other Complainant. It being thought a Wife's Duty to suffer everything without Complaint. *If all Men are born free*, how is it that all Women are born slaves? as they must be if the being subjected to the *inconstant, uncertain, unknown, arbitrary Will* of Men, be the *perfect Condition of Slavery?* and if the Essence of Freedom consists, as our Masters say it does, in having a *standing Rule to live by?* And why is Slavery so much condemned and strove against in one Case, and so highly applauded, and held so necessary and so sacred in another?

Discussion Questions

1. According to Mary Astell, what is women's customary status in society, and why? What evidence does Astell present to challenge this status?

2. What does the language Astell uses reveal about her style of thinking and basic intellectual beliefs?

3. Why do you think scholars characterize *Reflections upon Marriage* as a "feminist" work?

Comparative Questions

1. Although Equiano and the coffeehouse broadsheet belong to different literary genres, what do they reveal about late-seventeenth- and eighteenth-century Europeans and their customs?

2. How did both Voltaire and Peter I challenge the status quo with the hope of transforming society and politics? What do you think they would have thought of each other's tactics, and why?

3. Voltaire was a deep admirer of English society. What do you think he would have made of Astell's criticisms? What does this suggest about the limitations of Enlightenment ideals?

4. In what ways do Equiano, Voltaire, and Astell challenge conventional Christian authority and beliefs? What does this suggest about the place of Christianity in European society and culture at the time?

Acknowledgments

TEXT CREDITS

Bracketed numbers indicate document numbers.

Chapter 1

[1.1] Defining Humanity: *Epic of Gilgamesh*, c. 2000 B.C.E.. From *The Epic of Gilgamesh* (3rd ed., pp. 61–66), translated with an introduction by N. K. Sandars (Penguin Classics, 1972). Copyright © N. K. Sandars, 1960, 1964, and 1972. Reprinted by permission of Penguin Books, Ltd. (UK).

[1.2] Establishing Law and Justice: King Hammurabi, *The Code of Hammurabi*, Early Eighteenth Century B.C.E. From *Ancient Near Eastern Texts Relating to the Old Testament*, Third Edition with Supplement (pp. 164–78), edited by James B. Pritchard. Copyright © 1950, 1955, 1969, renewed 1978 by Princeton University Press. Reprinted by permission of Princeton University Press.

[1.3] Praising the One God: *Hymn to the Aten*, Fourteenth Century B.C.E. From *Ancient Egyptian Literature: Volume II: The New Kingdom* (pp. 91–92) by Miriam Lichtheim (The University of California Press, April 2006). Copyright © 1976 The Regents of The University of California.

[1.4] Writing Experiences: *Egyptian Scribal Exercise Book*, Twelfth Century B.C.E. From *Ancient Egyptian Literature: Volume II: The New Kingdom* (pp. 168–72) by Miriam Lichtheim. Copyright © 1976 by the Regents of the University of California. Reprinted by permission of the University of California Press.

[1.5] Allying for Peace: *The "Eternal Treaty" between the Egyptians and Hittites*, c. 1259 B.C.E. From *Ancient Near Eastern Texts Relating to the Old Testament*, Third Edition with Supplement (pp. 202–3), edited by James B. Pritchard. Copyright © 1950, 1955, 1969, renewed 1978 by Princeton University Press. Reprinted by permission of Princeton University Press.

Chapter 2

[2.1] Empires and Divine Right: *Inscription Honoring Cyrus, King of Persia*, r. c. 557–530 B.C.E. From *Ancient Near Eastern Texts Relating to the Old Testament*, Third Edition with Supplement (pp. 315–16), edited by James B. Pritchard. Copyright ©1950, 1955, 1969 renewed 1978 by Princeton University Press. Reprinted by permission of Princeton University Press.

[2.2] Monotheism and Mosaic Law: *The Book of Exodus, Chapters 19–20*, c. Tenth–Sixth Centuries B.C.E. From *The Jerusalem Bible: Reader's Edition*. Copyright © 1966 by Darton, Longman & Todd, Ltd., and Doubleday, a division of Random House, Inc. Reprinted by permission.

[2.3] The Quest for Individual Excellence: Homer, *The Odyssey*, Eighth Century B.C.E. From "Book 9: In the One-Eyed Giant's Cave" by Homer, from The Odyssey by Homer, translated by Robert Fagles, copyright © 1996 by Robert Fagles. Used by permission of Viking Penguin, a division of Penguin Group (USA) Inc.

[2.4] Two Visions of the City-State: Tyrtaeus of Sparta and Solon of Athens, *Poems*, Seventh–Sixth Centuries B.C.E. From *Early Greek Lyric Poetry* (pp. 48–49, 68–69), translated by David Mulroy. Copyright © 1992 by The University of Michigan. Reprinted by permission of University of Michigan Press.

[2.5] Economics and the Expansion of Slavery: Xenophon, *Revenues*, Fourth Century B.C.E. Reprinted by permission of the publishers and the Trustees of the Loeb Classical Library from *Xenophon: Volume VII, Loeb Classical Library Volume 183* (pp. 137–53), translated by E. C. Marchant, Cambridge, MA: Harvard University Press. Copyright © 1925 by the President and Fellows of Harvard College. Loeb Classical Library® is a registered trademark of the President and Fellows of Harvard College.

Chapter 3

[3.1] The Golden Age of Athens: Thucydides, *The Funeral Oration of Pericles*, 429 B.C.E. From Thucydides, *The Peloponnesian Wars* (pp. 65–72), translated by Benjamin Jowett, revised and abridged by P. A. Brunt. Copyright © 1963 by P. A. Brunt. Reprinted with the permission of Simon & Schuster, Inc. All rights reserved.

[3.3] The Emergence of Philosophy: Plato, *The Apology of Socrates*, 399 B.C.E. From *The Dialogues of Plato*, vol. 2 (3d ed., pp. 109, 111–16, 121–23), translated by Benjamin Jowett. New York: Macmillan and Co., 1892.

[3.4] The Advance of Science: Hippocrates of Cos, *On the Sacred Disease*, 400 B.C.E. From *Hippocrates: Volume II, Loeb Classical Library Volume 148* (pp. 139, 141, 143, 145, 153, 175, 179, 181, 183), translated by W. H. S. Jones, , Cambridge, MA: Harvard University Press, 1923. The Loeb Classical Library is a registered trademark of the President and Fellows of Harvard College.

[3.5] Domestic Boundaries: Euphiletus, *A Husband Speaks in His Own Defense*, c. 400 B.C.E. From *The Murder of Herodes and Other Trials from the Athenian Law Courts* (pp. 43–52), edited by Kathleen Freeman. Copyright © 1994 by Hackett Publishing. Reprinted by permission of Hackett Publishing Company, Inc. All rights reserved.

[3.6] Protesting War, Performing Satire: Aristophanes, *Lysistrata*, 411 B.C.E. From *The Comedies of Aristophanes*, translated by Alan Sommerstein, Aris & Philips, 1990.

Chapter 4

[4.1] The Conquest of New Lands: Arrian, *The Campaigns of Alexander the Great*, Fourth Century B.C.E. From *The Campaigns of Alexander* (pp. 360–66), translated by Aubrey de Selincourt, revised with an introduction and notes by J. R. Hamilton, Penguin Classics, 1958; revised edition, 1971. Copyright © the Estate of Aubrey de Selincourt, 1958. Introduction and Notes Copyright © J. R. Hamilton, 1971. Reprinted by permission of Penguin Books, Ltd. (UK).

[4.2] Imperial Bureaucracy: Zeno, Egyptian Official, *Records*, 259–250 B.C.E. Reprinted by permission of the publishers and the Trustees of the Loeb Classical Library from *Select Papyri: Volume I, Loeb Classical Library Volume 266* (pp. 269–77, 397–99, and 409–15), translated by A. S. Hunt and C. C. Edgar, Cambridge, MA: Harvard University Press. Copyright © 1932 by the President and Fellows of Harvard College. The Loeb Classical Library is a registered trademark of the President and Fellows of Harvard College.

[4.3] Everyday Life: *Funerary Inscriptions and Epitaphs*, Fifth–First Centuries B.C.E. From *Women's Life in Greece and Rome: A Source Book in Translation*, Second Edition (pp. 16–17, 190, 206, 219, 221–22, 263, 266–67, 274), edited by Mary R. Lefkowitz and Maureen B. Fant. Copyright © 1992 M. B. Fant and M. R. Lefkowitz. Reprinted with permission of The Johns Hopkins University Press and Bristol Classical Press, an imprint of Bloomsbury Publishing Plc. Epitaph #386 from "Greek Maenadism from Olympias to Messalina" by Albert Henrichs from Harvard Studies in Classical Philology, Vol. 82 (1978), pp. 121-160. Reprinted by permission of Harvard Studies in Classical Philology. Epitaph #39 from *Themes in Greek and Roman Epitaphs* by Richard Lattimore. Reprinted by permission of Steven Lattimore and Alexander Lattimore.

[4.4] In Pursuit of Happiness: Epicurus, *Letter to a Friend*, Late Third Century B.C.E. From "Letter to Menoeceus" in *The Way of Philosophy*, translated by Philip Wheelwright. Copyright © 1960 by Longman Publishing Group. Reprinted by permission of Pearson Education Group.

[4.5] Exacting Science: Archimedes, *Letter to Eratosthenes*, Third Century B.C.E. From *The Works of Archimedes* (pp. 12–13), edited by T. L. Heath, Mineola, NY: Dover Publications, 2002. Marcus Vitruvius Pollio, *Archimedes's "Eureka!" Moment*, 30–20 B.C.E. From *Vitruvius: Ten Books on Architecture*, translation by Ingrid D. Rowland. Copyright © 1993 by Ingrid Drake Rowland. Reprinted with the permission of Cambridge University Press.

Chapter 5

[5.1] Formalizing Roman Law: *The Twelve Tables*, 451–449 B.C.E. Excerpted from [8 "The Twelve Tables," including "notes" from pages 9–17 and [148 "Edicts of Augustus . . . ," including "notes" from pages 124–26 from *Ancient Roman Statutes: A Translation with Introduction, Commentary, Glossary, and Index* (pp. 9–17), translated by Allan Chester Johnson, Paul Robinson Coleman-Norton and Frank Card Bourne. Copyright © 1961 by University of Texas Press. Reprinted courtesy of the University of Texas Press.

[5.3] Status and Discrimination: *Roman Women Demonstrate against the Oppian Law*, 195 B.C.E. Reprinted by permission of the publishers and the Trustees of the Loeb Classical Library from *Livy: Volume IX, Loeb Classical Library 295* (pp. 413–21, 425–39), translated by Evan T. Sage, Cambridge, MA: Harvard University Press. Copyright © 1935 by the President and Fellows of Harvard College. The Loeb Classical Library® is a registered trademark of the President and Fellows of Harvard College.

[5.4] Cultivating Justice and Piety: Cicero, *On the Commonwealth*, 54 B.C.E. From *On the Commonwealth and On the Laws* (pp. 9–102), edited by James E. G. Zetzel. Copyright © 1999 Cambridge University Press. Reprinted with the permission of Cambridge University Press.

[5.6] Toward Empire: Julius Caesar, *The Gallic War*, 52 B.C.E. From Julius Caesar, *The Gallic War* (pp. 181, 183–84, 188–89, 191–94, 241–42), translated by Carolyn Hammond. Copyright © 1996 by Oxford University Press. Reprinted by permission of Oxford University Press.

Chapter 6

[6.1] An Empire Foretold: Virgil, *The Aeneid*, First Century B.C.E. From *The Aeneid*, translated by Robert Fagles. Copyright © 2006 by Robert Fagles. Used by permission of Viking Penguin, a division of Penguin Group (USA) Inc.

[6.2] An Urban Empire: *Notices and Graffiti Describe Life in Pompeii*, First Century C.E. From *Roman Civilization: Selected Readings, Vol. II: The Empire*, Third Edition (pp. 126–27, 237–38, 276–78), edited by Naphtali Lewis and Meyer Reinhold. Copyright © 1990 by Columbia University Press. Reprinted with the permission of Columbia University Press.

[6.4] The Making of a New Religion: Paul of Tarsus, *Letter to the Galatians*, First Century C.E. From *The Jerusalem Bible: Reader's Edition*. Copyright © 1966 by Darton, Longman & Todd, Ltd. and Doubleday, a division of Random House, Inc. Reprinted by permission.

[6.5] The Cult of Isis: Apulieus, *The Golden Ass*, c. 170 C.E. From *The Golden Ass by Apuleius*, translated by P. G. Walsh. Oxford University Press, New York. 1994. 218–222. © P. G. Walsh 1994. Reprinted by permission of Oxford University Press.

Chapter 7

[7.1] The Establishment of Roman Christian Doctrine: Arius, *Letter to Alexander, Bishop of Alexandria*, c. 170 C.E. From J. Stevenson, *A New Eusebius: Documents Illustrating the History of the Church to AD 337*, revised edition (pp. 326–27). Copyright © 1987 SPCK. Reprinted with permission of SPCK.

[7.2] The Struggle of Conversion: Augustine of Hippo, *Confessions*, c. 525 C.E. From *Confessions* by Saint Augustine, translated with an introduction by R. S. Pine-Coffin (pp.

170–71, 173, 175–78), Penguin Classics, 1961. Copyright © R.S. Pine-Coffin, 1961. Reproduced by permission of Penguin Books Ltd.

[7.3] The Development of Monasticism: Benedict of Nursia, *The Rule of St. Benedict*, c. 540 C.E. From *The Rule of St. Benedict*, edited by Timothy Fry. Copyright © 1981 by Order of Saint Benedict, Inc. Published by Liturgical Press, Collegeville, Minnesota. Reprinted with permission.

[7.4] Germanic Law in the Roman Empire: *The Burgundian Code*, c.475–525 C.E. From *The Burgundian Code* (pp. 17–24, 30–33, 40–47), translated by Katherine Fischer Drew. Copyright © 1972 by the University of Pennsylvania Press. Reprinted by permission of University of Pennsylvania Press.

[7.5] Emergence of Byzantium: Procopius, *Secret History*, 550 C.E." From Procopius, *Secret History* (pp. 40–44, 55, 58, 60, 75–76), translated by Richard Atwater. Copyright © 1961 by University of Michigan Press.

Chapter 8

[8.1] The Foundations of Islam: *Qur'an, Suras 1, 53, 98*, c. 610–632. From *Approaching the Qur'an: The Early Revelations* (pp. 35, 42, 44, 47, 104–6), introduced and translated by Michael Sells. Copyright © 1999 by White Cloud Press. Reprinted by permission of the publisher.

[8.2] Jihad and Jizya: *Islamic Terms of Peace*, 633–643. From *Islam: From the Prophet Muhammad to the Capture of Constantinople*, Volume 1, *Politics and War* (pp. 234–36, 238–40), edited and translated by Bernard Lewis. Copyright © 1974. Reprinted by permission of Walker and Company.

[8.3] Byzantine Life: *The Life of St. Theodore of Sykeon*, Early Seventh Century. From *Three Byzantine Saints* (pp. 115–20), translated by Elizabeth Dawes and Norman H. Baynes. Copyright © 1948 by Basil Blackwell. Reprinted by permission of Blackwell Publishing.

[8.4] A Noblewoman's Life: *The Life of Lady Balthild, Queen of the Franks*, Late Seventh Century. From *Late Merovingian France: History and Hagiography, 640–720* (pp. 119–27, 131–32), edited by Paul Fouracre and Richard A. Gerberding. Copyright © 1996 by Manchester University Press. Reprinted by permission of Manchester University Press.

Chapter 9

[9.2] Resistance from Constantinople: Liutprand of Cremona, *Report to Otto I*, 968. From *The Works of Liutprand of Cremona*, translated by F. A. Wright. Copyright © 1930. Reproduced by permission of Taylor & Francis Books UK.

[9.4] A New Islamic Dynasty: Ahmad al-Ya'qūbī, *Kitāb al-buldān*, Ninth Century. From *Islam: From the Prophet Muhammad to the Capture of Constantinople*, Volume II, *Religion and Society* (pp. 69–73), edited and translated by Bernard Lewis. Copyright © 1974. Reprinted by permission of Walker and Company.

Chapter 10

[10.1] Medieval Business: *Commenda Contracts*, Eleventh–Twelfth Centuries. From *Medieval Trade in the Mediterranean World*, Number LII of the *Records of Civilization, Sources and Studies*, edited by Austin P. Evans, translated by Robert S. Lopez and Irving W. Raymond. Copyright © 1961 by Columbia University Press. Reprinted by permission of the publisher.

[10.2] Sources of the Investiture Conflict: Emperor Henry IV and Pope Gregory VII, *Letter and Excommunication*, 1076. Gregory VII from *The Correspondence of Pope Gregory VII* (pp. 90–91), translated by Ephraim Emerton. Copyright © 1932 by Columbia University Press. Henry IV from *Imperial Lives and Letters of the Eleventh Century* (pp. 150–51), translated by Theodor E. Mommsen and Karl F. Morrison, edited by Robert L. Benson.

Copyright © 1962 by Columbia University Press. Reprinted by permission of Columbia University Press.

[10.4] Arab Response to the First Crusade: Ibn al-Athīr , A Muslim Perspective, 1097–1099. From Ibn al-Athīr, *The Chronicle of Ibn al-Athir for The Crusading Period* from *al-Kamil fi'l-Ta'rikh*, part 1, translated by D. S. Richards. Copyright © 2006 Ashgate Publishing. Reprinted by permission of Ashgate Publishing Ltd.

[10.5] The Power of William I: *The Anglo-Saxon Chronicle*, 1085–1086. From *The Anglo-Saxon Chronicle* (pp. 161–65), edited by Dorothy Whitelock. Copyright © 1961 by Dorothy Whitelock and David Douglas. Reprinted with the permission of Rutgers University Press.

Chapter 11

[11.1] New Learning: Peter Abelard, *The Story of My Misfortunes*, c. 1132.From *The Letters of Abelard and Heloise*, translated and introduced by Betty Radice (Penguin Classics, 1974). Copyright © Betty Radice, 1974. Reproduced by permission of Penguin Books Ltd.

[11.3] Courtly Love: Chrétien de Troyes, *Lancelot: The Knight of the Cart*, c. 1170s. From *Lancelot: The Knight of the Cart*, translated by Burton Raffel. New Haven: Yale University Press, 1997. Copyright © 1997 by Yale University

[11.4] Franciscan Piety: St. Francis and St. Clare of Assisi, *Selected Writings*, Thirteenth Century. From *Select Historical Documents of the Middle Ages* (pp. 344–49), edited by Ernest Henderson. Originally published by Bell and Sons (1921). Excerpts from *Francis and Clare: The Complete Works* (pp. 226–32), translated by Regis J. Armstrong and Ignatius C. Brady. Copyright © 1982 by Paulist Press. Reprinted by permission of Paulist Press.

[11.5] The Sack of Constantinople: *Annals of Niketas Choniates*, 1204. From *O City of Byzantium: Annals of Niketas Choniates*, translated by Harry J. Magoulias. Copyright © 1984 Wayne State University Press. Reprinted by permission of Wayne State University Press.

Chapter 12

[12.2] A Female Mystic: Hadewijch of Brabant, *Letters and* Poems, 1220–1240. From *Medieval Women Writers*, edited by Katharina M. Wilson. Copyright © 1984 by the University of Georgia Press. Reprinted by permission of the University of Georgia Press.

[12.3] Defining Outsiders: Thomas of Monmouth, *The Life and Martyrdom of St. William of Norwich*, c. 1173. From *The Life and Miracles of St. William of Norwich* (pp. 14–17, 19–23), translated by Augustus Jessopp and Montague Rhodes. Copyright © 1896 by Cambridge University Press. Reprinted with the permission of Cambridge University Press.

[12.4] Imagining Hell: Dante Alighieri, *Divine Comedy*, 1313–1321. From *The Inferno of Dante* (pp. 47–53), translated by Robert Pinksy. Copyright © 1994 by Farrar, Straus and Giroux. Reprinted by permission of Farrar, Straus and Giroux.

[12.5] The New Power of Medieval States: Boniface VIII, *Unam Sanctam*, 1302. From *Documents of the Christian Church*, ed. Henry Bettenson. Oxford University Press, New York, 1967. 115–116. Selection © Oxford University Press 1963. Reprinted by permission of Oxford University Press. King Philip IV of France, *General Assembly of Paris*, 1303. From *Medieval Europe*, edited by Julius Kirshner and Karl F. Morrison. University of Chicago Press. Copyright © 1986 by the University of Chicago.

Chapter 13

[13.1] Demographic Catastrophe: *The Black Death*, Fourteenth Century. From *The Black Death*, edited and translated by Rosemary Horrox. Copyright © 1994, Manchester University Press, Manchester, UK.

[13.5] Extolling Humanism: Giovanni Rucellai and Leonardo Bruni, *Florence in Quattrocento*, 1427 and 1457. From *Images of Quattrocento Florence: Selected Writings in Literature, History, and Art*, eited by Stefano Ugo Baldassarri and Arielle Saiber, New Haven and

Chapter 17

[17.2] A "Sober and Wholesome Drink": *A Brief Description of the Excellent Vertues of That Sober and Wholesome Drink, Called Coffee*, 1674. *Eighteenth-Century Coffee-House Culture*, vol. 1, *Restoration Satire* (pp. 129), edited by Markman Ellis. Copyright © 2006. Reproduced from *Eighteenth-Century Coffee-House Culture* with the permission of Pickering & Chatto Publishers.

[17.3] Westernizing Russian Culture: Peter I, *Decrees and Statutes*, 1701–1723. The Decree on "German" Dress, the Decree on the Shaving of Beards and Moustaches, and the Statute of the College of Manufactures from *A Source Book for Russian History from Early Times to 1917*, Volume 2, edited by George Vernadsky. Copyright © 1972 by Yale University. The Decree on the Invitation to Foreigners reprinted with the permission of Scribner, a Division of Simon & Schuster, Inc., from *Peter the Great* by Robert K. Massie. Copyright © 1980 by Robert K. Massie. All rights reserved.

[17.5] Questioning Women's Submission: Mary Astell, *Reflections upon Marriage*, 1706. From *The First English Feminist: Reflections upon Marriage and Other Writings* (pp. 69–76), edited and introduced by Bridget Hill. Copyright © 1986 by St. Martin's Press. Reprinted by permission of St. Martin's Press.

ART CREDITS

Page 61: The Art Archive/Museo Nazionale Terme Rome/Gianni Dagli Orti.   **Page 74**: Figures 6.2a–b from Susan Walker, "Women and Housing in Classical Greece: The Archaeological Evidence," in *Images of Women in Antiquity*, ed. Averil Cameron and Amelie Kuhrt (London: Routledge, 1993), 87.   **Page 108**: Statuette of a rider, Etruscan, late fifth century B.C.E. (bronze) by Detroit Institute of Arts, USA/ City of Detroit Purchase/ The Bridgeman Art Library.   **Page 109**: Scala/Art Resource, NY.   **Page 183**: The Bridgeman Art Library/ Getty Images.   **Page 283**: xff F1219.I.58 LAM .06, Courtesy of The Bancroft Library, University of California, Berkeley.